"CITY OF THE CENTURY"

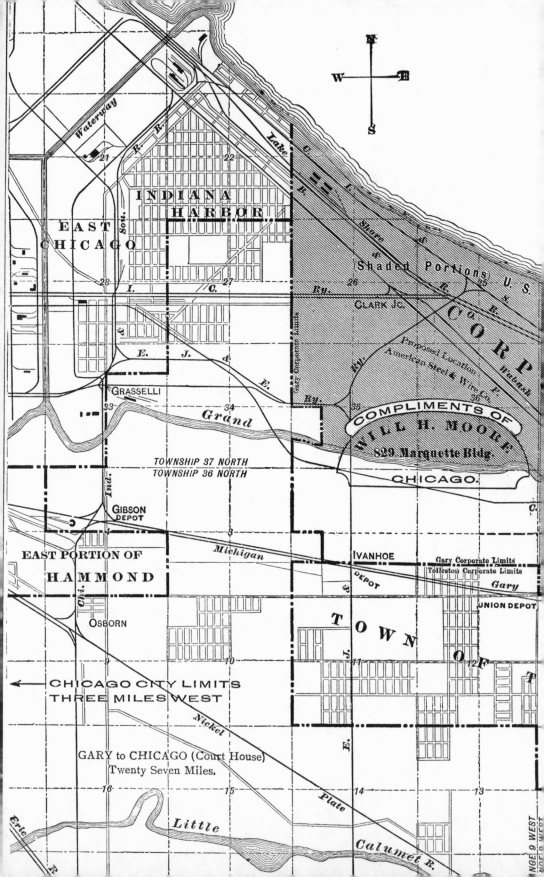

"CITY OF THE CENTURY"

A History of Gary, Indiana

James B. Lane

Bloomington
INDIANA UNIVERSITY PRESS
London

Manufactured in the United States of America

Library of Congress Cataloging in Publication Data

Lane, James B., 1942–
　City of the century.

　Bibliography: 307
　Includes index.
　1. Gary, Ind.—History.　I. Title.
F534.G2L36　　　977.2'99　　　77-23622
ISBN 0-253-11187-0　　　2 3 4 5 82 81 80 79

CONTENTS

ILLUSTRATIONS

(following page 116)

1. Shabanee; Alice Mable Gray, "Diana of the Dunes"; the Bailly homestead.

2. Leveling sand dunes for Gary Works, 1906; Carr's Beach, 1917.

3. Judge Elbert H. Gary; William P. Gleason, 1908; first iron ore shipment, 1908; pouring steel, about 1914.

4. Last of the shacks on Euclid Avenue; Broadway and 5th Avenue, 1907.

5. Water tower and pumping station, 1910; Town Board inspecting the sewer, 1908.

6. The Patch, about 1909; Broadway and 4th Avenue, 1907; Neighborhood House, 1910.

7. Town Board election, 1906; Ingwald Moe, 1908; Joseph Martin, 1908.

8. Paulino Monterrubio; Lorraine Duncan Washington; Marion C. Streeter; Dr. Antonio Giorgi; Tom Cannon.

9. Jovo and Dorothy Krstovich with Mato Chuck and John Wuletich and their wives; Wabash Freight Depot, 1909; night class, about 1913.

10. Mayor Roswell O. Johnson at Board of Works meeting, 1917; Mayor William F. Hodges, 1918; federal troops at Commercial Club, 1919.

11. Horace Mann students, about 1923; William A. Wirt; Froebel School.

12. E. A. Spaulding; Emerson School; Broadway and 6th Avenue, 1917.

13. John W. Kyle; Rabbi Garry Joel August; D. E. Sikes; Broadway and 7th Avenue, 1928.

14. William A. Forbis; J. Ralph Snyder; Erwin Crewe Rosenau; John Dillinger at the Crown Point jail, 1934.

15. Jacob L. Reddix; Ruth Wall Nelson; Mothers Club, Stewart House, 1930.

16. Wilbert W. Gasser; Gary State Bank Building, about 1930.

17. Waiting for President Roosevelt, 1936; City Methodist Church.

18. Horace S. Norton; John Mayerik; Frank N. Gavit; 5th and Broadway, 1936.

19. Tom Harmon; John A. Bushemi; Tony Zale with Boy Scouts.

PREFACE

DURING the late nineteenth century the United States underwent a period of unprecedented economic growth, and most of its people believed that the next hundred years would be, in the words of one editorial writer, "America's century." The industrial revolution caused dislocations in the fabric of society, however, and raised serious questions concerning the relationship between government and big business, the exploitation of the environment, the treatment of minorities, the upsetting of traditional moral values, and the preservation of individual freedom and economic opportunity. Conceived in a spirit of optimism and as a consequence of America's economic expansion, Gary's fate as a twentieth-century city depended on how these problems would be resolved.

"CITY OF THE CENTURY" proclaims the inscription on Gary's official seal, which depicts a globe being christened with molten steel. The United States Steel Corporation founded Gary in 1906 as an experiment in industrial urban planning, but the city never fulfilled the hopes of its pioneer boosters. Rather, in its travail it came to symbolize the plight of twentieth-century cities. In 1971 Edward Greer wrote that "in silhouette, the skyline of Gary, Indiana, could serve as the perfect emblem of America's industrial might—or its industrial pollution."

During Gary's pioneer period a power struggle ensued, with the so-called mill forces led by Gary Works Superintendent William Palmer Gleason and Gary Land Company Agent Horace Singer Norton pitted against the so-called "town forces" led by Mayor Thomas E. Knotts and a group of independent Southside entrepreneurs. The mill forces emerged supreme, defeating Knotts in the 1913 election; and until the 1930s they dominated the economic, political, and social life of the community. As one writer noted, they were the "founding fathers, power holders, executors of private economic policies, and symbols of authority." During the next generation, however, new ethnic and labor spokesmen challenged U.S. Steel's preeminence, and Gary changed from a Republican fiefdom to a Democratic stronghold. During the 1960s black people gained political power, but the downtown area went into decline and many white people began moving away—jeopardizing the chances of Gary's becoming a racially harmonious, economically diversified city.

Even though Gary underwent several transformations during the first 70 years of its history—as exemplified by the coming of collective bargaining at the mill in 1937 and the election of a black mayor in 1967—the city never rid itself completely of its frontier heritage or its company-town status. As Marshall Frady noted in 1969, "the city breathes with the mill." Peopled by immigrants representing more than 50 European nationality groups, as well as by newcomers from the American South, Mexico, Puerto Rico, and elsewhere, Gary has profited from its cultural diversity but has been fragmented economically and racially. Despite its unique history, the city has been profoundly affected by national business cycles, world wars, migration patterns, labor trends, civil rights developments, and the urban policies of the state and federal governments.

Chapter 1 of this book, entitled "Antecedents," links twentieth-century Gary with the previous history of the Calumet Region in order to demonstrate its impact on the area's ecology. The founding and peopling of the company town and the growth of its economic, political, social, and educational institutions are the subject of Chapters 2 and 3, which cover Gary's first decade. Chapter 4 examines the crisis years of World War I and its aftermath as seen in the 1919 steel strike, the rise of the Ku Klux Klan, and the persecution of dissenters. Chapters 5 and 6 examine the sanguine 1920s when, despite its problems, Gary seemed ready to become more than a satellite of Chicago and U.S. Steel. Such hopes waned with the onset of the depression, and Chapters 7 and 8 focus on the changes which took place during the anxious decade of the 1930s. Chapter 9 deals with the impact of World War II on Gary and its people, whereas Chapter 10 elaborates on the postwar strife evidenced in the schools, labor-management relations, and politics. The final chapter examines Gary's civil rights movement from the time when only a few voices were "crying in the wilderness" to the successful mobilization of black political strength during the 1960s. The book closes with an analysis of the problems faced by Mayor Richard G. Hatcher during his first two terms in office.

It has been my intention to write a general introduction to Gary's history with special emphasis on specific individuals—both common people and civic leaders. There are episodes of personal tragedy and heroism, of frustrated hopes and tarnished reputations. This book is written partially as an antidote to those who lament the passing of imagined "good old days" and also with the hope that a new spirit of civic pride might yet redeem Gary's promise as the "CITY OF THE CENTURY."

Many parts of this book first appeared in print in a somewhat different form as newspaper articles in *The Post-Tribune*. I benefited from the advice offered by *Post-Tribune* editors Terence O'Rourke, Carrol Vertrees, David Allen, Don Ross, Jerry Gengler, and Fay Donovan. Other staff members who provided valuable assistance were Mary Ellen McGrain, Louise K. Tucker, Marilou Popa, Mary Biegel, and Tom De Saintgene. *Post-Tribune* photographers David Fryer, Don Blume, Larry Bretts, John Mitchell, Jim McGill, and Robin Nelson helped compile the pictures. Gary S. Wilk of Indiana University Northwest's Fine Arts Department also took several photographs.

On many occasions while working at the Gary Public Library, I received aid from Mrs. Lee Sinai, David Swinehart, Henry Hastings, Larry Acheff, and Elsie Rodriquez. At Indiana University Northwest librarian Betty Shaw obtained many obscure journal articles for me. Staff members at Indiana University Press treated my book with professionalism and care.

I would also like to acknowledge the professional secretarial work done by Rosalie Zak, Carol Buchko, Toni Lane, Arlene Daunora, Jeralyn Dusich, Angie Rodriguez, and Debbi Zak.

Several lunch companions at the Gary YMCA—including Dr. E. C. Doering, Alvin F. Wood, Paul M. Ray, William Schmidt, Peter Bell, Harold Stiles, and Ragnar Kummen—frequently provided me with anecdotes, character sketches, insights, leads, encouragement, and good fellowship. I am also thankful to the many others who agreed to be interviewed and allowed me to phone them at all hours of the day.

I am especially indebted to several scholars whose research and findings made my work easier. These include Powell A. Moore, Raymond A. Mohl, Neil Betten, Dolly Millender, Richard J. Meister, Isaac J. Quillen, and Ronald D. Cohen. Dr. Cohen also helped found the Calumet Regional Archives at Indiana University Northwest, where important manuscript collections are located. Archives assistant Kathy O'Rourke secured several useful documents for me.

Indiana University Northwest provided me with a grant-in-aid and three summer faculty fellowships which allowed me to finish this project much sooner than otherwise. A contribution from the Gary National Bank made it possible to expand the number of illustrations. Several of my colleagues offered suggestions and encouragement, including Paul B. Kern, John S. Haller, Frederick B. Chary, James E. Newman, William B. Neil, Carl Allsup, Ronald D. Cohen, and Rhiman A. Rotz.

Finally, I dedicate the book to my wife Toni and my sons Philip and David, whose companionship and love have made my years in Gary happy ones.

"CITY OF THE CENTURY"

CHAPTER ONE

Antecedents

The dunes are a signature of time and eternity.

—CARL SANDBURG

FIFTEEN THOUSAND YEARS ago, a glacier covered northwest Indiana. As the ice melted and receded, a huge lake formed, dammed between the receding ice margin and the uplands to the south. The waters of this lake were more than 55 feet higher than the present level of Lake Michigan. Glacial movements and erosion of the lake's outlet stream gradually caused the water to recede, leaving a succession of sandy beaches across Lake County where mastodons once trod. Between 2,000 and 3,000 years ago, the southern shoreline of Lake Michigan approximated its present boundaries.

In time the Gary area was transformed into a series of wetlands and sandy ridges where white pines and cedars grew until chopped down by the first residents of Chicago, leaving scrub oak to grow in their place. Near the lake, during each of the ancestral Lake Michigan's several stages, brisk winds carried particles of sand and deposited them around reeds and trees, beginning a process by which dunes were formed and re-formed. Nestled among these huge mounds of sand were various sloughs, bogs, valleys, forests, and lowlands, constituting, in historian Powell A. Moore's words, "a treasure of plant life," including "more than 1,300 species of flowering plants and ferns" of the desert, woodland, swampland, and prairie variety.

THE POTAWATOMI: REMOVING THE INDIANS FROM INDIANA

Centuries ago, northwest Indiana was the temporary home of numerous Indian tribes. Although much of the terrain was a sandy wetland, fish, game, waterfowl, and berries were plentiful. There were also stately pines, maple groves for getting syrup, and "sacred" walnut trees. A network of trails connected the Woodland Indians of the Northeast with the Great Plains tribes. The "Old Sauk Trail," running through present-day Valparaiso, Merrillville, Schererville, and Dyer, was the most traveled of many routes that formed what historians have labeled the "Great Short Cut."

There were many Potawatomi villages on Kankakee River islets and in the prairie regions to the west, and some of their seminomadic clans traveled to present-day Gary to hunt and farm during the summer months. During the winter, Ottawa bands came from the north for an annual hunt. The Miami made seasonal visits to the area until they were forced out by the Potawatomi.

Potawatomi customs were similar to other Algonkian-speaking tribes such as the Chippewa, Cree, Ottawa, and Menominee. With a stable population of about 4,000 people scattered in the area around southern Lake Michigan, the Potawatomi had a rich culture that featured pottery making, hunting, trapping, and the harvesting of corn, beans, squash, and grapes. "In summer," historian George I. Quimby wrote, "they lived in villages and were agricultural. In autumn they separated into family groups and departed for their winter hunting grounds, where they remained until spring."

The Potawatomi had a loose political organization. The village leaders were the chief, the council (usually composed of family patriarchs), the shaman or medicine man, and, in times of emergency, war leaders. The chief, who was generally selected by the council from a group of hereditary candidates, ruled by consensus rather than fiat. He frequently had less influence over daily affairs than did the shaman.

Belief in supernatural spirits—evil ghosts and benign forces such as the sun, moon, and the four winds—played an important role in Potawatomi society. So did taboos. For example, when a girl reached puberty she fasted in isolation for more than a week. Females were considered unclean during menstruation. Pregnant women avoided deformed persons and did not eat turtles or rabbits. The Potawatomi believed in revelations through dreams. Visions guided the naming of children and the assignment of one's guardian spirit or *manito* and were sometimes induced by the smoking of peyote. "Religion was primarily an individual affair," wrote Robert and Pat Ritzenthaler, "and one that [the Potawatomi] practiced constantly."

Organized religious ceremonies, where sacrificial dogs were eaten and elaborate rituals performed, were special events reserved for funerals, a youth's first hunt, war dances, and the medicine dance, held to cure the sick and increase longevity. More important in everyday life were curative herbs, bloodletting and cupping, and mystical relics and good-luck charms carried in war bags and medicine bags.

When clans or tribes came together, the Indians held festive celebrations featuring lacrosse contests and ritual dances. In William F. Howat's *A Standard History of Lake County, Indiana, and the Calumet Region,* there is a description of such an event: "The Potawatomi would form a line according to age, the oldest first, the little children last. They danced in lines, back and forth, and the music was furnished by an old chief, a young chief, and a venerable Indian, who sat on the ground and shook dried corn in gourds. The song which accompanied these rattlings repeated the name of the principal chief over and over. After the dance all feasted on venison soup and green corn, stewed in iron kettles and served in wooden trenchers with wooden ladles."

The Potawatomi traveled by pony, birchbark canoe, and toboggan. In winter, men wore snowshoes and blankets over their breechclouts and leggings. There were three different types of headdress, designed for comfort, for use in festivals, or for warfare. Women generally wore broadcloth skirts over an underskirt and leggings. Both sexes wore tanned buckskin moccasins adorned with ribbonwork or beads.

Potawatomi marriages were usually arranged by families and followed an elaborate courtship procedure. There was no wedding ceremony, however, and separations were easily obtainable. Young women were rather modest compared to some other tribes. Intraclan unions were taboo. Monogamy was the rule, although some leaders had two or three wives, and the taking in of a wife's widowed sister was common practice.

Before the French came into the region, warfare was more like a dangerous sport, carried out for honor or revenge and with few casualties. In 1680, however, the explorer René Robert Cavelier, Sieur de La Salle, united the Miami and the Potawatomi to fight against their common enemy, the Iroquois. Succeeding generations of French fur traders and priests won the Potawatomi's loyalty to New France.

The Jesuits called the Potawatomi the "Fire Nation." In Algonkian the name meant "people of the place of the fire." The missionaries described them as intelligent, friendly, inclined to take life easy, and more humane and civilized than most tribes. "Calumet," the French designation for the region's two river arteries, stemmed from the word "reed" and referred to the Indians' ceremonial pipes. Originally "Calumick," the word was also used to describe "the act of smoking together."

In 1763 the British gained possession of the Calumet Region when the Peace of Paris ended almost a century of warfare with the French for worldwide supremacy. At that time, the principal Potawatomi campsite in the region was probably south of Turkey Creek, where the remains of a cemetery, workshop, and dancing grounds have been discovered.

The Potawatomi in 1763 joined the Ottawa and Chippewa in a bloody uprising against the English, known as Pontiac's Conspiracy. During the American Revolution, however, most of the Potawatomi remained loyal to the British, who furnished them with scalping knives and whiskey. A skirmish between Potawatomi braves and pro-American French settlers from the Illinois Country took place at Petite Forte, a stockade built in the 1750s by the French at the mouth of a creek now in Indiana Dunes State Park.

In 1794 the Potawatomi joined the Miami in fighting against "Mad" Anthony Wayne at Fallen Timbers in Ohio. Then in 1811 they joined the Shawnees in fighting against William Henry Harrison at Tippecanoe, and continued their warfare against the Americans during the War of 1812. With the coming of peace, they fared no better by striving for friendly relations with the United States government than they had by going on the warpath.

Once Indiana achieved statehood in 1816, the government moved steadily to force the Indians across the Mississippi River. In 1826 the Potawatomi in the Treaty of Mississinewa ceded a 10-mile tract at the southern extremity of Lake Michigan that included present-day Miller. The Treaty of Tippecanoe in 1832 and subsequent additions four years later deprived them of their other land in northwest Indiana. In 1827 the Indiana General Assembly wrote Congress that "the speedy concentration of the Indians, in some permanent situation, far from our frontier, offers the only practicable method of diverting them from indolent and vicious habits, to which, by their vicinity to our population, they are unhappily inclined." Governor James B. Ray added that they had "acquired all of the vices of the whites, with but few of their virtues."

The Potawatomi traded with agents of the American Fur Company, many of whom were former French and British subjects. Historians John D. Barnhart and Donald F. Carmony wrote that in return for mink, wolf, deer, raccoon, fox, muskrat, and opossum pelts, the Indians received such goods as blankets, hoes, rope, playing cards, rings, scissors, spices, belts, kettles, food, buttons, scalping knives, tomahawks, rifles, and whiskey.

Fur traders were among the tiny minority of whites who argued fruitlessly against wholesale removal. Among them was a black agent for the American Fur Company named Jean Baptiste Point du Sable, who was evidently the first non-Indian settler in the Gary area. His father had mercantile interests in Quebec and his mother had once been a slave. In the 1770s he operated a fur trading post on the Grand Calumet River until the Potawatomi forced him to move west to present-day Chicago.

The Black Hawk War, a series of skirmishes fought in 1832 in Wisconsin and Illinois, provided the excuse for the adoption of a forced migration policy, even though the Potawatomi had refused to join forces with the warring Indians. Removal took place gradually during the rest of the 1830s, culminating during the fall of 1838 in what Benjamin M. Petit called the "Trail of Death."

In 1924 a 99-year-old pioneer named James Monahan described how some Potawatomi marched through present-day Gary, probably in 1838, on their way to a Kansas reservation. "It certainly was a sad sight," Monahan wrote. "The Indians loved their homes as well as we loved ours. They sat around in their blankets looking sorrowful and dejected. Some, even the bravest, broke down and sobbed." They had been promised 10 cents an acre for their land, a pledge that was never kept.

A minor chief named Ash-kum bought back a tract of land that included what became the Gary Land Company's First Subdivision. But complaints by white settlers in nearby Liverpool caused the government to reverse its policy of allowing Indians to purchase land in Indiana.

A famous local Ottawa chieftain named Shabanee settled with his family on a small parcel of land in central Illinois. The son-in-law of an heirless Potawatomi chief, he was Tecumseh's second-in-command at the Battle of the Thames but after 1815 was known as a peace chief. Shabanee reared his daughters as Catholics and sent them to school at Notre Dame. During the 1840s, he frequently visited the Gibson Inn, which was located at the present site of Froebel School at 15th and Madison.

Henrietta E. Gibson, the daughter-in-law of Gary's first tavern-keeper, recollected that bands of Potawatomi continued to return periodically to hunt and visit burial grounds until the 1860s. They were her childhood playmates, and some worked at the Gibson Inn.

"The Indians were nice to you if you were nice to them, but it didn't do to anger them," she said. One of the last contacts she had with them was near the Calumet marsh, close to the present intersection of 25th and Broadway. The Potawatomi were cooking hard corn and muskrat soup in a large kettle and shared their meal with her.

During the 1890s, a final sighting of Potawatomi occurred in Glen Park, which was then named Kelly. William Reissig spotted three Indians riding up to an oak tree. They reportedly pulled a tin box from under its bark and then disappeared.

The vanquished Potawatomi were victims of a philosophy that equated might with right. Inevitable as their removal might have been, the policy was less an example of the march of "advancing civilization," as long-time Hoosier resident John B. Dillon claimed in 1897, than a combination of misunderstanding, racism, and avarice.

BETWEEN TWO CULTURES: THE SAGA OF MARIE BAILLY

Marie Le Fevre Bailly was the first woman settler in northwest Indiana. Her life symbolized the coming together of French and Indian culture in the Old Northwest and the destruction of that way of life by westward expansion. The young Marie predicted that when she was old she would live among strangers who would show her little respect. The fulfillment of that prophecy stemmed from her Indian and Catholic heritage.

Marie Le Fevre was born in 1783 in the fur-trading settlement of Rivière des Raisins near the present site of Monroe, Michigan. Her wealthy, eccentric father felt more comfortable in the wilderness outposts of New France than in Paris. Her mother was a vivacious woman of Indian and French descent.

When Le Fevre died, his relatives in France confiscated his estate, forcing his widow and their two daughters, Marie and Angeline, to live with her Ottawa relatives. Marie enjoyed Indian life except insofar as the customs conflicted with her Catholicism. After she reached puberty, her mother pressured her into marrying a shaman named De La Vigne. She bore him two children, but separated from him several years later.

Marie became known to French traders as the "Lily of the Lakes" because of her fair complexion, beautiful figure, and romantic background. Once when she had gone by canoe to Mackinac Island to sell handmade wares, she met Joseph Bailly de Messein, whose commercial contacts stretched from Quebec to New Orleans. That same day they decided to live together as husband and wife. He agreed to be a father to Marie's two daughters, Agatha and Theresa, and she accepted his four children from a former marriage.

The couple were much alike in their love of nature, devotion to children, and adventurous spirit. Contemporaries described Marie as quiet and reserved but a good storyteller, Joseph as boisterous and convivial. One Mackinac resident said of Joseph: "One was never at a loss to locate him, no matter what part of the island might contain him. His loud laughter and speech always betrayed his whereabouts. He was an exceptionally good-natured man, fond of entertaining his friends."

The War of 1812 interrupted the couple's life together. In 1814, while traveling through Indiana in search of pelts with their servant, John Baptiste Clutier, Joseph and Marie were halted by American cavalrymen. They accused Bailly of being a British spy and arrested him. Clutier fled with Marie, fearing the soldiers would rape her. Disguising themselves as Indians in order to get aid from sympathetic tribes, they began a long, arduous trek through Illinois and Wisconsin and finally returned to Mackinac Island. Soon afterwards the war's end brought a general amnesty that freed Joseph. Although the spirits of the reunited couple were high, their health was poor. Joseph suffered from malnutrition, and Marie's skin was blemished from having been darkened by the juice of walnut hulls.

After 1814 Marie stopped dressing in the European style and decided to carry out missionary work among the Great Lakes tribes. Her husband became an American citizen and obtained a trading license for the Calumet Region, after first settling in the South Bend area. In 1822 he built a trading post on the Little Calumet River in present-day Porter County (about 14 miles east of downtown Gary) for his wife and children. There were four offspring of their marriage: Esther, Rose, Ellen, and Robert. Their first domicile was wrecked by a flood that fall, and another homestead had to be erected on higher ground.

Soon after their arrival, the Baillys were visited by the chief Shabanee, who was a distant cousin of Marie. Joseph paid him tribute for dwelling on Indian land, and they smoked and drank cognac. Shabanee's people returned often with furs and received merchandise or money ranging from 25 cents for a squirrel pelt to a dollar for a mink skin. During one visit in late autumn, the chief predicted that the winter months would be unusually cold. His prediction, which enabled the Baillys to make adequate preparations to survive, proved correct.

During the 1820s the Baillys lived in relative isolation. Most visitors were Indians who set up their wigwams near a special cabin constructed for their use in storing belongings while on hunts. Itinerant priests occasionally heard confessions, performed baptisms, and celebrated mass in the Baillys' makeshift chapel. The Baillys sent their children to schools in Fort Wayne and Fort Dearborn (the future site of Chicago) and stocked their personal library with almost 300 books. Some of these were religious tracts in the Ottawa language.

At the trading post one of Marie Bailly's goals was to Christianize the Indian visitors. She found the Potawatomi much less receptive than the Ottawa, who came into the region each winter to hunt deer. Since many of the Ottawa had been captivated by the "miracles" of a half-breed medicine man, the Baillys explained that the magic tricks were done by hypnotism, electricity, and sleight-of-hand. Afterwards, numerous Ottawa became Catholic converts.

During the early 1830s, the Bailly homestead was made part of the permanent United States mail route. The old Indian trail that passed by their buildings was improved for use by wheeled vehicles. Travelers going west to Chicago or east to Detroit sometimes spent the night. One visitor described the Bailly compound as "six or eight log cabins of a most primitive construction, all of them gray with age and so grouped on the bank of the river as to present an appearance quite picturesque."

Improved roads brought more white settlers and less Indians. It was at this time that the Baillys' friendship with the Ottawa prevented a massacre of recently arrived settlers. After white youths almost raped two Ottawa maidens—who ran for protection to the Bailly homestead and fainted outside their house—the Indians prepared to avenge the insult. Marie and Joseph spent three days and nights convincing them not to go on the warpath.

Before long, the federal government began forcing the Potawatomi out of Indiana. In *Wolves Against the Moon,* a dramatized account of the Bailly family written by Julia Cooley Altrocchi, there is a scene, perhaps apocryphal, of cavalrymen escorting a long line of carts filled with hundreds of Indians who were bound to one another at the wrists and ankles. Others struggled along on foot, flanked by soldiers with whips and bayonets. The Baillys offered words of solace to their friends, but the humiliation of their captivity caused most victims to keep their eyes to the ground.

In December 1835 Joseph Bailly died. The French and Indian mourners who gathered at his grave to chant Catholic prayers in the

Ottawa tongue were like the last remnants of a dying species. Shortly before his death, Bailly had acquired property at the mouth of the Grand Calumet River in present-day Gary in the hope of founding a town. With his trading enterprise stricken by the changing conditions, he had planned to launch a career as a land promoter. He laid out the site at the present location of Marquette Park, naming streets after members of his family. But the "Town of Bailly" was not to be. After his death, a court-appointed trustee cheated his wife and their children out of the land. Because Marie was a woman, Porter County officials refused to allow her to control her husband's estate, even though Bailly had put his financial affairs in order before his death.

Seldom during the remaining 30 years of her life did Marie Bailly socialize with white people. For awhile Ottawa tribesmen continued to frequent the homestead. When these visits ceased, she lived with relatives in Chicago and then in Mackinac. In 1850, however, she moved back to the original homestead. Her granddaughter, Frances R. Howe, wrote that on occasion a group of Potawatomi "came up from Central Illinois to make maple sugar, in a fine forest of hard maple nearby; they would come and visit her and she would return their visits; otherwise she maintained a sort of cloister rule of never leaving the premises."

After she slipped on a hidden patch of ice and injured her spine, Marie Bailly died on September 15, 1866. Years later, local residents honored her memory, but during her lifetime she was much maligned and misunderstood. Some insensitive settlers regarded the elderly widow as a half-caste whose religion was heretical and whose habits were barbaric.

As a missionary, Marie Bailly had hoped that white settlers and Indians could coexist in harmony and that man's capacity for love could overcome his immorality and greed, but her dreams collapsed in the 1830s. The disillusionment of her remaining years was softened only by her enduring religious faith.

DREAM CITIES AND A MILLIONAIRES' PLAYGROUND

Lake County's first white residents were an assortment of misfits, speculators, and yeoman farmers. Some were escaping the disappointments of a painful past, while others desired new experiences away from society's restrictions. The virgin land did not attract the cautious, the contented, or the secure, but rather the boisterous, the unconventional, and the adventurous.

During the 1830s several groups of speculators drew up plans to build cities in present-day Gary, but their dreams never materialized due to natural calamities, human miscalculations, and economic reverses. A "phantom town," named Indiana City on the surveying blueprints and placed near the defunct "Town of Bailly," never had a single resident. Manchester and City West each sprouted a few buildings and then vanished. Despite the spirit of optimism and expansion characteristic of the nineteenth century, settlement stayed outside the Gary area except for a few peripheral villages.

In 1836 the federal government began selling former Indian land in northwest Indiana. Fearful of losing their homesteads, several hundred resolute settlers in Crown Point formed a squatters' union. When the government auctioned off their plots, they bought them for the base price of $1.25 an acre, silencing other prospective bidders with firearms and knives.

That same year George Earle, an Englishman, founded a settlement called Liverpool at the present site of Lake Station. Although he failed to attract many residents, he persuaded a state-appointed commission to designate Liverpool as the county seat. When the news reached Crown Point, townsmen pressured county officials into refusing quarters in Liverpool's hastily constructed courthouse in favor of their own facilities. The next year, when a reconstituted body of commissioners reversed the decision and awarded the county seat to Crown Point, Earle's ambitions for Liverpool received their death knell. Within a decade he relocated in another area that he called Hobart in honor of his brother, F. Hobart Earle.

To the Calumet Region's boosters, boom times seemed just around the corner, especially after railroads began cutting through the area during the next two decades. Many factors, however, retarded the area's growth. The region was sandwiched between the nearly impassable Kankakee marsh and an inhospitable Lake Michigan shoreline. Under the best of conditions a summer journey by teams of horses from Michigan City to Chicago took six days. The 1850 census recorded only 4,000 settlers in Lake County and virtually none within the present boundaries of Gary except for the proprietors of the Gibson Inn. Nonetheless, speculators dreamed that they could be city-builders if only they could manipulate a canal stop, a railroad terminal, federal money for harbor improvements, a county-seat charter, or a group of ingenuous settlers. To them Chicago's spectacular rise demonstrated what imagination and hard work could accomplish.

During the 1850s the villages of Miller and Tolleston sprang up on the site of present-day Gary. Miller's history began in 1851 when the Lake Shore and Michigan Southern Railroad was constructed. Several reasons have been given for naming the area Miller. There was an innkeeper named Samuel W. Miller who asked train conductors to drop off milk when they passed by, causing them to refer to the stop as "Miller Junction." A section boss named Miller was in charge of keeping the roadbeds in good repair. Finally, a foreman named John Miller, who was in charge of building a station house, may have christened the area Miller, after burying his child there.

The first residents of Tolleston, founded in 1857, were mainly Germans who worked for the Michigan Central Railroad. After the State Line Slaughterhouse was built in Hammond in 1869, its German, English, French, and Irish employees settled in Tolleston, which had 400 inhabitants by 1882. A few shacks were built in East Tolleston, an area near present-day Broadway, that one local wag referred to as the "Town of Plug Ugly."

During the 1890s a land boom began when the news spread that meatpacking czars Nelson Morris, Philip D. Armour, and Gustavus F. Swift were going to move away from Chicago as a result of a monetary dispute with the Union Stockyards and had bought land in the area. Not overly eager to relocate their enterprises, Morris, Armour, and Swift used their land acquisitions as leverage to win their fight. The bursting of the speculative bubble aborted two more planned cities on the present site of downtown Gary: Ivanhoe and Jerusalem. Despite this setback, the consolidation of holdings increased the possibility that the area would spawn a city.

Between 1896 and 1906 an enterprising man named Louis A. Bryan built a fledgling community called Calumet, laying out or improving 20 miles of streets, including Broadway. He established a furniture factory and a newspaper, and was a part-time postmaster and justice of the peace. In the words of Powell A. Moore, he deserved to be called "the first citizen of Gary." Because of his vast landholdings, he also became its first millionaire. Bryan's estate at 2300 Jefferson later became the Lake County Children's Home. On one of its walls a bronze tablet was hung in 1938 honoring the memory of "Louis Asahel Bryan (1855–1921), a leading resident of the older villages of Jerusalem, East Tolleston, and Calumet, one of Gary's incorporators, and its first treasurer."

During the late nineteenth century the future site of Gary was best known as a vacation place for wealthy Chicagoans. Such tycoons as merchant Marshall Field, railway executive John W. Gates, and meatpacker J. Ogden Armour enjoyed the sumptuous delights of the Tolleston Club, a resort founded shortly after the Civil War and located only an hour's journey from the Windy City (near the present intersection of 25th Avenue and Clark Road). A large staff of servants drove them from the railway depot to the club, kept their plates and glasses filled during meals and high-stake card parties, and tended their horses, pigeons, and hunting dogs.

Local residents resented the club members fencing off choice hunting, trapping, and fishing grounds for their own private pleasure and hiring wardens to keep trespassers away. The exclusivist policy seemed unjust in view of the abundance of wildlife on the club's 5,000 acres. Hunters of average ability commonly bagged a hundred ducks in one outing, and an enterprising marksman once shot 189 feathered victims before ten in the morning.

A long guerrilla war ensued between the wardens and the poachers, some of whom sneaked onto the property at night, set or checked their traps, and left. Others boldly came by daylight, using old-fashioned muzzle-loading rifles that made them easily distinguishable to the game wardens. According to historian Powell Moore, guards flogged poachers with brass knuckles and confiscated or smashed their boats, rifles, traps, and fishing gear.

Skirmishes occurred frequently, but two events especially mobilized community feeling against the absentee landlords. In 1893 a saloon altercation between 21-year-old townsman Albert Looker and two gamekeepers, James Conroy and John Cleary, ended abruptly when Looker shot and killed the other men. A local jury acquitted him on the grounds of self-defense, and he was celebrated in verse by postmaster Silas E. Green, who wrote:

> The trial is over and Looker is free;
> The people are glad and, of course, so is he.
> Lake County is rid of terrible pests,
> Their spirits gone hunting, their bodies at rest.
>
> All glory to Looker, let every one sing
> The praise of a man that would do such a thing.
> The Calumet marshes will miss their soft tread,
> For the terrors of Calumet Township are dead.

Three years later on the icy Tolleston Club marshland a score of men fought a bloody battle that resulted in one death and serious injuries to three men.

The issue of hunting privileges was not resolved until 1908 when a state law was passed that permitted hunting on uncultivated property. By that time, however, Gary's growth had diminished the site's attractiveness as a shooting club and wildlife area. In 1911 it became the Gary Country Club, featuring an 18-hole golf course. The owners shrewdly held onto most of the original property long after it had lost its vacation allure for them, finally selling it during the 1920s. In 1927 a developer paid $1,500,000 for the remaining 850 acres of land.

THE SINGULAR LIFE OF JONAS RHODES

Jonas Rhodes was neither Gary's first nor its most important pioneer, though he was close on both counts. An Englishman who migrated to New York alone and then to Michigan with a Canadian-born bride, Rhodes moved during the mid-1830s to the virgin territory which later was bounded to the north and south by 39th and 50th avenues and to the east and west by Mississippi and Massachusetts streets. The low marshy land was of poor quality for farming, but it abounded with wild game and berries and contained essential supplies of wood and water. In clearing the property and erecting a temporary homestead, Rhodes was gambling that he could overcome the challenges of the inhospitable terrain.

Contemporaries described Jonas Rhodes as short in stature with a large head and a rather wild shock of hair. He was quick-tempered but had a ready smile. Somewhat of a nonconformist who had little use for government or organized religion, he had a salty tongue and an irreverent wit. In later life, he became renowned for his generosity and geniality, but remained a free spirit who rarely amended his manners to satisfy the constraints of others.

Building a large log cabin that eventually accommodated 11 children, Rhodes and his family eked out a livelihood by growing vegetables, hunting and trapping wild game, raising cows, poultry, and pigs, and selling cranberries and butter in Crown Point, LaPorte, Hobart, and elsewhere. The entire family made an annual journey to Chicago to buy clothes, sugar, coffee, tea, candy, medicine, and novelties.

Necessity and choice kept the family close-knit. They sometimes broke the tedium of the evenings by making molasses candy and popping corn in the fireplace. Jonas organized spelling bees and asked the children to read from volumes of Shakespeare, Robert Burns, or the Bible. Like many pioneers, he feared that the frontier would have a barbarizing effect on his offspring if he did not remain diligent in educating them. The children received much of their preadolescent schooling at home, although some of them periodically attended a school in Hobart.

The Civil War was a personal tragedy for the Rhodes family. Four sons went off to face the pestilence and carnage of military life. William joined the Confederate Army after marrying a Southern woman whose dowry included numerous slaves. George, John, and Thomas fought for the North. Plagued with worry, Jonas and his wife, Susan, vainly tried to send food to them. On one occasion, Thomas evidently bought butter at the commissary and found a note from his mother in it. His subsequent efforts to get his money refunded failed. George Rhodes apparently died in battle, but his body was never found. Later Jonas walked over countless gravesites searching for some hint of where it lay. John and Thomas survived the war but died soon after coming home.

During the late 1860s Rhodes replaced his jerry-built log house with a large colonial structure. Baking, molding, and laying the bricks themselves, he and his family adorned their new home with plush carpets and walnut furniture. The estate became a sanctuary for travelers, who sometimes stayed for weeks at a time, and for friends who visited from Hobart.

In his twilight years Jonas became a convivial host and grandfatherly community pillar. At annual winter dances that followed sleigh rides, he played his English hornpipe and, dressed in cowhide boots, danced to the music of fiddlers. Claiming to be a practiced phrenologist, he enjoyed poring over children's heads and assessing their character and future from his analysis of the protuberances and shapes of their skulls. Alice Mundell Demmon, a neighbor, remembered him as a rather lonely old man who "was willing to keep any one who would stay and listen to him talk, and in fact, do all the talking; all he needed was someone to nod his head occasionally."

Rhodes took an interest in the first published history of Lake County and said, according to genealogist T. H. Ball, that its weather statistics were worth the entire price of the book. When his children taunted him for settling on such unfertile land, Rhodes admonished them to hold onto it after he died because it would one day embrace a great city. At his death in 1879 the vision seemed quixotic. Some of his descendants remained in Gary, but they did not have the prescience to profit from his advice.

SVANTI A. NORDSTROM AND BETHEL CHURCH

During the late 1860s famine struck throughout Sweden, causing widespread distress to thousands of peasants who, even in good times, lived close to the poverty level. In consequence, a tide of emigration commenced. In 1867, 9,000 Swedes entered America; in 1868, the numbers swelled to 27,000; in 1869 to 39,000. There were further increases during the 1870s and 1880s because of pressures of overpopulation due to a falling death rate and a rising birth rate. Most emigrants uprooted themselves from their native villages out of desperation. But there were pull factors as well as push factors at work. Letters from overseas, village gossip, and brochures from land companies and shipping lines all fostered hopes that America was a "Golden Land."

Some Swedes came to Miller, a tiny, out-of-the-way railroad junction whose sandy, swampy terrain was not conducive to farming. One of the first settlers, Svanti A. Nordstrom, had learned of the area from friends in LaPorte and Baillytown. Writing idyllic accounts of the outpost's scenic beauty and job opportunities, he in turn convinced others to join him. Life was hard for the newcomers. They hauled sand from pits, cut ice in winter, and kept the equipment of the Lake Shore and Michigan Southern Railroad in good repair for one dollar or less a day. The settlers also fished, picked berries, grew a few garden vegetables, and raised cows, pigs, and poultry.

Nicklas Nicklason and his family lived in Chicago for three years but moved to Miller after the catastrophic fire of 1871. Employed as a section man to drive spikes, level gravel beds, and inspect railroad ties, Nicklason once strapped a 220-pound barrel of salt onto his back and hauled it home from the train station. A devout Christian, he helped Nordstrom make plans for a community parish that would transplant the principles of the Swedish Evangelical Church unchanged and undiluted to the New World.

In the absence of an ordained minister, Nordstrom became the community's spiritual leader, holding prayer meetings in his home. For communion services, however, the settlers had to go to the Augsburg Lutheran Church in Baillytown. In 1872 Magnus Anderson's children, Jenny and Alfred, attended confirmation classes there twice a week, making the trip on foot along the Lake Shore tracks, on ice skates in winter across the frozen Long Lake, or by hitching rides on a passing train.

During the spring of 1874 Nordstrom and his neighbors drafted a church constitution so that, according to its preamble, "Everything [would] be decently and efficiently conducted." On June 26, 11 men signed the charter on behalf of their families. A twelfth founder, Mrs. Christina Maria Nelson, was prohibited from signing the document because of her sex. The members elected Nordstrom to be their first chairman and deacon.

The Reverend A. Challman of Baillytown attended these ceremonies and was the first to sign the charter; he returned every month or two to preach and hold communion services. In his absence Nordstrom was acting pastor. In October 1874 the congregation met for the first time in a one-room log schoolhouse (located at the present site of 651 South Henry Street).

During the 1870s the church had scant financial resources and a "barebones" budget. For example, in 1878 the yearly income was $31.04, exactly a dollar more than expenditures. The following year, the church raised $53.57 by assessing annual dues of 25 cents and asking for a special subscription to cover Nordstrom's $10.50 annual salary. Expenses for 1879, recorded in Swedish in a large ledger book, included: to Augustana synod—23 cents; to the church at Englewood —$1; for Inner Mission—$3.16; for poor seminary students—50 cents; and for the home-made communion wine—$2.

Svanti Nordstrom, a ruggedly handsome man with yellow, curly hair and a long, flowing beard, had tireless energy and an intimate knowledge of the Scriptures. The venerable Swede was a minister in all but title and was the church's guiding force for a generation. "He had the bearing of a man that you could not help but respect," said one of the parishioners.

Although he could not administer the sacrament of the Lord's Supper, Nordstrom performed emergency baptisms and regularly visited the sick and the elderly. He enjoyed composing religious homilies for young people on their birthdays. Once he told Signe Palm, who was moving away from the village, to remember her Psalms when she went out "into the world's big crowds."

One of Nordstrom's assistants was Hokan Hasselgren, who emigrated to Miller in 1880 after receiving a letter from Nordstrom describing the opportunities that awaited newcomers to the region. The 32-year-old sailor belonged to one of Sweden's most oppressed groups. As a youth, his father had been at sea for months at a time while his mother did back-breaking field labor in order to maintain her family in a one-room house. Not wishing to share the same fate, Hasselgren scraped together the 60-dollar transatlantic fare for himself, his wife Caroline, and their daughter Hanna, and together they embarked on the 12-day steamship voyage to America.

Caroline Hasselgren's experience as a midwife was a valuable addition to the Swedish-American community at a time when the nearest doctor lived in Hobart and, once contacted by telegram via Chicago, had to drive his horse and buggy over a tortuously slow route.

Soon after she arrived, a neighbor asked her to come to the aid of the storekeeper's wife. Conditioned by Sweden's rigid class system, she said in effect: "Oh no! I cannot go to that house!" After much urging, she went to a hovel that seemed incompatible with the merchant's station in life. A few months later, the man moved into a more luxurious house.

Both Hokan and Caroline Hasselgren worked for the Aetna Powder Company, which was built in 1881. Caroline made shells, and her husband packed dynamite into them. The plant provided income for the Swedish settlement, but the work was very hazardous. Explosions sometimes cracked the walls of the Miller schoolhouse. On these occasions, pupils were sent home to learn whether the tragedy had afflicted their family.

Taking an active part in church affairs, Hokan Hasselgren frequently preached sermons in a loud, intense voice that both entertained and awed his audience, especially since he stood in such close proximity to them, because as a layman he would not use the pulpit. On one occasion, while beseeching sinners to reform or face damnation, he smacked a chair with such fury that it crashed to the floor, causing one person to scream in fright.

For two decades, the congregation did not have its own place of worship and continued to use the school facilities. In 1890 Charles B. Daly, a wealthy Chicagoan with extensive real estate holdings in the area, donated a 50 X 150-foot plot of land at the southwest corner of 4th and Lake. Raising 900 dollars for the new building took four years and countless church suppers, needlework sales, and "free-will" offerings. In 1894 the new 28 X 40-foot frame structure, christened Bethel Church (meaning House of God), was ready for occupancy. Unfortunately there were still no funds to hire an ordained minister. Nordstrom remained acting pastor, and Hasselgren became superintendent of the Sunday School program.

"Old Bethel" was slow to lose its Scandinavian flavor. In Sunday School children learned Swedish Bible stories from books yellowed with age that had been brought over from the Old Country. Until 1905 church services were in Swedish. Males sat on the right, females on the left, until one morning when a woman remained with her husband on the "wrong" side of the aisle. With the tradition broken, others followed her example, and the segregated seating arrangement ended.

In 1905 the Reverend J. A. Berg became Bethel's first ordained pastor, thus enabling Svanti Nordstrom to go into semiretirement. Two years later, the 86-year-old patriarch published a book of poems and daily devotional essays. He died on Thanksgiving Day of 1910 and was buried in Miller cemetery, near the site from which he had first set eyes on his "Promised Land."

DIANA OF THE DUNES

The name, "Diana of the Dunes," suggests mythology, mystery, romance. The story of a woman who fled society to live in seclusion in the northwest Indiana dunes was ready-made for the sensational tabloids of the early twentieth century. In an era when Americans admired individualism and eccentricity, Diana's withdrawal from civilization contained irresistible elements of drama and pathos. In time legends grew about a carefree maiden who once swam naked in the lake surf and lived an idyllic life unencumbered by society's restraints.

In truth, the real Diana, a University of Chicago graduate with a Phi Beta Kappa key named Alice Mable Gray, was more complex. Her lifestyle was both a rebellion against the competitive, materialistic culture of urban America and a casualty of that world from which she tried to escape. Her very flight caused her in the end to become the center of unwanted publicity. A gawking public hounded her, made her a celebrity, and perhaps contributed to her death.

In October 1915, at the age of 34, she moved to an abandoned hut located in the wild dunes area northeast of Miller. While working as a stenographer and editor for an astronomy magazine in Chicago, she had made frequent excursions to the scenic marshes and sand hills. First inspired to "get away from the conventional world" by Byron's poem "Solitude," she acted out her fantasy of a "free life" upon discovering that she was being paid much less than men doing the same job.

Arriving with only a knife, spoon, blanket, jelly glass, and two guns, she slept on timbers protected from the wind and rain only by a linden tree. For a while she lived in a derailed boxcar, and then in an abandoned shack. In her words, "then I began housekeeping and all the furniture I have is made of driftwood. Everything is driftwood here, including myself."

The "woman hermit," as the Gary *Evening Post* called her, was first ridiculed by neighbors and called "Nellie Gray." As some of them got to know her, however, they found her to be intelligent, witty, and quick to laugh.

Alice Gray spent her time swimming, studying birds, flowers, and ferns, catching fish and wild animals, gathering driftwood, picking berries, and making wine. She sold some of these collectibles to buy bread, salt, and reading material. She read voraciously and wrote manuscripts about the history and ecology of the dunes. Not the complete hermit that some people portrayed her to be, she was a frequent visitor to the Miller Public Library and checked out books on travel, philosophy, and history. On occasion she visited her sister and brother in Michigan City, although they disapproved of her lifestyle. Gary attorney Armand Prete recollected seeing her often along the Miller lakefront carrying a gunny sack filled with books. He described her as small and rather dumpy but polite and sociable. Her gypsy ways would be less an oddity today, he concluded.

Matilda Burton, a fisherman's wife, described her in July 1916: "She wears her hair bobbed. She has no mirror and knows when her hair is too long by the length of the shadow it casts on the ground. . . . Her winter dress consists of a short coarse skirt, big boots, ragged waist[coat], and a little cap. In the summer she wears just an old light dress and the ragged waist[coat]. . . . She cooks outside her hut. She has a few boxes which she keeps scrupulously clean, and uses for chairs and tables. She has a sort of fireplace, and her only utensils are an old coffee pot and a cup she found on the railroad tracks."

Around the time of World War I, "Diana," as she was dubbed by the press, met a huge, quick-tempered fisherman and furniture maker named Paul G. Wilson, who was widely assumed to be a petty thief. Equipment disappeared periodically from Armand Prete's cabin until he hired Wilson to build him a boat. Then the pilfering ceased.

Samuel H. Reck, who befriended Paul and Diana, wrote that "their principal occupation was fishing. Paul had several boats and gill net equipment. Diana would hike to Miller with a gunny sack full of perch, sell them, and with the proceeds buy such things as were needed. . . . Her customary dress at the dunes was a pair of khaki trousers, leggings, and a khaki shirt. She usually wore a felt hat with a wide brim, though she did have feminine garments which she would put on on occasion."

In 1920 the couple moved to present-day Ogden Dunes. Sightseers frequently interrupted their solitude and were sometimes chased away by rifle fire. In May 1922 police suspected that Paul had killed a man whose body was found near their "Wren's Nest." It turned out that the victim had died elsewhere. The publicity brought swarms of curiosity seekers, some of whom broke into their primitive cabin.

During this time Paul and Diana tended to blame their problems on a deputy sheriff named Eugene Frank, who suspected them of vandalizing summer cabins and tampering with fishing nets and who had ordered them not to cross his beachfront property. Paul and Diana decided to go to Frank's house to complain about the harassment. An argument ensued; and Frank, who was allegedly drunk, shot Paul in the foot and pistol-whipped Diana, crushing her skull with the butt of his gun. She was taken to Gary's Mercy Hospital, setting off another flurry of publicity. Reporters had a field day, calling Paul "Diana's caveman mate." Meanwhile, souvenir hunters ransacked the "Wren's Nest." Deputy sheriff Frank was indicted for assault and battery but was not convicted.

In 1923 Paul and Diana took a boat trip down the Mississippi River. They returned to the dunes and intended to travel south again to settle permanently in the remote Texas badlands when suddenly on February 11, 1925, she became ill and died. Doctors diagnosed the ailment as uremic poisoning.

Diana's family refused to honor her request that she be cremated with her ashes spread among the dunes. Paul, who blamed his lover's death on the deputy sheriff who had fractured her skull, showed up at the funeral with a gun. Before her body was taken to Oak Hill Cemetery, the police put Paul in jail for disturbing the peace.

Wilson vowed vengeance on Diana's tormentors and was subsequently arrested for shooting at a train and assaulting a law officer. Later, he met an Indian widow named Henrietta Hyessa and moved with her to another isolated shack near Michigan City. In 1927 he was fined 100 dollars and sentenced to a penal farm for six months on two counts of assault and battery.

After she died, there was much posthumous glorifying of Diana by the very media people who previously had portrayed her as a freak. Nonetheless, an editorial in the Prairie Club *Bulletin* noted that "her fresh spirit and fair-mindedness left its impress, incorrigible individualist though she was."

Historian Powell A. Moore called Diana a "tragic recluse." The tragedy was not that she had shaken off the "shackles of conventionality," as the Gary *Post-Tribune* put it. She found considerable freedom and happiness in the dunes, at least for a time. Her quest for solitude failed because the world would not leave her alone.

DRUSILLA CARR: SHE STOOD HER GROUND

In 1872 Drusilla Benn moved from Valparaiso to a Miller lakefront fishery to join her brother as a housekeeper and cook. Two years later, she married Robert Carr and moved into a two-room pine cabin near the mouth of the Grand Calumet River. Their only neighbors were a boat builder named Allen Dutcher, a hunter-trapper of French and Indian descent named Jacques Beaubien, and an ex-fugitive slave named Davy Crockett. Drusilla was the only woman in the sparsely settled area.

The dunes country was so wild at this time that, according to Mrs. Carr, "the wolves stood back in the hills and cried like a woman." She told James W. Lester that "there were lots of white and blue cranes, and hundreds of bald eagles along the beach. When we went along the lake, we could see an eagle on every hill." Once, when one of the four Carr children was attacked by an eagle that a fisherman had adopted as a pet but had neglected to feed, Drusilla held the bird at bay with her sunbonnet until her husband heard the commotion and drove it off with a paddle.

Mrs. Carr often assisted her husband in his tasks as a fisherman and was adept at pulling in the nets and winding up the windlasses. She picked cranberries to sell in Miller, which was connected with their homestead by a rough, mile-long towpath. Most of the cranberry bushes died, however, after a man sold the dune moss, which protected them from frost, to be used in packing fruit trees.

The Carrs also traded at Clark Station, a settlement to the west founded by Germans in 1858 and named for George W. Clark, a railway engineer and land speculator. They traveled there by boat with sturgeon, whitefish, waterfowl, mink and muskrat pelts, and honey from Robert's bee colony.

In 1896 Drusilla befriended the French-born Chicagoan Octave Chanute, a civil engineer who conducted glider experiments for two weeks near her homestead. One of his planes had five tiers of wings and resembled a Venetian blind. Mrs. Carr fed his party and enjoyed watching the exciting experiments. Some other Millerites called Chanute the "Crazy Old Man of the Sand Dunes" and spread fables that his glider wings were thatched with chicken feathers, but Mrs. Carr was one of his staunch defenders.

After her husband's death in 1903, Drusilla lived for several months during the year in Indiana Harbor. But the scenic beauty and sense of being close to nature would draw her back to the lakefront for the rest of the year.

The founding of Gary upset Mrs. Carr's tranquil way of life. It precipitated a rash of claims to land that she considered to be her own. A dozen times she weathered legal battles only to face appeals and new suits. In 1908 Mrs. Carr attempted to secure her claim to a mile-long, 120-acre lakefront estate. Having lived there more than 30 years, she claimed title on the principle of squatter sovereignty.

Her legal position seemed to rest on solid ground since both Indiana and the federal government recognized the right of adverse possession based upon 20 years of peaceful, uninterrupted, and undisputed possession.

In addition to squatter's rights, Drusilla Carr asserted that a visiting Civil War veteran named Bingham had given her and her husband the land in gratitude for their hospitality after discovering that it was unsuitable for farming. Bingham allegedly promised to register the transaction and send back the deed but did neither. Without proof of a title transfer, the question of written title was open to debate. In 1832 the government had set aside several lakefront parcels for the Potawatomi, who, according to legend, bartered them away for "a barrel of whiskey, a handful of beads, and a pot of vermillion paint." Jacques Beaubien evidently sold a deed to William H. Hitt, whose heirs argued that Davy Crockett was his caretaker. Drusilla responded that Bingham had purchased the Hitt property. Several eastern families put forth additional claims of dubious validity. In 1920 Mrs. Carr succinctly summarized the weakness of her opponents' position. "No one ever told me I was on their property," she said.

During the 1920s Drusilla resided in a cottage located near the lake. She collected rentals on more than a hundred beach houses; lessees paid her a hundred dollars a year for the right to build a cottage on her property. The court fights aged her, friends noted, but left her spirit undaunted. She disliked publicity and was known to shake a broom at reporters. But newsman Arnold A. Coons wrote in 1920 that she was "perfectly free in her talk until her troublesome suits . . . are mentioned, when she freezes up and immediately gets suspicious."

In the 1920s, despite Miller's growth and annexation to Gary, the beachfront was still an exciting, primitive place to live. Mrs. A. C. Fonville recollected that on one occasion huge pieces of driftwood almost knocked over her rented home. On another occasion, beachcombers dismantled her wooden porch for firewood.

In 1927 a storm destroyed the old Carr homestead. As Drusilla described it, "the wind came along and blew in the roof, and then the sand pushed in the walls and covered everything. . . . I hated to see that old house go!" At this time, Carr's Beach at the end of Lake Street became Gary's most bustling summer tourist spot with such attractions as a miniature railroad, a shooting galley, a bath house, a pleasure boat, and several night spots. Drusilla's son Fred managed a dance hall and roller rink before a "super lake storm" destroyed it.

During a 17-year span of litigation culminating in 1929, Mrs. Carr won eight court decisions against three groups of plaintiffs. Nonetheless, she had to sell half her land to pay lawyers' fees. A *Post-Tribune* columnist captured Mrs. Carr's plight in the following poem: "Attorneys got her lake shore plot on quit claim deeds for acres, but still she harbors fight enough to challenge legal takers. . . . 'I'll lick 'em yet,' she says, 'You bet!'—when asked how things are going. If business ran like courts, 'twould soon be where it's never snowing." The poem concluded: "If doctors swathed a wound so ill and charged so much for cotton, their gentle blood we'd sweetly spill and bid them lie forgotten."

Attorney Armand Prete described Drusilla as a forceful, determined woman with a lot of grit who, although unschooled, knew her rights and would not be pushed around. Her main concern was that the lakefront ecology "not be desecrated by huge industrial smoke stacks."

That danger loomed in 1930 when Mrs. Carr's last battle commenced, this time against the Gary Land Company, a subsidiary of U.S. Steel. Between 1912 and 1917, lawyer Frank B. Pattee paid delinquent taxes on the Carr estate and subsequently sold his lien to the Gary Land Company. Mrs. Carr offered to assume the debt but the corporation refused and took her to court, arguing that the site was better suited for manufacturing than for "mere shacks."

On September 14, 1930, before a verdict was reached, Mrs. Carr died. The Reverend Frederick W. Backemeyer told several hundred mourners at Miller cemetery that "She was a heroic little soul who stood her ground when she thought she was in the right. . . . Strength, courage and dignity were her clothing."

Less than 45 acres remained for Mrs. Carr's heirs. They and the half-dozen lawyers who owned the balance of the disputed 89-acre tract (the rising lake level had wiped out the rest of the original claim) held the valid title, the court ruled. Nonetheless, the judge added that on pain of foreclosure they had to pay the assumed back taxes plus interest to the Gary Land Company.

After nine years of appeals, the decision still stood, but because of the compounding interest, the debt had risen to $92,000. Although the land was probably worth 50 times that amount, the trustees for the Drusilla Carr Land Corporation could not raise the money. Several times they almost obtained the necessary loan; and a number of clients expressed interest in buying parcels of land, including heavyweight champion Joe Louis, who wanted to open a recreation area and training camp. All the transactions fell through, partly due to pressure exerted by Gary Land Company officials, who had an informer keeping them abreast of the latest efforts.

In November 1937 the trustees attempted to sell half their property to the city of Gary for $100,000; but the City Council rejected the offer, 6 to 2, after mill spokesmen intimated that they would donate a similar tract. Prior to the vote, Carr attorney Armand Prete angrily declared: "The U.S. Steel Corporation has never given the city anything. It controls the most valuable property in Gary and has always received 1,000 percent profit on everything it ever 'gave' the city."

At a 1940 sheriff's sale, the Gary Land Company assumed official title to the 89 acres by bidding $92,632.78. Nonetheless, the depression had cooled U. S. Steel's ardor for expansion, and so the land was transferred to the parks department for approximately the amount of the auction price.

One person close to the case claimed that the mill "donated" the land for tax purposes and included so many stipulations that it could reclaim the gift by charging the city with violating the contract if and when it so desired. Had the Carr family not drawn them into a public battle, however, it is unlikely that Gary residents would have access to Drusilla's "stretch of beach."

Unprecedented in its length and complexity, the Carr case caused Indiana to tighten its "squatter sovereignty" statutes. A quarter-century later, the city of Gary used property laws, health ordinances, and condemnation procedures to oust fisherman August Sabinske from Marquette Park. After failing to intimidate the squatter with bulldozers ("they would run them up to my house and leave them idle for hours," Sabinske complained), municipal officials allowed him to live out his years there.

In 1964, three years before his death, Sabinske related how the beachfront environment had been poisoned since Mrs. Carr's day. "The fish are gone, the gulls are gone, everything is gone. The nuts have ruined everything," he said.

After U.S. Steel founded Gary, most old settlers made their peace with the new order or faded quietly out of sight. "Diana of the Dunes" tried to hide from society and became one of its "curiosity pieces." Drusilla Carr and August Sabinske were rugged individualists who were unafraid to stand their ground against overwhelming forces. They lost their land but not without a fight.

CHAPTER TWO

Twentieth-Century City

I see for Gary a future of rare commercial power and signal industrial greatness. . . . I see a city rise as if by magic, in proportions vast
and splendid, with a hundred busy marts of traffic and of trade,
with palatial homes unnumbered and seats of learning multi-
plied. . . . I see the multitude upon her streets as its atoms catch the
pulse-beat of strange new city life and then move to its ceaseless
rhythms urged on by the stimuli that come from crowd-pressure
and example. . . . I see countless toilers in factory, mill, and shop—
bare-bodied men who move like specters amid the heat and glow
of furnace and of forge, of molten streams of metal and red-hot,
yielding, lapping sheets of steel—and heaving wharfmen loading
cargoes on far-extending piers.

> —Governor J. Frank Hanly, in his
> speech at first banquet of the
> Gary Commercial Club, at the
> Gary Hotel, November 25, 1907

JUST AS THE Calumet Region was, according to Powell A. Moore,
"Indiana's last frontier," so was Gary the "youngest of the region's
industrial cities." In 1889 Standard Oil Company set up a refinery in
Whiting; twelve years later Inland Steel built a plant near East
Chicago. In 1906 United States Steel Corporation made its move to
the east of those cities. Graham R. Taylor called Gary both a "city by
decree" because it was the brainchild of U.S. Steel and a "satellite
city" because of its proximity to Chicago. Gary's resident boosters, on
the other hand, used the phrases "miracle city," "magic city," and
"city of the century" to describe their company town. In nine years
Gary was transformed from a barren wasteland to a second-class city

of 55,378 people. Serious dislocations accompanied the rapid growth, but to casual observers Gary truly seemed a city on the move.

In 1905 the United States Steel Corporation decided to build a new plant complex on the southern shore of Lake Michigan. The city of Gary came into being because of what historian G. Landen White called "the first example of the deliberate application of the principles of scientific location of industry in this century." Losing contracts because it was unable to satisfy the great demand for its products in the Midwest, U.S. Steel chose an undeveloped area accessible by water and rail to Minnesota iron ore, Michigan limestone, and Appalachian Mountains coal. Board chairman Elbert H. Gary originally favored a site near Waukegan, Illinois, but land agent Armanis F. Knotts, a former mayor of Hammond, convinced him that the Indiana site was less congested, better suited for tax purposes, and more closely linked to Chicago's railway arteries. The sparse vegetation and relatively level topography added to the site's attractiveness.

U.S. Steel acquired approximately 9,000 acres of land, including seven miles of shoreline, for about 7.2 million dollars, or 800 dollars an acre. A.F. Knotts made the transactions surreptitiously at first so as not to cause a boom in prices. At one point he carried more than a million dollars in a satchel to a New York office building. During the winter of 1905 construction engineers Ralph E. Rowley and Thomas H. Cutler began making preliminary plans for the railroad yards and plant. Knotts first showed Rowley the site on March 8, 1906. A month later, project engineer Arthur P. Melton began laying out a townsite south of the Grand Calumet River, which was regarded as a "moat" between the mills and the residential district. On April 18 the first stake was driven into the sand at 5th and Broadway. Melton's crew built a temporary bridge, dug sand wells, and surveyed the street boundaries. The workers had to contend with hornets, dune fleas, yellow jackets, and snakes as they made their way through swamps and thickets. By summer construction gangs were leveling and grading the land on the plant site, preparing the roadbeds and the elevations for 51 miles of railway track, and moving the Grand Calumet River 1,000 feet south of its former route. Powell Moore called the relocation project "an achievement of epic proportions," but Bradley J. Beckham took a somewhat different view of U.S. Steel's project, concluding that "what took nature thousands of years to mold, man in the guise of progress subverted in a few months."

While the work went forward, mill officials stayed in cottages at the Calumet Gun Club, which had been founded by affluent Chicagoans in 1885. Located at the site where the harbor for Gary Works was to be laid out, the clubhouse contained bowling alleys and billiard tables; nearby were facilities for trapshooting and a rifle range.

The work crews had less pleasant quarters and huddled together in tents pitched on the north bank of the Grand Calumet River. On the other side of the river a community was forming along a dirt road euphemistically called Euclid Avenue in honor of the Greek geometrist. Most of the newcomers lived in tents or tarpaper shacks; a few huts were dug right into hills of sand. The settlement's first "native" resident, a girl christened "Gary," was born to the Frank Huff family in September. Two months later, a six-inch snow knocked down half the dwellings and put most of the stoves out of order.

One of the first wooden buildings in Gary was a crude, windowless bunk house called McFadden's Flats, which contained 60 cots and had no indoor pump or bathroom. Major John McFadden got the idea of a rooming house from project superintendent William P. Gleason and charged customers 25 cents a night or one dollar a week. It was used mainly by workers, although quite a few people who later became community pillars (such as Mayor William F. Hodges) spent their first nights in Gary at McFadden's Flats. Women stayed there, too, with blankets hung around their cots.

All the while, U.S. Steel was going forward with its "urban experiment." The barriers separating mill officials, town leaders, and workers—symbolically seen in the first housing arrangements—remained hindrances to progress. The building of massive and impressive plant facilities took priority over the needs of the adjacent town. U.S. Steel allocated approximately 65 million dollars for the Gary projects; and when plant costs exceeded estimates, the money was taken from the town budget. The company applied the most modern techniques in constructing its mill facilities but paid little heed to scientific methods of urban planning. For example, Gary's grid street pattern was less efficient for twentieth-century traffic needs than a diagonal or circular design would have been, and the townsite was so close to the mills that the air was destined to be terribly polluted.

Company officials admitted that their main concern was profitable steel production rather than the creation of a "model" city. Adopting a "limited involvement" philosophy of town planning, U.S. Steel realized that it was absolutely necessary to create the rudiments of a city but hoped to avoid the thoroughgoing paternalism that had tarnished palace car tycoon George M. Pullman's company town in Illinois. "The most successful attempts at industrial social betterment in our country," Indiana Steel Company President Eugene J. Buffington wrote, "are those furthest removed from the suspicion of domination or control of the employer." Quoting poet James Russell Lowell, Buffington claimed that "one twig of experience is worth a whole forest of theory."

U.S. Steel modeled its policies somewhat on the planned community of Vandergrift, Pennsylvania, where most steelworkers owned their own homes, took pride in civic activities, and seemed less interested in strikes than had been the case at Pullman. The small, largely native-born population of Vandergrift made too rigid a duplication impossible, however, the company believed. For one thing, it was felt that Gary's foreign-born newcomers would not countenance prohibition, so the Vandergrift plan was amended to allow the sale of alcohol at four locations within U.S. Steel's 800-acre First Subdivision, which extended south to the Wabash Railroad tracks near 9th Avenue and was administered by a subsidiary, the Gary Land Company. Secondly, it was believed that the settlers should be given incentives for buying homes and keeping them in good order. Conditions were put on property sales, forcing buyers to develop their land within 18 months (in order to curtail speculation) and to build a certain distance away from the street, using specified materials. At first the company sold vacant lots; but when land sales lagged, it began constructing homes. Five hundred units were rented out to occupants, including 260 on the West Side to middle-class families, 190 on the East Side suitably priced for foremen and skilled workers, and 50 units for unskilled workers on the far Northeast—in apartments that were quickly nicknamed "double drygoods boxes."

The last project was a failure. Fearing that immigrants would rip up the floors for firewood, the Gary Land Company put in hardwood but did little to educate rural peasants about their new environment. The rents were so high and the housing shortage so severe that tenants took in boarders. As many as 20 people shared a four-room abode. Considering the settlement an eyesore, the company eventually shut it down, thereby compounding the housing shortage south of the Wabash tracks. Similarly, the Lake County Medical Society evicted homesteaders from Gary Land Company property where the first cluster of shacks had arisen in 1906.

In 1909 corporate executive Eugene J. Buffington wrote that "Gary is nothing more than the product of effort along practical lines to secure right living conditions around a steel-manufacturing plant." Six years later, however, urban planner Graham R. Taylor concluded that "the Gary town plan is likely to create in a decade conditions which can only be remedied by a Caesarean operation. . . ." Anthony Brook later concurred: "Hailed as the New Industrial Utopia, it rapidly degenerated into a dreary industrial conurbation."

Historians Raymond A. Mohl and Neil Betten concluded that successful city planning never became a reality in Gary, because U.S. Steel put less emphasis on the welfare of the community than on "efficient production of steel and stockholder profits." When difficulties arose in providing decent low-cost housing, for example, the company allowed immigrants to fend for themselves.

Gary grew up in the shadow of the mills and depended on them for its livelihood. In terms of economic power, Judge Elbert H. Gary's corporation reigned supreme even though the "founding father" never resided in the town and his local "baron," plant superintendent William Palmer Gleason, divided his time between a mansion at 7th and Jackson and an estate in Englewood, Illinois. U.S. Steel's political power in Gary was less secure, as reflected by the maverick policies of the town's first political boss, Thomas E. Knotts.

PROVIDING WATER FOR GARY

As overseer of the Northside, the Gary Land Company paved the streets of the First Subdivision, laid sidewalks, brought in top soil from Illinois, planted trees, and installed utilities and sewers. Perhaps the most important city-building task, however, was providing water. To that end, U.S. Steel created another subsidiary, the Gary Heat, Light, and Water Company, which hired the prestigious Chicago engineering firm of Alvord and Burdick to begin preliminary investigations in the summer of 1906.

John W. Alvord, formerly chief engineer of Lakeview, Hyde Park, and Cicero, was an inquisitive genius. During the late 1880s he had bicycled through Europe visiting famous waterworks. Hired to provide water for the 1893 World's Fair, he ran a pipe down from Wisconsin when reports of typhus microorganisms in the Chicago water supply threatened to keep away tourists. In 1902 Charles B. Burdick went into partnership with Alvord. A practical builder, he worked well in tandem with Alvord, who mapped out strategic decisions in Chicago's Hartford Building, while the 32-year-old Burdick supervised on-the-job operations to ensure that contractors complied with their specifications.

Prior to the tapping of Lake Michigan, Gary settlers got their water from sand wells. Pipes were driven ten or more feet into the ground, and suction pumps extracted the water. Alvord and Burdick drew up plans for a temporary pumping station to augment the community's short-term needs and a master blueprint for a permanent system of transferring water through a six-foot tunnel to a pumping station near 7th and Madison. Extending approximately 7,500 feet into the lake and another 7,500 feet underground, the tunnel was designed to connect with a land-based pump shaft, a shore shaft, and a lake shaft. The top part of the lake shaft would be removed after the installation of an octagonal crib which would rest on 76 piles and 3 range posts.

In February 1907, in an effort to hasten completion of the project, mill officials offered the Great Lakes Dredge and Dock Company a bonus and penalty contract. It was refused. Had it been accepted, the firm would have collected a year's bonus.

In the spring of 1908 the Great Lakes Dredge and Dock Company began work on the shore shaft. It took five weeks to sink the iron-encased structure down through 55½ feet of sand and 23 feet of clay. When excavation started at the base of the shaft, there was so much leakage that the project had to be abandoned. The problem, Alvord and Burdick believed, was that a submerged log had cut grooves in the shaft when dragged into the clay from its sandy resting place.

Work on a second shore shaft consumed three months. After filling it with water and using almost 300 tons of sandbags of achieve maximum penetration, a steel-plated air lock was installed in order to minimize the leakage. On July 27, 1908, air pressure was turned on. For eight hours the air lock performed adequately. Then the shaft suddenly exploded, leaving four cracks in the circular wall. A foreman later stated that it was a miracle no one was killed. For four weeks, the contractors tried to seal the fissure with oakum caulking, steel sheet piling, and concrete. The efforts were fruitless. New cracks appeared in late August, and the structure, like its predecessor ten yards away, was abandoned.

During the winter, Alvord and Burdick perfected a new air lock system. A third shore shaft, built the following spring, was finally ready for hookup with the intake crib, a huge apparatus built in South Chicago and towed to its underwater resting place. Innovatively designed by Alvord, the crib was one of the first clog-proof models of its kind. Previous Great Lakes systems were plagued during cold weather by gelatinous "frazzle ice" that blocked the intake entrances. Alvord discovered that the ice would not form at a depth of more than 35 feet if the velocity of the incoming water was less than three inches per second. The Gary crib, resting 43 feet below the lake surface, had an intricate series of passages which slowed down the water flow so that there never was an ice stoppage.

While lake operations moved forward, three teams of laborers toiled around the clock to install an underground tunnel through Gary's clay, sand, and gravel terrain. The sound of dynamite blasts was a frequent reminder to townspeople that the crews had come upon a layer of tough grubbing clay or hardpan. Once the cavity was hollowed out, laborers laid down tunnel sections that resembled foot-thick horseshoes.

Alvord and Burdick hired several contractors to install sewers, most of which drained into the Little Calumet River. Placing them through Gary's ubiquitous ridges required the use of well points to dry out the sand. Even after the removal of the well points, the brick sewers drained the ridges of water, as seen by the withering of the scrub oaks that had adorned them.

Digging tunnels and installing pipe lines and sewers was hazardous work, and tragedies occurred. For instance, on September 24, 1907, Mike Naughton was buried alive at a sewer site when lining boards caved in on him. Frantically, his fellow-workers dug through the sand, but he was dead by the time they reached him.

By June of 1909 the shafts and tunnels were complete. Engineers closed, unfastened, and removed the lake shaft. Then for a month the tunnels were disinfected with hypochlorite of lime. Finally, on July 16, 1909, the new network went into operation. A permanent station building and a new water tower were finished soon afterwards. The tower, located in Jefferson Park, would become the city's oldest permanent landmark. By 1917 a 58-mile network of street mains ringed Gary.

Despite criticism of the high water rates, it was generally agreed that the work of Alvord and Burdick was a success. Corporate leaders defended the water rates by citing the large financial investment necessary to build a system to provide water for more than 100,000 people. The company also noted that it gave home-owners almost unlimited water for lawn beautification by billing them during the summer an average of what they were billed the rest of the year. As a further inducement, free seeds were given to homeowners.

Gary's town board awarded franchises to the Gary Heat, Light, and Water Company for gas and electricity. Since these energy sources were, in the words of historian A. Michael Turner, "surplus by-products" from the mills, rates were low in contrast to the cost of water to consumers, but their quality was questionable. Visitors noted that the street lights seemed to flicker because of the low wattage, since the system was more in tune with the needs of the mill than the town.

A TOWN DIVIDED AT THE WABASH TRACKS

Because of U.S. Steel's limited concept of town planning, two strikingly different Garys emerged: one neat and scenic, the other chaotic and squalid. Symbolic of the contrast between conditions on each side of the Wabash tracks were the two genteel pubs on the Northside (the Binzenhof at 4th and Broadway and the Hotel Gary at 6th and Broadway) and the more than 200 saloons that had emerged by 1910 in the "Patch" district between Broadway, Madison, 10th, and 15th streets—including the First and Last Chance, Jack Johnson's Gambling Joint, and the Bucket of Blood. Northside businessmen, plant foremen, and skilled workers sought social isolation from the "other Gary" inhabited primarily by immigrants and blacks.

Gary Land Company agent Horace S. Norton directed the Northside's growth in a way that merged its interests with those of the company's parent organization, U.S. Steel. With careful scrutiny he approved land sales to merchant buyers. In the First Subdivision the Gary Land Company graded and paved streets, put in concrete sidewalks, brought in rich black soil, and planted grass and trees. In August 1907 Norton organized the Gary Commercial Club, which he headed for 33 years. At the time Broadway was only half-paved, and occasionally timber wolves were sighted crossing that street. By 1908 there had sprung up along Broadway two banks, two hotels, an assembly hall, and several dozen shops.

A Russian-born Jew named Morris Kahan opened the first permanent store on March 1, 1907, after having come to Gary the previous spring as a refugee from the San Francisco earthquake. One of the first restaurants was operated by Walter McNally at 577 Broadway. He opened at five in the morning to accommodate the mill-workers who started their shifts at six. His wash water came from a pump at 6th and Adams and his drinking water from Chicago. When McNally turned off his gas light at 9:00 P.M., the whole area down to the Wabash tracks was dark.

The center of social life on the Northside was the Binzenhof, which contained a restaurant, a large hall, club rooms, and professional

offices. It served as temporary headquarters for the town government, the Commercial Club, and several church congregations. Its
bar was nearly a hundred feet long, and on busy days, wrote newsman Tom Cannon, it "was manned by seven or eight barkeeps." On
paydays customers "lined up four deep along the bar," waiting for
a mug of Old Briar or Duffy's Malt.

By 1910 the Northside was becoming a civilized place for those
settlers who could afford to live there. But most newcomers could
not. Southside realtors took advantage of the Gary Land Company's
hesitancy in providing housing for them. Maurice N. Castleman per-
sonified the frontier spirit of Southside capitalists. Called "Battle
Axe" because of his expertise in spitting a brand of chewing tobacco
by that name, Castleman started out in Gary as a saloonkeeper and
became a real estate speculator, trolley car executive, and city councilman. He amassed a fortune by combing the Crown Point land files
and then buying out absentee owners or acquiring title simply by
paying delinquent tax assessments. Once, dressed in raggedy clothes,
he bought a choice plot for ten dollars after telling an unsuspecting
Chicago owner that the land was under four feet of water. He wanted
it for duck hunting, he said. Castleman and his colleagues distributed
pamphlets nationwide, such as E. G. Smith's booklet, *Great Gary,*
which lauded the virtues of "a city useful, a city healthful, and a city
beautiful."

In reality the Southside was a mockery of the boosters' brochures.
Many settlers lived in tents or tarpaper shacks. Landlords took advantage of the housing shortage and absence of health regulations or
building codes by charging inflated rents and selling property under
fraudulent liens that allowed them to terminate contracts if buyers
missed a single mortgage payment. Many workers lived in unven-
tilated barracks with cots lined up almost door-to-door. One apartment provided two-room flats (each room being nine feet square) at
rates so high that some tenants had to take in boarders. The marshy
Southside land attracted mosquitoes, and the pestilential outhouses,
unpaved alleys, damp cellars, and overcrowded dwellings were
breeding grounds for typhoid, malaria, and tuberculosis.

There was a spirit of camaraderie on the Southside among the
many nationalities sharing the crowded quarters. Blacks sometimes
taught immigrants English, and in turn some Negro children grew
up with a knowledge of Serbian or Croatian. Station agent John D.
Herr recalled that he roomed at an inn with people of every description. "We used to line up in the barroom about meal time," he said,
"and when the door opened to the dining room we made a grand

rush for the large table which was loaded with good substantial food, plenty for all, and large glasses of beer."

Life on the Southside was harsh and sometimes violent, however, and most inhabitants hoped that their stay there would be short. At first, married women were a rarity, and even by 1920 Gary's males predominated by more than 8,000 out of a total population of 54,000. Immigrant families gradually began clustering into little "shanty" communities where they raised pigs, chickens, cows, geese, and children. Mostly young, strong, and of peasant stock, they stuck together but adjusted their old-world lifestyles to new circumstances. Approximately half of Gary's ethnic populace came directly to Gary from the old country; the others had generally lived for awhile in New York, Pennsylvania, Ohio, or Illinois. Women carried on ethnic customs in their dress, speech, child-rearing practices, and religious activities. With the exception of the Russians, however, immigrant groups formed secular societies for mutual aid before they founded churches. One Hungarian grocer extended credit totaling more than a thousand dollars to impoverished compatriots.

The bawdy culture of the Patch stained the Southside. Laborers entered the omnipresent bars armed and ready to squeeze a few hours of action into their grim lives. Police Chief Joseph D. Martin referred to the area as "hell on wheels." For a time the red-light district was set off by a barbed-wire fence and, according to William S. Feuer, was "lined with saloons where the construction gang men could carry on unbridled roistering." Harry Hall remembered that it was commonplace for the pavements to be blotched with human blood, especially on Monday mornings. "Here men drank, brawled, and sometimes died," wrote historian Richard J. Meister. "Here charming streetwalkers sold their wares in a way any of the fifty plus nationalities could understand; here men either stashed away their wages in order to return to the homeland to a comfortable life or to bring their wife or mail order bride over or gambled and drank away every sweated penny."

Harry King, an early resident, recalled that many saloons had slot machines and around-the-clock poker games. "Gary sure was a wide open town then," he said. "The fellow who played a quarter slot machine was a piker. Most of the slot machines accommodated coins no smaller than a half-dollar."

Northsiders tended to blame slum problems on Mayor Tom Knotts, the saloonkeepers, and the bad habits of immigrants. One U.S. Steel official disavowed corporate responsibility for the conditions with the quip: "We are not in the summer resort business." But Southsiders in reality suffered from inadequate opportunity and prejudice. Raymond A. Mohl and Neil Betten wrote: "Gary quickly developed a slum of hovels, tarpaper shacks, and dingy boarding houses. . . . [which] reflected not only the nativism and bigotry of the period but Steel's ability to disregard the unskilled and unorganized immigrant worker. . . ."

In time, pleasant homes arose south of the Wabash tracks, but invisible barriers remained. The emergence of two Garys tarnished the so-called "miracle city." As Anthony Brook concluded: "The designers of Gary built only half a city—the speculators and the developers built the rest, but both were equally bad. The plan for Gary called for orderly efficient growth, but in both parts of town, planning objectives were ignored and entrepreneurial values prevailed. . . . Gary never solved the old problem of reconciling profit with humanity."

FOUNDING FATHER: JUDGE ELBERT H. GARY

Elbert Henry Gary's rise to prominence was an American success story. Born in Warrenville, Illinois, on October 8, 1846, and reared on a farm near Wheaton, he became a Chicago attorney and twice interrupted his lucrative corporation law practice during the 1880s to serve as a Du Page County judge. He also became mayor of Wheaton and taught about God and the work ethic in Sunday school. A protegé of steel tycoon John "Bet-a-Million" Gates, Gary became president in 1898 of Federal Steel Company, which merged with other companies three years later to form the United States Steel Corporation. One who admired power and despised weakness, Gary once said: "I think it is not in my nature to hurt anybody—at least I hope that is so. I know that is my policy; I don't believe in it. Of course, I am less aggressive now than I used to be. When I was in the public school and a new boy came, his place had to be settled, and I never shirked that!" Infatuation with order and status stayed with him always.

Judge Gary's refined manners, deep religious faith, and lack of practical training in steelmaking made him an oddity among the hard-nosed industrial magnates of his time. Although he once in a fit of pique called the judge a "boneless bootlicker," investment banker John Pierpont Morgan recognized Gary's managerial and public relations skills when he made him board chairman of U.S. Steel. His primary role was to conciliate the strong-willed steel barons who were on the executive committee and to convince a skeptical nation that the "Billion Dollar Trust" was beneficial to the general welfare. A true believer in business pieties, Gary preached the gospel of industrial statesmanship at board meetings as well as in public. Old-school tycoons such as Henry Clay Frick were openly hostile to him at first, but he gradually forged his diverse empire into a relatively harmonious unit.

Compared to his peers, Gary was an enlightened innovator who championed cooperation, balance, frankness, mutual interest, and good will. "Regarding the steel and iron industry as semipublic in character, Judge Gary has steadily worked to break down the defiant attitude of his colleagues in regard to what they called government interference with their operations—that what they did was nobody's business but their own," Ida M. Tarbell wrote. Gary believed that new realities called for minimizing cutthroat competition and using governmental agencies to advantage. He acquiesced in governmental scrutiny of corporation accounts and turned stockholders' meetings into open forums; he claimed to be the stockholders' servant rather than merely the agent of corporate directors.

A vain, humorless moralist, Gary paid much attention to appearances. He refused to play cards, saying that it was beneath his dignity. His recreational tastes ran to hunting, fishing, and horseback riding. His graying hair, manicured moustache, and firm posture went together with an air of haughty rectitude. He cultivated European royalty and collected Renaissance art and solid-gold china but bristled at other people's vulgar displays of wealth. He insisted that Gary, Indiana, bear his name rather than be called Corey in honor of the corporation's titular president (as was almost done). The postal service delayed approval of the name, fearing confusion with Gary, Md., until friendly Congressmen interceded.

Certain that he knew what was best for his employees, Gary opposed unions and was loath even to meet with labor representatives, whom he considered his social inferiors. Renowned for his fairness and candor, he assumed incorrectly that plant bosses and foremen would follow his lead. He quoted Scripture to support his labor policies but ignored the biblical injunction against working on the Sabbath. Although 228,000 people worked for him in 1914, he claimed that his door was always open to individuals with grievances. By 1919, however, workers were comparing him to the German Kaiser. One cartoon juxtaposed his statement, "the workmen prefer the longer hours," with pictures of tired, gaunt laborers. At a 1921 stockholders' meeting Judge Gary defended U.S. Steel's 84-hour week by claiming without foundation that "the workmen themselves are unwilling to have the hours of labor decreased. . . ."

Judge Gary took an avuncular interest in "his" town, although he never lived in it. "My home is in New York, but my heart is in Gary, Indiana," he once said. Contributing personally to several charitable causes, he had the Gary Land Company donate property for parks, churches, hospitals, a YMCA, a YWCA, and several public buildings. His wife Julia had Tiffany jewelers design the town seal with her husband's image and during an automobile tour enjoyed saying, "Look, there is a bank [or whatever] named after us."

Judge Gary's "inspection tour" on June 15, 1922, was billed as a "state visit." On that day he told 300 people at the Commercial Club that his company would help build "this city on a foundation that will stand. Good schools and churches, law and order." Upon his death on August 15, 1927, the city went into official mourning for two hours. Said Armanis F. Knotts: "To me, Judge Gary will always be the one great remarkable industrial genius of this and all times."

Elbert H. Gary bridged the gap between the "Public Be Damned" business mentality of the late nineteenth century and the sophisticated corporate anonymity of the twentieth century. A year before his death, on his 80th birthday, he said that the four people he had most admired during his lifetime were his father, his schoolmaster, J. P. Morgan, and Theodore Roosevelt. All were practical moralists, he believed.

The autocratic labor policies that tarnished Judge Gary's reputation sprang less from greed than from his naiveté about plant conditions and his aloofness from those at the bottom of the corporate ladder. His opposition to secrecy and his call for decent business ethics were admirable positions. On the other hand, with his limited social vision and reluctance to share power, he never achieved the perhaps impossible goal of applying the Golden Rule to business.

WILLIAM PALMER GLEASON: GODFATHER OF THE STEEL CITY

"He was *the* big man in Gary," recalled newsman Erwin Crewe Rosenau. "Nearly everybody kowtowed to him. He was held in awe and greatly feared."

For 30 years Superintendent William Palmer Gleason ran Gary Works like a feudal lord. Hard work and loyalty to the corporation were the means by which he rose to power, and he extracted these attributes from his subordinates, while treating them like cogs in his machine. Said one acquaintance: "Show me a man with any talent or ability, and I'll show you the man who can wring him dry: Gleason."

Gleason's childhood was laced with misfortune. In 1871, when he was six, his parents lost nearly everything in the Chicago fire. Seven years later, his father was killed in an industrial accident at the Joliet (Illinois) Iron and Steel Works. In order to help support his mother and his five brothers and sisters, Gleason went to work as a machine shop apprentice, tending the furnaces and greasing the wheels, axles, levers, and pulleys.

At the age of 17 Gleason was promoted to journeyman; at 19 he was a rod mill foreman. Despite working 12 hours a day and "double tricks" on alternate Sundays, he attended night school and took correspondence courses in mathematics and mechanics. When the Illinois Steel Company bought the Joliet mill, Gleason helped build an apparatus for mass-producing iron rails. By 1890 he was a master mechanic and married to the daughter of a wealthy contractor. The future looked bright.

Then a series of disasters struck. His daughter died of tuberculosis. The depression of 1893 caused the plant to shut down for 11 months. When it reopened, Gleason was put in charge of the repair and installation work necessary to make the machines operative. He virtually worked around the clock, taking meals on the run and naps on a cot. "We slaved like Trojans," he later recalled.

In 1895 Gleason's wife died of tuberculosis; to lessen his grief Gleason buried himself in his work more than ever and caught pneumonia. At this time he lost his brother John in a freak railway accident. According to E. C. Rosenau, the train had stopped "on a trestle over the DesPlaines River. For a joke some prankster, thinking to mimic the conductor, called out, 'Joliet!' John Gleason, roused from a doze, stumbled down the aisle, stepped off the train, and hurtled down into the river. He was drowned."

During a trip west to regain his health, Gleason took a job with the Colorado Iron and Fuel Company. His boss was George G. Thorp, a former neighbor in Joliet. By chance Thorp was picked by Illinois Steel Company to take charge of the Joliet plant, and he made Gleason his assistant. Although happy to be back with his family and friends—he remarried in 1898—on Thorp's orders Gleason went to Clairton, Pennsylvania, to supervise the construction of a new plant, the Crucible Steel Company. Gleason became the first superintendent of the company, which merged with U.S. Steel in 1903. Because of these experiences and Thorp's recommendation, U.S. Steel officials put him in charge of building their new plant complex in the Calumet Region.

Gleason first arrived at the Gary townsite on Memorial Day in 1906. After walking from the Tolleston depot along a cowpath and over rope bridges, he discussed blueprints that same day with the mill engineers and inspected the work already started—the laying down of railway bedding.

Gleason was responsible for coordinating a multitude of projects, including laying out a harbor and redirecting the Grand Calumet River. "I spent nearly all my time driving [on horseback] through hot sands and treacherous marshes," he later recalled, "hearing and adjusting complaints from one contractor and another, trying to keep them from dodging their responsibilities or misinterpreting their contracts. At the same time I had to build up an organization of my own and lend a patient ear to the laments raised by my men and their wives over the deplorable living conditions, sand, heat, mud, tumbleweeds. . . . Sometimes, now that I can look back, I wonder how we survived at all."

On July 23, 1908, several thousand people congregated on the shores of Lake Michigan to greet the arrival of the first shipment of iron ore, hauled by the freighter *Elbert H. Gary,* which, according to eyewitness Sam Woods, "entered the new harbor with whistles blowing, bells ringing, and cannon booming." The crowd cheered, sang "Garyland, My Garyland," picked up ore samples as mementos, and then paraded down Broadway.

Six months later, Gleason's daughter, Mary Louise, lighted a blast furnace whose eerie glare caused some distant observers to fear that the whole mill was aflame. By February 1909 Gary Works manufactured its first steel, and Gleason's position as plant superintendent was secure.

Believing that foremen were the key to running an efficient plant, Gleason frequently dined with them and, when angry, was known to lecture, curse, throw dishes, and otherwise browbeat them. He once fired a foreman on the spot who complained that his seven-day-a-week schedule prevented him from attending church.

Gleason tolerated no threats to his sovereignty at the mill. His employment manager, Hans O. Egeberg, had a legendary memory and blacklisted any troublemakers. An implacable foe of unions, Gleason also feuded with company officials not directly under his control, such as auditor A. M. Roberts, the plant managers at American Bridge Company (founded in 1909) and American Sheet and Tube Company (founded in 1910), and Gary Land Company agent Horace S. Norton. In fact, for a generation he and Norton jockeyed for the position of Gary's "first citizen." Gleason insisted on calling his rival "Mr. Norton," although everyone else used the title "Captain."

Gleason took an active part in Gary's civic affairs; but, as one resident concluded, his air of superiority was insufferable. He took pride in his hospital charity work and labored hard as head of Gary's parks department. A devout Catholic, he had Miller's beachfront park renamed in honor of Père Marquette and personally donated a statue of the missionary. But he opposed integrating Gary's parks and once justified his refusal to provide beach facilities for blacks, according to one witness, with the racist quip that they "would never use the beach if we provided one. The water's too cold. They can't stand that cold Lake Michigan." A black newspaper called him an "uncrowned czar" with a "phobia" about segregation. In 1932, as a consequence of Gleason's policies, the police prevented an American Legion baseball game between Gary and East Chicago from being played at Marquette Park because the visiting team had two black players.

Like many self-made millionaires whose early lives were filled with struggle, he loved the trappings of wealth—the maids, butlers, and chauffeurs and deferential respect of townspeople—and he had a myopic social vision when dealing with those who did not have his values, stamina, or opportunities. Like his hero, Napoleon, he was overbearing, egotistical, and tyrannical. E. C. Rosenau called Gleason the "Godfather of the Steel City." His motto was "IT CAN BE DONE," and when he wanted something, he had little use for those who questioned his methods.

MAYOR THOMAS E. KNOTTS:
HIS OWN MAN

His friends called him uncompromising, loyal, kindhearted, and shrewd. To his enemies he seemed stubborn, egotistical, devious, and dishonest. Thomas E. Knotts was an untypical man who inspired love and hate but rarely neutrality. His vigor and optimism made him a fitting leader of Gary during its formative years.

Born on an Ohio farm and a graduate of Valparaiso College, young Knotts taught Sioux Indians during the 1880s in Wyoming and the Dakotas. Settling in Hammond, he worked as a policeman, a realtor, and an editor of a Populist-leaning newspaper. During the 1894 Pullman strike, he was jailed for urging striking railway workers to defy a court injunction. That incident remained one of his proudest memories, and he named one of his five children Eugene in honor of the American Railway Union President Eugene V. Debs.

Tom Knotts moved to Gary soon after his older brother Armanis selected the site for U.S. Steel. His wife Ella was the first woman resident in the Euclid Avenue settlement. Upon seeing the pioneer village for the first time after a two-mile trek from the Tolleston depot, which took five hours, she exclaimed that it seemed like "a patch of white" at "the end of nowhere." Their four children attended classes at Gary's first schoolhouse which Knotts named Jefferson in honor of the "Sage of Monticello."

Securing a federal appointment as postmaster in July 1906, Knotts had an office in a frame building put up in May to be the headquarters of the Gary Land Company. He kept his stamps and money in a shoebox. On July 28 residents elected him to serve on the first town board, along with John E. Sears and Millard Caldwell. "We were just three bushwhackers," Knotts said, "and we had to learn how to manage public affairs as we went along." In balloting to select a board president, he demonstrated the instincts of a politician: Caldwell voted for Sears, Sears for Knotts, and Knotts for himself, thus carrying the vote, 2 to 1.

Many of Gary's early developments bore the stamp of Knotts' personality and political philosophy. He helped persuade the progressive educator William A. Wirt to become Gary's first school superintendent, and he literally changed the direction of the town in emphasizing southward expansion.

In 1907 a battle commenced between Knotts and Horace S. Norton, who represented mill interests. Norton had first arrived in Gary incognito to determine for Eugene J. Buffington why Gary Land Company sales were not doing well. After criticizing Armanis F. Knotts for concentrating on selling his own private holdings, Norton replaced him as general agent. Thereafter, Tom Knotts' "town forces" viewed Norton as a "mysterious and unwelcome stranger, an arrogant usurper, a man to be shunned."

The feud crystalized during a dispute over a trolley franchise. Knotts arranged for the town board to award it to the Gary and Interurban Company, which was owned by Frank Gavit and emphasized construction south along Broadway, rather than give the contract to the Gary and Hammond Traction Company, a U.S. Steel subsidiary interested in an east-west route along 5th Avenue. Thus, the U.S. Steel plan for primary expansion east and west near the lake front plants on company property never materialized. On the other hand, the price of property along Broadway south of the Wabash tracks skyrocketed twenty times its original value by 1911. Active in real estate at the same time that he was governing the city, Knotts later described his promotional ventures as "like picking leaves from trees." His brother sold a lot at 11th and Broadway for $1,200, six months after he had bought it for a hundred dollars.

In 1909 Gary became a fifth-class city, setting the stage for the first of its many rough-and-tumble mayoralty elections. Knotts hoped to outflank Captain Norton's mill forces with support from immigrant workers and independent businessmen. In the Democratic primary, Knotts defeated Norton's ally, William C. Crolius, who had labeled him the "Rotund Old Blunderbuss." Then Norton supported John A. Brennan, who had beaten contractor Ingwald Moe in the Republican primary. With the only newspaper, the Gary *Daily Tribune,* supporting Brennan, Knotts started a rival daily which he christened the Gary *Evening Post,* and told his hand-picked editors to "make it hot. . . . Give 'em hell." The *Evening Post* charged that Brennan's purpose was to convert Gary into a company town, "lock, stock, and barrel." Political vitriol dominated the pages of both papers as the election neared. Using a Slavic slang word meaning beer, Brennan called Knotts' forces the "Reevo Party."

Prohibition was dragged into the 1909 race because Gary had officially been a dry city since April. An Indiana statute mandated the suspension of liquor license permits for two years if more than half the number of voters who had participated in the previous township election signed a remonstrance petition. Since only 341 people had voted in the last election, a small group of Northside civic leaders met the terms of the law. Millworkers began taking their checks to other cities to be cashed and spent, to the chagrin of local merchants. In response Knotts allowed saloons to operate without licenses but gave the bar owners suspended jail sentences and levied fines that could be recouped in a few hours. His tactics were applauded by the Southside, as was his charge that Republicans had engineered the dry plot to discredit him. In 1910 prohibition ended in failure. The following year a jury acquitted Knotts of the charge of conspiring to violate the local option law.

On election eve the Republican county sheriff arrested Knotts and the entire Gary police force on a defamation-of-character warrant. Out on bail, Knotts convinced Governor Thomas R. Marshall to send state militia into the vicinity to counterbalance the county police and discourage violence. The governor allegedly complained, "I wish Gary would slide off into Lake Michigan."

Two near riots occurred on election day. The first incident arose when the Republicans brought in a boxcar full of immigrants. The city police would not let them vote. That evening, as the town board prepared to tally the vote, the county sheriff arrived to confiscate the ballot boxes. Knotts protested, until he noticed that the sheriff's men had him surrounded. He gave in but won anyway by 71 votes out of approximately 3,500 cast, on the strength of a 237-vote plurality from the Patch.

A resident named W. A. Woodruff composed the following poem about the 1909 election:

> Now father dons his shirt and mail,
> His cuirass and his greaves
> While mother dear, all wan and pale,
> Clings to him, ere he leaves
> The house, his rifle in his hand
> And pistols in his coat,
> A bowie knife between the teeth,
> For father's going to vote.

During Tom Knotts' tenure in office, Gary was a town on the move in terms of geographic expansion. Its growth often took place amidst swirls of controversy with critics charging Knotts with naked imperialism. The very first town ordinance of 1906, in fact, had extended Gary's borders west to Hammond and East Chicago, thereby incorporating the villages of Clark and Buffington. In 1907 Miller had been incorporated as a town because residents feared being annexed by their neighbor to the west. The next expansion occurred in 1909 into Glen Park, beyond the Little Calumet River to 45th Street (land farther south was added in 1926).

The annexation of Tolleston in 1910 coincided with a rivalry between Gary and East Chicago and was an outgrowth of Indiana's Towns and Cities Act of 1905, which facilitated municipal expansion through consolidation or annexation. Consolidation required agreement by the governing bodies of each area, but through an annexation ordinance a town board could simply announce its intent to add a contiguous area. If the people affected wished to contest it, they had to obtain the signatures of two-thirds of the area's qualified voters within 30 days, thereby annulling the procedure and preventing similar action for two years.

During the first three months of 1910, Mayor Knotts negotiated with Tolleston's trustees regarding consolidation. Most Tolleston residents worked in Gary and recognized the desirability of sharing the cost of schools, police and fire protection, and road building and repair. Tolleston's board president, W. S. Gallagher, favored consolidation but opposed unilateral annexation.

There matters stood in March 1910, when rumors arose concerning a plot by East Chicago's Mayor Alexander G. Schlieker to bring all of western Lake County under his domain. Calling Schlieker a tyrant, the *Daily Tribune* advised that "IT IS UP TO GARY TO ANNEX FIRST." The paper concluded: "Western frontier tactics are practically the last resort, that is, let Gary get the drop on East Chicago first, and then if there is to be any annexing done, let it be done by our own council."

Sounding his own alarm, Mayor Knotts declared: "They have gone clean crazy at East Chicago over annexation, and there is no telling what they are going to do." In the event that Schlieker moved against Gary, he worried aloud, it would take time, money, and 2,600 signatures to frustrate the scheme.

On May 27, 1910, the East Chicago council voted to annex neighboring Hammond. Early next morning, Gary's governing body passed an ordinance of annexation that incorporated East Chicago, Hammond, Whiting, Indiana Harbor, Tolleston, and Miller. Mayor Schlieker called Knotts' counterattack a stupid joke, but the *Daily Tribune,* in mock heroic phrases, heralded the birth of "Greater Gary." Never intending to carry out the scheme, Knotts pushed through the ordinance in order to help friends in Hammond who opposed the merger with East Chicago and also to forestall a move against Gary itself. Precipitating a showdown with Schlieker, he cajoled all the Lake County mayors into agreeing to a mutual hands-off policy. On December 20, 1910, a superior court judge dismissed the Gary ordinance against Hammond, East Chicago, Whiting, and Indiana Harbor without its being contested by Knotts. Nonetheless, Tolleston was swallowed up in the ploy, as their trustees could not obtain enough signatures to oppose it. On the other hand, Millerites succeeded in resisting annexation at this time.

With the annexation of Tolleston, Gary had a population of 16,802, half of them foreign-born and 11,521 of them males. The town stretched seven miles east and west and seven miles south from Lake Michigan. At a banquet on February 24, 1910, celebrating the completion of a trolley line between Hammond and Gary, Mayor Knotts said: "The city of Gary was conceived in the counting rooms and born in a jungle. It was nursed on faith and schooled in the fiery furnace of toil. It is peopled by men and women of every living tongue and creed, while in the marts of the world, it stands as the horoscope of good or evil symptoms in the final aspect of Christendom. As steel goes, so goes the world, and Gary is its prophet."

Knotts acted as quickly in facing a possible health hazard as he had in meeting the annexation challenge. In 1911 Gary housewives complained about the poor quality of milk from a new local dairy. Knotts took six bottles to the Emerson High School chemistry laboratory to be checked for impurities. He did not like what was found, and soon afterwards the council passed an ordinance requiring pasteurization and inspection.

While Knotts was mayor, the Republican-controlled Lake County government, headquartered in Crown Point, was a constant thorn in his side. On 14 occasions charges were brought against him ranging from perjury and election fraud to malfeasance and embezzlement. In one instance, Republicans planted a dictograph device in a hotel room and claimed they had a record of a conversation indicating that the mayor had taken a 5,000-dollar bribe. The evidence proved to be chimerical, although two councilmen fled town fearing they would be implicated. Even though Knotts was never tried for this or any other crime, the innuendos hurt his bid for reelection in 1913.

Knotts' chief rival in that contest was Roswell O. Johnson, who put together a coalition of Republicans, dissident Democrats, and Bull Moose Progressives and ran on the supposedly nonpartisan Citizen's Party ticket. A good stump speaker who had the blessing of U.S. Steel, Johnson claimed that Knotts was a divisive force in the community. Mill officials sought clerical allies for him by assuming the mortgages of a number of churches. Plant foremen monitored Democratic rallies and punished workers who attended them. They also acted as Republican whips on election day.

Knotts could not survive the tide. On the night before the election he privately conceded defeat to his friend Tom Cannon, saying: "I'm licked. No man can be twice elected mayor of Gary. The town is new, and it will be many years before they quit suspecting the actions of the other fellow." Johnson won by 1,516 votes.

Knotts was to be the only Democratic mayor of Gary between 1909 and 1935. After leaving office, he devoted the rest of his life to business affairs except for an unsuccessful race for county sheriff in 1916. His forced retirement from public office increased U.S. Steel's power. According to historian Powell Moore, Horace S. Norton "was said to be the real mayor of Gary during Johnson's first term." Norton's bodyguard, Pontius Heintz, was appointed chief of police. Mill engineer Ralph E. Rowley became president of the City Council.

Knotts died on March 26, 1921, and approximately 2,000 people attended the funeral service at the Orpheum Theatre. Delivering the eulogy was the famous trial lawyer Clarence Darrow, who said: "Tom Knotts did not cringe before the powerful nor was he content to drift with the tide. Such a man must naturally lead a stormy life."

Knotts made many close friends during his tenure as mayor. Perhaps his greatest strength was his ability to identify with so many of Gary's subcultures and to give them a line of communication with the government. Premier politician that he was, he showed many immigrants how to get their first citizenship papers. They nicknamed him "Papa" and were his most ardent supporters. One resident later described a Southside procession in which many ethnic groups came together "in native folk costume, each group with its band playing its own national airs, in one big political parade, shouting over and over again, 'Knotts, Knotts, Knotts.' " He added that it was the only word of English many of them knew.

CHIEF JOSEPH D. MARTIN AND THE "TURK RIOT"

On September 15, 1906, Gary's town board hired a Hammond policeman, Joseph D. Martin, to be its police chief. The first night on the job, Martin later recalled, he told his five-man squad: "All right, we are going to put the lockup to some use. The taxpayers' money has bought it, and we mustn't let it stay empty. Go out and get 'em." Before daybreak they had corraled 53 drunks and thrown them into "four cells and a bull pen."

In the ensuing months the police spent a good deal of time breaking up barroom disorders and getting drunks off sand hills, where they might tumble into sloughs and possibly drown. One way of rousting "stiffs" was the "hot foot"—hitting them on the soles of their shoes with a billy club. At night the police sometimes handcuffed them to trees and then released them the following morning upon payment of a fine. In winter Chief Martin commissioned a one-legged saloonkeeper named Jack Farrell, who was known as the "Boss of the Patch," to round them up in a horse-drawn buckboard so they would not freeze to death. Until December 1908, when a paid fire department was organized under Joseph J. Feely, the police led volunteer firefighting crews. Roy G. Parry recollected that "few fires were ever reached in time to do any good," because the police had only a small hose cart containing 200 feet of "second hand leaky hose."

Gary's first policemen and firemen did not have to pass any physical or civil service examinations. Patrolman John Bascovich was little more than four feet tall and barely literate. According to Parry, "he usually carried a razor, stiletto, and cheese knife, and sometimes it took the entire force to subdue Johnny." When the fire department was first organized, Joseph Feely came up with a simple test for the

50 or so applicants. "I lined them up," he later said, "and told them to run through the sand over a course which had been measured off.... The first men to finish were examined, and if found physically fit, got the jobs." Whereas patrolmen often got their jobs as patronage plums, Feely kept the fire department relatively free from politics.

Lawless behavior was commonplace in frontier Gary, where the population was overwhelmingly male and so transient that Louis J. Bailey claimed there was nearly a complete changeover every three months. A "Bread Riot" once erupted when a carload of supplies burned on its way from Chicago, causing shortages of vital foodstuffs. The wife of Dr. C. A. DeLong was so terrified of Gary's rough-and-ready ways that she accompanied her husband on his house calls. Mrs. William F. Hodges initially thought Gary to be "a terrible place."

One of the most famous altercations in frontier Gary was the so-called "Turk Riot," which erupted on the evening of January 15, 1908, and culminated in a gun battle between the police and a group of Serbian immigrants. The incident started as a practical joke when some construction workers pulled up the ropes of a tent belonging to a black junkman known as Mississippi Slim. When the victim tried to protest to their foremen, they scared him off by firing shotguns into the air. Three policemen investigated his complaint, but they were met by a volley of gunfire. Patrolmen William Miller was seriously wounded in the eye. Chief Martin then arrived with reinforcements and stormed the Serbian barracks, killing Peter Montrovich and wounding several others. The police took a score of prisoners to jail, flogged them to get confessions, and ultimately arrested Mike Jurich and Mike Berich on charges of assault and battery with intent to commit murder. The others were released.

The coroner ruled that Montrovich had died resisting arrest, but the Serbian consul in Chicago charged the police with using excessive force during the gun battle, and tried to get the county sheriff to arrest the entire Gary police force for mistreating prisoners. Rumors spread that the Serbians were buying weapons in preparation for another fight. According to *The Northern Indianian,* one foreigner shot a hole in a gunshop floor, and the police department was "in danger of being exterminated."

The fears expressed in the newspaper proved groundless. Martin placated the Serbian community (which constituted ten percent of Gary's population) somewhat by adding George Duchevich to his force. Charges were dropped against Berich, but in April, 27-year-old

Mike Jurich went on trial in Lake County Superior Court on charges of assaulting Patrolman Miller with intent to commit murder.

Testifying for the prosecution, Chief Martin labeled Jurich a "rude, insolent, and angry" prisoner who had acted "unlawfully, feloniously, purposely, and with premeditated malice." The defendant repudiated his "forced" confession, maintained his innocence, and complained that his internment until the day of the trial had prevented him from acquiring witnesses. His attorney, Gustave Heart, argued that two immigrants who had since moved away had seen the Gary police beat Jurich and that he was being singled out as a scapegoat. Nonetheless, Jurich was convicted.

In a motion for a new trial, Heart produced an affidavit from George Spolarevic stating that "on the night of the shooting . . . the defendant, Mike Jurich, was in bed with Mike Berich and the cook of the camp [and] . . . did not leave his bed until after the shooting was over." A statement from the cook, Pit Katic, substantiated the story. Heart's motion was denied, however, and Jurich was sent to the Indiana Reformatory.

No joking matter at the time of its occurrence, the "Turk Riot" later became one of Chief Martin's favorite anecdotes. He told it in a racist vein, with the black junk dealer as the butt of the story rather than the immigrants. Whether Mike Jurich was guilty of firing shotgun blasts at the police or was in bed with two fellow Serbians at the time of the riot remained undetermined. A jury pronounced him guilty, but his friends believed that he had been convicted unjustly.

INGWALD MOE AND VERN U. YOUNG: THEATRE IMPRESARIOS

Less than 18 months after Gary's founding, Ingwald Moe, a Norwegian-born contractor, obtained permission from Gary Land Company agent Horace S. Norton to construct a nickelodeon at 760 Broadway. Concerned that it would acquire an unsavory reputation, Norton reserved the right to censor all productions and extracted a promise to allow church services in the building. The town board, also worried about the effect of nickelodeons on public morals, had originally banned the showing of any silent films within the city limits. This ordinance was first amended to allow no more than one nickelodeon per block and then scrapped altogether in the face of public demand for more places of entertainment.

One Saturday night in 1908 Moe's Broadway Theatre closed early due to a power failure. The next morning the power suddenly came on during a Presbyterian service. The minister halted his prayer in mid-sentence when the automatic, coin-operated piano began playing the honky-tonk chords of "Hail, Hail, the Gang's All Here."

For five cents Moe's patrons could see several ten-minute silent films, generally of the slapstick or adventure variety, such as *Grotesque Figures, Soul Kiss, Beg Pardon, Yellowstone Park Hold-Up, Tragic Wedding,* and *One-Man Baseball.* Because movie film was highly flammable, it had to be handled carefully and rewound manually, which took almost as long as showing the film itself. To enliven these intermissions, Moe hired a woman to lead the audience in group singing.

The Broadway Theatre's first competitor, the Star and Garter, caught fire when a customer's lantern overturned. The wooden building was quickly destroyed. In September 1908 the Lyric Theatre closed for a few days because a film ignited and damaged the building. Similar mishaps and near-tragedies occurred at the Princess and Gem theatres, as well as at the Broadway and its companion theatre, the Derby, which was also built by Ingwald Moe.

By the winter of 1908 Gary had a diverse, if somewhat crude, entertainment industry, featuring a half-dozen nickelodeons, hundreds of saloons, and numerous brothels. The Victoria Hotel provided live music with evening meals (all for 50 cents), while Binzenhof's sometimes obtained prizefight films and booked touring entertainers such as Elwood the Wonder, a hypnotist. Road show troupes regularly performed at the Gary Theatre at 9th and Jefferson. Among the productions featured during the 1908 winter season were *Jesse James, The Devil, The American Girl, Eve's Ascension,* and *Jolly American Girls.* The latter, according to the *Daily Tribune,* featured "Pretty Girls ... Latest Songs ... Catchy Music ... [and] Elegant Costumes."

Primarily a contractor rather than a manager, Ingwald Moe's main contribution to Gary's entertainment industry was as a founding father and builder. On the other hand, his friend, Vern U. Young, a realtor who also arrived in Gary in 1906, remained active in theatre management for four decades. In 1908 Young bought a half-interest in the Majestic Roller Skating Rink and refurbished it as a theatre. It opened on March 19, 1909, with such local luminaries as William A. Wirt, William P. Gleason, Thomas E. Knotts, and C. Oliver Holmes in attendance. The vaudeville acts included Indian club swinging, acrobatics, comedy routines, and Hebrew impersonations. One reporter said that "the moving picture machine, after some adjustment, got down to business and threw on the screen some of the best pictures seen in Gary. The war scenes depicted were especially well received."

Anxious, as Moe had been, to achieve respectability for his enterprises, Young allowed the First Baptist Church to use his building. On occasion, according to one source, "a troupe of actors, practicing on Sunday morning, would use one side of the curtain and the minister the other."

In 1910 V. U. Young and C. J. Wolf built the ornate Orpheum Theatre near 8th and Washington, which housed such popular burlesque shows as *Pepple's All-Girl Revue* and *Petticoat Minstrels.* Young and Wolf also opened the Pastime Theatre in Tolleston and the Art Theatre at 620 Broadway. The latter had the town's first pipe organ, ran the first full-length motion picture, and used the first "natural color" projector. In 1914 the Art Theatre advertised its first "talkie," in which the actress Eva Tanguay sang "I Don't Care." The sound emanated from a phonograph located behind the screen and cranked by hand in order to synchronize the movie and the record.

Shortly before World War I, Moe built the "New Gary Theatre." Under the management of Fred Wheeler a variety of nationally famous vaudevillians, circus performers, exotic dancers, and scantily clad models performed on its stage. Wheeler also booked classical musicians and Shakespearean actors. More than 2,000 people turned out to hear Cantor Josef Rosenblatt. Sara Bernhardt's portrayal of *Queen Elizabeth* and the Marx Brothers' appearance in *The Cinderalla Girls* played to packed houses. There were some embarrassing moments, however. Once, the renowned actor DeWolf Hopper, starring in the play *The Better 'Ole,* became so irritated at the customers for not laughing at the proper times that he stopped the show temporarily and berated them for being a "bunch of hicks."

WORKING 84 HOURS A WEEK

By 1910 the huge mill complex north of the Grand Calumet River had proved a triumph of scientific planning. Stretching east to west, the integrated and self-contained facility contained coke ovens and coal storage bins; a large harbor slip; iron ore and limestone storage bins; blast furnaces and open hearths; and rolling tube, wire, sheet metal, tin plate, and steel hoop mills. A conveyor system carried molten steel directly to the mills. In time Gary Works contained a hospital, showers, and locker rooms; in-training classrooms; police and fire-fighting headquarters; huge repair shops; and railway facilities for 15,000 cars. When Judge Gary and his family first visited the site in May 1909, his brother, the Reverend O. J. Gary, declared in awed wonder, "Lord be praised."

A generation of technological progress had established American supremacy in manufacturing steel. Such inventions as electrical cranes, automatic rollers, skip hoists, the pig iron caster, and the Wellman charger had transformed steelworkers, according to historian David Brody, from "manipulators of raw material" into "tenders of machines." Mechanization abolished some of the worst tasks, such as hammering red-hot iron into shape and feeding the furnaces amid poisonous fumes and scalding heat. But if the changes reduced some of the horrors of production and increased productivity, they eroded the status of laborers, who were regarded as pawns in a system of cost accounting that minimized expenses while output was maximized. Management emphasis on efficiency led to the twelve-hour day, the seven-day week, frequent lay-offs, and hostility to unionization.

One worker later remembered how tired he would be after working a shift in the hot mill. "I used to come outa there," he said, "and I'd be shaky. Sometimes I'd get to the house, have supper, maybe a glass of wine, and fall asleep in my chair tryin' to read the paper. And I was a young man!"

Even though reformers were demanding government regulation of big business when Gary Works began operation, U.S. Steel enjoyed a golden age of prosperity until 1919. On good terms with the federal government, the company maintained its dominant position within the industry and staved off antitrust suits. Occasionally, however, there was a national outcry against the steel magnates. In 1910 the Federal Council of Churches called the 84-hour week "a disgrace to civilization," and a subsequent article by John A. Fitch entitled "Old Age at Forty" indicted unsafe plant conditions. In 1912 a Congressional committee characterized the industry's labor policies as a "brutal system of industrial slavery."

In response to public pressure U.S. Steel instituted a safety campaign. Spending 75,000 dollars a year on pamphlets, lectures, signs, advertising, and inspection trips, U.S. Steel allegedly reduced the rate of serious accidents in all its mills by 43 percent. But no amount of warnings and safety procedures could shield overworked men from the threat of injury or death. During the five years before World War I the company paid ten million dollars to accident victims, and this was but the tip of the iceberg in terms of wasted lives.

To maintain a stable and tractable work force, Gary Works developed "carrot and stick" policies that rewarded loyalty and purged troublemakers. Skilled workers, whose wages were adequate during good times, were offered pension plans, stock subscription benefits, low interest home loans, and the promise of advancement. David Brody wrote that "the modern steel mill developed a clear line of promotion. Each man was training for the next higher job and usually capable of filling it." During bad times, industrial spies and blacklisting muted discontent. Few men were irreplaceable, and their skills were, by and large, nontransferable to another industry. Ironically, fierce competition replaced labor solidarity within the mills just when competition among the companies diminished.

The skilled workers, mostly native-born or from Western Europe, tended to identify more with their employers than with unskilled immigrants. This attitude was fostered by the Gary Land Company's housing policies. The hope for permanent employment among skilled workers worked to the company's advantage, as did the transient habits of unskilled workers. Before Congress ended unrestricted immigration and until unskilled workers viewed Gary as their permanent residence, the rapid turnover rate minimized the threat of a strike. One unmarried worker, hoping to return to Europe, summarized his lifestyle in this way: "A good job, save money, work all the time, go home, sleep, no spend."

The strongest and luckiest immigrants managed to save money, even at 17 cents an hour, by working overtime and living in dingy boardinghouses. But nonresident aliens had no protection against employer negligence, and many suffered terrifying maimings. Enough immigrants were promoted to keep alive hopes for betterment. Gary Works *Circle* publicized success stories of people like Steve Augustinovitch, a repair crew foreman who was a homeowner with money in the bank and a large family ten years after emigrating from Croatia.

Nikola Tarailo's succession of jobs also exemplified the upward mobility possible within the mill's work force. On the very day in 1909 that he arrived in Gary he obtained work helping lay the foundation of an open hearth. Six months later, he quit after smashing his foreman's head with a shovel when instructed to "Go on . . . work over there." The command was similar to the Serbian word *govan*, which means excrement, and provoked Tarailo's militant response.

Tarailo next became a machinist's apprentice at American Bridge Company, taking home $9.60 a week for 60 hours' work. First a drill press operator and then a shop pusher, he quit after witnessing a young Croatian gored gruesomely when a drill press was accidentally turned on. Back at the mill, he became a rail straightener, picking up imperfectly finished pieces of steel with a wrench and manually slamming them on a hot bed. The work was very tiring, but he made more each day than he had at first made in a week.

Tarailo once joked about being the first Serbian to have gotten off his feet, because he had purchased a bicycle. In 1919 he participated in the steel strike and later remembered the machine guns on every corner and the ban on people walking in pairs during the period of martial law. During the mid-1920s he was promoted to the position of inspector and was one of the lucky few who had steady work after the depression struck. Once Tarailo had dreamed of going into business himself, but he stayed with U.S. Steel for 47 years.

Another immigrant worker at U.S. Steel was Duko Costo, who emigrated to Gary from Macedonia in 1912 at the age of 20 to avoid being drafted into the Turkish army. Two years previously, he had tried to join his older brother in America, but immigration officials at Ellis Island turned him back because of an illness contracted during the ocean voyage.

Finding a job at Gary Works, Duko lived in a Southside boardinghouse, sharing a bed with a co-worker who was on the other shift. At first, Duko's goal was to buy land in Macedonia, but that dream collapsed when he discovered that his brother back home, to whom he was sending money, was using it for his own purposes. As a result, Duko decided to stay in Gary.

In 1915 Duko married a 22-year-old Polish woman whom he had known for three weeks. She had worked in Chicago for four years as a dishwasher, handywoman, and maid, having left the province of Galicia because her parents could not provide her with a dowry. Attaining a job at a Gary boardinghouse, she accepted Duko's marriage proposal after being cheated out of her wages. She did not want to face the grim prospects of returning to Chicago without a job or of trying to find an honest employer in Gary.

By living first in a two-room apartment above a grocery store and then in a tarpaper shack, Duko and Mary saved enough money to purchase a four-room bungalow in Glen Park for 1,600 dollars. They paid a thousand dollars in cash and 25 dollars a month. The house had no bathroom, central heating, or running water except for a kitchen pump, but there was yard space for a garden and a chicken coop. Fortunately for Duko and Mary, their early married life coincided with the boom times created by World War I. But 1919 brought inflation and a worsening of working conditions. By the mid-1920s, their floors still had no rugs or linoleum. To make ends meet, Mary used flour sacks to make bed sheets and fashioned dresses from material costing five cents a yard.

At the onset of the depression the Costos lost their life savings of 150 dollars during a bank failure. The 1930s were years of economic insecurity, with the only silver lining being the coming of industrial unionism and the New Deal. Duko died in 1942, worn out from his labors at the age of 50. Mary outlived him for more than a quarter century.

Duko's three children never knew him intimately. His son Charles declared that, coming from Macedonia, Duko "was very closed-mouthed as are all people who live in an oppressed country full of occupation troops and police and secret political spies." Although Duko never talked about it, his son surmised that he participated in the 1919 strike, because "he always impressed upon me never to join the National Guard or Army because I would be fighting against him if he went on strike."

Duko and Mary were simple folk. Their dreams were of things that richer people took for granted—a roof over their heads, healthy children, a garden, a radio, a second-hand car in running order, a decent and steady job. The suspicions of the Old World and the hardships of America taught them caution. Their tranquil moments were a rare comfort in a strange world.

NEIGHBORHOOD HOUSE AND THE SOCIAL SETTLEMENT IDEAL

In February 1909 Kate and Jane Williams decided to establish a Christian mission in Gary. From their efforts sprang Neighborhood House, Gary's first social settlement, launched under the direction of the Home Mission Committee of the Indiana Presbyterian Synod and dedicated to meeting "the physical, mental, spiritual, and social needs of the community."

The two sisters ignored the warning of a Chicago businessman, who, upon hearing of their intentions, exclaimed: "Ladies, ladies, you should not venture into this Gary, of which we read so much in the papers." With the Reverend Fred E. Walton and Synodical officer Dr. George Knox they toured the Southside in a funeral car. After meeting with Superintendent William A. Wirt, they decided to sponsor kindergarten classes for immigrant children. Wirt agreed to provide a portable building free of charge, along with a piano and a janitor.

In May 1909 the preschool classes opened at 14th and Washington, followed during the summer by Bible School. In January 1910 the Reverend B. M. Baligrodski and his sister joined the staff, and in May they moved into a frame structure at 1525 Washington. Above its drab clapboards was a sign reading: "Presbyterian Mission. Bibles for Sale in all Languages. You Are Welcome." When the Gary schools established kindergarten classes the following fall, the center focused on other health, welfare, and educational needs, including a nursery, a used clothing store, language classes, a library, sewing clubs, and job counseling.

Staff members were concerned with saving immigrants from fast women, alcohol, and the evils of bunkhouse habitation. On one occasion Baligrodski took a load of Bibles to a group of boarders living above a saloon. Most of the men said they could not read, but one youth accepted the gift and began reading aloud from it. When he came to the Psalms, other immigrants began chanting the verses in their native tongue. After awhile, a man asked what stories were in the minister's newspaper, thereby establishing conversation. "Finally, after remaining as long as I could," Baligrodski recollected, "I had to leave on account of the closeness of the room and the foul air. It seemed that it was incredible that human beings could exist in such a place." He invited the men to visit the settlement, however, and before long they began holding meetings there.

Immigrants appreciated the settlement's practical services more than the Bibles. Nurse Sarah Burton, called "Dobri Pani" or the "Good Lady," filled such multiple roles as surrogate doctor, midwife, and charity worker. Making home visits by bike and on foot when the paved streets ended, she helped reduce the neighborhood's infant mortality rate by 25 percent in a year. Jane Williams furnished her with a second bicycle when someone pilfered her first one and allowed her to bring seriously ill children into the center for around-the-clock observation.

In November 1912 the settlement group moved into a new building at 1700 Adams. At the dedication an officer of the Presbyterian Women's Synodical Society declared that the two great tasks ahead were to save souls and brighten lives. The *Daily Tribune* reported that Mayor Tom Knotts and YMCA Director Charles M. Mayne attended the ceremony, as did a throng of Italians and Bohemians. During the next three years the city's improved library and medical facilities took some pressure off the settlement house, just as the schools had preempted the kindergarten. Yet such services as shower stalls and a public laundry remained necessary to families who had no running water.

Neighborhood House was a temporary domicile for many homeless immigrants and a haven of security in a hostile environment. The settlement's 1915 annual report declared: "When someone is sick or injured, when difficulties arise, the first resort for many families is our house."

In 1915 the Reverend Ralph Cummins moved to Neighborhood House and presided over its greatest growth. Trained in Yugoslavia, Cummins was well-liked by Eastern Europeans and tried to allow neighborhood needs to dictate settlement programs. He married Grace Mary Warmington, the staff member responsible for coordinating charity work and the day nursery for orphans and working mothers. A new wing built in 1916–17 contained residential quarters and an auditorium for dances, parties, plays, indoor sports, and folk festivals. Jane Addams of Chicago's Hull House delivered an address from its stage. There was also more space for game rooms, club rooms (Cummins was the boys' Scoutmaster), and classes in art, cooking, hygiene, civics, the English language, and ethnic customs. Italians, Hungarians, Rumanians, Mexicans, and other nationality groups used the chapel until they could build their own churches.

By World War I Neighborhood House had reached maturity and other settlement houses had sprung up, including Campbell House and Friendship House. In succeeding years Neighborhood House focused more attention on blacks and Mexicans, as European nationality groups were no longer so dependent on the center. Finally, in June 1973 Neighborhood House permanently closed its doors because of a lack of funding from the Presbyterian Church and Gary Neighborhood Services.

Although some slum dwellers resented middle-class "urban missionaries" telling them how to live, thousands of newcomers benefited from their programs. Historian Isaac J. Quillen wrote that "the settlement houses provided a place of refuge, guidance, and hope for Gary's newcomers and for its downtrodden or unassimilated old settlers. Here they could talk and play, dance and sing, get advice on their problems, help in securing a job, or relief if they were needy." Similarly, Raymond A. Mohl and Neil Betten concluded that the settlement houses "provided channels and facilities to make assimilation easier and more achievable."

CHAPTER THREE

Pioneer Life

And into this mill town men entered in streams—
Some merely for jobs, some mainly for dreams.

—Mark C. Roser

FRONTIER GARY ATTRACTED a multitude of adventurers and then tested their fortitude. At a time when western expansion was ending and the United States was becoming urbanized, Gary seemed unique in its wilderness setting and vocational opportunities. Many Americans regretted the vanishing of the frontier, worried about the nation becoming effete, applauded President Theodore Roosevelt's statements about the virtues of the "strenuous life," and made folk heroes of Paul Bunyan and John Henry.

Frontier Gary was like "prairie life and the gold rush," wrote Harry Hall. Bored with his desk job in western Pennsylvania, he had decided to start a fresh life in the new steel city. He later wrote: "I hadn't read much but what I read I remembered. One thing that stuck in my memory was the advice of Horace Greeley: 'Go West, young man.' Gary wasn't very far west but it was new. Besides, there was no other place for me to go."

For the thousands of immigrants unfamiliar with American ways, Gary was more bewildering than exciting. Bunco artists preyed on their ignorance, selling them fishing licenses for Lake Michigan and other needless things. A folktale common among ethnic groups told of the greenhorn who ate a banana without first peeling off the skin. The process of adjustment differed from person to person, but all newcomers suffered shocks of alienation.

ALBERT L. ANCHORS: HAULER AND BUILDER

On May 31, 1907, while passing through Chicago, 33-year-old Albert Lee Anchors noticed a sign advertising train fare to Gary for 35 cents. Intrigued, he "bought a ticket and went to have a look see." At the time, a derailed boxcar served as Gary's station house, and the only restaurants were fly-ridden shacks where customers came with guns at their side. "This is one tough burg, and don't you think it ain't!" a weather-beaten man exclaimed. Anchors later wrote: "When I got off the train and looked about one minute, I said to myself, 'this is my town.' . . . What I could see looked like a brand new gold mining camp. Everybody busy, everybody hurrying. Graders, carpenters, mill construction workers. I knew how to handle myself in a mining camp and knew what to do here." The primitive environment offered excitement and the promise of economic success.

Anchors' background was well-suited to adversity. In the mid-1870s his parents invested in a farm and then nearly lost everything in two disastrous fires. Relatives took care of their eight children until they could start over again. After a new house was built, 11-year-old Albert was put in charge of the farm while his father worked in a repair shop. The following summer Albert earned 70 cents a day for ten hours of labor in a glass plant. In the fall he arose at 2:00 A.M. to fold and deliver newspapers before school. He later worked for four years as a bookkeeper in a flour mill and then joined the Klondike Gold Rush. From 1897 until 1906 he prospected in the Yukon. Then after an unsuccessful oil-drilling venture in Casey, Illinois, which used up most of his ten years' savings, Anchors was on his way back to Alaska when he made the permanent detour to Gary.

Anchors put together a successful hauling business in Gary despite undergoing such problems as lame horses, inhospitable weather, dysentery, and having his eye swollen shut from poison ivy. Acquiring four teams of horses over a period of 18 months, he entered a partnership with Aaron H. Hale and formed the Gary Transfer and Storage Company. In his diary he recorded his arduous daily work schedule, including frequent trips to Chicago. He often hiked to Tolleston and once lived in an attic above a store, sharing a bed with a Methodist minister.

Anchors did not much mind Gary's lack of social amenities. On July 4, 1907, he noted that the holiday "passed very quietly in Gary. A few guns, some fire crackers and sky rockets. Lots of drunks was the order of things, but no speech making or demonstrations." In November

1909 he attended a Democratic victory party for Tom Knotts at a skating rink. Three years later, he supported the Bull Moose crusade of Teddy Roosevelt.

Women were a rarity in early Gary. Harry Hall later declared that the mere sight of one "made men lay down their tools and smile in sheepish pleasure." Anchors made a habit of befriending female schoolteachers who were arriving in town, and frequently held Sunday parties at Miller Beach, where he had a cottage. In this way he met Nellie E. Cary, who taught at Emerson. After their marriage in December 1921, Anchors sold his drayage equipment and went on an extended honeymoon. He later explained: "Having averaged 14 hours per day to that time, I was willing to take a breathing spell."

In 1922 U.S. Steel engineer Arthur P. Melton recalled the pioneer days when all sorts of businessmen had flocked to Gary, including many who were "here today and gone tomorrow." Anyone with "a front could start in and hold on for a while," Melton said, adding that "as the city has grown more stable, such men are less and less noticeable, all of which shows that Gary is getting into her stride as a substantial and solid community." Despite what Melton said, many people rued the passing of the very conditions that had attracted so many hearty, self-educated entrepreneurs, such as Albert Anchors.

During the 1920s Anchors built homes on the West Side and moved his wife and two daughters, Martha and Emily, into some of them until buyers were found. He later branched into real estate and insurance, as well as starting the Gary Storage and Van Company. He retired in 1945 at the age of 71 but remained very active. For example, he traveled by car with his wife Nell to some of his old haunts in Alaska. He bought several 30-foot lots near his house on Johnson Street and raised nearly enough vegetables for the entire neighborhood, as well as a colony of bees. On occasion, he dumped his wife's flowers over the fence to make room for more crops. She would do the same thing to his vegetables, whenever she found him out.

In 1952 Anchors became dissatisfied with his life; his gardening, in his words, "seemed so much like busy work." He bought a farm near Crown Point and grew crops there almost up until his death in 1963 at the age of 88. His widow recalled that Anchors was a thoughtful, unassuming man who always liked things running smoothly, perhaps in reaction to the inevitable problems arising from his multifaceted enterprises, which would have overwhelmed someone less patient or durable.

"WORK STUDY PLAY":
WILLIAM A. WIRT AND THE GARY SCHOOLS

For William A. Wirt frontier Gary offered a singular opportunity to construct almost from scratch an urban school system. Over the years his "work-study-play" concept came to be admired worldwide and copied by hundreds of localities. Randolph Bourne wrote that the Gary schools were "the most ingenious attempt yet made to meet the formidable problems of congested urban life and modern vocational demands which are presented to the administrators of the city school." He added that Wirt's success was due to "a very unusual combination of educational philosophy, economic engineering, and political sagacity."

Wirt's ideas reflected intellectual currents popular during the Progressive Era, especially the teachings of John Dewey. Dewey was less interested in formal logic than whether ideas worked; Wirt's litmus test was whether schooling prepared one for life. Universal public education was born during the mid-nineteenth century out of the notion that schools could facilitate social order and social mobility. By 1900, however, public schools were generally held in disrepute as being monotonous, inefficient, obsolete, irrelevant, and authoritarian. Wirt's plans dealt directly with these critiques and met educators' demands for curriculum reform and for child-oriented "learning through doing."

Born in 1874 on a farm near Markle, Indiana, Wirt graduated from DePauw University and became a school administrator in Bluffton, where he experimented with ideas of progressive education borrowed from European and American models.

When Wirt first visited Gary in the fall of 1906, the town's lone school—a portable building—was due to open in two days but as yet had no doors, windows, or seats. Two people taught there in 1906–7, Ora L. Wildermuth and R. R. Quillen. Wildermuth served also as a librarian and lawyer. One of his pupils recalled later that whenever someone came to his law office, a shack located across the sandy intersection of 4th and Broadway, "he left us to see if he could possibly be needed as a lawyer or if someone might want to borrow a book, since he had talked friends into giving or lending him books for anyone to borrow."

Demonstrating a tough-minded idealism and technical expertise in his meetings with town officials (who were as concerned about budgetary matters as educational theories), Wirt was hired as superintendent at an annual salary of 2,500 dollars, beginning July 1, 1907.

Enrollment, which was 35 the first year, swelled to 492 in the fall of 1907 and 1,100 a year later. By then Jefferson School had been remodeled, and William B. Ittner, a nationally acclaimed architect, had been hired to design Emerson, which opened in 1909, and Froebel, which opened in 1912. These schools had indoor swimming pools, auditorium facilities, and outdoor space for gardens and animals.

Under Wirt's "platoon" system students were divided into two groups, "Alpha" and "Beta," which were in school at the same time yet never interchanged in the classroom. Wirt declared that the "only important thing is so to departmentalize teaching and so to rotate classes that the teachers may render the greatest service with the least expenditure of energy, and that the maximum use may be secured from the school plant and other child-welfare facilities." His aim was to develop not only the child's intellectual and aesthetic instincts but also his manual and athletic skills, his mental and physical health, habits of industry and of patriotism, and his self-reliance and self-discipline. Schools, he said, should forget the distinction between the cultural and the utilitarian.

Wirt believed in "unit" schools that went from kindergarten through high school (later even college courses were taught). The school day was lengthened to eight hours, and work, study, and play received equal emphasis, at least in theory. Studios, laboratories, and shops for printing, forging, electrical, metal, carpentry, and plumbing work were an integral part of the curriculum. The students published their own newspaper and yearbook, repaired school equipment, and sold food and clothing with the aim of making the schools as self-sustaining as possible. The daily auditorium program was a central displayer of student productions, as well as a forum for debates, concerts, and the like. The elective system allowed for a wide variety of academic possibilities. Teachers were specialists except in the lowest grades. Older students tutored younger ones. Each pupil was classified as a rapid, normal, or slow learner, the differentiation applying not so much to curriculum as to length of time it took to graduate. This ranged from 10 to 14 years.

The schools' connection to community agencies was broad. Students received credit for working with settlement houses, churches, and city agencies or for taking music lessons. Doctors provided free health and dental care. Randolph Bourne labeled the Wirt schools miniature communities that aimed "to provide the practical natural education of the old school, shop, and home which educated our forefathers."

On November 29, 1913, urban reformer Jacob A. Riis was Wirt's guest on a guided tour of the Gary schools. Impressed by how quickly the city had grown in seven years, he commended the school superintendent for allowing children of all nationalities the opportunity to develop their talents fully. The next day Riis launched a series of 15 community forums sponsored by the YMCA at Froebel School. Praising the effectiveness and efficiency of the work-study-play system, he said: "If one of your boys is not able to take up classical work, he is not thrown out of the course nor handicapped because he cannot make the progress that the other students are doing. Instead he is given a place in the school where he can work for which he is adapted. I am glad to see the vocational side of the Gary educational institutions so highly developed."

The Wirt schools had classes at night for adults, who enrolled in numbers that occasionally surpassed the regular student body. Five nights a week there were "opportunity classes" in academic, commercial, citizenship, industrial arts, and crafts subjects, as well as community sings and patriotic programs.

A few people questioned whether schools—regardless of their quality—should dominate pupils' lives as much as the Wirt schools did, with their long days, after-hours activities, week-end sessions, and year-round schedules. Some people thought that all these programs to socialize and Americanize the students weakened family ties and reflected an anti-urban and anti-immigrant bias. Wirt believed that "cities have never been good places for the rearing of children" and fought against any sort of parental or neighborhood control. He also established policies of segregation, to the dismay of many black residents. The source of the most vocal complaints by white parents against Wirt's policies was the substitution of lockers for private desks, which was essential to the platoon system and much more practical in terms of space.

An attempt to establish the platoon plan in New York City met with opposite results to the Gary experiment. Hired as a one-week-a-month, $10,000-a-year consultant, Wirt helped coordinate a pilot program in the nation's largest metropolis. But attempts to expand the project produced week-long riots, as teachers, union leaders, and immigrants feared that it was a plot to train docile factory hands. In 1918 mayoralty candidate John F. Hylan swept to office on a slogan "a seat for every child," and the platoon system was dead in New York.

In defense of his "work-study-play" concept, Wirt argued that it was an open, experimental, developing outline that should be applied according to each separate community's needs. In Gary he allowed his staff a great deal of freedom, and each unit school tended to reflect the personalities of its principal, faculty, and student body. For example, white middle-class youths attended Emerson, whose principal for 40 years was E. A. Spaulding. Froebel, headed by C. S. Coons from 1916 until 1942, was known as the immigrant school.

Historian Ronald D. Cohen wrote that "at their worst, the Gary schools were places where bored, frightened students were endlessly herded from room to playground to auditorium; at their best they were free, exciting, creative environments, assisting and enriching the lives of rich and poor, black and white, native and immigrant children. For many they surely promoted opportunity."

"THE WILD BISON":
JOHNNY KYLE AND HIGH SCHOOL ATHLETICS

Johnny Kyle was one of Gary's first athletic heroes. A product and admirer of William A. Wirt's work-study-play system, he helped arouse great interest in high school sports with his football and basketball exploits at Emerson. During his subsequent 30-year coaching career at Froebel, athletics became a well-publicized, closely followed, large-scale operation.

John W. Kyle was born on a farm near Tyner, Indiana, on September 12, 1898, and moved to Gary in April 1907. The previous year, his father had obtained a construction job with U.S. Steel. The family of seven stayed first in the ramshackle Red Onion Hotel, then in a tent, and finally in a Gary Land Company house at 708 Pennsylvania. Kyle, whose first teacher was Ora Wildermuth, liked to chase rabbits on the swampy land upon which Emerson would soon be built.

The school's athletic program gave young people something to do and kept them out of mischief, Kyle recollected. There were tennis and basketball programs for his two sisters, and children had gymnasium classes as early as the first grade. Almost as soon as there were enough available players, Gary fielded a football team, coached by Ross Netherton, which played rivals in Hammond, East Chicago, and South Bend (at first Emerson and Froebel combined their players into one squad). Sports did not attract much publicity before 1917. Most parents had not competed in organized sports and did not understand football or basketball. There were no large stadia. A typical football game would find a few spectators milling around the sidelines.

During Kyle's senior year at Emerson in the fall of 1916 the Garyites won their first two football games, and sportswriters began heralding the coming of glory days. The next week the team lost 6 to 0, on an intercepted pass. According to the Gary *Evening Post,* fullback Kyle tackled the defensive receiver "like a battering ram," causing him to fumble, but another opponent recovered the ball and scored. A week later, the Gary team won 90 to 0, with Kyle scoring three touchdowns and six extra points. The Gary team went on to have a 6–1–1 record in 1916, routing Hammond, 40 to 7, for the regional championship and then defeating Sheridan, a visiting team from downstate, 21 to 0, for the unofficial state title. Only a few hundred people attended the game, despite perfect weather, demonstrating that city football had not yet become a craze.

The Emerson basketball team that year attracted large crowds and much publicity, however. Kyle was its captain and was selected as an all-state guard. Winning 21 straight games, the squad almost captured the state championship despite the small size of its players. After capturing the sectional by defeating Froebel, the team had to participate in a grueling 20-team tournament in Bloomington. As the players left Gary, well-wishers presented them with a huge basket of fruit.

Playing five games in four days, Emerson finally bowed to Lebanon, 34 to 26, in the finals. Lebanon was outscored 14 to 11 in the second half but used its overwhelming height advantage to score many tip-ins. The *Evening Post* wrote that "Kyle played a whirlwind game, displayed great coolness and shot basket after basket." He was the tournament's most valuable player.

The 1917 Emerson yearbook predicted that Kyle would go to Purdue, but Indiana University alumni persuaded him to go to Bloomington. There he gained the nickname of "Wild Bison of the West," which grew out of a cantilever-style pad he designed while working one summer at the mill to relieve pressure from a tender shoulder. It stuck up higher than contemporary shoulder gear. Combined with his low running style, the fullback's appearance, to some partisans, resembled a bison running amuck. Kyle's most memorable college feat was a dropkick against archrival Purdue in 1921 that provided the 3 to 0 margin of victory.

In 1922 Kyle became head coach at Froebel. Playing weekends with the semipro Gary Elks, he attracted the attention of the Cleveland Indians. For the next two years, he traveled to Ohio on Saturday nights, played professional football the next day, and then returned on the midnight train in time for work Monday. During the week he practiced Cleveland's plays with the freshmen players.

At various times, Kyle coached tennis, golf, swimming, wrestling, cross-country, basketball, and football. At first, he had no assistants to help him with the scores of youths from 30 or 40 nationalities coming out for practice. Ethnic rivalries hardly ever carried over to the gridiron because of Kyle's reputation for firmness and fairness. His prominently displayed but seldom used strap symbolized his disciplinary philosophy. In 1916 one of his high school teammates had been ejected from an important game for cursing. Kyle forbade profanity in his presence and severely punished any violators. He hoped that sports would serve as an alternative to the temptations of the street. He went to his players' homes, refrained from discussing religion or politics, and encouraged youths to continue their schooling. One year, 11 former athletes were playing for nine different college teams.

The 1927 Froebel football team was Kyle's best. High school football supremacy moved in cycles, depending on population trends, and the immigrant school's dominance set off a frenzy that somewhat embarrassed the coach. When Froebel beat Emerson, 22 to 14, for its ninth consecutive victory, fans snake-danced downtown, forced their way into movie theatres, and then burned coffins in effigy until firemen doused the flames. The following Monday, after police dispersed chanting Froebel students who had been "picketing" Emerson, there was a "pep fest" in the Froebel auditorium. That weekend the team played a championship game against Shortridge, an Indianapolis powerhouse that had not lost in two years. Froebel won, 70 to 0, setting off more celebrations.

Kyle's popularity did not escape the notice of politicians. Democratic party leaders once asked him to run for mayor. He remembered replying: "I'd like to think about it." That same night Republicans made him an identical offer. After talking with Superintendent Wirt, he turned them down, preferring to continue at Froebel rather than venture into the uncertain world of politics.

In contrast to the triumphs of 1927, Froebel's 1945 season was marked by futility. After winning the season opener, 6 to 0, Kyle's team did not score another point all year. During the third week of school, more than a thousand white students boycotted classes, protesting the integration policies of Principal Richard A. Nuzum. Parents asked Kyle to support their cause. Refusing, the coach continued to hold football practice with a decimated 20-man squad, earning the emnity of some former friends. The strike forced Kyle to forfeit half the remaining games. Ironically, Horace Mann's star quarterback that season was named Johnny Kyle, a youth not related to the coach.

On October 1, 1945, the Froebel strike temporarily ceased. The principal went on "vacation," and Kyle was put in charge of maintaining order. No further serious incidents took place. Kyle recollected that students were much calmer than their parents and much less militant in their hostility to blacks. He concluded: "We had these Negro children, and it was our job to educate them. . . . Froebel was a neighborhood school. If people lived there, they had a right to come."

Kyle retired from coaching in the mid-50s and spent a dozen years as a school athletic administrator. In retirement, he viewed sports with a detachment often missing in some overzealous coaches, players, and fans. Sports had been good to Kyle and healthy for Gary. But paraphrasing William Wirt, Kyle stated in 1973, shortly before his death, that sports was a preparation for life, not a substitute for it.

The growth of high school sports into a million-dollar business paralleled Gary's urbanization process. The tremendous emphasis on competition penalized children with poor motor skills and overvalued winning. Nonetheless, athletics became a path to college and an avenue of social mobility available to many youths, including a few famous professionals such as Hank Stram, Les Bingaman, Alex Karras, and Fred Williamson. In a fragmented city no other activity brought together such large numbers of disparate people or provided such excitement.

BLACK IMMIGRATION: NO LAND OF MILK AND HONEY

Black people were in Gary almost from its inception. More than 200 Negro construction workers helped lay out the townsite and plant complex. According to historian Dolly Millender, most disliked being "forced to live like the animals they were thought to be" and did not become permanent residents.

One worker who stayed was Samuel J. Duncan, who in 1906 had hired on as a cook at the millsite. Employed later by the Gary Heat, Light, and Water Company and the Gary State Bank, Duncan helped found the First Baptist Church and persuaded the Reverend Charles E. Hawkins, whom he had known in Louisville, to become its first permanent minister. His daughter Lorraine was, in all likelihood, the first black child born in Gary.

Numerous black settlers arrived in Gary in 1907, including John Preston (an ice and coal distributor), Shepherd King (a minister and carpenter), William Elston (a realtor and politician), William Seaton (an electrician), Charles Bird (a street paver), and Marion C. "Mack" Streeter. Streeter bought a plot of land near 22nd and Broadway for 625 dollars. "Broadway was the only street that you traveled," he recalled, "and the whole way was sand." He tried to convert a jerry-built shanty into a "tavern house," but the Gary Heat, Light, and Water Company refused to extend its services that far south. Streeter ultimately found work as a caretaker for Louis A. Bryan and Thomas E. Knotts.

Blacks sometimes became scapegoats for problems that arose from Gary's frontier climate. In June 1907, when a few blacks contracted smallpox, other blacks unaffected by the disease were put in quarantine with the afflicted patients in an isolated hut called "the pest house in the bush." A month later, a deranged man, falsely rumored to be black, shot a policeman. A posse took up the hunt, empowered with the right "to search every colored man." Blacks banded together for mutual protection until the apprehension of the white felon ended the crisis. Blacks were blamed for vice and dirty politics, as well as disease and crime. In 1909 the *Daily Tribune* complained that "colored" prostitutes at Dave Johnson's Flag House were fleecing customers. Right before the 1909 election, the *Evening Post* charged Republicans with planning to herd black outsiders to the polls.

By 1910 approximately 400 black people lived in Gary. According to historian Powell Moore, they "encountered racial barriers in the [Calumet] Region almost as severe as those they had known in the South." They were discouraged from using public parks and forbidden to attend some theatres. In 1911 a group of Tolleston residents formed the Sixth Ward Improvement Association in order to block construction of a boardinghouse for black people. Negro children, for the most part, attended school in a church basement until parents protested that it was too near the disreputable Dave Johnson's Flag House. Superintendent William A. Wirt, who said that "it is only in justice to the Negro children that they be segregated," provided them with a small portable building.

Gary's black lawyers, teachers, ministers, and other neighborhood leaders tried to dissociate themselves from the reputation of the Patch. In February 1909 they met at the First Baptist Church to discuss how to banish ne'er-do-wells from town. Desiring to participate fully in Gary's social, political, and economic life, they espoused moderate goals and genteel ethics little different from the white middle class. One early resident remembered how the Reverend Hawkins invited millworkers to come into his church to watch or

participate in spelling matches. Several other black churches were
founded by 1910, as well as such organizations as the Workingman's
Social and Political Club and the Classical Whist Club. Samuel Duncan helped establish a Big Brother Club and a Boy Scout troop in the
Central District.

The war boom between 1914 and 1918 swelled Gary's black population. Recruitment agents for U.S. Steel and stories in the Chicago
Defender attracted hundreds of rural Southerners living in conditions of near-serfdom. By the war's end, blacks comprised nearly
one-tenth of the mill labor force, although generally they held the
most dangerous and lowest paying jobs.

In 1916 the Gary NAACP prevented the showing of two objection-
able movies, *The Nigger* and *Birth of a Nation.* The influx of blacks
of high school age caused Froebel to integrate its classrooms, although black pupils were still barred from most social events. In 1918
photographer L. E. McIntyre organized the Gary Colored Commercial Club, which sponsored community forums and provided assistance to returning soldiers.

In 1919 the Calumet Church Federation asked John W. Lee, a
Philadelphia clergyman, to study Gary's burgeoning black neighborhoods. His survey reported the existence of three miniature ghettos
characterized by widespread poverty, squalid housing conditions,
and white ownership of the primary business and entertainment
establishments. Lee recommended that the Gary YMCA establish a
Negro community center and that building and loan companies
"which cater to the colored trade" enforce decent sanitary standards.
The YMCA did open a branch at 19th and Washington, but problems
caused by slum landlords remained. Lee's report mentioned an all-
black housing development bounded by Carolina, Georgia, 11th, and
13th streets that the Gary Land Company had built and recommended that it be expanded. Many black community leaders, however, objected to this indirect endorsement of segregationist policies
carried out by a U.S. Steel subsidiary.

During the so-called "Red summer of 1919" two dozen race riots
erupted across the nation. In October race tensions threatened to
boil over in Gary when white strikers manhandled black strikebreakers aboard a trolley. But the incident did not precipitate a race war.
A local black leader partially responsible for easing tensions was
NAACP official Louis Caldwell, a former Pullman porter and graduate of Northwestern University Law School, who urged blacks to
support the strike. Perhaps a residue of good feeling between the
common people of both races averted a major tragedy. Blacks and

Eastern European immigrants had shared a congested slum for more than a decade with a modicum of friction. Historian Elizabeth Balanoff concluded that segregation emanated not from working-class immigrants but from the racist policies of the cliché-wielding press, the Gary Land Company, and the corporate-dominated school, parks, and hospital boards.

Gary's first black residents suffered from substandard housing, job discrimination, inferior educational opportunities, inadequate hospital and recreation facilities, and inequitable law enforcement procedures. Effects of racism included high rates of infant mortality, tuberculosis, unemployment, and unsolved crimes committed against black people. Dolly Millender wrote that black newcomers did not find Gary "a land of milk and honey, but instead found ugly prejudice. . . ." The barriers became even more rigid during the next two decades.

EXTRANJEROS EN LA PATRIA: MEXICAN IMMIGRANTS

Manuel Lara was the first known Mexican to reside in Gary. Arriving in 1911, he worked in the tin mill, got married, served in World War I, and became a respected member of the community. Between 1917 and 1929 several thousand of his compatriots settled in the city, but most were unable to assimilate as readily as Lara had done.

Gary's Mexicans migrated mainly from the *mesa central* region north and northwest of Mexico City. Traveling from Laredo, El Paso, and other Texas towns along railroad routes, they were attracted to the Chicago-Gary area's stockyards and steel mills. Single males predominated, and even a third of the married workers left their wives behind. Six of ten were under 30 years of age, nine of ten under 40.

Recruiting Mexicans during the 1919 strike and after Congress drastically limited European immigration in 1921, U.S. Steel provided some housing units near the mills, but the arrangement was short-lived due to high rents and tenant discontent over company restrictions. Thus, almost all Mexicans came to live south of the Wabash tracks. "On the Northside they will not rent to Mexicans," one newcomer said but added: "We don't care about it; we could not pay the rent they charge down there anyway, and are just as happy here."

Most Mexicans lived in apartments which a Mexican consul described as wretched beyond belief. A settlement worker was shocked to find families in damp, noxious basements devoid of plumbing, beds, chairs, or tables. Poor housing, landlord exploitation, and dietary insufficiencies led to malnutrition, rickets, and tuberculosis. One social worker said: "The health of Mexicans seems to be worse up here. They have more money but less air and fresh vegetables, and they are more crowded."

Only rarely did these conditions attract public attention, and then usually because of a tragedy. For example, in the early morning of August 30, 1926, a flash fire erupted inside a ramshackle 28-room apartment at 1049 Jefferson after an exploding stove spewed kerosene throughout Vincent Billalon's cell-like flat. Flames spread up and down the long narrow wooden building. As dozens of tenants huddled outside in their nightgowns and undergarments, firemen fought the blaze for two hours. Billalon's charred corpse was found in his room, whose lone window was too small and too high from the ground to afford a means of escape. The body of his brother Alberto was across the hall.

The following day, the Gary *Post-Tribune* described how some Mexicans were forced to live: "Here's a family of five or six crowded into a single room, sometimes two rooms facing a dank hallway extending the full length of the structure. In another room 'down the way' may be crowded two men and their wives, or perhaps four or five roomers. . . . If the family is crowded to such an extent that there isn't room left in a corner of the sleeping room for a stove or is unable to provide itself with one, there may be the handy 'community kitchen' at the far end of the shack, where meals can be prepared à la 'first there, first served.'"

Mexican newcomers were easy marks for unscrupulous peddlers, grocers, and used-car salesmen. There were few Mexican merchants, due to the lack of investment capital. Until 1924, Mexicans had no parish, and four years later they owned just 27 businesses—a single grocery, two tailor shops, four barber shops, nine restaurants, and eleven pool halls. Grocer Frank Morfin, who had settled in East Chicago in 1924, built up a chain of six stores by 1930, including one in Gary (first located at 14th and Adams, then at 12th and Adams, and finally at 1237 Jefferson). Morfin slaughtered his own meat, was one of the first merchants to prepare Mexican food, and gave free tortillas and easy credit to needy customers.

Gary's theatres were off limits to Mexicans until 1925, as was the Hotel Gary, and the municipal cemetery had a separate Mexican section. Even more significant than these forms of racism were the prejudicial hiring practices of many small businessmen and the lack of advancement opportunities at the mill. One employer admitted:

"We use no Mexicans. We have more refined work and have not had to resort to the greasers. They use them [at the mill] for rough work and around blast furnaces."

By 1928 Mexicans constituted nine percent of U.S. Steel's work force (surpassing every foreign-born group except Poles), but only two percent of the Mexican employees held skilled jobs. One foreman dismissed an applicant's previous job record with the remark: "If you have not worked as a machinist in this country, then you are not a machinist."

During this nonunion era, when there was no job security, many Mexicans had to pay bribes to get work. One employment manager said: "When I hire Mexicans at the gate, I pick out the lightest among them. No, it isn't that the lighter-colored ones are any better workers, but the darker ones are like the niggers."

Family solidarity was a frequent casualty of city life. The shortage of women contributed to an increased desertion rate among wives, and children sometimes became alienated from their parents. The final passages of the folk song, "El Enganchado," revealed a lament common among patriarchs:

> Even my old woman has changed on me—
> She wears a bob-tailed dress of silk,
> Goes about painted like a *pinata*
> And goes at night to the dancing hall.

> My kids speak perfect English
> And have no use for our Spanish
> They call me 'fader' and don't work
> And are crazy about the Charleston.

> I am tired of all this nonsense
> I'm going back to Michoacan;
> As a parting memory I leave the old woman
> To see if someone else wants to burden himself.

Hardships sometimes reinforced Mexicans' ethnic loyalties. Economist Paul S. Taylor wrote in 1932 of their "strong emotional attachment to Mexico, a patriotism heightened ... by their expatriation, and by the attitude of superiority to which they frequently feel themselves subjected." Only a minority became naturalized, and quite a few wives returned "home" before childbirth to ensure that their infants would be Mexican citizens.

One agency that eased urban adjustment in Gary was the International Institute, founded in 1919 by the YWCA. A way station for refugees, it provided fellowship, language and citizenship classes, recreation, pageants, club facilities, job placement, casework guidance, referral services, and other valuable programs.

The International Institute was the initial home of Gary's first Mexican mutual aid society, La Sociedad Protectora Mexicana. It was first intended to be a woman's club, but, according to an institute secretary, the wives "sent their husbands to represent them, on account of babies, meals, and lunches for borders, etc., and . . . it turned into a men's club." The society moved to Neighborhood House, where the settlement's Spanish-speaking pastor helped rescue it from financial insolvency. Religious disputes between Catholics and Protestants caused the original organization to split into two new groups in 1928, the Sociedad Josefa Ortiz Dominguez and the Sociedad Hidalgo.

During the 1930s these mutual aid societies were hard-pressed to cope with the depression. Gary's Mexicans faced not only unemployment but an organized campaign to get them to leave town. The township trustee's office began to deny relief benefits to aliens, and mill officials made citizenship papers a prerequisite for a job. The American Legion suggested that Mexican aliens be "repatriated." Business, labor, political, and civic leaders took up the idea of providing them with free, one-way transportation. Horace S. Norton said: "The kindest thing which could be done [for] these people would be to send them back to Mexico. They do not assimilate and are unhappy here."

There was some precedent for removal. In April 1924 the police had begun an antivagrancy campaign, rounding up approximately 80 Mexicans whose only offense was not being able to prove they had a job. In a rooming house at 1009 Washington, they found 40 Mexicans whose quarters were, to quote an officer, "so overcrowded, so filthy, and so filled with vermin that they are worse than hog wallows."

The next day Gary City Judge C. M. Greenlee found 32 of the defendants guilty of vagrancy, fined them 25 dollars plus costs, and sentenced those without funds to 25 days in the penal farm. Then he issued a warning for unemployed "loiterers" to leave Gary or face arrest.

During the 1930s approximately 1,500 Mexicans were repatriated. Most went voluntarily, but historians Raymond A. Mohl and Neil Betten have concluded that for nine months, beginning in May 1932, local authorities—to the disgust of the International Institute—took coercive measures against unemployed Mexicans, including some who were American citizens. Similar campaigns elsewhere resulted in almost a half million Mexicans (approximately one-third of those in the United States) returning to their native land. Men generally were put on trucks, women and children on trains.

Before boarding a freight car, one girl said bitterly: "This is my country, but after the way we have been treated, I hope never to see it again. . . . As long as my father was working and spending his money in Gary stores, paying taxes and supporting us, it was all right, but now we have found we can't get justice here."

One Mexican who managed to remain in Gary was Paulino Monterrubio, who moved to Gary in 1922 at the age of 26. "People were discriminated against in those days," he recalled 51 years later. "We didn't have a very good life because we had nobody to watch over us."

Having emigrated north from Mexico City to escape the turmoil of the Mexican Revolution in 1915, Monterrubio learned halting English as a railway worker in Kansas, a foundry laborer in New Mexico, and a steelworker in Joliet, Illinois. In Gary he lived in a Southside boardinghouse and worked 12 hours a day. He recalled that if policemen spotted Mexicans on the streets after midnight, they asked them where they were coming from. Unless you had alcohol on your breath, you were all right if you replied, "the mill." After an eight-month stay in Gary, Monterrubio moved back to Joliet, got married, and returned with a wife and infant son the following year.

White people expected Mexicans to know their place, Monterrubio remembered; otherwise they were openly hostile. "I remember one time I went to a tavern on 5th Avenue with three friends," he said. "We decided to go in, and the bartender gave us a beer, but do you know what he did? He broke the glasses."

Monterrubio had little connection with neighborhood settlements, schools, or governmental agencies. The Italian church that a few of his acquaintances attended had little appeal to him. Most politicians paid such scant attention to the Latin community that "we didn't pay much attention to them." Monterrubio's social life revolved around family (he fathered six children), friends, and fraternal organizations such as La Sociedad Protectora Mexicana, which offered camaraderie, death benefits, and other forms of security against a hostile urban environment.

When work was plentiful at the mill, the long hours consumed much of his energy. Job hazards included dangerous manual labor and tough, unpredictable foremen. "Some were decent, some not," he remembered. Virtually none of them spoke Spanish, and disagreements arose over such diverse matters as bathroom privileges and tenure.

On one occasion, Monterrubio recalled, "a man at the mill asked me 'where do you come from?' I said, 'From Mexico.' He said, 'Well, why don't you go back?' At that time I talked a little more English than before and I told him, 'Why don't you go back to Poland?' "

When steel production slowed to a trickle during the 1930s, Monterrubio was laid off but escaped being repatriated. He rented a pool parlor at 13th and Adams, a block from his home. The establishment was a popular meeting place, but few "customers" had any money. Monterrubio went back to the mill, whenever there was work, and remained a steelworker until the early 1960s.

For those Mexicans who were able to remain in Gary during the depression the ensuing quarter-century brought a modicum of security, mobility, satisfaction, and acceptance. Not nostalgic about the past, Monterrubio nevertheless was proud of his family, his CIO membership card, his World War II civil defense hat, his American citizenship papers, his lack of a police record, and his many friends and acquaintances.

Until 1972 Monterrubio helped out as a bartender at La Sociedad Mutualista de Mexico, which he helped organize in 1933, but he curtailed his activities because he did not like to walk a mile home alone in the middle of the night. In his old age he lamented the dispersal of Gary's Mexican community that damaged ethnic solidarity and denied some young people the benefits of knowing about their heritage. "The only trouble," he said, "is that the Mexican people, we are scattered all over Gary."

JOVO KRSTOVICH: HE CAME TO STAY

In 1903 a 17-year-old youth from Trebinje, Serbia, emigrated to America. Three years later, he was part of a labor gang in Gary. Living in an overcrowded Southside boardinghouse and pouring concrete in sub-zero weather without gloves, Jovo Krstovich found that the mill town offered immigrants endless hours of drudgery with few redeeming pleasures save for dreams of a better tomorrow. After his death in 1972, his son George recalled that his most striking features were his huge hands, whose scars testified to his toil during Gary's early days when he had poured concrete for U.S. Steel.

Many Serbians viewed frontier Gary as a way station, a place to make money and then leave, perhaps to return to the homeland, but Krstovich had come to stay. Opposed to the exploitative economic order in his native land, he cast his lot with the expanding steel town. In 1907 he formed a partnership with Mato Chuck, John Wuletich, and Theodore Komenich to open a food store at 1724 Massachusetts called the Serbian Brothers' Market. Almost all nationality groups had their own little stores. Starting one did not require a large cash outlay, although operating it took ingenuity and long hours of work. Hungarians generally shopped at Bela Kelner's grocery; Slovaks at John and Mary Bilkovic's meat market. As a buyer, salesman, and deliveryman at the Serbian Brothers' Market, Krstovich negotiated with Chicago produce wholesalers and lugged orders down sandy pathways to bunkhouses. His nonstop pace, which he maintained for the half-century and more that he was in business, caused suppliers to nickname him "Hurry Up, John."

There was money to be made in servicing Gary's swelling population. A 19-year-old Serbian, John T. Marich, began selling groceries from a tarpaper shack in 1907, and with his profits built a brick store. When the Tittle brothers invested 13 thousand dollars in a meat market at 644 Broadway, skeptics predicted there would only be a few customers, but the merchants sold their entire stock the first day and were on their way to becoming successful businessmen.

Krstovich helped found the Sokol Lodge and the Sloboda Society, nationality clubs which fostered both Serbian solidarity and Americanism. During World War I some of his friends returned "home" to fight the hated Turks and Austrians. After setting up two new stores with partner John Wuletich, including Kirk Yard Market, Krstovich went into the American army and served as a military policeman at Newport News, Virginia. He was fond of telling friends later that he never had to unholster his weapon during the war. Under Krstovich's management during the 1920s the Kirk Yard Market at 295 Tyler Street expanded into the largest grocery outlet in the area, with more than 20 employees.

Krstovich once enrolled at Valparaiso University but quit within a week because the subject matter seemed so irrelevant. During a six-month visit to Yugoslavia, he married Dorothy Mandeganja, a woman 14 years his junior who gave birth to three sons in quick succession. When the depression and encroaching supermarkets cast their pall on his security, Krstovich and an Italian neighbor, Jack Nigrelli, started the J. and J. Tavern next to the market, one of the first post-prohibition taprooms.

Krstovich's frugality was armor against the economic ills of the 1930s. During the previous decade he had developed a liking for fancy automobiles. For instance, he paid out $2,265 in cash for a 1929

Reno Flying Cloud, after seeing one on display at the county fair. He made do with that car until 1941, despite his sons' remonstrances, arguing that belt-tightening precautions were necessary during the hard times.

Krstovich did not burden his family with business problems, but they shared work details. On occasion they prepared and ate the tavern's meal-of-the-day together. Krstovich never became very proficient at mixing drinks, but he sometimes helped out behind the bar on Friday nights. On one such evening men with Thompson machine guns burst into the taproom. Regarding Krstovich's cool demeanor while opening a safe with a weapon at his head, his son George recalled: "He was tough. They don't make guys like that anymore."

Business and family were Krstovich's two passions. Gradually he lost interest in the Serbian clubs and church because their stormy political feuds irritated him. His community service consisted of extending credit and loans to indigent families. One such creditor paid her depression food bill 35 years later. The blunt, outspoken merchant enjoyed the human contact of the neighborhood store. Only when business declined did his competitive nature cause him to lecture old customers whom he had helped during the lean years when they, after carrying chain-store shopping bags past his store, would later bring him their empty bottles for refund. He would admonish them to take their bottles elsewhere in tones that revealed the full force of his wrath.

By the 1960s, when poor health forced Krstovich to retire at the age of 83, the store's shrunken sales volume had long since failed to justify his enormous output of energy. But work had become his way of life and Kirk Yard Market an extra means of security for sons whose affluence far outstripped the need for the store except as a symbol of patriarchal sacrifice and devotion.

POOR PEOPLE'S PHYSICIAN:
ANTONIO GIORGI

Dr. Antonio Giorgi, an important pioneer physician in Gary, built the city's first hospital geared especially to the needs of the common people. When doctors were in short supply in the Central District and when other medical institutions turned away black people and discriminated against the poor, Dr. Giorgi treated people of all races and nationalities with respect. Bringing a diploma from Povia Medical College with him when he emigrated from Rome with his wife and four children, Dr. Giorgi lived in New York and Ohio for five years before settling in Gary in 1909 at the age of 49.

At that time Gary's only hospital was a weather-beaten, four-building complex run by Franciscan nuns and called St. Mary's. Six years later, it was superseded by a larger hospital called St. Mary's Mercy. Meanwhile, two other Northside medical facilities were built: Gary General (the forerunner of Methodist Hospital) and the Illinois Steel Company hospital for mill personnel.

In 1915 Dr. Giorgi built a three-story brick clinic in the 1800 block of Jefferson and called it St. Antonio's after his patron saint. From the outside it resembled a boardinghouse with bright potted plants along the front railing. It had a screened porch where convalescents lounged, gossiped, played cards, or read. Inside, the facilities were not as modern or antiseptic as the larger Northside hospitals. Multicolored curtains were used as partitions, and seasoned ethnic dishes were served to those patients whose constitutions would permit such a diet.

A resident later described Dr. Giorgi as a serious, dedicated man who never undertook an operation he could not handle. He was especially adept at appendectomies, Caesarean deliveries, and at stitching up victims of barroom brawls and industrial accidents who arrived at the makeshift emergency room at all hours of the day and night. Dr. Giorgi had a drawer stuffed with wage assignments, but compassion for impoverished patients often caused him to postpone indefinitely the filing of these garnishment notices.

Once a 325-pound saloonkeeper, known for his sadistic ways, checked into St. Antonio's with knife wounds. Somebody murdered him during the night. Dr. Giorgi's attorney recalled that the horrified doctor feared he would be held responsible, but the police told him: "Somebody should have killed the S.O.B. a long time ago. There will be no investigation."

Dr. Giorgi's immigrant background and all-purpose clinic made him more vulnerable to capricious suits than his Northside counterparts. During a malpractice suit, after a lawyer unfairly maligned him, he rose from his seat, muttered an epithet in broken English, stormed from the courtroom in a rage, slammed shut the door, and knocked over a man coming down the hall. Two days later, when he won the verdict, Dr. Giorgi rushed over to the jurors and shook their hands.

The long hours at the hospital would not have allowed most men to do anything else, but Dr. Giorgi somehow found the time to organize activities in the Italian-American community. Knowing that some Northsiders did not consider him a full-fledged physician because his training had been in Italy, Dr. Giorgi believed that his compatriots would not win the respect of others unless they banded together.

In 1913 Dr. Giorgi became the first president of the Italian-American Democratic Club. Soon afterwards he helped found the Francesco Crispi Lodge and the Theodore Roosevelt Political League. During World War I these groups marched in victory parades, sold Liberty Bonds, and participated in Americanization campaigns. Between 1917 and 1919 Dr. Giorgi set aside 10 of the 35 beds in St. Antonio's for armed services volunteers, draftees, and wounded veterans. Three other "free" beds were designated for indigents.

In the expansionistic 1920s the annual number of inpatients at St. Antonio's was over a thousand. More than 20 physicians used the facilities, which by this time included a fourth-floor wing. In 1925 Dr. Giorgi was appointed to the Gary Health Board and the Red Cross Fund-Raising Committee.

In 1930 Dr. Giorgi ran unsuccessfully for county coroner in the Republican primary. On April 22 an advertisement in the Hobart News claimed that he was "the quintessence of well-bred urbanity and kindly, considerate, and true to the standards of honor that mark the gentle-born." After stressing his philanthropy, patriotism, and liberality, the write-up concluded: "Every creed, race or color receives the same consideration."

Shifting allegiance back to the Democratic party during the depression, Dr. Giorgi was appointed physician for the county poor farm in 1936. He hosted a testimonial dinner for Governor M. Clifford Townsend, and shortly thereafter Townsend appointed him to the Central Indiana State Hospital Board. In 1938 he once again became president of the Italian-American Democratic Club.

In 1947 the Indiana Medical Association honored Dr. Giorgi, who had recently retired, for a half-century of medical service, including 30 years in Gary. He died six months later at the age of 87.

Dr. Giorgi's public life demonstrated both the opportunities and limitations awaiting immigrant professionals who came to Gary during its formative years. His old-world loyalties kept him close to the common people, and he served them well.

TOM CANNON:
EARLY GARY'S REPRESENTATIVE MAN

"When I got off the train, the housing was confined to a few shacks, tents, and temporary frame structures," Thomas Harvey Cannon reminisced. "In the woods nearby the wolves were howling. When the real estate men who swarmed around incoming trains found that I did not come to buy real estate, they set up more howling. And when I found that I had to walk nine blocks through the sand . . . to get a drink, I started howling."

For more than a quarter century, Tom Cannon was Gary's foremost newspaperman, booster, poet, humorist, and social historian. A founder of the Gary *Evening Post,* editor of a two-volume history of the Calumet Region, and publicist for the preservation of Indian trails and the establishment of the Dunes State Park, Burns Ditch, and Gateway Park, Cannon had an enormous impact on Gary, especially considering that he was more than 60 years old when he took up residence.

Born on St. Patrick's Day in 1849 in Parke County, Indiana, Cannon was an adventurous youth whose hero was Simon Bolivar and whose reading matter concentrated on the Mexican War and the California Gold Rush. At the age of 16 he ran away from his parents' farm and joined the Union Army. Six days later, General Robert E. Lee surrendered at Appomattox, Disappointed at missing combat, the young would-be soldier then enrolled at Wabash College in Crawfordsville, Indiana. Although his parents hoped he would become a minister, he preferred law. Before graduating, however, he was expelled for being involved in a shooting spree in a nearby hamlet. Journeying to Missouri, he worked as a reporter and eventually became a member of the bar. When his law partner took over a defunct newspaper, he became its editor.

A couple of years later, the lure of prospecting prompted him to go west, where for two decades he was a miner, journalist, negotiator of Indian treaties, and guide for a geological expedition. If his autobiography is to be believed, he killed buffalo with William F. "Buffalo Bill" Cody, became a blood brother of the Utes, got into a scrape with James B. "Wild Bill" Hickok, and fought skirmishes against Geronimo's Apaches. After hauling a printing press by mule cart across the Rocky Mountains, he founded the first newspaper in western Colorado. During the trip, he lost the "f" type and had to substitute the letters "ph" in his first issues.

In 1890 Cannon became a reporter for the Chicago *Times.* Between assignments to political conventions, labor disputes, and the 1893 World's Fair, he visited the Calumet Region to cover the stockyards land boom, the Tolleston poachers' war, and the construction of the first gravel road between Hobart and Miller.

In 1906 Cannon wrote several stories about the creation of Gary, including "The Three Industrial Musketeers," a biographical sketch of engineers Ralph E. Rowley, Arthur P. Melton, and Thomas H. Cutler. "I found a city in the raw," he wrote. Save for the omnipresent sand, he might have been back in a Colorado mining camp.

Three years later, at the age of 61, Cannon moved to Gary to start a newspaper. He later explained: "Chicago had become drab. . . . I longed for further adventure into the land of romance." He uprooted himself from his steady job in response to the urging of his friend Tom Knotts, who was taking an editorial beating from Homer J. Carr's Gary *Daily Tribune,* the town's lone paper since the demise of the *Northern Indianian.*

By October 1909 Cannon and three other staff members were ready to put out a four-page daily called the Gary *Evening Post.* Their political coverage contributed to Knotts' narrow victory. Although the Mayor was more radical than Cannon would have liked, the journalist retained a lifelong admiration for him. In his words, Knotts "was brusquely outspoken, because he was a genuine Gary boomer and above all because he was never known to go back on a friend."

Following the 1909 election, Knotts lost interest in the *Evening Post.* Cannon had to sell stock to keep it afloat. In 1910 the Snyder family of Ohio bought the controlling interest in it but retained Cannon. For the next half-century the brothers H. B. "Bud" Snyder and J. R. "Ralph" Snyder would play a dominant role in shaping public opinion in Gary.

A gruff, hard-shelled, self-trained newsman schooled in the "heroic" style of personal journalism, Cannon wrote stories with a flair for the dramatic. He did not treat Gary as a mere appendage of Chicago but as an important industrial center worthy of first-rate news coverage.

During the 1912 presidential campaign Theodore Roosevelt visited Gary and then traveled to Wisconsin, where he was shot and wounded slightly. The following day, in a story entitled "MIGHT HAVE HAPPENED HERE," the *Evening Post* announced that police "believe the would-be murderer of Colonel Roosevelt was in Gary yesterday" but had had no good opportunity to fire at him.

When Democratic presidential aspirant Woodrow Wilson campaigned in Gary, he disappointed local Democrats by refusing to ride in the fire company's new "motorized hose cart," which was normally used for state occasions such as the funeral procession for newsboy Billy Rugh, a 41-year-old cripple who volunteered for a skin graft operation to save a woman's life and died as a result of the sacrifice. Although the Democratic candidate won the election, Roosevelt carried Gary.

One of Cannon's favorite stories concerned an "Indian Uprising" that erupted when some members of a "Wild West" troupe stayed too long in a Southside saloon. Receiving complaints of a loud disturbance, Mayor Knotts helped calm the Indians by speaking to them in the Sioux tongue.

Cannon also got lively copy from the exploits of Maurice "Battle Axe" Castleman, one of six saloonkeepers on the City Council, whom Cannon labeled the "stormy petrel" with a "racketeer complex" whose "hand was against every official he could not control." Castleman once kidnapped an opponent in a fit of pique and periodically enjoyed taunting mill officials with ordinances calling for transportation routes through their property.

Two of Cannon's most dramatic stories took place during World War I. The first was the unsolved murder of Reverend Edmund E. A. Kayser in August 1915, which some people attributed to the clergyman's outspoken espousal of the German cause against England. The other was the catastrophic Hagenbeck-Wallace train crash of 1918, which claimed the lives of scores of circus entertainers because of the negligence of a troop train engineer.

During World War I Cannon served on several mobilization committees and was an ardent supporter of harsh measures against dissenters. His patriotism tended to blur his vision of injustices inflicted on immigrants. An informer for the Secret Service, he once got a man interned for the duration of the war for speaking out against the draft.

A onetime admirer of such Midwestern iconoclasts as Mark Twain, William Jennings Bryan, John Peter Altgeld, Eugene V. Debs, Robert Ingersoll, and Clarence Darrow, with age Cannon grew uncomfortable with unionists, socialists, free thinkers, feminists, and anyone who said a bad word about Gary. His elitist political views were reflected in his statement that "We have far too many people voting than we ought to have. . . . Only about thirty-five percent of our citizenship is qualified to vote."

Cannon's conservatism became apparent during the 1919 steel strike. He sympathized with management and characterized the union leaders as "incendiary irreconcilables." Mill officials did not allow journalists inside Gary Works until the strike lost momentum. Then they took Cannon on an exclusive tour. The newsman later boasted that his report about the bustle of activity at the mill contributed to the "complete collapse of the strike."

During the 1920s, Cannon edited the "Flue Dust" newspaper column, making use of contributors' poetry, sayings, and anecdotes interspersed with his own salty aphorisms regarding prohibition, gangsters, "Vampire" drivers, bathing suits, and the like. "A pessimist is all right in his place," he quipped, "but he never goes there until he dies." Regarding the Wall Street Crash, he wrote on November 13, 1929: "The stock market slump is now called a readjustment. It's a good word to remember when you go broke in a poker game."

Cannon's poetry generally reflected a spirit of booster optimism. In 1924 he paid this tribute to his adopted city:

> In thy pillared smoke uprising,
> Gary mine, Gary mine,
> Dwells the soul of thy emprising,
> Gary mine, Gary mine,
> Hands of steel and heart of gold,
> Swift of purpose, strong and bold . . .
> Thy wondrous story ne'er grows old,
> Gary mine.

Cannon also wrote satirical essays under the pen name "Lud Wrangler." The observations of this "old traveler" encompassed everything from the generation gap to eating habits. On January 28, 1930, he wrote: "My first revolt took place when I was only three years old. Mother undertook to get a bowl of spinach down in my infantile tummy and I became a bolshevist on the spot. . . . Spinach should be fed to the cows. It has no place in the internal economy of man. It's a wise child that knows its own fodder—and spinach is far from being that."

In his old age, Cannon was Gary's most famous celebrity and received the esteem of mill managers, municipal officials, and civic leaders. His Hotel Gary suite and newspaper office cubicle attracted many visitors. His annual birthday banquet was a social event for scores of "Flue Dusters" with such exotic pen names as Hen Peck, Me 2, Hayseed, Paddie Kak, Greyhead, Chuckles, Mollie O., and Manda Linn.

On his eightieth birthday Cannon danced an Irish jig and remarked: "I've lived a pretty full life, and I'm ready to go whenever 'the old man with the scythe' figures it's time to put my number up. Funny thing is—during my life I've violated about every code that was ever written. I've been addicted to most of the popular vices, lived hard and furiously, and here I am, outliving men who should have survived to crack 100."

Eight months later, Cannon gave a talk on specialization in the modern world. "If we set out to master all lines of knowledge, we do nothing well," he declared but added: "Developing a specialty is a good deal like developing a boil on the back of the neck. When fully grown it prevents one from looking at the sun, moon, and stars, except with painful effort." Happy to have grown to maturity in a less complex era, Cannon categorized himself as "a singer of simple songs, an humble minstrel singing at the outer gate of a material world."

On December 24, 1929, Cannon reminisced about Christmas in early Gary, when most residents spent the holidays elsewhere, leaving a "ghost town" atmosphere for "the few of us who stayed home and 'kept house,' ate our Christmas dinners at the restaurant, and celebrated the gladsome season at the round bar of the old Gary Hotel."

In 1930 the *Post-Tribune* published Cannon's serialized autobiography. It evoked nostalgia for an era when Tom Knotts put all the local mail in a shoebox and there were less than a half-dozen cars on Broadway. Even though his autobiography appeared at the dawn of the depression, its theme was faith in the city's progress and growth.

On August 27, 1937, Cannon left the *Post-Tribune* newsroom complaining of stomach pains. He died the next day. In an editorial entitled "A GREAT SCOUT IS DEAD," he was eulogized as a man who in 26 years had "passed from a blustering, tempestuous worker to a lovable character full of wit and the wise saws of many experiences." Cannon himself had told a colleague that his epitaph should read: "The Last of the Mad Cannons."

Among Cannon's mourners was Horace S. Norton, the personification of the close corporate ties with civic affairs. "I loved Tom Cannon as I loved my own brother. I do not think I ever had a better friend nor a stauncher defender," Norton said.

Cannon was Gary's ideal bourgeois statesman, to paraphrase what historian Richard Hofstadter said of President Grover Cleveland. With his old-fashioned beliefs in rugged individualism and self-help and his curious blend of romanticism and pragmatism, he was the flower of "Steel City" culture during its frontier age.

CHAPTER FOUR

World War I
and its Aftermath

I asked the Mayor of Gary about the 12-hour day and the 7-day
week.

And the Mayor of Gary answered: more workmen steal time on the
job in Gary than in any other place in the United States.

"Go into the plants and you will see men sitting around doing
nothing—machinery does everything," said the Mayor of Gary
when I asked him about the 12-hour day and the 7-day week.

And he wore cool cream pants, the Mayor of Gary, and white shoes,
and a barber had fixed him up with a shampoo and a shave and
he was easy and imperturbable though the government weather
bureau thermometer said 96 and children were soaking their
heads at bubbling fountains on the street corners.

And I said good-by to the Mayor of Gary and went out from the
city hall and turned the corner into Broadway.

And I saw workmen wearing leather shoes scruffed with fire and
cinders, and pitted with little holes from running molten steel,

And some had bunches of specialized muscles around their shoulder blades hard as pig iron; muscles of their fore-arms were sheet
steel and they looked to me like men who had been somewhere.

> —Carl Sandburg, "The Mayor of
> Gary," written in 1915 and pub-
> lished in *Smoke and Steel* (1920)

THE COMING OF World War I speeded up Gary's growth process,
caused housing shortages, revitalized the vice trade, increased black
migration from the South, and infected the body politic with an
intolerant mood. Once the fighting stopped, the city experienced
inflation and worker layoffs, suffered from a traumatic steel strike,
and was put under martial law. By 1919 less than a third of Gary's

60,000 residents were foreign-born, compared to 50 percent in 1910. Although Gary went on to enjoy its most prosperous era during the 1920s, there was an enduring undercurrent of polarization that manifested itself in the rise of the Ku Klux Klan as a force in local politics and in the mistreatment of aliens, dissenters, and minority groups.

MOST AMERICAN OF AMERICAN CITIES

On April 28, 1917, a huge procession cascaded down Broadway. Caught up in the martial spirit and anxious to quash rumors that its "hyphenated" populace lacked patriotism, 30,000 marchers stepped to the beat of 26 bands. Mayor Roswell O. Johnson, dressed as Uncle Sam, was the parade marshal. Astride a pureblood horse, Superintendent William P. Gleason led a 7,000-member contingent from Gary Works. Lending color to the pageant were floats from a score of civic groups and ethnic clubs. Labeling Gary the "Most American of American Cities," the *Evening Post* wrote: "Some people have been wondering if there is any spirit of patriotism in Gary, but after the tremendous, the unprecedented demonstration of Saturday night, no one will ask that question again."

World War I had a momentous impact on Gary's economy. When faced with a serious recession in 1914, Gary Works had required that its employees reside within the city limits. The slump caused such hardship that Mayor Johnson set up several relief centers for the unemployed. Even so, hundreds of immigrant children invaded the Northside at night, picking through garbage cans for food.

In contrast, by the end of 1916, the company had increased its profits fivefold and rescinded the residency order, as the mills were operating at full capacity. When the United States declared war against Germany on April 6, 1917, Superintendent Gleason had good reason to sit tall in the saddle behind the banners of God, country, and U.S. Steel. The company even adopted the slogan "Shells, More Shells for the Huns," in an effort to motivate workers to reach higher production levels.

Anxious to attract new residents, the city published a brochure that proclaimed: "Cosmopolitan Gary, the Magic Steel City, welcomes all comers to its confines, where health, wealth, and pleasure combine to make it the most wonderful city of the present century. Thrice welcome! Ye patriotic peoples of the universe."

The high intensity of war fever had a pernicious effect on civil liberties. Peace groups and radical labor organizations, such as the Industrial Workers of the World, were suppressed. The local papers printed the names of "slackers" who allegedly were avoiding the draft, and police arrested loiterers. The Loyalty League forced aliens to buy bonds, while the American Protective League filed reports of subversive activity with the government. Anything German was held in scorn. One local organization even proclaimed that "the war of the Revolution in 1776 was not the fault of the British people . . . but was brought about by George III, who was. . .a German by descent, a German by education, a German by racial instinct, and a German of hereditary brutishness." Even though most residents supported the war, there was much worry over the patriotism of Gary's immigrants. The federal government kept a close watch on foreign language newspapers and churches, and millworkers were urged to be on the lookout for saboteurs.

Gary's business aristocracy exhorted residents to help the "boys in the trenches" through homefront sacrifices. Horace S. Norton directed the county chapter of the National Council of Defense, which coordinated more than 20 subsidiary committees. These groups urged Garyites to observe heatless Mondays, meatless Tuesdays, and wheatless Wednesdays; and they disseminated propaganda to churches, schools, newspapers, unions, businesses, civic groups, and the general public. Thousands of people started home garden plots. Liberty Loan and War Relief drives met with an enthusiastic response far in excess of quotas set for the city.

U.S. Steel collected money for the Red Cross by deducting a day's wages from workers every two weeks. The method used was to issue special checks stamped "Red Cross" in workers' pay envelopes. Officials strongly recommended that the checks be donated to the Red Cross and punished those who objected. Not surprisingly, the corporation commonly reported 100 percent participation in its Red Cross drives.

One year after America entered the war, the Liberty Loan Committee held another unity parade. Its ads admonished: "You Should Think of Nothing Now But Your Duty to the Government. . . EVERYONE MUST BE IN THE BIG PARADE." Inclement conditions held the crowd to half of what it had been a year previously, but one participant said: "If our boys . . . could see us marching in the rain and mud, they would be all the more ready to go over the top in France."

The Gary Theatre presented several propaganda films, including *The Brute of Berlin,* which, according to a local reviewer, portrayed Kaiser Wilhelm's "different moods of passion, cruelty, and mental terror. . . ." The showing of *The Brute of Berlin* was cut short by a nationwide influenza epidemic that closed down all Gary's theatres, schools, and churches and, according to some estimates, killed more Americans than did the Germans.

From time to time, the local papers, in an effort to promote "100 percent Americanism," printed letters sent home by soldiers. The first batch from boot camps tended to be cheerful and cocky, despite occasional complaints of poor food and callous treatment by officers. The trainees expressed eagerness to "Kill the Kaiser" and "Swat the Huns." The letters from overseas, however, were more somber, and the soldiers were less naïve about the glory of war. The confidence and acceptance of duty were still there, but so, too, were the horror of trench warfare, the sounds of explosives, the smell of mustard gas, and the fear of cholera, typhus, and gangrene.

The letters testified also to the brutalizing impact of war. John Bancsi of Tolleston told his sister Alma: "I have killed nine Huns myself with my automatic rifle. Believe me, I was happy when I saw a Dutchman's brains flying all over, and I could hold my position." Fred Englehart wrote: "I often said I would kill the first prisoners I took, but when they throw up their hands, cry for mercy, and throw their arms around your neck...why it's mighty hard to bayonet them."

Emphasizing his heroism, the *Evening Post* on September 19, 1918, recounted how Private Forrest A. Ragon captured two Germans while separated from his outfit for eight days. During that ordeal, Ragon wrote, "I staggered and wandered around, shells dropping far and near from me, [and] didn't know whether I was in hell or Gary—about half crazy I guess."

Soon after the Armistice, Elmer W. Holm wrote Mrs. Myrtle E. Werber, his former piano teacher, that he had lost a leg when a shell exploded near him. "My wounds are all healed now and am waiting for them to build me a new leg. As soon as I get it, I will be all right and will hop back to old Gary," wrote Holm.

Some of Holm's friends never returned. Gary furnished many more combatants than the national average, and 97 of them died in action. The "Honor Roll," wrote historian Richard J. Meister, "included the Russian Balcius, the Hungarian Razin, the Welsh Davies, the Swede Carlson, the Serb Dubraja, the Italian Saladina, the Pole Peichochi, and the Irish Moore."

The United States went from a victorious war to a bankrupt peace with reform moribund, idealism drained, and President Wilson an invalid in the White House. Labor strife and a Red Scare hysteria were consequences of a noisome new mood that enveloped Gary, as well as other parts of the country, in the war's wake.

THE 1919 STEEL STRIKE

At 4:40 P.M. on Saturday, October 4, 1919, a disturbance broke out along Broadway. Steelworkers surged onto a streetcar transporting several dozen strikebreakers to the mill. The trolley had stopped and then stalled at a railway crossing, and the subsequent heckling and name-calling disintegrated into a minor riot. Pitched battles erupted up and down the street, and the first two patrolmen to arrive on the scene were manhandled by the crowd. Reinforcements soon arrived. Patrolman Max Quandt later said: "Just as I reached the mob, I saw one man pick up a brick and draw back to hurl it. . . . My club descended on the would-be assassin's head with a thud, and two special police lifted him into a waiting machine and hurried him off to the station."

Aiding the police were members of the Loyal American League, an antiunion vigilante organization that had pledged to crush the "subversive parasites" who had gone on strike two weeks previously. Three deputized members beat up Councilman Frank Spychalski while he was trying to disperse the crowd. "Every one of us had a deputy's star in his pocket, a heavy gun under his left shoulder, and a blackjack in his right hand," said one Loyal American Leaguer.

The disturbance quieted down by nightfall with the aid of a timely rain. In all, 34 strikers were arrested and several hospitalized. Union officials blamed the violence on agents provocateurs hired by U.S. Steel.

The following day Mayor William F. Hodges banned public gatherings and asked Governor James J. Goodrich to send the state militia into the area. The previous May, Hodges had placed a similar edict on outdoor meetings in order to forestall a Socialist-sponsored parade protesting Eugene V. Debs' incarceration by the federal government. The rally was held instead at the Romanian Hall, and afterwards a mob of superpatriots, including 50 policemen and 25 deputy sheriffs, beat up departing participants. Both local newspapers applauded the vigilante action.

Most of the state troops sent to Gary at Hodges' request had avoided serving in World War I. They were ill-trained and not respected by most local residents. On Monday, October 6, the strikers held a march and rally at East Side Park that the state troops were unable to prevent. Thousands of people, led by 500 men in uniform, participated in the parade, singing war songs and union songs and shouting "Run the tin soldiers home." Hodges thereupon requested that Gary be placed under martial law. Governor Goodrich relayed the message to General Leonard Wood at Fort Sheridan, and 1,500 troops of the U.S. Army, Fourth Division, were sent to the city under the command of Colonel William S. Mapes.

This was the turning point in the strike, which had begun on a wave of rank-and-file bitterness over the 12-hour day, the 45 cents an hour pay scale for unskilled laborers, and the 7-day work week. The federal troops made little pretense of neutrality and introduced the red herring of "Bolshevism" into what had been a dispute over collective bargaining. At first, strikers hoped that the federal troops would be fairer than local authorities, but they found out otherwise.

During World War I there had been much talk of industrial democracy and worker-management partnership in the task of waging the war to make the world "safe for democracy." In the face of postwar inflation and unemployment, the American Federation of Labor began a mass organizing crusade. Management's response was to fire activists and to rally behind the principle of the open shop.

In the fall of 1919 the AFL hierarchy believed a walkout would be untimely because of the Red Scare and the enormous power wielded by the steel industry. Nevertheless, the intransigence of management on the issue of collective bargaining pushed matters to the boiling point. This intransigence was evident in an editorial appearing in the August-September issue of the Gary Works *Circle*, a company newsletter. It branded unionists as unpatriotic troublemakers and added sarcastically: "When the Creator had made all the good things, there was still some dirty work to do, so He made beasts and reptiles and poisonous insects; and when He had finished, He had some scraps that were too bad to put into the rattlesnake, the hyena, the scorpion, and the skunk, so He put all these together, covered it with suspicion, wrapped it together with jealousy, and marked it KNOCKER."

Union demands included an eight-hour day, a six-day week, double pay for overtime, reinstatement of union organizers, provisions for a seniority system, wage increases "sufficient to guarantee [an] American standard of living," and—most important—the right to bargain collectively. During the first week of the Gary strike, which coincided with similar walkouts across the country, steel production nearly halted. The overwhelming majority of workers remained off the job, despite Judge Gary's testimony to the Senate Committee on Education and Labor that, with "very inconsequential exceptions," the company was on "the best of terms" with its workers. He added: "I think the relationship . . . is pretty intimate and pretty friendly, and has been growing more so year by year and day by day."

During the first days of the strike, the mill's public relations department announced that 82 percent of the work force opposed the strike, and it issued false work lists. The company, rumor had it, even burned tar so that smoky skies would advertise "business as usual." Agents began recruiting "scabs" in American Legion halls and in black ghettos. Between 500 and 1,000 strikebreakers were smuggled inside the mills and provided with cots, entertainment, and overtime pay. On one occasion, mill officials paraded a large number of blacks through the streets in an effort to demoralize the strikers (some black residents accepted money to be in the demonstration and then went home afterwards rather than into the mill). The strikebreakers had less effect on the outcome of the dispute, however, than the fact that many skilled laborers broke ranks and returned to work. Had the workers remained together, the strikebreakers would have made no difference. But the corporation exploited skilled workers' feelings of superiority over the primarily Southern and Eastern European unskilled workers.

U.S. Steel's greatest weapon was its friendly relationship with the government. Mayor Hodges, a conservative Republican elected in 1917 with mill support, pledged that the city would maintain order and protect the rights of both striker and strikebreaker alike, but he limited the number of union pickets to 50 and abdicated to military rule at the first sign of trouble, which was just what the corporation wanted.

By October 7, 1919, Gary had become an armed camp. Although General Wood told strikers that his mission was "to see that you get justice and that everyone else gets justice," his troops ransacked the home of union lawyer Paul P. Glaser, raided the headquarters of the local Socialist party, and jailed several strike leaders without formal charges. Some of the federal troops were quartered in the Commercial Club. Its president, Gary Land Company agent Horace S. Norton, later said that the soldiers caused damages to the club estimated at 7,000 dollars, but that the members did not seek reimbursement because they "considered it to be a contribution to the community."

Anxious to win the 1920 Republican nomination for President, General Wood turned the strike into a highly publicized witch-hunt. On October 10 Colonel Mapes announced that his men were "housecleaning radicals from Gary." Four days later, he declared that "the steel strike in Gary was fostered by Reds and Revolutionists in the hope of plunging the entire country [into] a nationwide revolt. . . ." Strikers were arrested and then released on the condition that they go back to work; otherwise, military officials put them on labor gangs.

AFL organizer William Z. Foster later charged that aliens were threatened with deportation and citizens with violating sedition laws unless they capitulated to company terms. The military also enforced eviction notices against strikers in company-owned dwellings.

On October 23 the charismatic labor organizer Mother Jones told unionists: "I am going to help you win your fight against the blood-sucking robbers who are trying to enslave, crush, and crucify you." By then, however, the strike had deteriorated. With many workers impoverished and winter approaching, the mills were soon functioning at near capacity.

On January 8, 1920, the union officially capitulated. Federal troops left town three days later, but their presence was not soon forgotten. They had patrolled streets, issued directives, commandeered buildings, and even raided moonshiners (some of their contraband eventually made its way back to the black market). "Those soldiers were tough cookies," one resident recollected. "They were the law, pure and simple, for better or for worse."

The strike left a bitter legacy. Mayor Hodges defended the Draconian military measures as necessary because "Reds" were threatening American institutions. The *Evening Post*, rather even-handed in its strike coverage at the outset, ended by blaming Gary's problems on "the foreigner [who] will not educate himself."

The steel strike exposed inequitable mill conditions and the extent to which Gary was a company town. It split the city, according to historian David Janott, into warring factions whose tempers "didn't cool in the January cold." Gary had always been fragmented; but during the winter of 1919, wrote Isaac J. Quillen, "the gap at the Wabash tracks became a canyon," dividing churches and families, fostering contempt for law and government, and breeding cynicism and disillusionment. Thus, at the dawn of the 1920s, Gary had lost its innocence and some of its illusions of grandeur.

THE KU KLUX KLAN IN LOCAL POLITICS

In May 1921 some local residents formed a Ku Klux Klan chapter. Posing as defenders of patriotism, morality, and clean government, and exploiting racial tensions, anti-Catholicism, anti-Semitism, hostility toward immigrants, and fear of labor radicalism, the Klansmen influenced Gary politics for several years.

In the early 1920s Indiana was the largest Klan bastion outside the South with an estimated 350,000 members. This was mainly because of the organizational talents of the Klan's midwestern grand dragon, David Curtis Stephenson, a former coal dealer from Texas in his early thirties, who crisscrossed Indiana in an airplane, selling "Klavern" regalia and delivering demagogic speeches. He built up a loyal following, wrote historian David A. Shannon, "through rallies that were masterpieces of showmanship. . .and appeals to dark and latent prejudices easily exploited because of the rapid changes that were occurring in the half-urban and half-rural state."

In July 1921 the *Post-Tribune* described the Klan as a bulwark against anarchy and Bolshevism and a disseminator of "simon pure American propaganda." Two months later, however, the paper questioned its structure, tactics, principles, and integrity and asked: "How is it possible to sell such a collection of tomfoolery, cajolery, hate, suspicion, buncome, rot, idiocy, and unAmericanism to the American people?"

Without the support of the press or the city government, the Klan remained a covert organization whose power was indirect and hard to measure. In 1923 the Gary "Kleagle" announced that 1,375 local residents belonged to the Klan. The figure was probably inflated, but many nonmembers sympathized with its aims.

The Klan was opposed by immigrants, Catholics, Jews, blacks, liberals, and other people of conscience who decried its gospel of hate. When Klan agents attempted to sell copies of the newspaper *Fiery Cross,* they were frequently manhandled. Methodist Hospital returned a Klan donation in response to public pressure. The newspapers *Tolerance* and *Americans All* were issued to counteract Klan propaganda, and the Lake County Good Government Club (a white organization) and the Fraternal and Loyal Knights of the Constitution (a black group) were organized for the same purpose.

In the spring of 1923, four crosses were burned, and the Klan tried to hold a masked parade and a meeting in a public park. Mayor R. O. Johnson, a Republican, refused to allow the events to take place, so the Klan met in surrounding areas such as Hobart and Hammond. One rally in Hammond drew 5,000 people.

The Klan posed as the enemy of prostitutes and bootleggers, and the Mayor was alleged to allow vice to flourish and racketeers to violate the prohibition laws with impunity. In the 1924 Republican county primary a Klan-endorsed anti-Johnson slate swept to victory. The *Post-Tribune* gave "the so-called Klan ticket" an aura of respectability, claiming that it comprised "one of the best Republican tickets ever placed before the voters of Lake County at a general election."

At this time Klan influence in nearby Valparaiso was so great that Valparaiso University trustees offered to sell their institution to the

KKK on the condition that it spend one million dollars to erase the debt and improve the college. The deal fell through when the Klan reneged on the money; but on July 4, 1924, 10,000 people attended an all-day Klan picnic at the Valparaiso Fairgrounds.

At the state level, the Klan helped Republican Edward Jackson attain the governorship. The Klan hoped to persuade the state legislature to outlaw parochial schools and pornographic movies, and once prevented the showing of a biblical epic because the actor portraying David was Jewish. The Klan distributed thousands of leaflets which said: REMEMBER EVERY CRIMINAL, EVERY GAMBLER, EVERY THUG, EVERY LIBERTINE, EVERY GIRL RUINER, EVERY HOME WRECKER, EVERY WIFE BEATER, EVERY DOPE PEDDLER, EVERY MOONSHINER, EVERY CROOKED POLITICIAN, EVERY PAGAN PAPIST PRIEST, EVERY SHYSTER LAWYER, EVERY K. OF C., EVERY WHITE SLAVER, EVERY BROTHEL MADAM, EVERY ROME CONTROLLED NEWSPAPER, EVERY BLACK SPIDER IS FIGHTING THE KLAN. THINK IT OVER. WHICH SIDE ARE YOU ON?"

The 1924 Lake County elections exposed the division within the Republican party in Gary between the so-called good-government forces and the Johnson machine politicians whose roots were in the immigrant and black precincts. Disgusted with corruption and popular rule, the conservative wing had tried in 1923 to place Gary under a city-manager appointed by the City Council. A referendum to replace the mayoralty system with a city-manager form of government failed due to the near-unanimous opposition from the Southside. Stung by the defeat, many Northsiders joined in an unofficial alliance with the Klan under the fourfold banner of Americanism, morality, clean government, and white supremacy.

In the 1925 Republican city primary, both the Klan and the good-government faction endorsed undertaker Floyd E. Williams. So did three black candidates for city council, giving rise to a rumor that Gary had a black Klan chapter. Williams denied KKK membership but did not repudiate Klan doctrines. William J. Fulton, the former city controller who became mayor on March 28, 1925, after R. O. Johnson exhausted his appeals and was jailed for conspiring to violate the prohibition laws, was Williams' major opponent in the Republican primary. Not only did Williams win, with 9,349 votes compared to 7,988 for Fulton and 1,126 for C. Oliver Holmes, but so did five Klan-sponsored councilmen-at-large. In November, after Republicans smoothed over their differences, Williams won more than 80 percent of the vote.

That same month D. C. Stephenson was convicted of second degree murder after allegedly drugging and molesting a young woman.

Since the Klan claimed to be the moral guardian of the nation, the scandal came as a mortal blow. Williams dissociated himself from the Klan and maintained a low profile on controversial issues but was the target of Southside charges of police brutality, racism, and municipal indifference to the plight of the poor. Pardoned by President Calvin Coolidge, R. O. Johnson swept back into office in 1929. Nonetheless, the fact that a conspiratorial organization founded on hate could have gained a political foothold, if only for a brief period, demonstrated the degree of division in Gary's body politic.

PAUL P. GLASER: STORMY PETREL OF THE BAR

Paul Pavlovich Glaser was the most controversial local lawyer of his era. He combined a romantic attachment to the dispossessed with a distaste for corporate capitalism. Because of his temerity in championing the rights of workers, the government tried for more than a decade to deport him and succeeded for awhile in revoking his American citizenship and preventing him from practicing law. At his death the *Post-Tribune* characterized him as a "gimlet-eyed, acid-tongued barrister whose adventurous life and flamboyant career would have made an absorbing study for Alexander Dumas."

The son of impoverished Ukrainian Jews, Glaser left home in 1887 at the age of nine. After living a vagabond existence for some time, he was adopted by a Cossack general named Paul Klaus, who provided him with a classical education of the type usually afforded only the rich. Glaser studied linguistics and religion at the Greek Orthodox Theological Seminary and spent a year in Palestine in preparation for the ministry. He became disenchanted with the political machinations of the Russian church, however, and decided to obtain a law degree at Kazan Imperial University. He took courses in political economy from Ilya Ulyanov, the father of Vladimir I. Lenin, and became, in his own words, "one of the original bolsheviks."

After postgraduate work at the University of Heidelberg, Glaser accepted a position as Czar Counselor in the small Ural Mountain town of Ufa. In 1905 he participated in an abortive revolt against Czar Nicholas II and was sent to a Siberian prison as a traitor. His wife Sarah, the niece of an influential archbishop, arranged for his escape to England. Six months later, they emigrated to America and settled in Chicago.

Glaser's education gave him an advantage over the hundreds of thousands of unschooled immigrants who "flooded America's gates" in 1906. He became a part-time faculty member at Northwestern

University Law School and took night courses there as well. Two years later, he obtained a doctorate in civil law from DePaul University while working for the Chicago Church Extension Committee. His fluency in 15 foreign dialects—"the most remarkable linguistic ability we've ever encountered," said one customs official—enabled him to provide valuable service at the immigrant-aid center.

In 1909 Glaser started a private practice in Gary. The following year he helped found a Socialist party chapter and a Russian lodge. He was a part-time organizer for the AFL, and in 1917 he ran unsuccessfully for city judge with the endorsement of organized labor. During World War I Glaser was classified 4-F because of poor eyesight but served on Liberty Bond and Red Cross committees as well as the local Selective Service Board. His support for the government ceased after the Armistice, however, and his admiration for President Wilson evaporated in the wake of hostile governmental policies toward American workers and the Soviet Union.

An attorney for Gary's striking steelworkers, Glaser gave a militant speech at the East Side Park rally that Mayor Hodges used as an excuse to call in federal troops. The soldiers subsequently broke into his house, seized some of his personal papers, sacked his library (considered the finest in the city), took him to jail, subjected him to intensive questioning, and warned him to halt his radical agitation. Commenting on his release 24 hours later, the *Daily Tribune* noted that Glaser's appearance was haggard and that he looked "years older."

After Glaser complained publicly of having been manhandled by his captors, his enemies opened a campaign to have him deported as a "Bolshevik" agent. The press and the military referred to him as a dangerous menace. In Indianapolis Federal Judge A. B. Anderson cited him for criminal contempt because he had allegedly advised three strikers to plead innocent to charges of stealing goods from a train after they had supposedly admitted their guilt to him. At a hearing in January 1920, Glaser charged that his former clients had fabricated a faulty version of what had been a privileged conversation in return for leniency. Unmoved, Judge Anderson replied: "You are too active up there. You have caused a great deal of trouble in Lake County. You have been lawless for years and never should have been admitted to the bar."

Shortly thereafter, United States Attorney Frederick Van Nuys demanded that Glaser be stripped of his citizenship on the ground that in 1913, when he took his oath to support and defend the Constitution, he was not acting in good faith. Claiming that Glaser was a

Soviet agent, Van Nuys vowed: "Communism shall not take root in Indiana; all foreign-born 'reds' will be deported."

Glaser called the charges ridiculous and pointed out that in 1913 the Soviet Union had not even been in existence. His union activities had gotten him in trouble, he charged, declaring that prior to the strike, nobody had ever accused him of being a poor citizen.

During a subsequent hearing to determine Glaser's citizenship status, Judge Anderson repeatedly ridiculed the defendant. Commenting on the "rough handling" and "hot remarks" emanating from the bench, one reporter concluded that Anderson "had lots of fun with Glaser and his queer methods. . . ."

In the absence of a jury it was not surprising that Judge Anderson found Glaser guilty. On May 28, 1920, he denied a rehearing and told the defendant: "Glaser, you have not shown the spirit of American citizenship; the evidence introduced demonstrates that you have paraded under a red flag before obtaining your papers. . . . I am forced to revoke your citizenship papers, and from now on you are considered an alien."

Although Glaser sympathized with the Soviet Union and was even offered several positions in the Lenin regime, he had no desire to leave America and believed that his espousal of socialism—which he distinguished from communism—did not detract from his being a good citizen. Thus, he began a decade-long fight to have Judge Anderson's decision overturned.

Friends cautioned Glaser to maintain a low profile until he got his citizenship back, but he paid no heed, arguing that the Bill of Rights was meaningless unless one was free to say controversial things. He frequently spoke at radical meetings; and at a Worker's party rally in May 1923 he raised 86 dollars toward buying a Ford tractor for Russian peasants. A month later, he appealed his citizenship revocation to the Supreme Court, claiming that he had become a naturalized American with the full intention of meeting the duties and obligations of citizenship. At the time he was involved in one of the most important labor cases of his career: the so-called "Million-Dollar Express" case.

At 2:18 A.M. on August 19, 1922, when a Michigan Central freight train crashed on a desolate section of track east of Gary, fireman Elmer Lubs and engineer William Coy were killed and two other persons were seriously injured. Half of the 22 freight cars derailed, and 200 feet of track were torn up. One of the cars contained a million dollars in cash. Since the disaster occurred during a nation-wide railway strike, there was immediate suspicion of foul play. The

Michigan Central offered a five thousand dollar reward for information leading to the conviction of saboteurs, and the press intimated that union agitators were to blame.

Several days later, Albino Olessio, a paid informer for the railroad, told police that he had seen three Chicago unionists—Charles Uselis, John Petrowski, and Joe Popovich—commit the crime for the Brotherhood of Railroad Shopmen. At a union rally the previous evening, Olessio alleged, Uselis had declared that "the only way to win the strike [was] to throw red pepper in the eyes of the strikebreakers, throw bombs, club the 'scabs,' and wreck trains."

Gary Police Chief William A. Forbis asked Chicago officials to round up the three suspects. Three days later, haggard and bruised, they signed confessions. In his statement, Uselis charged that Olessio had instigated the crime—transporting them to Gary after the union meeting, providing them with a crowbar to pull out the spikes, and helping them dismantle the fishplate which held the rails together. Uselis added that he merely wanted to halt the train and was sick at heart when Olessio gleefully told him the details of the crash the following day.

On August 30 the *Post-Tribune* reported the confessions under the headline, "Read This and Form Your Opinion as to Guilt or Innocence of the Michigan Central Wreckers." If the men were found guilty, the article concluded, "all agree, it seems, that . . . the electric chair is too good for them." The following day, the newspaper characterized the suspects as foreigners with a jungle mentality, who had been spurred on by revolutionary propaganda.

After the police had rounded up the three suspects, the Brotherhood of Railroad Shopmen hired Glaser to be their attorney. Government agents had been breaking into their offices all week and accusing their leaders of radicalism, and union officials suspected that the wreck was being used as an opportunity to turn public opinion against the strike.

Glaser had not been permitted to visit the defendants prior to their confessing. At their first meeting they said that they had only signed the statements "to save our lives." Uselis told Glaser that he had gone shopping after the union meeting and was with friends at the time of the crash.

While they were in the custody of the Chicago police, the defendants claimed to have been struck with blackjacks and garden hoses and told that they would be cut up into little pieces and thrown into a stove if they did not admit their guilt. More of the same treatment awaited them when they were turned over to the Gary authorities.

One interrogator knocked them against the wall; another repeatedly kicked them in their genitals. From time to time, railroad detectives took part in the inquisition. One police eyewitness said later, "I thought the Czar of Russia was cruel, but he was an angel compared to these police."

When the sabotage case went to the grand jury in October, the prosecution presented an Interstate Commerce Commission report that listed "malicious tampering" as the probable cause of the wreck. Although Glaser presented indisputable evidence that the defendants had been beaten while in police custody, the grand jury voted to indict Uselis. Charges against Popovich and Petrowski were dropped, and the informer Albino Olessio was named as a co-conspirator, although this had not been recommended by the prosecution.

During the four months prior to the trial, Glaser tried in vain to get Uselis released on bail, charging that he was not safe in the hands of his captors. He also claimed that the case was a cynical attempt to frustrate the union movement.

A huge crowd was on hand on February 12, 1923, when Charles Uselis went on trial in Lake County Circuit Court for the murder of engineer William Coy. Glaser and two associates were being paid by the Brotherhood of Railroad Shopmen, while Special Prosecutor Ralph Smith, whose salary was subsidized by the Michigan Central Railroad, headed the government team of attorneys. During jury selection Glaser summarily discharged anyone who expressed opposition to unions or strikes, while the prosecution excused those who questioned "Third Degree" police methods or the death penalty.

The chief prosecution witness was company spy Albino Olessio, who claimed to have seen Uselis uproot railway spikes at the scene of the crash. Glaser charged that Olessio's testimony could not be trusted and suggested that company negligence rather than labor sabotage caused the disaster. Railway personnel admitted that the train had been traveling at an excessive speed and that the gear lever had been broken. A switchman stated that the wooden ties near the crash were so rotten that spikes would not stay in them. Glaser made a motion to take the jury to the accident site in order to demonstrate the poor condition of the rails, but Judge E. Miles Norton denied the request.

Glaser assembled a large number of defense witnesses. Some claimed to have been with Uselis at a party at the time of the crash; others testified to his battered condition at the time he confessed. Sheriff William H. Olds said he was in bad shape when brought to the county jail. Two physicians described the bruises and abrasions in all their gory detail. Judge Norton not only forbade the submission of the confession as evidence but also castigated the police for torturing Uselis and preventing him from consulting his lawyer. Nonetheless, the prosecution found indirect ways of getting the confession into the record through the testimony of law enforcement officials. After Uselis took the stand to proclaim his innocence, the prosecution team subjected him to a bitter cross-examination interlaced with such sarcastic remarks as "Why don't you tell the truth once?" and "Have you lost your memory since Glaser quit questioning you?"

Upon receiving the final summations and Judge Norton's instructions, the jury deliberated almost two days and still could not reach a decision. After Judge Norton discharged them, it was learned that the final tally had been 9 to 3 for acquittal.

A second trial took place two months later. Its most newsworthy moments occurred when a policeman admitted beating Uselis because he wanted to collect the reward offered by the Michigan Central and when Glaser took the witness stand to describe how he had been turned away from the station house while Uselis was being worked over. The prosecution scored what seemed to be a major victory when Judge Norton allowed the confession to be introduced into evidence, in contrast to the first trial. Nonetheless, the jury after 30 hours acquitted Uselis. The defendant kissed the hand of each juror before he left the courtroom a free man after ten months of confinement.

While the "Million-Dollar Express" case was in progress, several local attorneys questioned whether Glaser had the right to practice law, given his legal status as an alien. Glaser claimed that the state law that required that lawyers be American citizens could not be applied to him *ex post facto* since it was not on the books when he started his practice.

In 1925 the Gary Bar Association opened hearings on whether Glaser should be disbarred. Although his radicalism and alien status were the primary issues, much attention focused on two unfounded charges: that Glaser had passed a fraudulent check and that he had driven a client onto the relief rolls. In the first instance, Glaser had merely postdated the check and was exonerated in a civil suit; in the other case, the woman, whose husband was accused of slaying their son, would have needed welfare no matter who argued her case.

After fighting the Gary Bar Association for nine months, Glaser resigned voluntarily from the Indiana Bar until his citizenship case was resolved. In return the Gary Bar Association dropped its disbarment suit. As a result, Glaser's professional status went into limbo for four years, and he worked mainly as an adviser for his two law partners: his daughter, Marguerite, and his son-in-law, Albert Block. (In 1955 Marguerite Glaser would become president of the Gary Bar Association.)

Glaser's last case prior to his temporary retirement involved two defendants charged with uttering seditious statements at a 1923 May Day rally. Claiming that his clients had been stripped of their freedom of speech, Glaser declared: "Anybody who comes into Gary with a newspaper that the steel company doesn't like the smell of is thrown in jail." One of the defendants pleaded guilty in return for the minimum sentence, a hundred dollar fine. In 1926, after numerous delays and appeals, the case against the second radical was dismissed when it was discovered that the informants who said that they had heard him advocating the violent overthrow of the government could not understand Slovak, the language in which he had spoken.

Glaser was still regarded as an eccentric radical in the late 1920s. He was indeed a colorful personage. An excellent equestrian, he was a familiar sight in Fourth of July parades because he always wore Cossack costume, a sealskin hat, and a ruby ring (stolen, rumor had it, from the Russian church). Although few persons were more dedicated to labor's cause than he, his habits were more those of a distinguished emigré than of a union firebrand.

In 1930 Glaser finally regained his American citizenship. Granted a retrial by the Supreme Court, he went before special referee Harry Long, who was appointed by Governor Harry G. Leslie after two judges disqualified themselves from hearing the case. What probably turned the decision in his favor were character statements from State Senator C. Oliver Holmes, a neighbor, and Judge E. Miles Norton, who presided in the "Million-Dollar Express" case. On July 8, 1930, the *Post-Tribune* announced: "Man Without a Country for Ten Years Takes U.S. Oath Again." The accompanying article quoted Glaser as expressing faith in the Constitution, professing no desire to return to Russia, and pledging to "continue to be true to my adopted country."

Glaser's jubilation was short-lived. The following day he was arrested for allegedly forging a bail bond, and the immigration department announced it would appeal the referee's verdict. The forgery charge arose from the fact that his accuser had lied about agreeing to insure the bond in order to escape his wife's wrath after the released defendants jumped bail, thus forfeiting the bond money. Although Glaser never lost confidence that he would win back his civil rights, the ordeal left scars. As one observer stated: "They persecuted him, slandered him, hounded him, tried to ruin his reputation . . . and put a terrible strain on his health."

During the 1930s Glaser resumed his role as a "people's lawyer," taking on such unpopular cases as the defense of "hunger marchers" and blacklisted workers. A member of the Indiana Civil Liberties Union, the International Labor Defense Council, and the Steel Workers Organizing Committee, Glaser's primary goals in public life, according to his son-in-law, were to preserve the Bill of Rights and to help workers get a fair return for their labor.

During the depression many people down on their luck stopped at the modest Glaser home in Glen Park for a small loan or some of Sarah Glaser's homemade soup. Once, after noticing a neighbor putting socks on her children's hands during the winter, Glaser pilfered gloves for that family from a downtown department store. When the neighbor protested, he said: "Never mind, they owe me millions!" Although he had more debts than assets, Glaser was so free with his money, one friend recollected, that he frequently gave away all his change and then would not have trolley fare to ride home. His brother Samuel, a clothing merchant who operated the Paris Fashion Shop on Broadway, was the capitalist in the family; Paul was the visionary.

Neighbor Polly McNough described Glaser as a seemingly aloof man with a brilliant mind, "exquisite grammar," and a passion for good books and tea "Russian style"—served warm in a glass with jelly at the bottom. Some people considered his bluntness ill-mannered and his heavy accent a sign of gruffness, she said, but he hated mediocrity and had a sensitivity toward children and poor people that revealed a tender nature.

On May 13, 1941, Glaser died of a heart attack. Near the end of his life he had become increasingly disturbed over the persecution of Jews in Germany. The Stalin-Hitler pact, according to Polly McNough, "broke his heart." He had never liked Joseph Stalin very much, and the Russian leader's alliance with the Third Reich was more than he could bear.

In an editorial entitled "Citizen Glaser Passes On," the *Post-Tribune* eulogized him as a brilliant, tenacious friend of the underdog, who had been "astonishingly indifferent" to making money. The newspaper concluded: "Truly he was a unique character, hurling billingsgate and baiting learned government lawyers in a manner inimitable with one breath, and waxing dreamy and gently philosophical over a pleasurable horseback ride or a prized passage from Swinburne, Heine or Milton with the next."

Glaser paid a high price for his ideals and outspokenness. Much of his energy was expended in defensive battles to regain his citizenship and his law license. How much easier it would have been to have disavowed his kinship with his native Russia and dissociated himself from political pariahs. As it was, his public career became a test case measuring the degree to which free speech existed in Gary between the wars.

Twenty years before his death, when a federal judge asked him to relinquish his citizenship papers, Glaser refused, saying that would not happen until "I am in my casket." His pugnacity, combined with a keen legal mind and remarkable patience, allowed him to make good his promise.

CHAPTER FIVE

Boom Years

She is only just a maiden,
With years not heavy laden;
The prospects of her future sure are great.
So, like the bantam rooster,
We will work to crow and boost her
Till she's the largest city in the state.

—"Flue Dust" poem by "E.Z.
Stuff"

IN 1920 THE CITY directory boasted that Gary was "the Greatest and Most Prosperous City for its Age, with Wonderful Results Accomplished and Growing Greater Day by Day." In reality the city was still reeling from the 1919 steel strike and soon sank into a sharp recession when mill operations shrank to 29 percent of capacity. The city tried to ameliorate the plight of 5,000 unemployed workers with a placement bureau, free lodging houses, and veterans' benefits but ended up with a million-dollar budget deficit.

The economy improved markedly in 1922, however, and U.S. Steel opened a new subsidiary, the National Tube Company. By 1923 the mills were operating at full capacity, and U.S. Steel, bowing to governmental pressure, instituted the eight-hour day for most of its employees, whose hourly wages rose 25 percent to compensate for the shorter work day. Despite dire predictions by Judge Elbert H. Gary, there was no appreciable loss of profits to the company.

A year later, the Federal Trade Commission forced U.S. Steel to end its "Pittsburgh Plus" system by which the costs of its products were computed as if they were shipped from the home office. Powell Moore concluded that "the abolition of this pricing system contributed to plant expansion in Gary and to the high rate of production in the local mills from 1924 to 1929."

The booster spirit reached its zenith in Gary during the 1920s. Downtown merchants, resentful of mill dominance in the Rotary and the Commercial clubs, organized the Lions Club and the Chamber of Commerce. Another splinter group formed the Kiwanis Club. There was talk of a "New Era" of economic diversification, though, in the end, U.S. Steel resisted such plans and Gary's prosperity remained wedded to its mills. By 1930 the "New Era" had ended, and the Chamber of Commerce merged with the Commercial Club.

GARY'S AUGUSTAN AGE

A tremendous building boom commenced in Gary in 1923 and continued for six years. The city's physical appearance underwent a dramatic transformation with the construction of the Hotel Gary, the Palace Theatre, the Gary National Bank building, the Memorial Civic Auditorium, City Methodist Church, City Hall, Lew Wallace High School, the Gary Armory, the Salvation Army Citadel, and the Elks and Moose temples. Perhaps the most impressive new edifice was the ten-story Knights of Columbus building, which employed a rare setback architectural design and contained shops, a restaurant, clubrooms, a gymnasium, a ballroom, bowling alleys, and more than a hundred hotel rooms.

Despite the proliferation of new buildings, urban planning was of secondary importance in guiding the expansion. In March 1920 Mayor William F. Hodges established a 21-member Civic Service Commission to recommend ways of facilitating future growth. Dominated by mill spokesmen such as Horace S. Norton, Ralph E. Rowley, and Arthur P. Melton, the commission hired the Chicago firm of Bennett and Parsons to draw up a comprehensive master plan. The report suggested that Gary needed rational zoning laws, a boulevard along the Grand Calumet River, a civic center, diagonal highways to relieve mill traffic, elevated railway crossings, and more transportation routes to surrounding areas. Hodges' commission won approval for one diagonal street, a new park, a civic center, a street-widening program, and more downtown parking space. Railroads opposed interference with their crossings, however, and U.S. Steel balked at giving up land needed for a Grand Calumet Boulevard. Said Superintendent William P. Gleason: "The steel corporation has no apologies to offer for the way the city was first laid out and the company's accomplishments."

In 1921 the Indiana legislature passed enabling legislation for a permanent nine-member City Planning Commission, but its powers were extremely limited. Zoning laws gradually emerged, but they reflected the wishes of businessmen and did not reverse previous mistakes. Citizen complaints did cause a ban against funeral homes in residential areas, but filling stations, luncheonettes, and grocery stores still proliferated in many neighborhoods. Scores of accidents occurred at railroad crossings, and Gary's traffic congestion problems were among the worst in the nation. State officials generally regarded Gary as a "Hoosier step-child," and funds necessary for better linkage highways were not forthcoming. Tom Cannon quipped: "It is reported from Indianapolis and points south that the state highway commission is planning an expedition to discover Gary."

The Gateway Plan, proposed by the Commercial Club in 1924, included building a park, a city court building, and a new city hall along 5th Avenue at a cost of three million dollars. Civic leaders argued that the unsightly billboards and scruffy vacant lots along its main thoroughfare and commuter railway line were bad for Gary's image. "The city is going to clean up the front yard, mow the lawn, and trim the hedge," the *Post-Tribune* stated on March 19, 1924.

Between 1918 and 1924 Gary annexed Miller and Aetna, and some boosters believed the day was near when Hobart, Merrillville, East Chicago, and other surrounding areas would become part of "Greater Gary." Ever since the administration of Mayor Thomas E. Knotts, Gary had been interested in Miller's beachfront. In 1915 Gary and Miller formed a joint parks department. When vexing land purchase problems crippled the committee's effectiveness, Gary resolved to annex Miller and condemn the desired park property. In December 1918 Miller's Town Board signed a resolution to the effect that "it is desired and deemed necessary that the territory now comprising the Town of Miller be annexed to the city of Gary. . . ." Some owners of the proposed park property sought redress in the courts, but U.S. Steel headed off the dispute by purchasing more than 100 acres of land and donating it to the parks department. Since Miller faced prohibitive costs for police, fire, and general services, most residents resigned themselves to annexation.

Rumors of Aetna's annexation had circulated as early as 1906. In 1881 the Aetna Powder Company had constructed two dozen buildings on 240 acres of wilderness between Miller and Tolleston. Farmers all over the Midwest used the explosives for uprooting tree stumps and boulders. The company purposely isolated itself, set up a tiny village for its mostly male population, and incorporated Aetna as a town in 1907. Miller and Gary residents regarded the powder plant as a menace, especially after an explosion in 1912 killed six workers. An even more spectacular detonation in 1914 shattered windows as far away as downtown Gary. In 1917 a great conflagration destroyed half the plant, but World War I gave the company its greatest period of prosperity, with the number of workers increasing three-fold to a thousand men. After the war, the plant shut down, and Aetna became virtually a ghost town with less than a hundred residents. In 1924 the city of Gary moved to annex it, a process that took four years.

During the 1920s Gary faced serious housing problems caused in part by the doubling of the city's population. On January 6, 1921, a newspaper article stated that "a real estate dealer recently placed two advertisements . . . to let two- or three-room suites in an apartment building and he almost developed a riot." The building boom minimized housing problems for the affluent, with the construction of such sumptuous apartments as "The Ambassador" at 574 Monroe. Nonetheless, health officers, juvenile court officials, and civil rights organizations all lamented the overcrowded conditions for low income groups. In 1923 the Health Department ordered all substandard shacks in the Southside evacuated—thus bringing an end to the old "Patch" dwellings and forcing 1,500 people to find other quarters.

Despite the problems of Gary's "other half," the committee for the 1926 "Greater Gary Exposition" proclaimed that a "Wonder City" rested on the southern shores of Lake Michigan. Gary was a lively, lusty place and became Indiana's leading convention city. When 12,000 conventioneers visited in 1928, hotels, shops, theatres, restaurants, speakeasies, and brothels flourished.

EVANGELIST BOB LEWIS
AT CENTRAL BAPTIST CHURCH

In October 1925 Evangelist Bob Lewis came to the Central Baptist Church at 529 Jefferson for a month-long Christian crusade. Lewis represented the fiery type of fundamentalist preaching made famous by Billy Sunday and Aimee Semple McPherson. A former lumberjack, he entertained audiences with magic tricks and graphic illustrations of Bible stories as well as with his theatrical speaking delivery. During his stay in Gary, however, Lewis set off a storm of controversy because of his negative remarks about the city.

Lewis found a receptive audience among Gary's numerous white Southerners who had recently migrated from Tennessee, Kentucky, and southern Indiana in order to work at the mill. For them, the revival was a social event as well as a way to reinvigorate their faith. Many older members of Central Baptist Church also believed that the revival was useful because a visiting evangelist had more freedom than a resident minister to "shake up" the congregation.

Central Baptist Church's history dated back to January 1909, when 19 people met in the home of Mrs. Harriet Cathcart. The congregation used the Majestic Theatre for its services for eleven months before it was able to move into the basement of its partially built church, which had dirt floors, a leaky roof, and "a coke salamander with no stack that kept the room filled with smoke." The building was completed in 1912.

The Reverend Oliver B. Sarber was the parish's second permanent pastor, having succeeded the popular Reverend H. E. Wilson in January 1920. A learned, humanistic man, Sarber worked tirelessly to build up attendance and repair his church building, often taking up saw and sledgehammer himself. In January 1924 his fourth annual report stated: "I have worked hard, but perhaps not always wisely; I have been zealous, but not always with 'a zeal according to wisdom'; but God and you have been patient and together we have gathered some sheaves to lay at His dear feet."

Sarber was not eager to bring Lewis to Gary, but parishioners convinced him that a revival would rekindle faith within the church and the outside community. Lewis got off to an auspicious start when he patched up a long-standing feud that had begun when nonunion laborers had been hired to construct Central Baptist Church. In retaliation Gary's union council of skilled craftsmen fined any member who attended functions there. Lewis went to union headquarters and hired its band to lead his kickoff parade in return for an end to the boycott.

Making use of newspaper advertisements and leaflets, Lewis built up interest in his sermons. When he announced that he would speak on the state of moral decay in Gary, he attracted an overflow audience. Herbert Merwald later recalled that "the place was jammed," with hundreds of people standing outside, including prostitutes and alcoholics. Pointing to some well-displayed bottles of bootleg whiskey, which he had evidently obtained on a clandestine tour, Lewis charged that in Gary it was easier to purchase liquor than a good meal. Then he launched into a diatribe against dancing, smoking, petting, evolution, sissified boys, and flappers who wore "short, tight 'sleazy' [outfits] cut high at the bottom, to the knee or above and low at the top."

The spectacle of huge throngs listening to hell-fire-and-brimstone sermons was a ready-made news item, but the *Post-Tribune* was unsure how to handle it. The story was good copy, but Lewis leveled many wild charges that contradicted the image that the paper wished to convey about Gary. For example, on November 8, Lewis charged that "the bars are down and vice runs rampant. This city is wide open with every known vice flourishing as I have never seen in any city of the same size." At first the *Post-Tribune* gave Lewis valuable publicity by having the following alliteration adorn its front page: "BOB'S BIG BERTHAS BOOM BROADSIDES . . . BOOZE BOMBS BLARE; BIFF-BANGS BURST . . . BOOTLEGGING BATTLER BLESSES, BLAMES AND BLASPHEMES." The accompanying article summarized in colorful detail Lewis' theatrical performance and insured a large turnout for his next service.

Local officials reacted gingerly to Lewis' attacks, with the exception of Gary City Judge C. M. Greenlee, who called him an extremist. Police Chief William J. Linn offered him a deputy's badge, and Lake County Prosecutor August A. Bremer invited him to testify before a grand jury, which Lewis did. After four days of indecision the *Post-Tribune* decided to attack Lewis for smearing Gary with exaggerated and unfounded statements—such as the scurrilous claim that it was easier to find a prostitute in some sections of town than a virtuous woman. The *Post-Tribune* also published complaints from Froebel and Emerson students of charges that immorality was rampant at these schools. Lewis was an "acrobatic loud-speaker" who should be unplugged, the paper concluded.

In turn, Lewis labeled the *Post-Tribune's* statements "contemptible lies." At a "Sunshine Night" rally, he branded his enemies as "dirty Bolsheviks" who should go to Russia. Five days later, he charged that the *Post-Tribune* was a tool of City Hall.

The *Post-Tribune* retaliated by reporting a visit Lewis made to its office, allegedly for the purpose of quashing a story about a friend who assaulted a policeman. Describing the minister's appearance as rakish, the *Post-Tribune* declared: "He wore a pair of sheikish multicolored, rubber-soled slippers, the mingled colors being banana yellow and coffee tan."

Thereafter, the *Post-Tribune* ceased coverage of the crusade, justifying the "silent treatment" with the rationale that Lewis' "lies" did not merit publication. As columnist Tom Cannon put it, "Maybe if Rev. Lewis would say nice things like Flue Dust, he could get all the newspaper space he wants." The *Post-Tribune* also adopted the strategy of differentiating Lewis from resident minister Oliver B. Sarber, characterizing the former as a demagogue and the latter as a respected man of the cloth. Once Lewis departed, the newspaper promised, there would be full coverage of Sarber's very next sermon.

In truth, the Reverend Sarber was less than sanguine over the notoriety surrounding the crusade and disapproved of the anti-intellectual thrust of Lewis' fundamentalism. The evangelist sensed the coolness and interpreted it as jealousy and a lack of spirituality on Sarber's part. Sarber was tremendously relieved when the five-week crusade finally ended. During its final stages, Lewis had become openly critical of a sermon Sarber delivered in which he said that the Son of God shines His light equally on all races of people, just as the sun shines its light on all the colors of the church's stained glass windows. Lewis, in contrast, viewed integration as a heretical example of "modernism."

On November 30, 1925, the *Post-Tribune* reported on Sarber's post-revival service. Now that the emotionalism has abated, Sarber reportedly said, Christians had to come off the mountaintop and face the commonplace routine of life. Faith is tested by the way we handle everyday problems, he concluded.

The "Bob Lewis–*Post-Tribune* war" was an interesting example of journalistic and evangelistic techniques used during the 1920s. The adversaries each had a product to sell and trafficked in sin and moralism. As chief publicist of Gary's booster image, the *Post-Tribune* could tolerate no charge that the "queenly city" was comparable to Sodom and Gomorrah. As a self-proclaimed defender of the faith, Lewis could countenance no accusation that he was a charlatan. Neither side had a monopoly on virtue or wisdom. According to church member Nina Traver, Lewis was a foxy showman who would do anything for a good offering and "loved to start a rumpus." Similarly, the *Post-Tribune* sought out macabre, bizarre, and titillating stories in order to turn a good profit. The episode was a colorful footnote to Gary's religious and social history during an age of ballyhoo and bombast.

There was one sad footnote to the affair. Because of the Lewis-Sarber feud, a small but vocal faction within Central Baptist Church continued to castigate Sarber's "modernist" views. This friction helped precipitate his resignation in February 1926. His successor, William Ward Ayer, was a fundamentalist-leaning traditionalist who set up a "Little Brown Church" atop a Ford automobile for street meetings and prayer services. Ayer's opinion of integration was summed up in a letter he wrote to a black newspaper, the Gary *American,* in response to a query as to whether he favored racially mixed church services. Ayer replied that such a phenomenon would cause everyone discomfort and added: "I am not blind to the differences with which the races have been endowed by the Creator. . . ."

Ayer shared Lewis' jaundiced view of the big city and considered Central Baptist to be "a light in a dark place." He left Gary in 1932 to take over a parish in Canada. His successors, who stayed an average of five years, set up suburban missions which in time rivaled and even surpassed the "Mother Church" in size. In 1975 Central Baptist relocated in Porter County.

WILLIAM GRANT SEAMAN AND CITY METHODIST CHURCH

"From the heart of a city radiates its life and influences. That is why our church was put where it is," said Dr. William Grant Seaman on October 10, 1926, at the dedication of City Methodist Church at 6th and Washington. Seaman hoped that his beautiful new cathedral would spur a moral awakening and become a multipurpose community center offering social, recreational, commercial, educational, cultural, and religious activities to inner city residents.

There were 98 churches in Gary in the 1920s, and the oldest of the Protestant congregations, First Methodist Episcopal Church, held its initial service at Binzenhof Hall in October 1906. Its name was changed to City Methodist 20 years later. Its members included skilled laborers, mill foremen, and middle-level management personnel. Gary's social elite were mainly Presbyterian, while ethnic churches served the poor. During the free-spirited 1920s the churches were mostly the preserve of the old, the very young, and women. One clergyman remarked, with slight exaggeration, that "the industrial worker is divorced from the church."

Born in 1866 in Wakarusa, Indiana, Seaman was a graduate of Boston University School of Theology. He had taught philosophy at DePauw University, and came to Gary in 1916 from the presidency of Dakota Wesleyan University. Nicknamed "Sunny Jim" because of his confident, enthusiastic personality, he once told the Optimist Club that the most admirable person was the one who accepted the lemons given to him and made lemonade from them. On another occasion, he told the Emerson High School graduating class to set high, noble goals because "even donkeys go better when a wisp of hay is dangled in front of them."

One Sunday afternoon, Seaman took 500 children to a Miller Beach rally for lunch, a hike, and devotional services. His sermon that day attempted to affirm Christianity by the use of historical, philosophical, and scientific evidence. "The agnostic is merely an immature mind, or a man who has not the power to think straight through," he said.

The 50-year-old pastor became steward of an inauspicious $31,000 building at 7th and Adams, a small 315-member congregation, and a mere $3,500 annual budget, including his salary. In quick order he began a $20,000 Sunday School building drive and stalled plans for constructing another Methodist church in Ambridge, arguing that a centralized urban plant was more practical than many little parishes. In 1919 Methodist leaders of the Centenary movement persuaded Judge Elbert H. Gary to help finance such an inner city church, and the plan was launched.

Seaman told civic leaders that his church would be a civilizing influence on those who ordinarily were outside the pale of organized religion. In February 1920 he wrote Horace S. Norton that "the downtown church is moving out to the suburban districts. Down in the city [are] . . . boarding houses, apartments, and tenements full of people. Down here are saloons and dance halls and brothels where God is forgotten. The church moves and makes its rest in the peaceful suburbs where this is needed, certainly, but not as deeply as in the thick of the city's life."

Before the building drive could go forward, other needs had to be met. Raising money for Methodist Hospital demanded much of his attention until 1923. He also helped raise money for the John Stewart Memorial Settlement House, which provided vital social services for Southside blacks. By the end of 1924, however, enough money had come into the building fund to allow the ground-breaking ceremony to be held for the new church complex.

Seaman's personality was a blend of aloofness and geniality. A former member of the children's choir remembered him as dignified, precise, scholarly, and rather unsuited to young people's tastes. Nonetheless, at Wednesday socials Seaman joined in games of drop-the-handkerchief. With reddish skin, white hair, and a paunch, he reminded one parishioner of a beardless Santa Claus.

Seaman's wife Laura, a Vassar graduate, participated in women's auxiliaries and took more interest in politics than did her husband (his major crusade had been prohibition). In 1921 she had joined a

good government club opposed to mayoralty candidate R. O. Johnson. During the final week of the campaign, Johnson accused her and
two colleagues of defaming his wife's character. Fellow-Republican
James A. Patterson added that he was ready to "tar and feather
them." Mrs. Seaman charged that Johnson had manufactured the
whole incident.

Seaman tried hard to combat racism in Gary. While full-scale integration was not part of the city church concept, due to opposition
within his congregation, Seaman arranged special joint services with
the black Trinity Methodist Episcopal Church, and he spoke out for
racial tolerance. Southern-born Hazel McDaniel recollected how he
once called her aside upon seeing her discomfort when a dark-
skinned child joined her Sunday school class. "That little girl is an
Indian," he told her. "Then I realized how foolish I was," Mrs.
McDaniel said.

As one of the 18 members of the Methodist Hospital board, Seaman
battled unsuccessfully for the admittance of black patients. What
made the segregationist policy especially odious was the fact that
blacks had contributed to the institution's fund-raising drive. During
the summer of 1923 Seaman met with black ministers at Stewart
House to devise a plan to integrate the hospital. Hearing about an
ailing light-skinned Negro named Mrs. John W. Russell, Seaman suggested having her pass as white, thereby establishing a precedent for
integration (the segregation policy was an unwritten custom as yet
not officially approved by the board). Mrs. Russell thought that the
idea of "sneaking" into the hospital was degrading, however; and
after inquiring by phone whether blacks would be admitted and
being told "No," she went instead to Dr. Antonio Giorgi's clinic.
Seaman's plan thus fell through, and at subsequent board meetings
he failed to reverse the ban on black patients.

In December 1924 Seaman and four other local ministers pressed
Mayor Johnson to halt an Orpheum Theatre presentation of *Birth of
a Nation*. Seaman felt the movie "would arouse racial prejudices"
because it portrayed blacks as heinous and glamorized the Recon-
struction role of the Ku Klux Klan. Johnson unearthed an old ordinance barring all motion pictures within the city limits, but the
showings went ahead anyway, playing to overflow audiences. The
manager paid a ten-dollar fine, and ultimately the City Council re-
voked the ordinance.

Racial incidents increased after the showing of *Birth of a Nation*,
as Seaman had feared. For example, on December 10, 1924, four
white men accosted a black youth walking west from Miller. They

poured gasoline on him and set him ablaze, seriously burning him. They were never caught.

Few people saw a connection between this outrage and the ground-breaking ceremony of City Church which took place a month later. But racial polarization was one of several factors that torpedoed Seaman's dream of an inner city church that would bring together Gary's fragmented community under the banners of faith and brotherhood.

Building City Methodist Church took 21 months. U.S. Steel donated $385,000 in matching funds after Judge Elbert H. Gary allegedly silenced opponents at a board meeting with the tart remark: "Hell, men, they want to build a church in our town!" The Judge also personally donated an ornate, four-manual Skinner organ. The Methodist Board of Home Missions contributed several hundred thousand dollars to the building drive. Smaller amounts came from individual members, the proceeds of church bazaars, and the sale of the old church to a mortician.

City Church had three main wings: a worship area, a social-educational unit, and a commercial section. The goal was for the building to be self-supporting. Explaining his philosophy of an urban-oriented Christian gospel, Seaman wrote in a commemorative pamphlet: "The sturdy maker of iron and steel, the active man in commercial life, the busy woman, and the growing youth are best convinced of the living Christ by seeing His influence every hour of the weekday as well as an hour or so on Sunday. Thus, into the downtown church came a plan of service, a plan for a comprehensive ministry, for a church open seven days a week, a church presenting the beautiful in architecture, a church providing Christian educational features, healthful recreation, appealing and clean entertainment for youth and aged, and above all, a church bringing the spirit of Christian friendliness into the heart of the city."

On October 3, 1926, Seaman preached for the first time in the impressive Gothic structure of Indiana Bedford limestone. The next seven days were taken up with nightly celebrations. Tom Cannon wrote a poem entitled "Dreams of the Twilight—The City Church," which predicted that "there in the heart of a rushing, bustling city, there amid a greedy, grasping throng, it shall ... hold out its quiet arms to the weary and oppressed." Seaman proclaimed the events to be the climax of his ministerial career.

By 1927 Seaman's 1,700-member congregation had a paid staff of six, including the pastor, assistant minister William F. Switzer, directors of athletics and Christian education, a music master, and a secretary. Especially interested in cultural affairs, Seaman recruited lecturers to speak in "Seaman Hall," suggested scripts to the dramatics club, showed travel films, and sponsored interfaith pageants. The music program was reputedly the best in the country. There were also joint projects with the Boy Scouts, the YMCA, the YWCA, and settlement houses. Seaman helped establish a Bible School program with the public schools that was serving 5,000 pupils by the late 1920s.

Despite these bright spots, City Church was plagued by serious problems. Dissidents complained that the ornamental design not only smacked of popery but was Seaman's monument to himself. Some had said from the beginning, "If he wants to build the thing, let him build it, but don't ask me to pay." Envious ministers of other faiths feared competition, as did an influential Methodist restaurateur, who stalled completion of the cafeteria. Plans for a bowling alley failed. So did a projected roof garden atop the commercial unit due to the turbulent Lake Michigan wind currents. Stories spread of children cursing in the gymnasium, which was so located as to require athletes to troop through the heart of the church building. Young people shunned church parties because dancing, smoking, and card playing were banned. Millworkers preferred to unwind at speakeasies and pool halls, where they could drink and not have to watch their language.

There were further troubles. Seaman underestimated the maintenance costs, and budget-slicing measures torpedoed otherwise sound programs. Too many members regarded the opening of the new building as the culmination rather than the beginning of their mission. Conditioned to look toward Chicago for culture, many reacted apathetically to the Seaman Hall forums and artistic productions and looked askance at interfaith services involving minority groups.

In September 1929 these dilemmas led to Seaman's removal. His transfer to Lancaster, Ohio, was not an unusual Methodist policy, but it reflected lay criticism from the Pastoral Relations Committee, whose consultations were relayed to the bishop. People who wanted a new minister rationalized that Seaman had done his part, and now what was needed was an efficient man, not a liberal visionary.

Seaman expressed his regret at leaving Gary in this manner: "I love the city; I have had more fun here than I ever had before in my life. . . ." He added that, in his opinion, Gary had "a truly western spirit of progress and hospitality." As was his custom, he showed no outward bitterness against those who had worked for his transfer.

In 1944 Seaman died in an automobile accident, and his ashes were

Shabanee, an Ottawa chief.
(Gary Public Library)

Alice Mable Gray, "Diana of the Dunes."
(Chicago Historical Society)

The Bailly homestead on the Little Calumet River.
(Gary Public Library)

Leveling sand dunes on site of Gary Works, 1906.
(Calumet Regional Archives)

Carr's Beach, Miller, 1917.
(Calumet Regional Archives)

Judge Elbert H. Gary.
(Gary *Post-Tribune*)

William P. Gleason, superintendent,
Gary Works, 1908.
(Gary *Post-Tribune*)

First iron ore shipment arrives, June 23, 1908.
(Gary Public Library)

Pouring steel, Gary Works, about 1914.
(Calumet Regional Archives)

Last of the shacks on Euclid Avenue.
(Gary *Post-Tribune*)

Intersection of Broadway and 5th Avenue, May 2, 1907.
(Gary *Post-Tribune*)

Water tower and pumping station, Jefferson Park, July 14, 1910.
(Calumet Regional Archives)

Town Board inspecting the sewer, August 12, 1908.
(Gary *Post-Tribune*)

The Patch, about 1909.
(Calumet Regional Archives)

Broadway and 4th Avenue, 1907.
(Calumet Regional Archives)

Neighborhood House, 1910; in doorway, Rev. B. M. Baligrodski.
(Calumet Regional Archives)

Town Board election in first post office, 1906; left to right, Thomas E. Knotts, Eddie Fitzgerald, Louis A. Bryan, and John E. Sears.
(Calumet Regional Archives)

gwald Moe, theatre impresario, 08.
(Calumet Regional Archives)

Police Chief Joseph Martin, 1908.
(Calumet Regional Archives)

Paulino Monterrubio in 1973.
(Robin Nelson)

Lorraine Duncan Washington in 1974.
(Don Blume)

Marion C. Streeter in 1956.
(Gary *Post-Tribune*)

Dr. Antonio Giorgi in 1930.
(Mrs. Paul Giorgi)

Tom Cannon, editor of "Flue Dust" column.
(Gary *Post-Tribune*)

Jovo and Dorothy Krstovich, at left, with Mato Chuck and John Wuletich and their wives.
(George Krstovich)

Gary Transfer and Storage Company wagon at Wabash Freight Depot, 1909.
(Calumet Regional Archives)

Night class, Gary Schools, about 1913.
(Calumet Regional Archives)

Board of Works meeting, 1917; far right, Mayor Roswell O. Johnson.
(Gary Public Library)

Mayor William F. Hodges, 1918.
(Calumet Regional Archives)

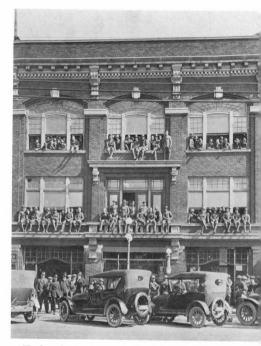

Federal troops at Commercial Club during
steel strike, 1919.
(Gary Public Library)

Horace Mann students in a portable building, about 1923.
(Calumet Regional Archives)

William A. Wirt, superintendent of schools, 1907–1938. (Inset)
(Calumet Regional Archives)

Froebel School opened in 1912.
(Calumet Regional Archives)

E. A. Spaulding, principal of Emerson School for 40 years. (Inset)
(Gary *Post-Tribune*)

Emerson School opened in 1909.
(Calumet Regional Archives)

Broadway and 6th Avenue, May 1917.
(Calumet Regional Archives)

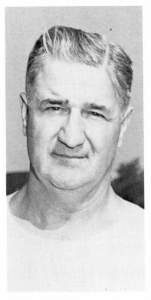

John W. Kyle, coach at
Froebel for 30 years.
(Calumet Regional
Archives)

Rabbi Garry Joel Au-
gust in 1974.
(Don Blume)

D. E. Sikes in 1976.
(Gary S. Wilk)

Broadway and 7th Avenue, 1928.
(Gary *Post-Tribune*)

William A. Forbis, police chief under four mayors.
(Gary *Post-Tribune*)

J. Ralph Snyder of the
Gary *Post-Tribune.*

Erwin Crewe Rosenau
in 1952.
(Gary *Post-Tribune*)

UPI photo taken at the Crown Point jail, February 1934. Left to right: Sheriff
Lillian Holley; her brother; Chief Deputy Sheriff Carroll Holley; Lake
County Prosecutor Robert Estill; John Dillinger; East Chicago Police Chief
Nicholas Maker.
(UPI)

Jacob L. Reddix, founder of the Gary
Consumer Cooperative, 1932.
(Calumet Regional Archives)

Ruth Wall Nelson, administrative
assistant, Gary College.
(Calumet Regional Archives)

Mothers Club, Stewart House, 1930; far right, Rev. Frank S. Delaney.
(Delaney Methodist Church)

Wilbert W. Gasser, president, Gary State Bank. (Inset)
(Gary National Bank)

Gary State Bank Building, about 1930.
(Gary National Bank)

Waiting for President Franklin D. Roosevelt, August 1936.
(Calumet Regional Archives)

City Methodist Church.
(Calumet Regional Archives)

Horace S. Norton, general agent, Gary Land Company, in 1932.
(Gary *Post-Tribune*)

John Mayerik, president for 15 years of Gary Works local 1014.
(Gary *Post-Tribune*)

Frank N. Gavit, attorney, in 1935.
(Gary *Post-Tribune*)

Fifth and Broadway, June 20, 1936.
(Gary Public Library)

Tom Harmon, all-American football player, 1939, 1940.
(Gary *Post-Tribune*)

John A. Bushemi, army photographer killed at Eniwetok, February 1945.
(Mary Ellen Cessna)

Tony Zale, middleweight champion, with Boy Scouts.
(Gary *Post-Tribune*)

Anna Rigovsky Yurin
in 1952.
(Gary *Post-Tribune*)

Martin Zelt in 1974.
(Gary S. Wilk)

Rev. Vencelaus M.
Ardas, pastor, Holy
Trinity Church.
(Calumet Regional
Archives)

Karogeorge Singing Society, 1936.
(Calumet Regional Archives)

Richard A. Nuzum, principal at Froebel School.
(Gary *Post-Tribune*)

Charles D. Lutz, superintendent of
schools.
(Gary *Post-Tribune*)

Frank Sinatra at Memorial Auditorium, November 1, 1945.
(Gary Public Library)

Joseph C. Chapman, executive secretary, Gary Urban League.
(Gary *Post-Tribune*)

Reuben Olsen of Anselm Forum.
(Gary *Post-Tribune*)

Dr. Lester K. Jackson, pastor, St. Paul Baptist Church.
(Gary *Post-Tribune*)

Rev. Bernard Spong, Metro Holovachka, and David Stanton.
(Gary *Post-Tribune*)

Mary Cheever and Lew Wallace High School students.
(Gary *Post-Tribune*)

Women's Citizens Committee march on City Hall, March 7, 1949.
(Gary *Post-Tribune*)

Blast furnaces, Gary Works.
(Calumet Regional Archives)

Strikers during steel strike, 1952.
(Gary *Post-Tribune*)

Election victory celebration, 1951; Mayor Eugene Swartz holds up the hand of Mayor-elect Peter Mandich.

(Gary Public Library)

Mayor George Chacharis, Presidential candidate John F. Kennedy, Congressman Ray J. Madden, and Bishop Andrew Grutka, at Hellenic Hall, February 4, 1960. (Gary *Post-Tribune*)

Mayor Lee B. "Barney" Clayton.
(Gary *Post-Tribune*)

Mayor Ernst L. Schaible.
(Gary *Post-Tribune*)

President Harry S Truman, Governor Henry F. Schricker, and Gary Mayor Eugene Swartz, October 1948.
(Gary *Post-Tribune*)

Mayor Joseph Finerty.
(Gary *Post-Tribune*)

seph B. Radigan, Re-
blican candidate for
ayor, 1967.
(Gary *Post-Tribune*)

John Krupa, Demo-
cratic county chair-
man.
(Gary *Post-Tribune*)

Mayor A. Martin Katz.
(Gary *Post-Tribune*)

Gary in 1962.
(Gary *Post-Tribune*)

Rev. Julius James of the
Gary Freedom Move-
ment.
(Gary *Post-Tribune*)

H. Theo Tatum, princi-
pal of Roosevelt High
School.
(Gary *Post-Tribune*)

Hilbert L. Bradley of
the Fair Share Orga-
nization.
(Gary *Post-Tribune*)

Fair Share Organization demonstration at the Anderson Company.
(Gary *Post-Tribune*)

Emerson basketball team, winner of
first Hall of Fame Classic, Indianapolis, November 1977.
(Toni Lane)

Dozier T. Allen, Democratic city chairman, 1970.
(Gary *Post-Tribune*)

Steve Morris of Concerned Citizens for Quality Education, 1968.(Gary *Post-Tribune*)

Alexander S. Williams, county coroner, 1964.
(Gary *Post-Tribune*)

Mayor Richard G. Hatcher, Senator Robert F. Kennedy, and East Chicago Mayor John Nicosia.
(Gary *Post-Tribune*)

Mayor Hatcher with Rev. Jesse Jackson, 1970.
(Gary *Post-Tribune*)

Mayor Hatcher speaking at an anti-war rally, May 1972.
(Gary *Post-Tribune*)

placed in the sanctuary of City Church. Two years earlier, historian Isaac J. Quillen concluded that "Gary's experiment in religion for the market place failed because of the prejudice and disunity of members of the Church and the lack of adequate financial resources to compete successfully with commercial recreation and the facilities of the schools and the parks."

Had Seaman succeeded in bringing Gary's disparate people into City Church, he would truly have worked a miracle. But it was not to be. The crusade had too few resources, and Seaman had too few allies. His successor, Richard M. Millard, failed to ignite enthusiasm and lasted only three years; and his replacement, William E. Clark, endorsed many of Seaman's ideas, but the depression reduced the church budget. By the late 1940s, despite the existence of shops and college classes and music studios in the commercial wing, the congregation had turned inward. Satellite churches in Miller, Glen Park, and Ambridge drained away younger people. Membership surpassed 3,000 during the religious revival of the early 1950s, but after that, there was an irreversible decline. In 1973 the membership had slumped to 320 and, with a median age of 62 and white disenchantment with the inner city rising, only a third of the members attended regularly. Two years later, the church closed down.

SALES GIMMICKS: CHERRY LAMONT, THE XPLORER, AND CAPTAIN JACK ATKINSON

Cherry Lamont's five-day ride through Gary was an example of the stage-managed advertising spectacles that abounded during the "Roaring Twenties." Although Lamont was portrayed to Garyites as a daredevil sportsman out to break a world's endurance record, the veteran stunt driver under contract to General Motors came to town as part of a promotional venture to sell cars.

It was commonplace for sports celebrities to endorse products during the 1920s, a decade when the public seemed to have an almost obsessive need for heroes, perhaps out of fear that the rise of a machine-dominated, consumer-oriented society threatened to deemphasize individual accomplishment. The mass media lionized such captains of industry as Samuel Insull, the utilities tycoon whose takeover of the Gary Heat, Light, and Water Company in 1931 preceded by a year the collapse of his poorly managed holding company empire. For each corporate magnate who got his picture on the cover of *Time* magazine, there were thousands of local entrepreneurs who tried to copy his style.

In 1926 White-Sarber Auto Sales, Gary's main Pontiac distributor, hired Cherry Lamont to drive an Oakland Sedan for 106 hours while handcuffed to the steering wheel. Lamont was to leave the show-room at 7:00 A.M. on Wednesday, September 22, and travel continu-ously until late Sunday afternoon. The ignition would be wired in such a fashion that it could not be turned off without opening the hood. The wheels would keep moving at all times, even during stops for fuel, which would require that gas station attendants service him on the run. The promoters even announced contingency plans for changing flat tires without stopping the car.

On September 21, 1926, the *Post-Tribune* ran a photograph of the red-haired stunt driver and invited people "to take turns in riding with him day or night, to guard against any attempts to discredit the sincerity of his performance." The next day a reporter noted wryly that Lamont seemed to be "in his right mind" as he pulled out of the White-Sarber parking lot.

On Thursday a huge newspaper advertisement proclaimed that the whole town was watching the "sensational attempt to break the world's record" of 103 hours, set two weeks previously in Milwaukee. In the center of the ad was a picture of an Oakland Landau, priced at $1,295 and featuring four-wheel brakes, tilting beam headlights, a six-cylinder engine, and a rubber-silenced chassis with "an epochal and exclusive feature eliminating disturbing noise and rum-bling. . . ." Prospective buyers were reminded of the General Motors time payment plan, which brought luxury items within the reach of the masses. As a matter of fact, the outward prosperity of the 1920s rested in large part on the expansion of this type of credit buying.

It should be noted that other Oakland models sold for $1,025 and $1,195, still quite expensive by 1920s standards but available on the General Motors time payment plan. Pontiacs cost 200 dollars less, and Chevrolets could be purchased for as little as 500 dollars. Pack-ards, however, cost approximately 3,000 dollars.

Other Gary merchants touted their supporting roles in the test of endurance. Appearing like satellites around the White-Sarber ad were five smaller commercial announcements from Lighthouse Electric, whose fixture display Lamont would pass four times a day in order to attract potential customers; Plummer Motors in Glen Park, which also would be visited four times daily; Ridgely Phar-macy, which was supplying Lamont with a steady diet of malted milkshakes; Herman Zimmerlie Auto Repair, which offered a Strom-berg carburetor to the customer who best predicted Lamont's mile-age (the odometer had been taped to keep the information a secret);

and Minas Furniture, which lent a bedroom suite to the White-Sarber showroom for Lamont's use after he completed his labors.

Lamont provided newsmen with a constant flow of quotes in order to build up human interest and had a nurse and his wife accompany him on various legs of his journey. On September 23, the *Post-Tribune* pronounced him "Strong After 29 Hours" and repeated his claim that he "would soon be able to drive blindfolded through Gary." Lamont told reporters that he was usually so weak after such a ride that people had to lift him from his car. "The worst of it is they won't let me sleep when I get through," he added. "They seem to be afraid that I will sleep myself to death, I guess. Anyhow, they only let me pound my ear for four or five hours at a stretch and then wake me up and make me drink some tea or something like that."

On Sunday evening, just as he was completing his 107th hour, Lamont turned into the White-Sarber lot, cheered on by a large throng. He was helped from the car and given a quick medical examination. The doctor found his pulse to be normal but his blood pressure very high. He then went to his Olympic Hotel suite for a shave and a shower. Returning a half hour later wearing blue pajamas, he ate a bowl of hot noodle soup and then shuffled over to the Minas Furniture bedroom suite and fell asleep.

Sponsors then removed the tape from the Oakland's mileage gauge, and it was revealed that Lamont had traveled 819 miles, averaging less than eight miles per hour. Two weeks later, the irrepressible stunt driver traveled for 108 straight hours through the streets of Wheaton, Illinois. By that time, however, Gary had been visited by a gimmicky roadster called the Xplorer, which was painted red and green and adorned with the likeness of a thousand movie stars' eyes.

Les and Dempster Beatty, the owners of the Xplorer, announced in the *Post-Tribune* that they would tour Gary, conduct interviews, survey the city's industrial enterprises, and then write articles about the city. The first "Xploration" column was a rather prosaic description of Gary's history, location, population, water system, and major industries. Next to the column, in a separate box, Les Beatty asked people to "Tell Me What to Xplore Tomorrow." The following day, under the banner "BOOST YOUR CITY TO YOUR OUT-OF-TOWN FRIENDS," another "Xploration" article described such points of interest as the public library and the YMCA.

Unbeknownst to most *Post-Tribune* readers, the Beatty brothers had been hired as advance men to boost land sales at a new subdivision in Aetna on behalf of the Xen-McNair corporation. On October

9 the newspaper ran an advertisement extolling the virtues of Aetna and announcing the Xplorer's forthcoming appearance at a rally on the property site. Les Beatty was quoted as predicting a huge population increase for the city with subsequent rises in property values. If people desired a more comprehensive description of real estate opportunities in Gary, Beatty advised them to fill out an enclosed form and send it to him in care of the Xen-McNair corporation.

Also appearing at the Aetna rally was aviator Jack Atkinson, who performed a variety of flying stunts (including the "Dip," the "Dash," and the "Flash") for potential land buyers. At a subsequent performance on October 23, Atkinson supplemented his nose dives, tailspins, and upside-down stunts with an illuminated flying performance. Flying into wire circuits, he touched off a massive fireworks display. Afterwards, he signed up people interested in flying lessons.

Seven Gary merchants lent their names to the promotion of Atkinson's feats. The Lake Hotel Dining Room acclaimed itself as "Captain Jack's" favorite eating spot in Gary and announced a special dinner in honor of the illuminated display. Publicizing the items which they furnished for the flight were People's Hardware (tools), George J. Dunleavy (helmet, goggles, gloves), Lighthouse Electric (electrical work), U.S.L. (batteries), K. and S. (boots, coat, breeches), and Alger and Hirschberg (gas, oil, spark plugs).

In the 1920s Madison Avenue advertising techniques reached new levels of sophistication, spawning hundreds of extravagant schemes designed to separate the consumer from his money. The exploits of Cherry Lamont, the Beatty brothers, and Captain Jack Atkinson exemplified the excessive commercialism of the 1920s. Nonetheless, these spectacles were relatively harmless when compared with the stock swindles, insurance and loan frauds, door-to-door bunco schemes, and extralegal enterprises of organized crime that also went unregulated, for the most part, during the era.

PACKING THEM IN AT THE CINEMA

The 1920s were the heyday of Gary's theatre industry. More than a dozen movie houses offered a variety of silent films, vaudeville acts, and burlesque routines. With wartime censorship over, a hedonistic spirit prevailed. Nearly twenty thousand people were attending the movies each day, and by 1923 the *Post-Tribune* expanded its amusement section to include pictures of such screen idols as Clara Bow, Mary Pickford, Norma Talmadge, and Rudolph Valentino. Box-office hits that year included *Slave of Desire, Dulcey: The Story of a Delightful Dumbbell, Trifling Women, One Week of Love,* and *The Super Sex.*

The Gary Theatre supplemented its vaudeville and film fare with Charleston contests, beauty pageants, boxing, wrestling, amateur nights, auctions, and give-away drawings. In November 1923 the management booked Crystal Bennett and Peggy Doyle, two "physical culture experts" who appeared first in gowns, then in gym suits, and finally in one-piece bathing suits—in order, according to an admiring reviewer, to perform their exercises unencumbered and to show off their "perfect form."

Perhaps the most important entertainment development in the 1920s was the construction by Ingwald Moe of V. U. Young and C. J. Wolf's Palace Theatre. It had a seating capacity of nearly 3,000 and chandeliers imported from Spain. At the gala dedication on Thanksgiving Day of 1925, Horace S. Norton, who had reluctantly approved Moe's Broadway Theatre 18 years previously, remarked: "We didn't know where we were going then, but we were driving fast to get there. But now we are doing things that make life worthwhile."

Another "million dollar" theatre, the Tivoli, was built before the end of the decade, causing some of the older theatres to lose customers. The Orpheum stopped showing films in 1929 and was briefly refurbished by V. U. Young as a miniature golf course. The Gary Theatre, once called the "City's Pride," occasionally enticed patrons with "Adults Only" movies such as *The Road to Ruin,* advertised as containing scenes of "CLOSED CARS PARKED ON SHADY LANES—FAST ROAD HOUSES—STRIP POKER PARTIES—LOVE, PASSION, REMORSE, AND DESPAIR."

In the fall of 1929 the Gary Theatre began presenting burlesque shows featuring strippers, chorus girls, models, and such "entertainment queens" as Little Egypt, Fanny McAvey, Hindu Wausau, Midgie Gibbons, Olga Mae and her "Red Hots," and Babe Archer, the "Shimmy Shaking Queen." Matinee shows generally maintained a modicum of propriety, and women and children sometimes attended. Evening shows were more erotic, especially the "off comes the lid" Saturday jamborees.

As burlesque became popular, it also became the subject of criticism by the Gary Lions Club in the winter of 1930. Attending a performance of Babe Harris and the Big City Burlesk Revue, a delegation of civic leaders claimed that the show was obscene in its "language, gestures, and nudity."

Shortly thereafter, the Board of Safety ordered police to shut down

Gary's "sin meccas." Police Chief Stanley Bucklind told touring companies to "cut out the smut or get out of town." The Gary Theatre soon switched to vaudeville and talkies, and the strippers were relegated to night clubs such as Neal's Barnyard, which featured such acts as "The One and Only Zorine and Her Nudists."

DORTHY E. SIKES: JACK-OF-ALL-TRADES

Dorthy E. Sikes was one of the many black emigrants to Gary during the 1920s. A farmer, grocer, millworker, carpenter, and mechanic, he was a man of much resourcefulness who just barely "got by" in the insecure urban environment that became his home for more than 50 years.

Born in 1886, Sikes grew up in the hamlet of Commerce, Missouri. His family grew wheat and corn on a half-square mile strip of land and as sharecroppers gave the owner a third of their earnings. Life was perilous. Dorthy, or D. E., as he was called, had few clothes without patches. At the age of eight he was operating a threshing machine. In frolicsome moods he drove it through the three blocks of town. Because his family needed his labor, he only attended school three months a year but was a bright student who effortlessly mastered figures. Once, he later claimed, he told his teacher that there was not a mathematics problem that he could not solve. Given a complicated cube root, he worked it out to the eighteenth decimal. The instructor left the answer on the board all year and gave him a grade of 98, telling him that nobody was more perfect than that.

On his eighteenth birthday, his father gave Sikes a ten-dollar bill for a 160-mile trip north to the St. Louis World's Fair. He spent a week there before the money ran out. Upon his return his father put him on a 50-cents weekly salary which rose to 65 cents three years later. For relaxation he toured surrounding towns with a Negro baseball team and became a veterinarian's assistant. After awhile, neighbors brought their diseased animals to him for free treatment.

In 1913, after the farm's crops were ruined by floods and then drought, Sikes was hired by the Aetna Powder Company in nearby Fayville, Illinois. His ability to handle unforeseen situations and to get along with people earned him a rapid promotion to foreman. But making dynamite and nitroglycerin was dangerous, and the effects of inhaling perfume gas led to chronic arthritis and respiratory problems. In 1917 his wife finally persuaded him to quit after an explosion knocked out their house lights a mile away from the plant.

Shortly before he left the Aetna Powder Company, a superintendent who was moving to Gary to take charge of a tin mill asked Sikes to join him. Demurring, he settled instead in Charleston, Missouri. For five years he practiced carpentry, laid bricks, finished concrete, and managed a general store; but the dim economic prospects eventually drove him north. Leaving his wife Kimmie to tend the store, he arrived in Gary on a Wednesday and became a steelworker the following day. Sikes remembered: "Six hundred people were begging for work at the mill gate. They hired nine, and I was one of them. I never stopped walking. The foreman pointed to me and said 'do you want a job?' I said 'yes' and had one."

Within a week Sikes discovered that a cousin resided just a half-mile from his rooming house. He moved in with him until he saved enough money to send for his wife and five-year-old son Melvin (a daughter, Dortha, was born after he came to Gary). He augmented his $3.50 daily salary by working for a service station owner named Gorski. Several months later, the man cajoled him into becoming a full-time employee at a salary of five dollars a day plus tips. The arrangement lasted several years until the station failed. Sikes bought some of the equipment at a government sale and set up business on his own, the first of several such ventures. "Gorski cleared 73 dollars a day—can you imagine?—but he drank and gambled," Sikes said. "I knew the inventory prices better than he did. But the family was nice. The young son even tried to teach me Polish."

Sikes paid a thousand dollars apiece for two lots near 21st and Adams that were "nothing but sand." He put down a dirt foundation and built a house. Several white families lived on the block, including an immigrant storekeeper. Gangs of Mexican and Polish youths often hung around his place of work, learning how to fix cars.

Once Sikes enrolled in a mechanics class at Froebel night school. The students were told to take all the wires off an automobile and, afterwards, to rewire it. "They couldn't do it, and neither could the teacher," Sikes remembered. He wired it for them and left, never to return for another lesson.

A family man who spent most of his time at home or at work, Sikes belonged to the First African Methodist Episcopal Church and to the Masonic Lodge. He disliked liquor because "it made me tremble like a leaf." He spent most of his spare time conversing in a wooden swing, watching softball games at the nearby freight yard, or being with his children. On special occasions they went to western movies at the Roosevelt Theatre or bought hot tamales from a street vendor. Once a year a circus troupe unloaded wild animals from railway cars within sight of their house and then paraded the elephants, lions, and tigers down Broadway.

The depression forced Sikes once again to look for work. Dwindling income from repairing cars made him thankful for such supplemental Works Progress Administration money that he earned by building bridges and installing sewers. New Dealers set a wage ceiling of 75 dollars a month for work relief, and thus he could only labor "seven days and one hour" for the government.

Declining health forced Sikes to retire in the 1950s. Interviewed in 1973 at the age of 86, he had few regrets about the past, although had he not been poor and black he might have become a veterinarian, a professional baseball player, a plant foreman, or the owner of a large shop. Proud of his family (his son became a psychology professor at the University of Texas), he wished only that he could have seen more of the world and that his social security checks were larger. He passed away in 1977.

IMAGES OF GARY:
ARTHUR W. SHUMWAY AND GARRY J. AUGUST

In January 1929 a 23-year-old former reporter for the *Post-Tribune* named Arthur Shumway published a biting satire about Gary's culture, or lack of it, in the magazine *American Parade*. The article was entitled "Gary, Shrine of the Steel God: The City That Has Everything, and at the Same Time Has Nothing." In a style at times similar to that of H. L. Mencken and Sinclair Lewis, Shumway wrote: "Gary, whatever else, is a paradox. It is busy; it is dull. It is modern; it is backward. It is clean; it is filthy. It is rich; it is poor. It has beautiful homes; it has sordid hovels. It is a typical overgrown mill-town; it is a unique new city of the old world. It has a past, but it has no traditions. It has a feeble glow of culture, yet the darkness of prehistoric ignorance."

Shumway took aim at Gary's most prominent community pillars. He labeled School Superintendent William A. Wirt the "Little Father," whose work-study-play system was an "overrated" scheme to keep children busy for the longest time in the least expensive manner. Shumway also hooted at the Gary Quill Club because it sought to lionize Hoosier poet William Herschell for writing such verse as "Ain't God good to Indiana? / Ain't He fellers? / Ain't He though?"

According to Shumway, Gary was a materialistic, smoke-belching "incubater-child" of "St. Elbert" and his steel barons. Rather than face up to the problems created by an absentee landlord, a "squirming handful" of boosters christened their "half-raw, dirty sort of a hole" the "Miracle City of Hoosierland" and the "Wonder City of the

World." Gary "lies in the gutter and looks at the stars," Shumway concluded.

The boosters actually retarded progress with their tranquilizing rhetoric, Shumway believed. These "Brewers of Slogans" and "Creators of the Great Illusion" used such phrases as "melting pot" and "Americanization process" to suggest social harmony. But, in reality, Shumway charged, "a good share of those you see on Broadway, especially when they are coming *from* the Works, are devoid of the foolish appearance of optimism; their big backs droop; their feet drag; their eyes look dull; it is conceivable that . . . many want to flee from blazing furnaces, from lonely sand drifts. . . ." Shumway added: "A melting pot, this Gary? In 50 years, perhaps."

In Shumway's opinion, Gary's cultural mecca was the Southside, the place the conservative Northsiders condescendingly labeled "Hunkytown." He wrote: "This is living, breathing, sweating, drinking, cursing, laughing, singing Gary." Shumway eulogized the exotic cafes and stores, the smell of foreign cooking, the flags and the posters adorning nationality clubs, the Balkan coffee-houses that sheltered "gossiping, card-playing men who read papers with the L's and P's crazily inverted. . . ."

In the Southside, Shumway went on to say, "hawkers wander along, leading sad-faced horses and shouting their wares in all versions of the bewildering jumble of tongues; children skip and run, half-naked, in the streets; mothers sing to dark babies strange, alien lullabies, remembered from European hearth sides—all this is Gary's real charm."

One of Shumway's targets was the *Post-Tribune*, which he characterized as "a vast, crazily made-up, overgrown, jumbled sheet, giving a heavy armload of advertising, entertainment, and news for a mere three cents, along with editorials that (save on rare occasions) won't give anybody a twinge or cause any of the true Garyites to think any harder than is their usual custom." The paper replied editorially that Shumway had an alluring style but that there were "rifts" in his "lute." The newspaper published a broadside from a Presbyterian minister who labeled the author "an evil influence on formative youth," and it solicited a rebuttal from Rabbi Garry Joel August, one of the few Garyites praised by Shumway.

A Phi Beta Kappa scholar at Western Reserve University in his native Cleveland and a graduate of Hebrew Union College, August came to Temple Israel in 1926 from St. Joseph, Missouri. An admirer of H. L. Mencken, Sinclair Lewis, and Theodore Dreiser, the reform rabbi shared much in common with Shumway in his literary tastes and dislike of cant. Both were much interested in the theatre and in classical music. Shumway described the rabbi as a "young man of infinite culture, who reads continually and searchingly ... and who, in the pulpit, preaches with intelligence, force, and clarity on anything under the sun."

In "Gary—An Interpretation," a two-part reply to Shumway's essay, Rabbi August asserted that Gary was similar to other young cities, past and present, and was not abnormally sick or backward. Roughhewn and sharp-witted speculators founded towns, he said, not harpists, philosophers, and professors of Sanskrit. He noted that boosterism was inevitable in the evolution of a city, and then asked: "We run up gaudy banners, we toot and pound ... what is all this harmless nonsense but an indication of a pioneer complex? And where, within our broad shores, is it not in view?" August said that Shumway was a clever writer who employed hyperbole for its shock effect and was commenting on foibles common to all American cities rather than things unique to Gary. He concluded: "Gary is America. Every American city is Gary writ large or small."

The Shumway-August dialogue came near the end of Gary's most prosperous era. Shumway had bemoaned Gary's dependence on U.S. Steel, saying that until economic diversification occurred, the city would "rattle along in the same old rut." August also found disturbing tendencies in the city's social and economic fabric, but his essay was free of the rhetorical excesses contained in the reporter's broadside.

Following his move from Gary, Shumway's star seemed on the rise. He became a columnist for an Evanston paper, wrote prizewinning short stories and a novel, and was on the staff of *Esquire.* Then, in April 1934, he committed suicide while in Florida recuperating from a disease of the nerves and a broken marriage.

During the 1930s Rabbi August was in the public eye as a popular lecturer, critic, and patron of the arts. He wrote book reviews for the *Post-Tribune,* arranged interfaith services, was a member of the library board, and became the first president of the Gary Symphony. The Reverend Thomas S. Pierce described his oratorical delivery as like that of a magnificent actor, with perfect elocution and a deep resonant voice. In 1932, debating the merits of prohibition with the Reverend Frederick W. Backemeyer, he delighted the audience and infuriated his abstemious adversary by predicting that "when your boys grow up, they'll be drinking beer."

August retired in 1951 but remained in Gary. Earlier he had rejected attractive offers in Chicago, Montreal, Baton Rouge, and elsewhere because of the freedom that his job afforded him. Chicago's attractions were accessible, and he did not feel that his adopted city was a cultural wasteland. In fact, he enjoyed observing the diverse customs of Gary's many ethnic groups. At a banquet honoring his 25 years of service to Temple Israel, August said that "my congregation had a heart that was warm, a loyalty that was always intense, an imagination that was always alive, and love that was always profound." He quoted Robert Ingersoll's advice to the effect that "Happiness is the only goal, justice the only worship, truth the only torch, humanity the only religion, and love the only priest."

R. O. JOHNSON AND THE 1929 ELECTION

Roswell O. Johnson's election as mayor in 1929 confounded the critics who had written his political obituary a half-decade earlier when he went to jail in the wake of a liquor scandal. Most Northsiders regarded him as a somewhat disreputable character, but Johnson remained the toast of the Southside until the depression caused most working-class voters to vote Democratic.

Born on a farm near Decatur, Indiana, on April 23, 1872, Johnson attended Tri-State Normal College for three years before becoming a teacher, a lawyer, and then a customs collector and judge in the territory of Arizona. In 1905 he set up law practice in Kendallville, Indiana. Opening a law office in Gary in 1909, he went into realty and became president of the Indiana Sales Company.

A "born mixer" who "never forgot a name or a face," Johnson "knew no peer in Lake County as an orator," according to one writer. He frequently emphasized his points with the expression, "By the eternal," and could curse or quote classical poetry with equal facility.

In 1929 Johnson secured a full pardon from President Calvin Coolidge and entered the Republican primary against incumbent Mayor Floyd E. Williams in hopes of duplicating his 1913 and 1921 victories. "Growing bald and appearing somewhat dissipated, he was still imposing in appearance," wrote historian Isaac J. Quillen, and was "able to associate with everyone. He could meet people on their own level in the saloon, dance hall or office."

In the 1929 primary the *Post-Tribune* warned that a Johnson victory would deliver Gary over to the lords of vice. Johnson's main editorial support came from the Glen Park *News*, a small weekly that embellished its stories with such headlines as "MAYOR LOCKS BARN DOOR . . . HORSE ALREADY STOLEN" (concerning vice) and "BEAT INNO-CENT WAR VETERAN TO A PULP" (in reference to police brutality).

Johnson won more than 14,000 of the 24,000 votes cast in the primary. Emmet N. White, his Democratic opponent in the general election, obtained the support of several Republican civic leaders and hit hard at Johnson's criminal record. Most residents, perhaps cynical of all politicians, sat out the November election. Johnson won by 2,600 votes out of 22,495 cast.

Refusing to accept defeat, White filed suit to prevent Johnson from taking office on the grounds that his pardon was not affixed with the Great Seal and that President Calvin Coolidge had not specifically returned his "political rights," just his "civil rights." Disgruntled Republicans joined in these machinations. Three weeks before his term expired, Mayor Williams resigned to take a job with the Gary Real Estate Exchange. He was succeeded by City Controller Henry G. Hay, who vowed to stay in office to "protect the financial credit of the city" if there was no "qualified successor" to take up the reins of government.

The Gary *American,* a black weekly which had supported Johnson, spoke out against the White-Williams-Hay "conspiracy," writing that "the town has gained notoriety enough. The stink of bossism has become unbearable." And the Glen Park *News* warned of civil war if Johnson was not sworn in, a threat rendered moot by Johnson's vindication in the courts on the eve of his inauguration.

After the 1929 election the *Post-Tribune* launched a series entitled "If I Were Mayor," asking readers for ideas on improving city government. The responses ranged from a student's request for shorter school hours to an appeal by Tom Cannon to de-politicize City Hall.

One woman wanted prostitutes off the street corners; another wanted a crackdown against drunks, gamblers, and foul-mouthed ruffians. There were complaints about inadequate garbage collection and downtown parking space, requests to ban smoking on street cars, protestations about unequal economic and educational opportunities for blacks, and calls for economic diversification and the repair of muddy and pot-holed streets. Gary merchants were criticized for their ugly signboards, the poor quality of their products, and their low wage scales. One resident, claiming that some employers made salesgirls work 14 hours a day, wanted to "put some of these slave-drivers into line with Americanism."

Many letters complained about the low level of city politics and the resultant damage to Gary's image. Taking exception to the mayor-elect's demeanor, one resident wrote: "I would not be seen outside the Hotel Gary door every day garbed in the raiment of a sport headed for Tia Juana [*sic*], with my hat tilted at a reckless angle, and the end of my cigar meeting the brim of my hat."

Most of these letters dealt with problems that had accompanied the quick growth during the prosperous 1920s—such as traffic congestion, bad roads, and the like. Because Johnson took office at the onset of the depression, his third term was destined to be more trying than almost anyone imagined. Ironically, Johnson had had to deal with depressions at the outset of each of his previous two administrations. But the economic downswings of 1914 and 1922 were mild compared to the crisis conditions throughout his unhappy third term.

CHAPTER SIX

Law and Justice
in the Steel City

A lack of respect for law and order, for honesty and justice, lay
deep in the body politic of the city of Gary.

—Isaac J. Quillen

THE IDEAL OF equality under the law was unrealized in Gary during
the postwar generation. Many factors made this so. The police department, the news media, and the judiciary were allies of a business
and social elite that valued order more than justice. Respect for the
law was compromised by prohibition, a politically apathetic elector-
ate, and Gary's frontier legacy. If a person was poor or a member of
a minority group, or both, he felt the full brunt of the law much more
than affluent Northsiders did.

WILLIAM A. FORBIS AND POLICE ENFORCEMENT

During the 1920s the police department was Gary's most powerful
municipal agency. Under Chief William A. Forbis, it grew in size and
became more professional. Forbis established a detective bureau,
competitive testing, a classification system of criminal identification,
and closer ties with regional and state institutions. He had traffic
lanes painted on the city streets and compiled a book of statutes for
patrolmen. Extremely interested in the welfare of his men, Forbis
founded a police pension fund and the Gary lodge of the Fraternal
Order of Police. "He had a lot of class and was well-liked; you could
sit down and talk with him," recalled Carl "Bud" Ingersoll, who
headed the motor division which consisted of some Model A Fords,
a Cadillac touring car, and six motorcycles.

Despite these accomplishments, Forbis was chief during an era when police used "Third Degree" tactics against suspects, carried out no-knock raids and vagrancy roundups, and paid little heed to such legal guarantees as the writ of habeas corpus, the presumption of innocence, or a defendant's right to remain silent. In May 1921, for example, his officers interrogated seven alleged bootleggers for 36 hours. As reprehensible as these techniques were, they were sanctioned and even encouraged by Gary's civic leaders.

Born in Ohio in 1869, Forbis had been a police clerk, a railroad detective, a secret serviceman, and a doorkeeper for the U.S. House of Representatives before moving to Gary in 1909. He worked for four years as a mill inspector. When his friend R. O. Johnson was elected mayor, he became an assistant to Police Chief Pontius Heintz and set up a Bertillon Squad (now the Bureau of Identification) for keeping fingerprints and criminal-history records. When Heintz retired in 1915, Forbis succeeded him.

Tall and heavy, with a round, distinguished face, Forbis was an armchair crimefighter who, according to the *Post-Tribune,* "took it as his main duty to sit in his office and receive reports and callers." The paper described him as a "cracker-barrel philosopher" whose "powerful frame, droll anecdotes, tall stories, and bristling mustaches . . . are known to hundreds of men and women."

Forbis cultivated the image of an affable public servant. His friend Tom Cannon periodically reprinted his witticisms in "Flue Dust," such as the remark that "what this country needs is a good five-cent place to park." One day Forbis wired his office chair and, as a practical joke, shocked visiting newsmen and city officials with electrical jolts.

Forbis usually left the distasteful task of questioning suspects to Captain William J. Linn, who had a reputation for using brutal interrogation techniques. Forbis denied that his men used terror tactics to extract confessions but admitted that "in many cases it is necessary to use harsh language and, in a measure, be free with the hands."

In September 1922 Governor Warren T. McCray ordered an investigation into charges that the Gary police mistreated prisoners. State Senator C. Oliver Holmes produced affidavits from people who claimed to have been pummeled with rubber hoses, blackjacks, and railroad spikes, as well as having been threatened with hanging. Holmes believed that "Third Degree" tactics retarded law enforcement by casting doubt on all confessions.

Former policeman W. L. Wall testified that some of his colleagues had slapped around a black woman out for a walk until she signed a false confession that she was a prostitute. Captain Linn labeled Wall an agitator and told the *Post-Tribune* that, rather than print his lies, the paper could better use its space "by advertising jaw or brain treatment followed by a testimonial."

Operating under the glare of publicity, the police were under some restraints to behave properly, but in the absence of clear-cut community support for prohibition or for running gamblers and prostitutes out of town, the force was susceptible to corruption and partisan politics. In its policies toward minorities and dissenters, the department was the willing ally of conservatives who wanted deviant and threatening behavior curbed. In fact, the press often supported questionable police techniques against radicals and minorities. Reporting on the killing of a black teen-ager named Jake Herbert, who was running between buildings and failed to obey a warning to halt, the *Evening Post* said it was the youth's own fault for not heeding his mother's advice to be careful where he played. The article concluded: "The shooting of Herbert is the first notch of Police Chief William Forbis' campaign to stop wholesale robberies, holdups, and attacks on women and girls on the West Side."

Fear of radicalism also caused the press to sanction police curbs on the right of assembly, such as the breaking up of a Socialist rally on May 5, 1921. On this occasion, Forbis declared that "these disloyal foreigners should be taken to their port of entrance, rowed a hundred miles or so, and then made to swim back." After Attorney Paul P. Glaser filed an injunction to prevent the police from interfering with another meeting, Forbis threatened: "If he enjoins the police, there may be some red-blooded Americans left in the city. This ought to bring them out."

Public opinion, press coverage, and government policy all contributed to discriminatory law enforcement practices. In a single issue the *Post-Tribune* criticized the surpise "no-knock" entry into a white man's house but applauded the raiding of disorderly black homes. On one occasion, Judge C. M. Greenlee released a half-dozen gamblers for lack of search warrants but fined a black woman 130 dollars and sentenced her to 60 days in jail because a gallon jug of moonshine whiskey was found in her chicken coop. After white policeman Julius Gunther was killed by a black man, the ensuing manhunt and unrelenting roundup of suspicious characters dominated headlines until police extracted a confession from the prime suspect. But when a black maid vanished after having last been sighted at the shack of a white man (who had been seen crying while scrubbing his floor), the suspect was quickly released. There was no search for the woman, and the case was soon forgotten.

On July 19, 1929, the Gary *American* complained that "local police take more pains to arrest law violators of color" than to apprehend white criminals. Typically, whenever a felony occurred on the Southside, "many innocent people are rounded up in droves." If the laws were upheld fairly, the black newspaper concluded, then more citizens would respect and obey them.

The newspapers of the 1920s were filled with cases of policemen who were found wanting in wisdom, tact, honesty, and common sense. Five officers were suspended at one time in 1925, seven on another occasion in 1926, for negligence and corruption. Honest policemen attracted less publicity, and their reputations suffered from the failings of some of their peers.

In Gary, as in other cities, the individual patrolman was the key to maintaining order and justice. Performing both service and law enforcement duties, he was often in the ambiguous position of having to decide when to assert his authority and when to use discretion. For example, stopping the elopement of teen-agers and picking up "suspicious" characters in wealthy neighborhoods were typical "service" functions that pleased some people but alienated others. Most arrests involved minor offenses, such as traffic violations, loitering, gambling, drunkenness, and disorderly conduct, in situations where the patrolman's prejudices and personal values could easily affect his judgment.

It would be inaccurate, however, to lay the chief blame for corruption on the individual policeman. In an age that glorified materialism, sanctioned racism, hooted at prohibition, and exhibited little respect for the poor and the powerless, it was natural for policemen to use their jobs as paths toward upward mobility and to reflect the prejudices of the larger society.

On August 19, 1924, the Chamber of Commerce charged that the police department was a political football, that discipline was "notoriously lax," that some speakeasies operated with police blessing (off-duty patrolmen were sometimes hired as bouncers), and that "the situation calls for surgical methods." The police response was to carry out a series of "Sponge Squad" raids designed to give the public an impression of vigilance. This special police detail would break down tenement doors, climb through windows, and comb the Calumet marshes from time to time. Stills of every description were on display at the station. One week the "Sponge Squad" confiscated 80 of them.

On July 20, 1925, the police raided a "blind pig" whose owner had failed to maintain good relations with the force. The *Post-Tribune* wrote that "the bar was battered beyond hope of further use, [and] the tables, chairs, and other equipment were shattered to pieces" with axes and sledgehammers.

In 1926 the City Council launched an investigation into alleged police inefficiency. A week later, the department unearthed the largest still ever discovered in Lake County, one capable of producing 2,500 gallons daily. Due in part to the publicity surrounding that fortuitous success, the City Council turned to other matters, such as making it a crime punishable by a fine up to 300 dollars and 30 days in jail to make suggestive gestures, utter vile epithets, or seek an introduction in public to someone of the opposite sex except for the purpose of conducting legal business.

Chief Forbis served under four mayors, but because his position was an appointive one, he had to be a shrewd politician. A staunch Republican with close ties to the R. O. Johnson machine, he also cultivated the support of business leaders who were members of the conservative wing of Gary's Republican party. Even so, in 1925 Forbis lost his post for several months during the caretaker administration of Mayor William J. Fulton. Although Mayor Floyd Williams reappointed him in 1926, the episode was a sobering testament to the precariousness of Forbis' position.

In his 14 years as chief, Forbis stayed clear of personal scandal. As former Mayor William F. Hodges said: "Never once has anyone been able to point a finger at Bill Forbis and say, 'There is a dishonest man.'" Nonetheless, as in the Tammany Hall maxim, "if you want to get along, go along," prudence sometimes dictated that he be blind to the indiscretions of others.

Chief Forbis had a propensity for exaggerating his accomplishments. Once, after arresting four people on adultery charges, he announced that he had struck at the heart of the underworld. "We've got them on the run, and we intend to keep them going," he said. Month after month, he declared that the liquor laws were being enforced. But this item in Tom Cannon's "Flue Dust" column, May 7, 1926, was closer to the mark: "Gary policeman found a needle this afternoon, and the entire force is scouring the city for the haystack." On June 29, 1927, Forbis reached new heights of hyperbole when he labeled Gary the driest city in the country.

On January 26, 1929, the *Post-Tribune* suggested putting the police under civil service regulations and increasing their salaries. Forbis concurred with these suggestions. The paper summarized the state of affairs in this manner: "Nobody expects you to live on $180 a month; your bosses expect you to graft another $75 or $100 a month. I'll see that you are paid $100 every month if you let my place run. Don't be a numbskull. They all do it. Feather your nest while you are able."

On August 23, 1929, Forbis set forth his views regarding prohibition in a letter to George W. Wickersham, chairman of President Herbert Hoover's Commission on Law Observance and Enforcement. Recommending the legalization of beer, he said that the prohibition laws bred corruption and caused "more enemies than any other one thing." The middle and upper classes drank their whiskey with impunity, he wrote, but "the poor hard-working fellow who needs a glass of beer and cannot get it . . . then cooks up anything to make a drink." The result, Forbis concluded, was persecution of the working class and grief for their families.

Less than two months later, a federal grand jury indicted 20 policemen for violating the prohibition laws. Although Forbis was not named as a coconspirator and although most of those arraigned escaped conviction, the episode prompted his demotion to the Bertillon squad. In October 1930, at the age of 60, he was given the rank of captain. Nine years later, when he retired after 25 years of service, Chief William J. Linn said, "The department won't seem the same when 'Cap' is gone. He will be missed."

Replacing Forbis as chief was a token gesture that did little to end malfeasance and did bring harsher policies toward poor people and dissenters. In December 1931 Inspector A. S. J. Woods, a criminologist from Berkeley, California, whom R. O. Johnson had hired 21 months previously to make the force more efficient, resigned in protest over the continuing political interference and corruption within the department. The repeal of the Eighteenth Amendment lessened the opportunities for graft somewhat, but other problems remained.

ANNA CUNNINGHAM: THE "POISON MOTHER" CASE

The headline "GARY POISON PLOT," appearing in the April 11, 1925, issue of the *Post-Tribune,* climaxed a nightmarish series of ordeals for 48-year-old Anna Cunningham. The general public came to know her as a deranged murderer, but she was the victim of a tragic miscarriage of justice.

The day before the bizarre case broke, 22-year-old David Cunningham, Jr., lay in critical condition at Chicago's Columbus Memorial Hospital, suffering from a hereditary congenital deficiency. Fifty pounds underweight, almost totally paralyzed, and unable to speak above a whisper, he evidently had the same ailment that had taken the lives of several of his brothers within the past few years.

David's nurse, Helen Cummings, watched his condition deteriorate with growing alarm and began to suspect that he had been stricken with arsenic poisoning. David had told her that his trouble began soon after he had eaten a strange-tasting apple which his mother had put in his lunch pail. When Nurse Cummings mentioned this to David's aunt, she was told that Mrs. Cunningham had once threatened to kill her entire family with a butcher knife. After a staff doctor admitted the plausibility of the poison theory, David's aunt called the police, who interviewed the hospital staff, took statements from Anna and David, and asked Gary police to search the Cunningham house at 458 Buchanan.

The subsequent probe uncovered two empty boxes of arsenic. Mrs. Cunningham was then taken into custody for observation and interrogation. Hours later, she suffered a paralytic seizure and lost consciousness, then awakened and tried to choke herself with a torn sheet. Attending physicians diagnosed her condition as epileptic psychosis and assigned matrons to be with her at all times.

In response to these developments, Lake County Prosecutor August A. Bremer ordered the bodies of two of the dead Cunningham boys exhumed and their vital organs studied by the Cook County coroner's office and a team from Purdue University. After Bremer learned that the analyses showed traces of arsenic which, in Coroner Oscar Wolff's opinion, "strongly indicated" foul play, he arraigned Mrs. Cunningham for murder.

At this time Bremer believed that Mrs. Cunningham was probably insane but that it was up to her lawyers to prove it. His objective was to obtain a confession with the aid of Sheriff Ben H. Strong. During her first three days in custody Mrs. Cunningham was in a trance, with her expression fixed in an "ironical glassy stare." Then under pressure from the sheriff she signed a statement to the effect that she had fed arsenic on buttered bread to four of her children so that they might join their father in heaven. On each occasion, the document said, she had poisoned the one she loved most—first Isabelle, then Charles, then Walter, and finally David. Her daughter Mae escaped death, the confession stated, because "she treated me so mean and caused so much trouble staying out at dances and places and never telling me anything. I wouldn't have killed her."

Mae Cunningham's reaction to her mother's confession was a combination of shock and incredulity. "I don't believe it," she screamed repeatedly. A day later, Mrs. Cunningham disavowed the confession, claiming to have been in an amnesiac trance for the past several days. "People must have put words in my mouth," she declared.

As a matter of fact, Anna Cunningham's sheltered life and tenuous health left her ill-prepared to cope with the enormous pressures that suddenly descended on her. Ever since 1918, when a son accidentally killed a playmate with a gun, she had periodically sunk into fits of depression. She shunned contact with her neighbors in Blanchley's Corner, who regarded her a queer recluse.

In 1919, when her husband David died of an intestinal inflammation, his relatives tended to blame her for failing to nurse him back to health (in her "confession" Anna insisted that she did not poison her husband).

After her husband's death, Anna moved to Gary so that her oldest sons could work at U.S. Steel. A plague of misfortunes seemed to stalk her; four of her six children died within four years—Isabelle, after an appendectomy; Harry, after having become ill in the army; Charles, after eating a large quantity of frozen peaches; and Walter, evidently from a congenital heart defect.

After Walter's death, Anna suffered a nervous breakdown. Her family doctor advised her to enter a sanitarium, but she said she was needed at home to take care of David, one of whose arms had been partially paralyzed since birth. Her grief at the loss of her ten-year-old child remained unabated, according to neighbor Marie Bauer, who heard her frequently lament: "My poor Walter boy. He was all the world to me. I can't see why it is that such sorrow should be mine to bear."

"I don't believe there has been or is anything wrong with the deaths in the Cunningham family," Marie Bauer concluded. "Any charges that have been or may be made are the result of interfamily strife fostered by relatives of Mrs. Cunningham in Chicago," she added, referring to sisters of Anna's deceased husband, who refused to believe that he might have had a congenital disease.

On the strength of the confession and the autopsy, the prosecutor's office obtained an indictment against Anna on the charge of murdering Walter. Mae Cunningham blamed the "foolish" grand jury action on the strong-arm tactics of publicity-hungry officials. She told reporters that she herself had bought one of the arsenic boxes to exterminate plant germs and rats, and the family did not have it in the house at the time of Walter's death. She added that the traces of arsenic came from the drug Neo Salvarsan (arsphenamine), which family doctors had prescribed for Walter and David.

The *Post-Tribune* expressed certainty that the defendant had poisoned her children but questioned whether the case was not "material for the sanity court." On the eve of the trial, the paper proclaimed: "It has been quite evident from the start that Mrs. Cunningham is not normal and her confession is sufficient proof that she should have been committed to an insane hospital years ago."

The Lake County *Star's* assessment of the case noted that the defendant's confession seemed inconsistent, disconnected, and disordered. The *Star* added: "Almost without exception, officials and newspapermen who have been investigating the case accept the theory that if the woman did administer the poison, it was done at a time when she was not mentally responsible, or her normal self. . . . Anyone looking into those sad eyes, that stricken, sorrowful, but still kindly face could hardly believe otherwise."

On July 8, 1925, Anna Cunningham was brought to trial for allegedly putting lethal doses of arsenic on her son Walter's buttered bread. Although the case rested largely on the repudiated confession, the prosecution alleged that her primary motive was to collect her child's life insurance during a time of financial distress. This thesis not only contradicted the confession but was difficult to prove. Anna received approximately 330 dollars from Walter's insurance policy, hardly enough to cover the burial. In summoning 35 witnesses to the stand, including policemen, relatives, nurses, medical consultants, neighbors, and insurance agents, the prosecution presented more evidence linking Anna to David's illness than to Walter's death, which caused some court watchers to speculate that the prosecutor's office should have waited to see if David died. In essence, the prosecutor's office, desiring a quick murder conviction in order to obtain maximum political mileage, was asking the jury to believe that what had recently happened to David had also been done to Walter.

For example, the prosecution relied heavily on the testimony of David's nurse, Helen Cummings, and a woman named Minnie E. Ginder who had looked after Walter during the last two weeks of his life. While Nurse Cummings was very definite in her knowledge and opinion about David's medical condition, Nurse Ginder had only a vague idea of what had been wrong with Walter or what type of medication he had been taking. She merely confirmed that his symptoms were the same as those described by Nurse Cummings.

In fact, the prosecution's star witness was David Cunningham, who, paradoxically, maintained that his mother was innocent. Deputy Prosecutor James McNeff was counting on "the mute testimony of his wasted limbs [and] the wan and drawn appearance of his features . . . to get to the jury," the *Post-Tribune* wrote.

On July 18 David was carried into court. Not having seen him in three months, Anna rushed over to his stretcher and screamed: "You know I didn't do it!" "Yes, mother, I know you didn't do it," David whispered back. David's formal testimony, limited to his medical history, was cut short by his physician. As he left, Mrs. Cunningham fainted.

The most critical issue was whether Mrs. Cunningham's confession should be admitted as evidence. With the jury sequestered, experts gave conflicting testimony as to whether Anna was sane and rational at the time she signed the document. Judge Smith ruled for the prosecution, saying that it was the jury's obligation to decide the matter of the confession's validity.

Defense attorneys Frank and Al Gavit hoped to destroy the credibility of the confession, to discredit the greed thesis, and above all, to demonstrate that Walter had died from natural causes. The defense had already beclouded the prosecution's claim of irrefutable proof that Walter had been poisoned. In his cross-examination of Dr. Frank P. Hunter of Purdue University, Frank Gavit established that the medical team had only done a qualitative analysis of Walter's vital organs and that, in the absence of a quantitative analysis, there was no scientific evidence on which to base conclusions regarding cause of death.

The Cook County coroner's office had done a quantitative analysis. Two members of its staff claimed that the amounts of arsenic exceeded ordinary medical dosages; but Dr. Albert Tannebaum, the chemist in charge of the postmortem analysis, testified that test results showed less than half a grain of arsenic in Walter's body, a "very minute amount" which in all probability was the result of Neo Salvarsan injections.

The defense summoned an impressive group of community leaders to testify on behalf of Mrs. Cunningham's character. Druggist Peter Honorof rebutted the confession's accuracy in regard to the manner in which the arsenic found in the Cunningham household was purchased. Mortician Floyd Williams described how Mrs. Cunningham insisted that her children receive the most expensive funeral arrangements. The Reverend O. E. Tomes characterized the defendant as a Christian mother whose grief caused her to lapse into shock following Walter's death. During times of stress, neighbor Marie Bauer testified, Anna's behavior was irrational; a stranger might think her normal, but she said things that did not square with reality.

A battery of medical experts also buttressed Anna's case, including two physicians who had examined her shortly before her confession and who concluded that she was temporarily insane. Dr. T. B. Templin said that she had been unconscious, with her hands clenched, her body rigid, and her pupils dilated, until awakened by stimulants and turned over to the custody of Sheriff Strong. She was prostrate, irrational, and extremely susceptible to suggestions and accusations at that time, Dr. Templin concluded.

Family doctor A. A. Watts told the court that Mrs. Cunningham insisted on consulting several specialists even after having been told that Walter's condition was hopeless. Three of these physicians testified how eye and spinal fluid and blood tests confirmed the existence of a congenital defect. Dr. B. W. Harris told of prescribing Neo Salvarsan, a drug containing arsenic, as an antidote for Walter's symptoms.

Anna Cunningham told the jury about her humble origins in Manotowe, Wisconsin, of quitting school after fourth grade to do farm chores and having no social life apart from her children. She described the trance-like spell that overtook her for several days after having been taken into custody as similar to the breakdown which she suffered after the deaths of her children. All she could remember about these episodes, Anna said, was hearing strange voices speaking to her. She vehemently denied the confession's statement that she was resentful toward her surviving daughter. "I loved Mae as much as I did any of the children, and I loved them all dearly," she said.

In their final arguments the defense attorneys declared that David's illness was not at issue, that one could not be convicted on the strength of a confession alone, and that there had not been enough poison in Walter's body to "kill a canary." The prosecution, on the other hand, stressed that the multiple deaths showed a recurrent pattern of suspicious events from which there was only one possible conclusion: premeditated murder. Before the jury retired to consider its verdict, Judge Martin Smith ruled out the possibility of a compromise decision, declaring that the defendant was either guilty or not guilty of premeditated murder.

The jury remained deadlocked for more than 26 hours. "God won't let them convict me—for He knows that I am innocent," the defendant exclaimed. That evening she and her daughter prayed together in her cell. Next morning the jury asked for a mathematics textbook to compute the amount of arsenic found in Walter's vital organs. Judge Smith denied the request on the ground that the material was not already in evidence. By 3:20 P.M. the jury had reached a verdict of guilty and recommended a sentence of life imprisonment. Told of the verdict in his hospital bed, David Cunningham said, "I know my mother didn't do it."

The *Post-Tribune* called the verdict just, even though it disagreed with the prosecution's contention that Mrs. Cunningham was a sane, cold-blooded murderer. In its headlines it had done much to prejudice the case against the "Poison Mother," and on one occasion an arsenic bottle was juxtaposed directly below her photograph.

The *Post-Tribune* coverage also was unfair to Anna's daughter Mae, taking its cue from the unflattering confession portrait. Even though Mae stood behind her mother and obtained good counsel for her, the press scolded her for not visiting the jail every day and for getting married a few weeks before the trial.

For three months, Anna Cunningham remained in a Crown Point cell while her lawyers unsuccessfully appealed the decision. Then on October 12, 1925, she entered Women's Prison in Indianapolis. There she stayed for seven years.

Meanwhile Mae doggedly fought to free her. Aided by the Gavits and two family doctors, Mrs. Cunningham won a parole board review of the case when Nurses Minnie Ginder and Helen Cummings amended their crucial trial testimony and admitted that David's symptoms might not have stemmed from arsenic poisoning. After an exhaustive investigation, the parole board concluded that Mrs. Cunningham had been the victim of a miscarriage of justice and should be set free. When Prosecutor August Bremer, Sheriff Ben Strong, and Judge Martin Smith raised no objections, Governor Harry G. Leslie commuted Anna's sentence and ordered her released in her daughter's care.

Thus, on October 12, 1932, the 57-year-old inmate returned to Gary to stay with her daughter, her son-in-law, and 30-year-old David Cunningham, who had recovered from his paralytic disease. Her release did not make the front page of the *Post-Tribune,* and few people realized that she had been cleared of poisoning her children.

"WE WON'T GO BACK UNTIL EMERSON'S WHITE"

"The devil came back Monday morning to worry the Negro citizenry of Gary, to stir the state of Indiana, and to arrest the attention of the whole world," wrote the Gary *Sun* about the 1927 Emerson School strike. At issue during the five-day boycott were the questions of integration and equal educational opportunities for black students. The "cruel, stupid, and un-American mob action," to quote the Chicago *Tribune,* retarded racial progress, led to the adoption of Jim

Crow practices, and stained the reputation of the city's educational system.

For several years prior to 1927 a few blacks had been attending Emerson without incident. Why then did the transfer of a mere 18 black students from Virginia Street School cause such a stir? School officials selected intelligent, well-mannered, light-skinned youths to minimize the likelihood of friction. Nonetheless, white parents feared it was the opening wedge to integrate the Gary schools. School officials expected some opposition to the transfer and hoped to promote sentiment in favor of constructing a new school in order to keep up with the large-scale black migration to Gary.

Rumors of a boycott spread following the arrival at Emerson on September 19 of the transfer students. Resentment tended to be strongest among those who came from the least affluent Northside families, from those who worried about the possibility of too intimate social intercourse between the races and the effect that this would have on their children's manners and morals.

The strike began almost by accident on September 26 when a janitor neglected to unlock the auditorium doors in time for first period class, causing a crowd to congregate in the corridors. As two black girls walked by, someone exclaimed: "Let's get out of here until they get rid of the niggers." Others took up the chant and began snakedancing down the halls, calling out for their friends to join them in a walkout.

Approximately 600 students paraded down Broadway with make-shift placards that proclaimed, "We won't go back until Emerson's white." Two-thirds of the students returned to school in time for the 10:15 roster check, but the others held a rally at East Side Park and proclaimed their intention to take a "school holiday" until the black students were ousted.

Principal E. A. Spaulding had harsh words for the "foolish show-offs" who participated in the boycott and predicted that things would be back to normal the following day. But on Tuesday morning, as 800 students milled around the school grounds and refused to go inside, Spaulding announced a special assembly open to strikers and non-strikers alike for the purpose of having Superintendent Wirt explain why the transfers had taken place.

Overcrowding and a limited budget made integration a temporary expedient until funds could be found for an all-black school, Wirt told the students. He blamed the crisis on false predictions concerning more transfers of blacks into Emerson. He stated that all but 50 of Gary's 3,000 black pupils were in segregated classrooms and concluded that those in the audience who went on to college would probably encounter more Negroes there than at Emerson.

Hecklers interrupted Wirt's remarks on several occasions with jeers and strike chants. During the question period, leaders of the boycott beseeched classmates to join the cause. According to the *Post-Tribune*, when one student cautioned patience, "he was howled and hissed down by the noisy students."

Wirt's public position that "segregation is impossible now" was echoed by school board member Henry G. Hay, who announced that segregation would be lawful only if there was a black school equal in quality to Emerson. Rather than defend integration as a laudable goal, Wirt and Hay argued that it was a regrettable necessity. For some time, Wirt had believed that the best solution to the "race question" would be the construction of a new black high school. He now used the strike as an excuse to lobby for the necessary appropriations.

Had Gary's civic officials been committed to integration, they could have enforced the truancy laws against those strikers under the age of 16 and suspended the older ones. Early in the week, the police were mobilized to prevent strikers from trespassing on school property or marching in the streets, but at the last minute they were told not to interfere with boycott activities.

On the third day of the boycott, half of Emerson's students stayed away from classes. The boycott gained momentum because school officials allowed the dissidents to use facilities at Emerson for strategy meetings and opened negotiations with the strike leaders. These actions permitted a holiday atmosphere to intrude upon a gravely serious situation and indirectly legitimatized the boycott.

At a mass meeting in the Emerson auditorium on Wednesday morning, senior class president Sam Chase and student council member Jack Keener opposed the strike. Chase argued that ample channels of communication existed for the arbitration of student grievances. Added Keener: "I think you should return to school and settle this question sanely. . . ."

There was a hostile reaction to these pleas for tolerance and moderation. Leonard Boynton, who claimed to have been the first person to leave Emerson on Monday morning, suggested that Keener and Chase be removed from their student government posts, and a cry went up for new elections. Later it was decided to parade down Broadway again, and the strikers stormed out of the school. As the march proceeded downtown, Mayor Floyd E. Williams doffed his hat and applauded the Emerson band, as it passed by him in full uniform playing a fight song.

Although it was generally believed that most Emerson students supported the strike, student leader Keener thought that a small but vocal pressure group had stagemanaged the incident and that city officials and the press had played into their hands. Keener's opposition sprang from his religious convictions and from his acquaintance with several black people, including Emerson track star Bob Anderson and his postman, a college-educated music teacher who could not obtain a position equal to his talents. "I was planning to go off to college myself," said Keener, "and I took a dim view of a man with a college degree having to handle the mail."

On Thursday, September 29, Superintendent Wirt warned students to be back in school by 8:15 the next morning or face severe reprisals. That evening, however, the strike committee won its demands for amnesty, in the form of excused absences, and for the ouster of all blacks within 90 days except for graduating seniors who had not recently transferred to Emerson. The decision was reached by the school board in consultation with a number of community leaders brought together by the mayor, including William P. Gleason and Horace S. Norton. As part of the deal, Mayor Williams and prominent councilmen promised to support enabling legislation for a new black high school. At a special council session, a bill appropriating $15,000 for a temporary school building and $600,000 for a permanent structure at 25th and Harrison passed first reading.

Early Friday morning, Emerson students filed into the auditorium to hear the terms of the agreement. Less than 15 minutes after the meeting began, they voted overwhelmingly to return to classes. The boycott was over. For most Emersonians, thoughts turned to football and other rites of autumn.

Until Roosevelt High School was ready for occupancy, however, there could be no pretense that the black students being retransferred out of Emerson—or, for that matter, the other 3,000 Negro pupils in the city—would receive "separate but equal" education. Perhaps the cruelest fate befell the handful of black undergraduates already at Emerson before the transfer issue arose; they were soon moved to an inferior institution.

Even before the strike settlement was reached, the black community had mobilized in opposition to the establishment of a segregated redistricting plan. Under the direction of Dr. James H. Garnett, a citizens' committee circulated petitions protesting actions which "will blight the noble work that has heretofore been done and bring about irreparable injury to this school system as well as inculcate a spirit of mob violence in the youth." Most Negroes in Gary viewed the agreement as a rejection of equal opportunity for their children. Some doubted that the promised permanent school would even be built. In any case, the most articulate spokesmen in Gary's black community advocated an integrated school system.

On October 3, 1927, as the City Council met to consider final approval of the strike settlement, the room was filled with black demonstrators who presented a resolution asking that the ordinance sanctioning a new segregated school be tabled. One speaker declared that the $15,000 earmarked for the temporary building would provide little more than a "telephone booth" and that the proposed site was swampland with no sidewalks, lights, or sewers.

The council rejected a motion to table the ordinance. Then Councilman A. B. Whitlock spoke against the proposal. Castigating the surrender to "mob rule," he said that whereas "poor white trash" had fomented the trouble, Gary's best citizens had now come upon a day of reckoning because if they passed the ordinance under consideration, they would be telling members of his race that they were unwelcome in the city. Whitlock concluded by asking that his written remarks be registered as a part of the official minutes. Chairman Merritt Martindale, paymaster at Gary Works, ruled his request out of order.

Prior to the final vote, Martindale made an appeal to his three black colleagues on the council, William Burrus, A. B. Whitlock, and Dr. S. R. Blackwell, to vote for the ordinance in the interest of harmony. According to the *Post-Tribune,* Martindale said: "Now I'm talking to you, Bill, 'A. B.,' and 'Doc,' and I want you to listen to me. We've got to vote for this ordinance and make it possible for those colored youngsters to go to school, where they can learn and learn right."

Oblivious to the looks of disbelief in the audience, Martindale continued: "Gary needs its colored folks, boys, and this council needs you. Gary couldn't do without you and you know it, but there is that difference in our color and race which we cannot overlook. These colored children shouldn't be in Emerson school among those white children and you know it . . . because they don't belong there."

The council then passed the ordinance, 10 to 3, with Burrus, Whitlock, and Blackwell dissenting. It later was ruled that the council had exceeded its authority in appropriating the $15,000, and a temporary building was never built.

The black community reacted to the plans for Roosevelt High

School with mixed feelings. Some people, reflecting the philosophy of black separatist Marcus Garvey, argued that an all-black institution would foster race pride and would be preferable to blacks being treated as second-class citizens at predominantly white schools. For example, at the dedication ceremonies four years later, Roosevelt's first principal, F. C. McFarlane, declared that "every race has its own contribution to make to cultural progress. At Roosevelt we will try to teach the Negro youth to value his own background with its African overtones."

The NAACP continued to protest the retreat from integration. National officer James Weldon Johnson came to Gary in November 1927 to lend support to legal action to prevent the segregation arrangement from being implemented. In December, however, Circuit Court Judge Grant Crumpacker dismissed the NAACP suit.

In January 1928 Superintendent Wirt informed the eight female transfer students who still remained at Emerson that they were being sent back to the Virginia Street School. When they complained that there were inadequate college preparatory courses there, he promised to supply them with tutors. After this failed to mollify them, Wirt allegedly replied that the matter was out of his hands and that his superiors "want the schools of Gary to be like those of Birmingham, Alabama."

Three of the eight girls fought their ouster from Emerson. In seeking aid from the NAACP, one girl wrote that facilities at the Virginia Street School were so crowded that both sexes had to take gym classes together. There were no lockers, labs, or library there. She also complained that several Emerson teachers had segregated the black students in corners of their rooms and tried to forget about them, but she added that she needed the language courses there in order to get into college.

NAACP attorney Edward McKinley Bacoyn argued the civil rights case on the narrow basis of whether a school board could transfer someone from an accredited to a nonaccredited school on the basis of race. In the summer of 1928 Judge Grant Crumpacker ruled against the three plaintiffs, who had spent the rest of the academic year commuting to a private school in Chicago.

With the institution of segregation in the public schools, Gary's black people were forced to make the best of a bad situation. They took pride in Roosevelt High School, but as NAACP leader Joseph A. Pitts noted, it took 40 years to complete all its promised facilities. Some blacks continued to attend Froebel, but they were put into separate classrooms, could not join the band or most clubs, and could only use the swimming pool on the day before it was cleaned. They could participate in sports but not take showers with the white athletes. These practices, some felt, were designed to encourage blacks to transfer voluntarily to Roosevelt.

The Emerson School strike succeeded because civic leaders were not committed to integration and too willingly bowed to the vigilante actions of a small pressure group which may or may not have reflected student opinion or community sentiment. Principal Spaulding later condoned the strike and remembered how "some white kids [had] chased a Negro boy down the street, caught him, and painted him white." Chuckling as he finished the anecdote, he said: "You know, they did it just for a prank. The colored boy knew it, too. He didn't care. He took it like a man."

In the November 26, 1927, issue of *School and Society* C. Victor Cools wrote that "the whole country has been stirred one way or another by the strike." Most Southern newspapers treated the walkout favorably, but in the North the view prevailed that it had been a setback for integration and the reputation of the Wirt schools.

PROHIBITION: THE PATH NOT TAKEN

Throughout the 1920s, it was easy to obtain illegal alcoholic beverages in Gary. Inside hotels, soft drink parlors, luncheonettes, pool halls, and private homes, people brought out their beer mugs, popped champagne bottles, filled their cocktail tumblers, emptied their shot glasses, and sampled the latest bootleg import or "alky" home brew. The proliferation of such speakeasies as the Chicken Shack, the Chicken Farm, and Louisiana May's Kitchen attested to the failure of the "Noble Experiment." The worst of them attracted prostitutes and gamblers and were a lucrative source of revenue for underworld czars, "night mayors" looking for payoffs, and petty racketeers of all types. At the Chicken Farm, for example, call-girl "Little Eva" lured men to her apartment and tranquilized them with chloroform so that two accomplices could mug them. The racket ended when Eva took pity on a client and warned him in time for him to call the police.

Most Garyites did not receive the Eighteenth Amendment with elation and refused to obey it. Rather than purifying lives, prohibition bred disrespect for the law, increased tensions between immigrants and native-born Americans, and corrupted the processes of government. Speakeasies such as the Broadway Inn, the Jefferson Inn, and the Senate, located between 10th and 14th avenues, attracted a mixed clientele of doctors, lawyers, junior executives, reporters, and millworkers. For 75 cents one could purchase a shot of the best Canadian bourbon. A bottle of "Needle" beer sold for 25 cents, as did low-grade moonshine made from such sundry ingredients as potato peelings. Most drinkers could not afford a regular diet of imported liquor but made do with the cheaper but much more powerful variety, sometimes even brewing their own. Once in a while, an old resident declared, "you would get some bad stuff and land in the hospital."

In 1921 mayoralty candidate R. O. Johnson campaigned openly for the "wet" vote, causing the *Daily-Tribune* to warn that his victory would open the gates for such vice barons as Gasperi Monti, "Big Jim" Caesar, and "Dago" Mangano. Johnson's victory was to some extent a "nay" vote on prohibition enforcement. In fact, according to Erwin Crewe Rosenau, the mayor had one of the best supplies of corn liquor in the city and from time to time gave free samples to reporters.

Within a year of Johnson's inauguration, a federal grand jury began investigating links between city officials and the liquor trade. In 1923 Mayor Johnson was convicted of conspiring to violate the Volstead Act; and in 1925, after his appeals were exhausted, he went to a federal penitentiary in Atlanta, Georgia.

Ninety percent of the 4,000 criminal cases in city court in 1923 involved liquor violations. This represented, of course, just the tip of an iceberg of criminal activity. One man caught with 1,500 gallons of wine told the judge that the police had searched his cellar on seven previous occasions and just winked at him. Others discovered that fines for liquor and gambling violations were so small that speakeasies could recoup their losses in an hour and go right on about their business. County officials were generally more vigilant enforcers of prohibition than the city police. The prosecutor's office operated on a fee system and pocketed 25 dollars for each fine collected.

Mass arrests, however, failed to amend most people's drinking habits. Even the bold midday assassination of gangster Gasperi Monti failed to erase the charismatic appeal that men of his profession enjoyed in some quarters. Carried out by gunmen who sped by the Italian Club at the precise moment to trap Monti, the rival gang had planned its "hit" with such precision, the *Post-Tribune* marveled, that the victim did not even have time to get his hands out of his pockets.

At middecade, one federal judge threatened to "shut up the whole town of Gary if we cannot stop liquor law violators there any other way." Mayor Johnson's successors did not reverse the situation, except to order a few ritualistic crackdowns on the most notorious nightspots and on small-time owners of stills. Chicago mobsters periodically "cooled their heels" at the Hotel Gary, where they were furnished with call girls. Prohibition lacked both the public and the political support necessary to make compliance a realistic possibility.

The manner in which Gary's news media handled the prohibition issue from 1920 to 1933 reflected a changing sentiment from "high hopes" to disillusionment concerning the feasibility of legislating morality. After advocating compliance and strict enforcement during the early 1920s, the press lost interest in the crusade.

At first, the *Daily Tribune,* and the *Evening Post,* (which merged during the summer of 1921), blamed liquor violations for the upswing in marital discord, sexual depravity, crime, lunacy, arson, and other wanton behavior. On January 21, 1921, the *Evening Post* reported that a father had given whiskey to his 11-year-old daughter and then had allowed a man in his sixties to take liberties with her. A month later, the paper told of a moonshine-crazed husband who tore off his wife's clothes and threatened to kill her. Commenting about a drunken suicide victim on March 3, 1921, the *Evening Post* declared that the consumption of bootleg alcohol commonly resulted in maniacal behavior. Three months later, the paper ran the following headline: "MOONSHINE BLAMED FOR WAVE OF INSANITY CASES IN CITY; AVERAGE ONE DAILY."

The tendency to blame all cases of aberrant behavior on moonshine whiskey sometimes backfired. On July 10, 1922, the *Post-Tribune* dramatically announced: "WIFE KILLS LIQUOR CRAZED MATE." The article claimed that a woman had rescued her infant from her drunken husband and, in mortal danger, shot him in self-defense. When subsequent investigation indicated that the couple had previously engaged in a heated quarrel and that she had paid up his life insurance policy three hours before his death, the *Post-Tribune* headlined its next story: "WIFE WHO SHOT HUBBY FACES MURDER CHARGE."

On April 10, 1922, the *Post-Tribune* castigated those who did not take the drinking laws seriously. "Have you noticed how many otherwise law abiding citizens are boasting about their acquaintance with hooch vendors?" the paper said. "In some quarters," the editorial continued, " 'my bootlegger' is becoming as common an expression as 'my barber' or 'my doctor.' This is something new under the sun —a criminal aristocracy."

While the *Post-Tribune* criticized Gary's professional elite in the

"My Bootlegger" editorial, most of its prohibition articles dealt with poor people. For example, on January 21, 1924, the paper announced that an immigrant had shot his wife's lover, writing that the "killer" was "broken in health" and showed the "outward appearance of having been conquered by the demon, moonshine whiskey. . . ." The following day, after the man gashed his head on the floor of his cell, the paper speculated that he was deranged. Two months later, he was found guilty and sentenced to life imprisonment.

In September 1924, reporting that an intoxicated alien had attacked and murdered a nine-year-old girl, the *Post-Tribune* stated that the child-slayer looked "the part of the foul fiendish killer of a little girl. . . . His face is weak. His eyes are unsteady. He is shy and meek. . . . His cheeks are sunken. His chin is sharp. . . ." At the man's trial the victim's mother tried to hit him with a paving brick. He was convicted and received the death penalty.

In contrast to the banner stories of moonshine tragedy and the somber editorial pronouncements of the *Post-Tribune,* humorist Tom Cannon poked fun at prohibition. A man who did not allow the Eighteenth Amendment to deter him from his noontime and evening "constitutional," Cannon in 1922 and 1923 put these items in his "Flue Dust" column: "The Gary man caught with imitation books containing liquor probably picked his library from the best cellar"; "Where moonshine comes from—is a secret still"; "Every week is clean-up week for Gary bootleggers"; "In Gary everybody used to duck when a man reached for his hip pocket. Now they crowd around him"; and "Now is the time for Gary bootleggers to have a rum-age sale of the old stuff."

During the late 1920s the *Post-Tribune* amended its attitude toward strict enforcement. Reporter E. C. Rosenau speculated that someone might have been paid off, or that the managing editor might have regarded continued defense of the Volstead Act as futile. He himself frequently patronized speakeasies. At any rate, by 1930 prohibition had proved a failure in Gary, and R. O. Johnson returned triumphantly for a third term as mayor. A survey revealed that six of seven Garyites opposed strict enforcement.

The last big federal undercover raids against Gary bootleggers occurred in September 1932. Six months later, incoming President Franklin D. Roosevelt announced his support for repeal of the Eighteenth Amendment. The "Sponge Squad" was officially disbanded, and Hoosiers voted to ratify the Twenty-first Amendment, by a seven to one margin in Gary. The *Post-Tribune* saw the result as proof that "too rapid progress is often made at the cost of wrecking the whole journey."

When prohibition was finally repealed in December 1933, celebrants rang the bell in the Crown Point courthouse for the first time since World War I.

The *Post-Tribune* reported that "bars are back in all their shining glory. Footrails disguised as steps and top pieces for elongated cuspidors running the full length of the bar, are back."

If the Twenty-first Amendment succeeded in raising government revenue and reducing hypocrisy in government, it did not end organized crime. Gangland slayings continued unabated in Gary among factions trying to monopolize the business of smuggling liquor into the city without paying taxes.

Because Indiana passed a law preventing the selling of hard liquor except in drug stores, a vestige of prohibition remained on the statute books, but like the more publicized laws, it went unenforced. As the *Post-Tribune* declared on December 5, 1933: "Anyone who wanted a drink of anything and had the price could walk a block or so and buy it."

THE ARLENE DRAVES CASE

No single local event in Gary's history received more notoriety or unleashed more passion than the Arlene Draves case. In November 1930 an attractive 18-year-old girl was repeatedly raped and beaten to death. Her assailants at first seemed to be typical examples of Gary youth. The man primarily responsible for the crime, a 20-year-old millworker named Virgil Kirkland, had been the victim's date during her final night of terror, and he was a former high school football star.

Arlene "Babe" Draves had met Kirkland in 1928 at the Gay-Mill Ballroom in Miller while she was a sophomore at Emerson and he a senior at Horace Mann. According to one of Arlene's classmates, he became "her hero, her god. . . . Everybody talked about him—not just everybody in school, but people all over town, everywhere."

Despite this infatuation, Arlene apparently did not see much of Kirkland until two years later. She was not allowed to go out on dates, and so their meetings were restricted to a few chance encounters and a visit she paid him, accompanied by a friend, when he was briefly hospitalized by a football injury.

In her senior year Arlene became engaged unofficially to someone else. In the fall of 1930, however, Kirkland visited her a few times at her married sister's house where she had gone to live following graduation. Caught between conflicting desires—her old flame and settling down to marriage—Arlene went to several parties with Kirkland without telling her fiancé. Kirkland seemed to enjoy wooing

Arlene and once even announced that he was going to marry her. He privately told an acquaintance, however, that he was frustrated at not "getting anything off Babe" but that things would be different the next time they were together.

That fateful occasion occurred on November 29, 1930. Virgil took Arlene to a party in Glen Park. It was a lively but not abnormally wild party, as charged later in the press, although quite a bit of alcohol was consumed. The 17 or 18 guests talked, popped corn, flirted, spooned, and danced to the radio.

Around 11:00 P.M. Virgil took Arlene out to the front porch. He had had several highballs and was "a little drunk but could still walk straight," a friend remembered. Arlene had been nursing a tumbler of wine most of the evening (she disliked hard liquor) and was "quite sober" according to several guests.

Fifteen minutes later, another couple joined Virgil and Arlene outside. The man heard them arguing, while seated on a settee. When she repeatedly begged to go home, he slapped her. Suddenly she fell on the floor. When the onlooker went to her aid, Kirkland warned him to leave them alone, that they were just having a lovers' quarrel.

Kirkland then rounded up some friends for the alleged purpose of getting something to eat, and they drove off with Virgil and Arlene in the back seat. On the way to a restaurant, he told the driver to stop at a secluded spot near 43rd and Connecticut and raped the dazed girl. At his urging others joined in the assault.

An hour later, the men returned to the party and began joking in hushed tones about "the one in the car." Kirkland and four friends then walked to the roadster where Arlene's body, naked from the waist down, lay limp and unmoving. Several men raped her or—to quote from two of their statements to police—started to and then "became disgusted" or impotent from alcohol.

When the party broke up, a woman noticed Arlene's unconscious and disheveled body in the back seat of the car. Touching it, she found it unnaturally cold. Kirkland chased her away and told her to mind her own business. Kirkland then wrapped a coat around Arlene and sped off with six friends. After four of them were dropped off, the others cruised around until Kirkland finally decided that Arlene needed medical attention. She had been unconscious for a long time and showed no signs of life, even after Kirkland rubbed her face with snow.

Arriving at the home of Dr. R. O. Wharton at 3:00 A.M., Kirkland dressed Arlene as best he could and carried the body inside with the help of his two friends. After the physician pronounced her dead, the men ran out his front door. Wharton told them to halt, fired shots at the fleeing automobile, and then called the police.

Meanwhile, Kirkland went to the home of Arlene's sister and brother-in-law and told them that "Arlene is dead. She fell and killed herself." As the husband telephoned the police, Virgil exclaimed: "Well, I'm sunk."

By 6:00 A.M. Arlene's battered body was at the city morgue. Coroner Chester A. Owen and Dr. James Burcham, who performed the autopsy, took note of two dozen cuts and bruises on the forehead, chin, neck, face, elbows, breasts, and knees. There was also a blood clot "the size of a hen's egg" by her skull. They determined that she had died shortly after midnight from an intracranial hemorrhage and from shock induced by criminal attacks. In the presence of several witnesses, Kirkland confessed to having sexually violated her. Four of his friends subsequently admitted their participation in the attack.

News of the Draves murder electrified the city. The five prisoners were former high school sports stars. One was the son of the fire chief. Friends described the victim as a vivacious, morally upright girl of considerable popularity and talent. The previous year she had starred in Emerson's "spice and variety show."

The *Post-Tribune*'s first reports blamed the tragedy on bootleg alcohol. A search was on, the paper stated, to apprehend the person who sold the youths the "poisoned hootch." A defense attorney took up this theme, telling reporters, "Don't blame the boys, blame prohibition liquor. These boys are not criminals. They are the victims of the laws which govern the society in which they live." Similarly, a defendant's mother was quoted as saying, "I blame the wicked prohibition law."

To Arlene's father this line of reasoning was nonsensical. Pointing out that, according to eyewitnesses, neither Arlene nor Kirkland was drunk, he demanded that those found guilty be sentenced to death. "There are hundreds of parties held every week in which booze plays a vital part, but there aren't young girls criminally attacked at them," Charles Draves said.

The Chicago *American*, a Hearst tabloid, treated the defendants sympathetically. Without proof, it insinuated that Arlene was a loose woman and charged that the police coerced the "boys" to confess, that a lynch mob mentality had engulfed the "Steel City," and that there was a drinking problem of "staggering proportions" among Gary students.

Viewing these accusations as scurrilous, the *Post-Tribune* began increasingly to emphasize lack of parental control and individual misbehavior as causes of the crime rather than prohibition. Furthermore, the rumor that the liquor consumed at the Glen Park party was poisonous proved false. Mayor Johnson asserted that Gary was a better governed city than Chicago and a more desirable place to live. He repeated an oft-given vow to make Gary the driest city in the state.

In a similar vein, Superintendent William A. Wirt denounced the Chicago press for having misrepresented the defendants' ages and for having erroneously implied that they were presently students. In fact, one of them had been out of school for seven years. Kirkland had been expelled for "immoral conduct" and had never graduated. They were wild adults, not teen-age boys, Wirt concluded, adding: "The Draves tragedy, so far as I can see, took place outside of school."

On December 9, 1930, a grand jury indicted the five defendants on counts of assaulting, criminally attacking, and murdering Arlene Draves. Kirkland's lawyers won motions for a change of venue to Porter County and for a separate trial to begin in Valparaiso on February 23, 1931, in the courtroom of Circuit Court Judge Grant Crumpacker.

From the first gavel, the "Whoopie Trial" or "Orgy Murder," as it was tastelessly labeled by the news media, attracted hordes of spectators. On one occasion, the courtroom became so unruly that Judge Crumpacker moved the proceedings across the hall to a larger chamber. The incident almost provoked a riot, a reporter wrote, as spectators "propped themselves on railings, squeezed themselves into corners . . . , and defied all efforts to eject them."

Kirkland's mother told reporters that her son was the victim of a witch-hunt. Nonetheless, the defendant appeared to be enjoying the notoriety and told reporters that except for missing the basketball sectionals, "I've enjoyed my stay with Sheriff Burney Maxwell."

Jury selection was a tedious task since the case had attracted so much pretrial publicity. After 12 men were finally sworn in, the *Post-Tribune* reported their marital status and the ages of their children, thus dramatizing the paper's editorial position that the crime was an offense against the institutions of womanhood and family.

Lake County Prosecutor Robert G. Estill and his assistants presented a formidable case against Kirkland. Although Judge Crumpacker disallowed the confession, which had since been repudiated, police told of Kirkland's conduct at the city morgue in the early hours of November 30, 1930, when, confronted with the battered corpse, he put his head on a policeman's shoulder and "admitted every-

thing." Several witnesses, including Coroner Chester A. Owen, testified that Kirkland confessed to having attacked Miss Draves three
times. Among the incriminating pieces of evidence were a blood-
stained seatcover, Kirkland's bloody shirt, two shirt buttons found in
the car, and the victim's torn undergarments.

Two witnesses declared that, prior to his last date with Arlene,
Kirkland told them that he was going to seduce "Babe" or "beat the
hell out of her." During cross-examination one of them was asked
how well he knew Kirkland.

"Casually," he answered.

"Wasn't it a rather intimate conversation you carried on with a
mere acquaintance?" he was asked.

"It wasn't intimate among the young people of Gary," he replied.

Testimony describing the events at the snack bar, where Kirkland
and his friends went after first raping Arlene, revealed the apathy of
bystanders toward her plight. An employee recollected that Kirkland came inside several minutes after his friends, slapped his fist into
his palm, and said: "Boy, I sure gave it to her that time." Then he told
someone who called him "rat" that there was "a girl out there
drunker than hell." Kirkland bragged to several customers about his
conquest. A policeman nearby did not involve himself in the affair,
even though he saw blood on Kirkland's hands. Neither did several
passersby outside who noticed Arlene's limp body in the car. After
buying hamburgers, Kirkland asked a man to feel Arlene's pulse. "I
believe she's dead," Kirkland told him. Asked on the stand why he
did not raise an alarm, the man replied that he thought the woman
was just in an alcoholic stupor.

The defense team, led by the renowned Chicagoan Barrett
O'Hara, claimed that Miss Draves had died from an accidental fall
while under the influence of alcohol. The coroner had concluded,
however, that the alcoholic content in Arlene's stomach was inconsequential, that her multiple wounds ruled out accidental death, and
that there were unmistakable signs of criminal attack.

After the prosecution rested, O'Hara demanded that the corpse be
exhumed. Judge Crumpacker granted the motion; and the next day,
in the tiny hamlet of Reynolds, 300 spectators hiked through eight
inches of snow to see what one local resident called the "biggest
event in White County in years."

On March 4 a Chicago physician hired by the defense claimed that
the original autopsy findings were in error and that there was no
conclusive evidence of criminal assault. Questioned about the multiple wounds, he replied lamely that the victim had delicate skin and

bruised easily. His conclusions were later challenged by prosecution experts.

The defense team then attempted to convince the jury that Miss Draves had willingly engaged in intercourse with Kirkland. Although several witnesses told of Arlene's attachment to Kirkland, this claim rested solely on the unverified testimony of the defendant himself, who took the stand on March 6.

Under O'Hara's guidance, Kirkland recounted his relationship with Miss Draves. According to reporters, his expression during the early phases of the trial had been one of apathy, but now he frequently sobbed, causing O'Hara to say, "Brace up, boy. . . . Just tell the truth."

Tension in the courtroom peaked as Kirkland described the front porch episode at the party. This is how the *Post-Tribune* reported the scene:

> O'Hara: "Virgil, when you were on the settee, were there any sexual relations? You've got to answer, boy. You have got to answer."
> Virgil hung his head.
> Deputy Prosecutor John Underwood: "Oh, he'll answer all right."
> O'Hara: "You've got to answer, boy. You've got to answer."
> Underwood: "I object to this line of questioning."
> O'Hara: "I'm only trying to be decent in the presence of this tragedy . . . go on, Virgil."
> Virgil wept, then raised his head and said, "yes," through trembling lips.

Regaining his composure, Kirkland described how Arlene appeared dazed after the seduction, so he gently rocked her head with his hands cupped over her ears. At his lawyer's request, Kirkland sat on the arm of the witness chair and imitated the rocking motion several times as O'Hara assumed the role of Miss Draves.

"Did the jury see that?" the barrister asked.

"Yeah, they saw it," Underwood replied sarcastically, drawing laughter from the audience.

Ignoring the sarcasm, O'Hara resumed his questioning until the judge implored: "Get out of the chair and let the witness sit down."

Kirkland denied slapping Arlene, as he had told police, but mentioned that she stumbled onto the floor and then "became kinda sleepy" so he thought a car ride might be good for her. He denied attacking her but could not swear that the others had not raped her while he was in the restaurant or back at the party.

Realizing that the four defendants had refused to testify on grounds of self-incrimination, he implied that they might have framed him. His lawyers took up this refrain in their final summations.

Telling the farmers and small-town businessmen on the jury that he was a simple country lawyer, defense attorney Ronald Oldham tried to persuade them that Kirkland was a victim of big city injustices. "The city coppers," he intoned, "are not to question why, they're to sleuth and lie." He charged that the prosecutors wanted to splatter Lake County with "Blood! Blood! Blood!" Oldham concluded with a description of the horrors of the electric chair and asked jurors to be guided by the biblical demand: "Thou shalt not kill."

The prosecution team replied that Kirkland was a "young hoodlum" whose belated expressions of love for Arlene were hypocritical and base. "Not even a dog or a wolf would have allowed another dog or wolf to violate its mate, as he did," one prosecutor said. Robert Estill concluded the prosecution's case by asking the panel to "vindicate Arlene Draves so that the white in the flag might still stand for purity and the red for courage."

The jurors deliberated a little more than two hours before finding Kirkland guilty of murder in the first degree. They fixed his punishment as life imprisonment. Eleven jurors had voted to send Kirkland to the electric chair, but the twelfth held out for a lesser penalty.

Kirkland remained calm after Judge Crumpacker read the verdict. He congratulated Estill on his "stirring" final speech, then winked at a friend and said: "Well, that was a tough game to lose." On the way back to his cell, he hummed the tune to a popular song entitled "Just a Gigolo," which contained these lines: "And when death comes I know, I'll be just a gigolo. And life goes on without me."

Before leaving, Barrett O'Hara embraced Mrs. Kirkland and said: "Be brave like those Spartan mothers who sent their sons forth to battle.... We'll have him home again with you in six months."

A month later, Judge Crumpacker threw out the decision on the grounds that the evidence did not support the requirement of premeditation. This made necessary a retrial.

The ruling unleashed a storm of protest, and the fact that Judge Crumpacker's son was one of Kirkland's attorneys added fuel to the flames. The brutal manner in which Miss Draves had been raped and beaten convinced many people that his life sentence had been, if anything, too mild.

Prosecutor Estill angrily announced that the defense strategy of having the first trial annulled would land Kirkland in the death house. Questioned about rumors that some of Kirkland's friends had offered to testify if given immunity, he rejected any plea bargaining on the grounds that he already had an "airtight" case.

When the second trial began, Judge Crumpacker denounced a published report that he would allow live radio coverage and forbade the selling of an illustrated pamphlet entitled "The Inside on the Virgil Kirkland Murder Case," which had become a best-selling newsstand item.

As in the first trial, the defense challenged all potential jurors who believed in the prohibition laws or who acknowledged a familiarity with the case. After hundreds of prospective jurors had been dismissed, Kirkland's lawyers admitted that their objective was to demonstrate the impossibility of a fair trial. Judge Crumpacker finally chose the 12-member panel himself from a random sample of Porter County residents, refusing to countenance further challenges by either side. This resolved the immediate stalemate but made questionable the quality of the jury.

The highlight of the second trial occurred when two of Kirkland's codefendants took the stand against him. They allegedly agreed to speak out without immunity over the objections of their lawyers because Kirkland's lack of remorse over what he did to Arlene disgusted them. When informed of their decision, Kirkland quipped, "I'll have to get some new pals now."

Both former "pals" corroborated the prosecution's charge of criminal attack and indicated that Kirkland had gotten others to rape Arlene in order to implicate them. One of them said that Kirkland had taunted him to assault Arlene with the words: "Go ahead—don't be a baby." The other recollected Kirkland urging friends at the party to go out to the car.

Realizing the damage done to his case, Kirkland added new details about his alleged love relationship with the deceased girl when he testified in his own defense. He claimed that their past intimacy nullified any need for him to have forced his will upon her and said that he once played strip poker with Arlene and two other friends (they denied it under oath). Maintaining his innocence, he charged that one of his two accusers had admitted raping Arlene and was now slandering him in order to save his own neck.

In an effort to establish "reasonable doubt," the defense held out the possibility of a gang rape without Kirkland's knowledge and the proposition that Miss Draves "became so drunk that she fell and killed herself." The deceased teen-ager was labeled a "shameless" temptress who loved "gin parties," whereas Kirkland was called a victim of "monstrous perjuries." One defense attorney even suggested that jealous wives might have beaten Arlene to death.

After much disagreement and confusion, the jury returned a verdict of guilty on the single count of assault and battery with intent to commit criminal attack. After the judge read the decision, Kirkland smiled broadly, but one of his lawyers was punched twice and called a "dirty rat" by a man whose daughter he had maligned.

During the ensuing confusion Estill tried to get Judge Crumpacker's attention in order to poll the jury individually. He was not recognized. The jurors were dismissed and filed out of the noisy room, followed by the judge. Reporters later learned that the 12-member panel had at first voted 10 to 2 for a first-degree murder conviction. Those ten jurors later released a statement to the effect that when they agreed to the verdict, they believed that it carried the death penalty. Judge Crumpacker had evidently given them no written instructions, and they recollected his saying that the crime of attempted rape resulting in death was a capital offense.

Crumpacker sentenced Kirkland to a 1–10 year sentence, a decision that was roundly criticized by the Attorney General of Indiana, who said that the statute called for 5 to 21 years. "The greatest tragic-comic farce in the history of Indiana courts"—that was State Senator C. Oliver Holmes' assessment of the trial and verdict. Another observer recollected: "If they would have been five Negroes, they would have been strung up."

Estill vowed to put pressure on parole boards for the next ten years in order to keep Kirkland behind bars for the maximum penalty. But in the judge's chambers, the prosecutor was less belligerent in his parting meeting with the defendant. "Be a good boy, Virgil," he advised. "Let this be a lesson to you."

Estill dropped charges against the other four defendants on the questionable rationale that further trials would just be exercises in futility. He told reporters: "I guess we may as well give the others medals and turn them loose."

That news drew this retort from Ed Draves, Arlene's brother: "If they won't try Kirkland's pals for murder, they can try me for murder.... Gary is not big enough for those boys and me, too."

The *Post-Tribune* viewed the decision as a defeat for law, order, and decency. The paper heaped scorn on Crumpacker for adjudicating one of his son's cases, for nullifying the original conviction, for allowing a "circus" atmosphere to reign in his courtroom, and for meting out such a light sentence.

For the Draves family, the decision was the culmination of a night-marish ordeal that had begun in shock and ended in bitterness. At the expense of an innocent victim, Kirkland's defense team had exploited a sexist value system that held women accountable for being raped unless their virtue was proved beyond a reasonable doubt. Perhaps it was this same moral cant that caused so many people to be unconcerned about Arlene Draves during the last hours of her life.

On August 27, 1937, Virgil Kirkland was paroled from Pendleton Reformatory on the condition that he not return to Lake County. "What more can we do or say?" an anguished sister of the dead girl said when notified of the decision. Her family had protested the release, but authorities said Kirkland was rehabilitated. On the day he got out of jail, reporters went to the Draves house for their comments. They found it boarded up.

CHAPTER SEVEN

The Onset of the Depression

Ye horrible depression!
Ye've turned my hair to gray;
All things in my possession
Ye've stolen quite away.

. . . .

My house is almost fallen down,
The rats run on the floor
I am the poorest man in town;
The wolf is at my door!

—"Flue Dust" poem by
"Quetzalcoatl"

FOR GARYITES THE depression left deep emotional scars and unpleasant memories of soup lines, flophouses, bank failures, sheriff's sales, and armies of the jobless gathered in hobo camps, lined up at mill gates, or protesting in the streets. For thousands of residents it meant the loss of a business, a job, a home, of self-respect or a sense of purpose. Fathers unable to provide for their families irrationally blamed themselves for seeing their children go without eyeglasses or winter coats or dental care. The humiliations often drove men to the brink of desertion.

GETTING THROUGH THE HARD TIMES

"How to get by?" That was the dominant dilemma in countless Gary households. Poor people converted their back yards into vegetable gardens, spent many hours canning, patched and repatched old

161

clothes, and sewed good parts of old sheets together. They bought day-old bread, haggled with the grocer for free soup bones, served their children black coffee instead of milk or juice, and outfitted them in 50-cent tennis shoes.

Just as President Hoover repeatedly claimed that prosperity was just around the corner, the *Post-Tribune* publicized every hint of an economic upswing. One resident remarked wryly that his alarm increased in direct proportion to the frequency and intensity of the paper's rosy forecasts.

On November 21, 1933, after conditions improved slightly, the *Post-Tribune* admitted that the Calumet Region had been one of the worst hit in the country. Even before then, news items belied the editorial optimism. For example, in 1932 there were large numbers of tax delinquencies, and two-thirds of Gary's hospital patients failed to pay their bills in full. School nurses reported many cases of malnutrition. During the summer the health department warned of the hazards to public health resulting from so many people having had their water turned off. Garyites were buying 40 percent less milk in 1932 than in 1930 despite a five-cent price reduction to nine cents a quart. In its advertisements Clover Leaf Dairy warned that children denied Vitamin D milk were susceptible to rickets.

According to historian Richard J. Meister, in 1932 "thousands of car owners in Gary drove their autos without plates." Less people used Gary's trolleys, and some customers became adept at sneaking past the driver. Many men walked downtown in order to save the nickel fare for fresh pastry or a glass of beer.

One of the most significant depression statistics concerned employment at the mills, which had sunk below 30 percent of capacity. Jobs were so scarce that rumors of openings attracted thousands of applicants. The bleak conditions caused some people to join Communist-led hunger marches or express their anger in even more violent ways. For example, while Cornelius Vanderbilt, Jr., was driving into Gary on the night of June 15, 1931, a large brick suddenly crashed through his window. He stopped his car and said, "What's the big idea?" From out of the darkness came the reply: "Just to teach you, you goddam millionaire, not to drive around in that bloody car of yours.... All rich guys ought to be strung up."

Seeing himself surrounded, Vanderbilt asked: "But who are you?"

"We're the fellows that'll do the stringing," came the reply.

Later, a hotel clerk told Vanderbilt that people in Gary were ready to do "much worse things any day now," because "their patience is at an end."

Shoplifting increased during the depression. Groceries, department stores, and pharmacies were hardest hit, but some thieves even haunted church coat racks. In court some defendants requested jail terms rather than suspended sentences so that they would not be forced into stealing again. Judges were sometimes lenient to petty thieves, but once a black man was sentenced to life imprisonment for stealing a 20-dollar tire on the dubious grounds that he was a third offender.

From time to time, the *Post-Tribune* ran poignant stories about depression victims. During the 1931 Thanksgiving holiday a charity officer found an abandoned 18-year-old woman and her sickly infant son on the steps of the Salvation Army citadel at 824 Washington. After the paper wrote about their plight, a Glen Park family offered them shelter.

In reporting a funeral arranged by the welfare department for Edward Garret, a retired druggist and night clerk who had fallen upon hard times, the *Post-Tribune* wrote: "His threadbare figure— always neat and white linen clean—could have been seen in a line awaiting sustenance at a soup kitchen on Adams Street."

The suicide rate did not skyrocket during the 1930s, as once believed, but public preoccupation with the phenomenon reflected the anxieties of the age. The self-inflicted death of a bank president precipitated the first of Gary's bank panics. A pioneer food dealer and a popular lunch stand proprietor shot themselves when faced with bankruptcy, and a 47-year-old unemployed steelworker swallowed carbolic acid because he was unable to provide for his wife and three children.

Many people registered their frustrations in the *Post-Tribune's* "Voice of The People" column. With jobs so precious, there was resentment that non-Garyites, aliens, "Hill Billies," and women were taking work away from the more deserving. One letter, signed by "Helpful Henrietta," urged wives to quit work. It sparked a spirited debate. One of Henrietta's critics declared: "I was once a taken-care-of wife, too, but Hubby's job was closed out, and after four years of unsteady work he is now making $20 a week."

Readers frequently complained about wild dogs turned loose by owners too poor to care for them. Mothers allegedly had to guard their children "with brooms to keep off the homeless animals that range over the East Side in packs, like wolves."

A rash of dog-biting incidents raised fears of blood poisoning or a rabies epidemic. Revising an old newspaper maxim, Police Captain William A. Forbis declared: "If a dog bites a man, that's not news. But if seven dogs bite seven persons, that's very serious and very bad news."

To combat this menace, the police shot dogs that had no collars or muzzles. Patrolmen could earn "pin money" by selling the carcasses to the Chicago stockyards. Because the most dangerous dogs were the hardest to catch, the police concentrated less on killing wild dogs than domesticated pets, which they sometimes gunned down in full view of the children to whom they belonged. In June 1937 there was considerable anger over the shooting of a dog named Boots who had entertained downtowners for more than a decade with his tricks and affable personality. A month later, Health Inspector William F. Smith warned that 9,000 strays were still on the loose and were a danger to the public health.

DEPRESSION ENTERTAINMENT

The hard times caused people to adjust their recreational tastes somewhat. Parlor games came back in vogue. The radio was an enormously popular form of entertainment. In 1931 librarian W. J. Hamilton announced that circulation had risen dramatically, especially of practical books about gardening, budgeting, medicine, and the like.

During the 1930s, movies remained a relatively inexpensive means of forgetting, for the moment, about the harsh realities of life. Managers attracted customers with double features, amateur nights, jitterbug contests, bingo games, and raffles. The Tivoli once offered all women patrons a piece of "Pettipoint Cockatoo" chinaware, and rival theatres responded with similar giveaways.

The Palace Theatre's "Bank Night" offered prizes to lottery winners on the condition that they attended the drawing. One man reported: "Sitting on the steps on the top of the balcony, I spied an elderly woman almost in rags. In her hand was a holy rosary. She was wishing, hoping and even praying that she might win in order to purchase for her children clothes, food, and coal. . . ."

The depression killed off vaudeville and ended most theatre stage shows. The Gary Theatre fought against an income squeeze by showing such "adults-only" films as *This Nude World, Polygamy, Elysia: The Valley of the Nude,* and *Marihuana: Weed with Roots in Hell.*

Live entertainment could be found in such taverns and night clubs as the Boogy Woogy Club, which offered "wine, dine, and dancing." The new Miramar Gardens advertised a "Hi-Hat Revue," while Budweiser Café patrons could eye "shawl dancer" Carmelita Mondoza, "soubrette" Bobby Baker, and exotic dancer Olga "Hotter Than Hades" Petrovich.

Many of Gary's 220 bars had live combos. One observer captured the frenetic mood at a typical 1930s night spot: "Couples plastered against each other moved as a body in the oneness of a dance hall tango. Paunchy salesmen with ten-cent-store girls hanging from their necks stomped dumbly around the floor. As the crooner crooned about the moon in June, thin-haired waspish soda jerkers emitting strong aromas of lilac vegetal or medicinal soap moaned in falsetto voice to their switchboard girl friends. Without allowance for a conclusion to the slow hesitation waltz, the leader drew a tiger rag from his musicians. Couples started tearing around the floor, stimulating the hot musk and sudden blaze of lights. Round and round they whirled until they saw nothing but a revolving blear of lights, faces, and table covers."

Walter J. Kelly, a gambling "czar" who had moved to Gary in 1935 after serving time in federal prison for selling narcotics, hoped to attract an integrated clientele to a lavish cabaret at 1819 Washington. Although it had a magnificent bar, three dance floors, a stage, and an outdoor garden, so few customers patronized it that Kelly said: "If I ever open another joint, it'll be one with a swinging door and sawdust on the floor." Soon afterwards, Kelly was gunned down by Chicago gangsters, and his club became a poolroom.

In May 1935 a chain-letter phenomenon swept Gary. By paying out four dimes and circulating four lists of names, people were told to expect as much as $1,562.50 in return contributions. The post office was swamped with more than twice as much mail as normal, and dimes went into short supply. Racketeers moved in with one-dollar and five-dollar schemes, and a half-dozen merchants offered exchange services which bypassed the post office. One pharmacy, charging a 25 percent transaction fee, cleared 3,000 dollars in a single day. With lists flooding the market, most people either threw them away or added their name without paying out any money. The craze soon passed with few people any richer, except for the shysters.

That same month, the Xen-McNair corporation launched a "Kentucky Derby Sweepstakes." The lottery was billed as a charitable enterprise to obtain property in Aetna for a disabled veterans' convalescent home, but ticket salesmen were recruited with lavish offers of 40 percent commissions. Xen-McNair eventually paid out only four percent of the promised prize money (20 Gary winners received a total of $48.11) and never built the convalescent home.

Gary had an unenviable reputation of being a cultural wasteland without museums or other monuments to the arts. Nonetheless, as Richard J. Meister wrote, "Gary had a few moments during the thirties when the activities of the fan and belly dancers had to take second place to the productions of the Gary Civic Theatre or to the annual production of the 'Messiah' by a joint effort of Gary choruses."

The building of Memorial Auditorium and Seaman Hall during the 1920s had sparked interest in highbrow entertainment. Citizens groups founded the Gary Municipal Chorus, the Gary Philharmonic Orchestra, and the Gary Concert Association. In 1935, 3,000 people attended performances by Sergei Rachmaninoff and Fritz Kreisler. But subsequent concerts by less famous artists were poorly attended.

In 1936 a heated debate concerning the merits of "Steel City" culture was waged in the *Post-Tribune* "Voice of the People" column, with charges of "hick" and "snob" hurled back and forth. Several people complained about poor attendance and uncouth behavior at concerts. Others replied that they would not be bullied into supporting unenjoyable shows or made to feel stupid if they applauded too soon, sneezed a few times, or left before the encore. Despite a vigorous registration drive, the concert guild could not sell enough season tickets to establish a permanent series featuring famous guest artists.

At this time, however, several ethnic choral groups, including the Chopin Choir, the Serb Karogeorge Choir, and the Croatian Pera- dovic Choir, achieved national recognition. In addition, the semi- monthly productions of the Gary Civic Theatre allowed an aspiring actor Mladen Sekulovich (Karl Malden) to gain experience and expo- sure.

W. W. GASSER AND THE BANK PANICS

Under the leadership of Wilbert W. Gasser, the Gary State Bank was a solitary symbol of stability during a time of bank failures. It was the only financial institution in the city that did not collapse in the wake of the depression.

After graduating from Michigan State University in 1907 and working briefly as a government engineer, Gasser cofounded a bank in his home town of Sherman, Michigan. When it burned down two years later, he took a job as a cashier in Beebee, Arkansas. In 1922, after a succession of transfers and promotions, he became vice-presi- dent of the Union National Bank in Marquette, Michigan.

Gasser's credentials impressed the United States Steel Corporation officials who had founded Gary State in 1908 and controlled its board of directors. In the spring of 1928 the bank was in a period of transition, and a ten-story skyscraper at 5th and Broadway was almost ready for occupancy.

Bank official Joseph J. Schuster later described the circumstances regarding Gasser's appointment: "Up to now bank presidents of Gary State were part-time men who only spent a few hours in the bank each day. . . . With the construction of the new bank building the Board of Directors thought we needed a full-time dynamic and experienced bank man . . . to justify the expenditure of a million dollars for a new bank building." Schuster recalled that Gasser had some misgivings about taking the job after seeing the "tumbleweeds rolling down the sidewalk and into the store fronts [and] many taverns that lined the streets. . . . But being somewhat adventuresome because of his Michigan logging background, he cast his lot and came to Gary."

After a brief apprenticeship as vice-president, the 42-year-old Gasser replaced retiring president Lawrence W. McNamee on June 25, 1928. The following year, the Wall Street crash sent shock waves reverberating throughout the country. In June 1930 Gary's 13 banks appeared sound, with deposits totaling 21 million dollars, but four successive panics within two years caused them to fall like dominoes until only Gary State remained.

On August 11, 1930, the suicide of American State Bank President Albert DeFries precipitated mass withdrawals that forced it into receivership. Within a week, there were ruinous runs on the Gary Labor Bank, the Mid-City Bank, the 5th Avenue Bank, and the Miller State Bank—whose president, former Mayor William J. Fulton, had committed suicide the previous month after losing a primary race for county commissioner. The reason he shot himself evidently involved charges that his campaign manager had engaged in ballot-box stuffing. "They might just as well have shot me," Fulton had said at the time.

Christmas withdrawals in 1930 bankrupted the Glen Park State Bank, People's State Bank, Central Trust and Savings, and the First Indiana State Bank. More ominously, the reorganized Miller and American State banks collapsed, dashing predictions that the closings were temporary and that depositors would receive full compensation.

Bank failures made a mockery of traditional business pieties about thrift. Life savings evaporated without warning. Perhaps a customer might retrieve a fraction of his money, but there was no guarantee of this. Most bankers blamed the problem on customers, whose panic allegedly brought on a needless chain reaction. On January 7, 1931, the *Post-Tribune* claimed that the banks "were closed by the tongue of the gossips." But Gasser himself believed that many bankers had "courted disaster" by their reckless policies of easy loans and speculation.

In July 1931 the Gary Trust and Savings, founded by the Knotts brothers in 1909 and headed by the highly respected Harry Lee Arnold, bolted its doors. It did not reopen until the fall of 1932. By summer's end, the number of closings had reached ten, with losses in excess of five million dollars.

That left just two of Gasser's competitors, the First National (Gary's oldest and second largest financial institution) and the National Bank of America (founded by William A. Wirt, Henry G. Hay, and Harry Hall and known for the stone sculpture of a flying eagle over its entrance). Both these supposed bastions of security failed in January 1932.

These developments offered Gasser no joy. In the words of former bank officer Edith Wise, "it really frightened us when they closed. Then the panic really began."

Gasser opened the bank doors early on the morning of January 6, 1932, hoping to quash rumors that there was anything to fear. He had a nurse on duty to deal with those who fainted and a doctor on call nearby. Telling reporters that the bank had recently gained $800,-000 in new accounts, Gasser declared, "The Gary State Bank is standing on its own foundation as solid as the rock of Gibraltar."

By midmorning, overflow crowds had spilled onto the corner of 5th and Broadway. Joseph J. Schuster remembered that there was "much pushing and shoving to get to the window first. You could see the tension in the faces and in the air." Board members, including Superintendent William P. Gleason of Gary Works and Plant Manager P. W. Seyl of the American Bridge Company, gave impassioned speeches telling edgy customers not to panic.

There were some humorous moments amid the anxiety and confusion. One customer only wanted a free calendar for the new year. Another demanded all his savings—a total of four dollars. Mrs. Martha Neil, whose husband was unemployed, withdrew the few hundred dollars that separated her family from poverty. After she got home, she had second thoughts about its safety and returned it to the bank. Others did likewise. In fact, one person withdrew his money twice the same day and returned it each time.

Underplaying the run on the bank, the *Post-Tribune* reported business as brisk but orderly. The mood was one of apprehension that changed to relief when a person reached a teller. The following day, business was close to normal, but no one knew when the next panic might erupt.

To boost morale, Gasser had a *Bulletin* printed with lists of new depositors, jokes, and inspirational messages. On February 19, 1932, he told his workers: "None of us know what discouragements may enter into the life of another. . . . We today are inclined to be easily scared. If we showed one-hundredth part of the stamina that [George] Washington displayed back in 1777, we would go through any difficulty that might arise."

The following day, having discovered a quote to the effect that thoroughbred horses ran until they could not go another mile and then kept running anyway, Gasser wrote in the *Bulletin*: "It seems that this depression is going to bring out the thoroughbreds in business. If one feels his job is hard and he can not keep on, it is well to remember the thoroughbred and keep going. It pays dividends in the long run."

How did the Gary State Bank survive the rash of bank panics? A key factor was its association with U.S. Steel. Gary Works was its largest client and issued payroll checks through the bank, as did other corporate units such as American Bridge Company, Elgin, Joliet and Eastern Railroad, and Gary Sheet and Tin.

Nonetheless, Gasser's leadership was crucial. As optometrist E. C. Doering stated, he did not throw money around promiscuously as had some of his colleagues. His goal, achieved in 1938, was full liquidity. To achieve this he rejected many loans and slashed interest rates on savings accounts (down to 2½ percent by January 1934 and 1 percent in 1940). Although he did not make customers sign intent slips days before withdrawing their money, as did some other banks, during successive crises that struck in the winter of 1932–33, he limited individual withdrawals—first to 500 dollars and then to a fixed percentage of one's total account. On March 1, 1933, when it looked as though America's banking system was near collapse, Gasser bragged that he could produce more than $1,750,000 on a day's notice.

The image of bankers plummeted during the early 1930s as the public searched for depression scapegoats. In 1932 a grand jury investigated the former president of Central Trust and Savings for overdrawing funds. That same year Mid-City's president was indicted for embezzlement, and Miller Bank executives were found to have loaned 30 percent of their mortgage funds to relatives.

Gasser was probably the least tarnished of Gary's bankers, but the steps he took to liquidate losses were sometimes unpopular. Stressing his obligations to depositors, Gasser turned down many loan requests. During the 1920s it had been easy for Garyites to get credit. Perhaps because of the competition among the more than dozen lending institutions, mortgages were commonly approved without requiring collateral or fixed repayment plans. Gasser set about reversing these practices, and his conservatism angered many people. At one Kiwanis meeting a realtor shouted out that "the S.O.B. ought to be killed."

Joseph J. Schuster wrote that Gasser became known as "a hard man to do business with. . . . Many epithets were hurled against him as the 'hard nosed' banker who would not give you a loan unless you could put up sufficient cash to cover it and then you would not need the loan." Schuster added, however, that Gasser's "strategy paid off when the forced liquidation began in the early 30's."

Gasser stayed very close to the daily operations of the bank, especially in the loan department. Each afternoon he inspected all overdue notes over 50 dollars and, to quote E. C. Doering, "if you owed his bank money, he was not afraid to come out and ask you for it."

Gasser usually eschewed his private office for a floor desk to the right of the 5th Avenue entrance, where he greeted people with a smile, a handshake, a slap on the back, or a scowl, depending on whether or not the person was a good customer. Astute in ingratiating himself to others, he frequently sent congratulatory notes and clippings to people who had been mentioned in the newspaper.

In March 1933, on the eve of Franklin D. Roosevelt's inauguration, Gary State employees labored until 2 A.M. to assemble collateral statements so that they could obtain funds to weather the most recent panic. At the time of FDR's "Bank Holiday," the Gary State was fluid, but Gasser welcomed the moratorium because it contributed to public confidence. Soon afterwards, he accepted a local position in the National Recovery Administration, the most important New Deal program of 1933.

That winter, Gasser angered Mayor R. O. Johnson by refusing to purchase $500,000 in tax warrants at four percent interest in order to allow the bankrupt city government to pay employees and continue municipal services. Gasser, who had come to the city's aid on previous occasions, believed the warrants to be a bad risk.

Gasser was a board member of the Gary-Hobart Water Company, the South Shore Railroad, and the Hotel Gary. He served as president of the Chamber of Commerce, the Rotary Club, the YMCA membership committee, and the Indiana Bankers' Association.

He lived at 630 Jackson with his second wife Mildred and their four children. While one of his two daughters was attending Northwestern, he wrote her: "Guard your Morals, Be Industrious, Be Cheerful, Be Original, Be a Good Sport, and Be Honest." His two sons would later become board chairman and president of the Gary National Bank.

In his spare time, Gasser played golf, cooked outdoors, and entertained at his Dune Acres cottage. He sang in a loud tenor voice and once played the lead in a charity play entitled "The Dream of a Clown." A teetotaler and nonsmoker, he offered a hundred dollars to any employee who gave up cigarettes. "At our bank parties," wrote Schuster, "no alcoholic drinks were served, but soda, tea, and coffee and he would take delight in serving it. He would do this at Rotary or Kiwanis meetings and this became a reputation of his."

After the depression waned, Gasser's bank grew tremendously (the name changed to Gary National in 1943). Suburban branches were established in a dozen neighborhoods, beginning with Glen Park in 1937. Resources quintupled during his 30-year reign. Although critics claimed that more liberal policies would have spurred even faster growth during the 1940s and 1950s, the fact that Gasser's fiscal policies had kept the Gary State afloat during the hard times enhanced the bank's prestige.

Gasser's singleminded conservatism brought him both respect and scorn, both accolades and death threats. During the depression, politicians, debtors, and fellow bankers wanted him to come to their rescue. Gasser believed that, like a man who could not swim diving into turbulent waters to save a drowning friend, it would be suicidal to deviate from his rigid banking principles. People either thought him to be a great man or a son-of-a-bitch, one resident recalled.

Gasser directed his corporate enterprise like the patriarch of a large extended family. This displeased some people but was one of his greatest strengths. Even after he suffered a stroke during the 1950s, which badly impaired his speech, he still roamed the floor hailing old customers and overseeing operations. He died on April 24, 1958, after suffering a heart attack on his way back from the bank cafeteria.

BUOY IN A STORM: R. O. JOHNSON'S THIRD TERM

In January 1930 R. O. Johnson began his third nonconsecutive term as mayor. One of his first acts was to appoint as city attorney his son Roswell, Jr. According to the press, when the 27-year-old law school graduate peered into the mayor's chambers, he quipped, "By golly, this is some throne room, isn't it, dad?" Shortly after the inauguration, Johnson suffered a physical breakdown which incapacitated him for several weeks. Worse misfortunes would soon beset his city and imperil his political fortunes.

Johnson was ill-equipped to deal with the depression crisis. Responsibility for relief lay primarily with private agencies and the Calumet township trustees. In the winter of 1930, after thousands of job layoffs had crippled the existing system, the Gary Relief Council raised money for crash programs. With Mayor Johnson as director and YMCA secretary A. B. Dickson as chief administrator, the Gary Relief Council hired able-bodied unemployed workers to repair roads, pick up litter, refurbish parks, and clear lots donated by the Gary Land Company to ease downtown parking. The council bought food wholesale and operated two shelters for transients. High school students conducted surveys to locate needy families, and civic leaders held charity benefits and solicited money, goods, and services. Policemen, firemen, and teachers pledged one day's pay per month to the cause. During the winter of 1930–31, the relief council aided more than 6,500 families.

Despite its auspicious beginning, the Gary Relief Council faced formidable obstacles. For example, in 1932 bank failures and defaults on pledges wiped out nearly half its assets. As well-intentioned as were its programs, they met only a small fraction of the community's needs. Occasional handouts and make-work projects were poor substitutes for steady jobs.

Johnson's power eroded during his third term. Altercations over patronage and unpaid campaign bills lost him the support of the Glen Park *News* and the Gary *American*. His firing of more than 30 policemen, including Chief William J. Linn, drew fire from the *Post-Tribune*, as did his laxity toward mobsters who controlled Gary's bookie joints, slot machines, and brothels. Half-way through his term, Johnson brought Linn back onto the force, saying, "I need someone like him to knock the ears off some of the tough birds that have been giving the department a lot of trouble."

In 1930 Johnson launched a drive to get his political allies nominated to county offices. Taking advantage of the bitter intraparty divisions, the Democrats, who had garnered less than ten percent of the primary vote, swept the general election, winning every contest except where Republican judges ran unopposed.

These unprecedented Democratic gains indirectly led to Johnson's indictment for allegedly using city equipment and workers to build him a beach house and rock garden. The malfeasance charges were ultimately dropped (Johnson apparently paid the city for improving his property), but the Democrats in Crown Point remained a thorn in his side. During the crisis Johnson appointed his son city controller so that he would be next in the line of succession. "Self-preservation, they say, is the first law of nature," the mayor explained, "and there is no telling what these hounds may do."

In January 1932 the Reverend F. W. Backemeyer delivered a sermon entitled "What's the Matter with Gary?" The municipality, charged the minister, was "swamped and befogged by selfish pursuits and exploitations. . . ."

At the next City Council meeting, Johnson delivered what reporter E. C. Rosenau called "a blood and thunder" defense of his administration. Rather gentle in chiding the Reverend Backemeyer for his political naïveté, by the time he got to Councilman Louis C. Christopher, who controlled the Glen Park *News*, Johnson's "face was purple, his whole frame was shaking, and he stuttered with rage." "I received 15,000 votes for mayor in 1929," Johnson said, "and I swear that to date I've received that many applications for jobs from jobless men. Naturally, I had to turn most of them away and some of them got peevish."

A month later, Council President Ralph E. Rowley proposed that city officials take a voluntary 20 percent salary cut to help balance the budget. Annual deficits were in the hundreds of thousands of dollars despite decreases in departmental budgets. The city even lacked the money to pay for license plates for police cars and other city vehicles.

In reply to Rowley's suggestion, Johnson said: "It cost me $10,000 to land this job and another $7,500 to hold it. I earn every dollar I'm getting and anybody who thinks I intend to refund any part . . . is plumb crazy."

On July 1, however, Johnson reluctantly approved a ten percent pay cut for all city employees, including himself, in order to prune an estimated hundred thousand dollars from the budget. Perhaps disenchanted with the perils of being a depression mayor, Johnson ran for Congress in the 1932 primary but fared very poorly except in Gary's Central District.

In 1933 the Democratic-controlled Indiana legislature passed a "skip-year" law which moved city elections to even-numbered years and thus extended Johnson's term in office to five years. Touted as an economy measure to save 300,000 dollars in election expenses, the Democrats hoped to gain "coat-tail" votes from New Deal supporters who would tend to vote a straight ticket in local and national elections.

In 1934, after losing the four-man Republican mayoralty primary by 831 votes to John Holloway, Johnson claimed that the skip-year law was unconstitutional. His law suit to remain in office another three years failed, and his days of power were over. Running for Congress in 1936, he finished a distant sixth in the Republican primary.

In 1938 Johnson made one more fight for a fourth term. "By the eternal, I am going to be Gary's eighth mayor, just as I was Gary's second, fourth, and sixth," he vowed. The highlight of Johnson's campaign was a mammoth rally in the Central District. It was a sentimental evening, but the New Deal had caused most ghetto residents to transfer their loyalties to the Democratic party. In the May primary Johnson received only 1,221 votes and finished far behind the two major contenders.

Johnson became seriously ill soon after the election; and on June 18, 1939, he succumbed to a cerebral hemorrhage. People of all backgrounds mourned the death of the once-dapper politician who, according to historian Richard J. Meister, had been equally "at home at a Negro revival, a Polish wedding, or an Episcopalian tea." At his funeral the Reverend J. M. Johnson compared "R. O." to "a buoy in a storm, always bobbing up." He was ultimately a political victim of the depression, however, which sapped his strength and dampened his spirit.

REVEREND FRANK S. DELANEY AND STEWART HOUSE

In the spring of 1920 the Reverend Frank S. Delaney became pastor of the Trinity Methodist Episcopal Church. During the next 19 years he built Stewart House into a vital neighborhood center for Gary's black people and won the respect of rich and poor alike.

Trinity Church originated in 1916 when a few people began holding prayer meetings in their homes. In the four years before Delaney's appointment, the parish had a new preacher each year, including a part-time shoemaker and a ministerial student. For a while services took place in a tent that collapsed on worshipers during windstorms. At the time of Delaney's arrival the congregation was using a rented building at 15th and Carolina. Six months later, Trinity Church moved to a site donated by the Gary Land Company at 15th and Massachusetts.

Delaney later wrote that Gary was "a bit different from anything

I had ever experienced. In many parts it resembled a huge mining or lumber camp with long sheds and tarpaper shacks." He realized that combatting the housing evils, the unsanitary living conditions, and the high rent rates would "challenge all of my energy, talent and time."

A native of Ohio and a graduate of Gammon Theological Seminary in Atlanta, Georgia, Delaney had been working for the Methodist Sunday School Board in Chicago when he was assigned to Gary at the urging of two local physicians, W. A. Hardy and H. R. DeBra. Delaney had visited the "Steel City" a few times in fulfillment of his duties as a social worker, adviser, and problem-solver for struggling parishes. Short, balding, and a little overweight, he did not look the part of a dynamic innovator, but he soon transformed the little church into a haven for the hungry and the homeless.

Delaney's involvement with settlement work was a consequence of the 1921 depression. At the request of women's auxiliaries of veterans' organizations, Delaney started programs to aid unemployed ex-soldiers as well as other needy residents. These included free lodging, meals, clothing, and furniture, plus medical, legal, and nursery school services.

These activities were continued after the economic crisis abated. Hundreds of black immigrants needed help in easing the cultural shock of life in a strange city. "Getting folks settled" was how Mrs. Mayola Spann Young described Delaney's work. On January 26, 1922, the *Post-Tribune* wrote: "Reverend Delaney has the interest of his people at heart, and his vigor and enthusiasm are certain to make his institution one that will accomplish big things."

In 1924 construction started on a permanent settlement house, to be named in honor of a nineteenth-century Indian missionary named John Stewart. Architect William W. Cooke, a member of the congregation, designed it without fee. The 70,000 dollars raised for its construction came from a variety of sources, including the Snyder family, the Gary Land Company, and the Methodist Board of Missions. Delaney's congregation pledged a total of 10,000 dollars. The settlement director was most proud of the numerous contributions from former "down and outers" who had been helped during the 1921 depression.

Dedicated to "Christian Ideals and Racial Goodwill," Stewart House focused on the practical needs of relief, employment referral, recreation, health care, and education. Delaney often counseled several dozen people each day and frequently visited a branch mission on 25th Avenue. Adult education classes featured courses on black history, civics, Spanish, dressmaking, home decoration, lamp shade making, budget management, hygiene, and nutrition. Youngsters could play volleyball, baseball, basketball, or tennis, and they could join the Dramatics Club, the Boy Scouts, or the Campfire Girls. On summer evenings, women often canned vegetables grown in home garden plots. In the winter, there were sewing circles and Bible study groups.

Stewart House was a family enterprise for the Delaneys. The pastor's wife, Leila, headed the Baby Clinic and the Mothers Club. His sister, Gussie, ran the Nursery School. One morning, a woman dropped off her infant and never returned. The Delaneys, who were childless, adopted him.

Stewart House's critical period came during the 1930s. The fate of thousands of people depended on whether it could meet the needs of the neighborhood. Homeless people flocked to Stewart House for a place to sleep at night and a hot meal at dinner time. Grocers donated day-old bread and slow-moving items, and coal dealers extended credit, trusting that the settlement director would make good when times were better.

Delaney's "Tenth Annual Report," written on November 11, 1930, reflected the strain put on the settlement's resources: "The calls for help and employment have been so often more than we were able to supply, and the fact that we were compelled to turn away unfortunate, suffering people . . . became a source of regret and embarrassment."

A year later, Delaney hosted a Thanksgiving dinner consisting of pork, potatoes, yams, corn bread, coffee, and dessert. A few spartan grocery baskets were distributed. Delaney said apologetically, "We'd send turkeys and hams if we could, but this year our budget is stretched to its limits, and we can't afford frills."

After teachers donated part of their salaries to finance a free lunch program, Stewart House fed a hundred pupils at a cost of 15 cents per meal. When funds ran short at one point, Delaney continued the hot lunches without payment. "If anyone wants to know what penny-pinching means, the *Post-Tribune* editorialized, "he can find out by watching Rev. Delaney buy his supplies."

By 1937 the bleakest period of the depression had passed, but 500 people a day still depended on Stewart House for food, shelter, counseling, recreation, and medical aid. Delaney received funds from the Community Chest and the National Youth Administration, and the Works Progress Administration constructed a playing field and parking lot behind the settlement.

On January 28, 1939, Delaney died from a kidney ailment. Under his leadership Stewart House lived up to its motto: "Here let no man be a stranger." Delaney had "an outstanding quality of humility," his good friend H. Theo Tatum concluded, "the humility of a man truly dedicated to a religion or a calling." Tatum added: "He wasn't a politician; he wasn't a businessman; he wasn't an eloquent speaker although he was interesting because he believed so much in what he was doing. He was simply a good Christian worker."

In October 1939 Gary's first federal housing project was designated "Delaney Community." Momenta Weaver, a Roosevelt High School senior who suggested the name, wrote of Delaney: "Not content was he to preach the word of God alone, but he labored unceasingly to supply the underprivileged with shelter, nourishing food, educational training, and work, thus enabling them to maintain their physical being as well as [their] self-respect."

FOLK CELEBRITY JOHN DILLINGER

No celebrity received more attention locally during the 1930s than bank robber John Herbert Dillinger. The swashbuckling manner in which the former Indiana farmboy leaped over railings, wisecracked with tellers, backed roadsters out of alleys, and hoodwinked the police captured the imagination of many residents and appealed to their fantasies. Law enforcement officials and the news media enhanced Dillinger's reputation even as they branded him a notorious public enemy. At a time when prohibition and the depression diluted respect for authority, Dillinger's crimes seemed no more heinous than the machinations of businessmen or the payoff arrangements among municipal officials and vice lords, bootleggers, and numbers racketeers.

Born on June 22, 1903, Dillinger was a free-spirited youth who disliked school and farm chores and loved motorbikes, fast cars, baseball, pool halls, and pretty women. In 1924, after deserting from the Navy and entering into an unhappy marriage with a 16-year-old Mooresville neighbor, Dillinger took part in an unsuccessful holdup and received a 10 to 20 years prison sentence. Following three futile escape attempts, he fell in with a group of professional criminals headed by Harry Pierpont.

Dillinger was paroled from Indiana State Prison in Michigan City on May 22, 1933. After attending his stepmother's funeral—delay in processing his commutation papers had prevented him from being at her deathbed—Dillinger set out to raise enough money to arrange for his friends' escape. Recruiting gangsters and selecting banks from a list prepared by Pierpont, which the depression had rendered somewhat obsolete, Dillinger carried out a series of daring heists in New Castle, Daleville, Montpelier, Bluffton, and Indianapolis.

In September 1933 Dillinger threw three loaded guns wrapped in newspapers over a 30-foot wall to a prearranged spot inside Indiana State Prison, but they were discovered before Pierpont got them. Next, he bribed a thread company foreman into hiding guns in a 200-pound barrel shipped to the prison's shirt shop. It was marked with a red "X" to tip off Pierpont. Before it arrived, Ohio police captured Dillinger, but four days later Pierpont and nine other convicts broke out of prison.

The ensuing manhunt sparked a controversy between the state police and radio station WIND. The station sent a crew headed by broadcaster Steve Trumbull to a wooded area eight miles south of Chesterton where a woman had reported seeing two of the felons. Dissatisfied with the lack of action, Trumbull persuaded a Gary policeman to turn on his siren and backfire his motorcycle while he shouted into the microphone: "Listen closely, folks; listen to that deadly patter of lead!"

The contrived gun battle provoked hundreds of telephone inquiries and led Captain Matt Leach of the Indiana State Police to divert most of his troopers to the scene. He was not amused when he learned that there were no convicts in sight. Blaming the radio crew for ruining his search plans, he held Trumbull overnight on charges of obstructing justice. Leach also vowed to have WIND stripped of its broadcasting license. The *Post-Tribune* branded the broadcast a disgraceful hoax. When Trumbull was fired, Leach softened his criticism of the radio station, and the incident faded away.

Pierpont and most of his companions eluded the manhunt and sprang Dillinger from the Lima, Ohio, jail. The gang then held up several more banks before heading to Florida for a Christmas vacation. In January 1934 Dillinger returned north to pick up his girlfriend Billie Frechette. Before joining his companions in Tucson, Arizona, Dillinger robbed the First National Bank of East Chicago, Indiana. During the getaway he shot and killed Patrolman William Patrick O'Malley.

Three weeks later, Dillinger was captured in Arizona after a freak fire destroyed the gang's cover. "Somebody has dealt me a rotten hand," he complained. "We had come to Arizona to quit and rest. We were through. None of us liked it anyway."

When Lake County officials heard of Dillinger's capture, they made plans to arraign him for the murder of Officer O'Malley. In charge of the extradition arrangements was the politically ambitious county prosecutor Robert Estill, who discovered that he was competing with several other jurisdictions for the captive. Successful, however, in winning custody of Dillinger, Estill escorted him to the supposedly "escape proof" Crown Point jail. Dillinger was so scared of the airplane ride, Estill said later, that he shook like a leaf.

Local politicians considered it a feather in their caps to have gained custody of Dillinger and posed amicably with him. The most widely publicized shot showed Dillinger and Estill with their arms around each other. FBI Director J. Edgar Hoover later declared that no photograph ever disgusted him more, and Captain Matt Leach referred to it as the "petting party picture."

Although the prosecutor maintained that the pressure of space had caused him to grasp the outlaw involuntarily, the photograph ultimately ruined Estill's political career. He later was made a scapegoat for the laxity of others and blamed for fostering the impression that Dillinger was neither so bad nor so dangerous as his reputation. Ironically, Estill had been repulsed by the festive mood that greeted Dillinger's arrival and had argued in vain for his transfer to Michigan City.

When Dillinger was first taken to the new jail, the warden illuminated the building with floodlights and had a machine gun constantly aimed at the prisoner. Gradually these procedures were discontinued.

Shortly after 9:00 A.M. on March 3, 1934, Dillinger and a black prisoner from Gary named Herbert Youngblood escaped from the Crown Point jail. A myth arose—started by Dillinger himself for reasons of bravado and to cover up the true story—that he used a "toy gun" carved from a wooden washboard and darkened by shoe polish. In all probability, however, a judge, bribed by Dillinger's attorney Louis Piquett, provided him with a real pistol. Dillinger first turned it on trusty Sam Cahoon, who called for fingerprint expert Ernie Blunk to "come back and bring the keys." After subduing Blunk, Dillinger and Youngblood made their way out a series of doors with their hostages, secured some machine guns, and then sped away in Sheriff Lillian Holley's car, which had just been serviced with a full tank of gas.

Afterwards, there was so much confusion that authorities at the jail failed to notify the state police about the escape until late in the morning and then gave out an incorrect license number on Sheriff Holley's car. "If I ever get John Dillinger back," Sheriff Holley vowed, "I'll shoot him in the head, with my own gun." Dillinger later quipped: "A jail is just like a nut with a worm in it. The worm can always get out."

A grand jury later castigated the sheriff's staff for negligence and indicted Cahoon and Blunk for abetting the escape. They were found not guilty. Sheriff Holley mellowed in her opinion of Dillinger. "There were twenty in the jail I'd less rather have dealt with than Dillinger," she said.

Within hours after their escape, Dillinger and Youngblood were in Chicago. Their only mistake was in driving the stolen car across the state border, which violated federal law and allowed the FBI to enter the case.

Joining up with other gangsters, Dillinger orchestrated a few more robberies but spent most of his time trying to avoid the police. On March 16 Youngblood was killed during a gunfight in Michigan that left three officers wounded. Dillinger barely escaped a trap in Wisconsin, then returned to Chicago, had a face lift, and started making inquiries about fleeing to Mexico. His behavior on several occasions was rather brazen. Once he visited a police station, and at Wrigley Field he walked up to Louis Piquett and said, "Hi, counselor."

In July 1934 an East Chicago policeman named Martin Zarkovich informed Special Agent Melvin Purvis, who was in charge of the Chicago FBI office, that he would deliver Dillinger into a trap in return for reward money and amnesty for Anna Sage, a 42-year-old Romanian immigrant who had run afoul of the immigration authorities. For several years Anna Sage had managed the Kostur Hotel, a Gary brothel which contained in its basement the notorious "Bucket of Blood" saloon. In 1930 she had been fined 60 dollars for operating a disreputable place of business and was ordered to leave Gary following subsequent arrests. Mrs. Sage had procured for Dillinger a woman named Polly Hamilton, who had formerly been married to a Gary policeman.

On Saturday, July 21, Mrs. Sage told the FBI that Dillinger was planning to take her and Polly Hamilton to a movie the following evening at either the Biograph or the Marbro Theatre and that she would wear a bright orange skirt if Dillinger decided on the Biograph. Next evening, having been tipped off by Mrs. Sage—known later as the "Lady in Red"—Purvis, Zarkovich, and a large contingent of lawmen waited for Dillinger to emerge from the Biograph, whose Sunday feature was the gangster film "Manhattan Melodrama." Dillinger was killed as he fled toward an alley amid a hail of bullets with a Colt automatic in his hand. The site was just a few blocks from the scene of the St. Valentine's Day massacre.

The body was put on public display at the Chicago morgue, ostensibly to quash rumors that Dillinger was still alive. One vendor sold handkerchiefs dipped in blood to souvenir hunters; another claimed to have locks of the dead man's hair. Police joked about a part of the gangster's anatomy which had become legendary. Reporter Fred Myers wrote that "an operating table—used in post-mortem examination—held Dillinger in a half vertical position, facing the passing throng. Close-lidded eyes stared at a gray wall. His lips were parted, revealing grinning teeth."

Dillinger's Quaker father brought the body back to Mooresville. "He might have been different," he said, "if his mother hadn't died when he was a little boy, or if the law had given him a chance when he made his first mistake." The elder Dillinger turned down 10,000 dollars for his son's body but later gave talks on the subject "Crime Does Not Pay" and became a caretaker at a Dillinger museum in Wisconsin.

During the months following the Biograph shoot-out, the FBI killed "Baby Face" Nelson and most other members of the Dillinger gang. Harry Pierpont was electrocuted in October 1934, after failing to break out of death row with a soap-carved likeness of a gun. Anna Sage received 5,000 dollars for "fingering" Dillinger but was deported two years later despite her claim that she had been promised immunity from her previous scrapes with the law. She died in Timisoara, Romania, in 1947. Billie Frechette joined a carnival tour after serving a two-year prison sentence. She told rapt audiences that "Johnnie liked to dance and liked to hunt. . . . I think he liked gravy better than anything else. He liked bread and gravy."

Some Garyites, who saw Dillinger as a symbol of rebellion, refused to believe that he had been outwitted by the police and were certain that he had set up someone else at the Biograph in order to make good his "permanent escape." He was such a flamboyant maverick that the majority of letters to the press about him were complimentary. One "Group of Citizens" wrote: "We say Hurray! Hurray for John Dillinger. . . . He is really a man Indiana should be proud to know."

John Toland wrote: "The myth and the man, in death, as in life, are hard to separate. The mythical Dillinger was first created by Matt Leach and then exaggerated and embellished by newspapers. Yet the myth was not mere fiction, for the man himself was possessed by it and lived up to it finally; and, at times, such as when he escaped from Crown Point, he even exceeded it."

CHAPTER EIGHT

Gary in Transition

Can you visualize a buzzing industrial town of over 100,000 people
—a town in which big things are taking place, such as unionization
of its workers, a renters' strike, an alleged vice racket, etc.—yet no
fathers to guide the community? . . . Gary is nothing to sneeze at.
It is quite an important community. . . . Gary steel is used to build
automobiles, rails, airplanes, ships, and what have you. So, you see,
the country needs Gary. Still, it has no city fathers.

—Ethel Stewart in a letter to the
Post-Tribune, April 23, 1937

THE 1930s WERE A transition period in Gary's history, a time of
change and of continuity. The depression cast a pall upon the era and
underscored Gary's dependence on the health of the national economy, but President Franklin D. Roosevelt's New Deal programs provided jobs for thousands of unemployed people and lifted their
spirits.

Largely on the strength of Roosevelt's popularity, the Democrats
captured city hall for the first time in a quarter century. In regard
to patronage matters and laxity toward organized crime, Democratic
policies resembled those of outgoing Republican R. O. Johnson. More
important than the bureaucratic turnover and the continuing corruption, however, was the shift in political allegiance of white ethnic
and black voters that caused Gary to change from a one-party Republican fiefdom to a Democratic stronghold.

Although Gary remained essentially a polluted, vice-ridden, racially segregated milltown whose fate depended on decisions made
in Washington and Pittsburgh, steelworkers became unionized during the 1930s, and blacks were more vocal in protesting discrimina-

tion, though their gains came at a snail's pace. Many pioneer residents were passing from the scene, and an age of uncertainty was at hand. Prior to the 1930s, according to political scientist Warner Bloomberg, U.S. Steel's top managers "formed the core of a business elite which also dominated the upper class social life and, behind the scenes through the local Republican party, the political affairs of the community." Although the mill influence remained strong, U.S. Steel had to reckon with new social forces, and power was not monopolized by a few guardians of the old order.

By the winter of 1940 defense spending had brightened Gary's economic outlook. Gary Works was operating at full capacity, and auto dealers were making record sales. A minor building boom began, and skilled laborers were much in demand, especially in the construction industry. In contrast to the 1930s, more people were moving to the city than were leaving it.

WORKING FOR THE WPA

At a time when the city's economy was near collapse, the New Deal gave people a sense of hope. "It was only with federal funds that Gary made it through this decade of crisis," wrote historian Richard Meister. During his first "Hundred Days" in office, beginning in March 1933, President Roosevelt prompted Congress to enact a flood of bills important to cities like Gary, including a bank protection act; a measure to refinance delinquent mortgages through the Home Owners Loan Corporation; the National Industrial Recovery Act, which authorized the drawing up of industrywide codes of fair business practices regarding wages, hours, prices, child labor, collective bargaining, and production quotas; and a plan to employ young people in the Civilian Conservation Corps. By the end of May nearly 200 Gary youths had begun working in Indiana's "Forest Army," many at tasks in the Dunes State Park. We have "a leader at last," exclaimed the *Post-Tribune.*

Although economic recovery was the primary New Deal goal, the Roosevelt administration also provided relief to depression victims. Throughout the summer and autumn of 1933 the Federal Emergency Relief Administration (FERA) funneled millions of dollars to hard-pressed local agencies. When FERA funds were exhausted, Roosevelt appointed Harry Hopkins as head of the Civil Works Administration (CWA). During the winter 4,500 local CWA workers refurbished parks, repaired railroad crossings and highways, built a football stadium at Horace Mann High School, and maintained a transient center. The CWA was phased out in April 1934, when more money was appropriated for FERA, which continued most of the CWA programs.

In 1935 FERA was superseded by the Works Progress Administration (WPA). Frederick A. Niestadt, a former CWA and FERA director, coordinated WPA projects in northwest Indiana. He expanded the adult education program so that one could study subjects as diverse as philosophy, civics, public speaking, tap dancing, swimming, life saving, and astrology. Hundreds of women participated in canning and sewing projects. Thousands of men repaired streets and alleys, school buildings, post offices, and other public property. They worked on the Marquette Park pavilion and on a 9-hole golf course for blacks at Gleason Park, where there already was an 18-hole course for whites.

While most WPA jobs were of the pick-and-shovel variety, unemployed musicians gave concerts and instrument lessons, artists painted murals in public buildings, historians wrote guidebooks and collected library and archival materials, and engineers surveyed Gary's housing and traffic problems and put together a city atlas.

The most ambitious youth project was an arts center in Aetna started by Mrs. Betty Kessler Lyman. Having previously directed children's puppet shows, Mrs. Lyman expanded her activities with aid from the WPA Federal Theatre Project. Soon 600 youths were producing plays and puppet shows and forming choral and orchestra groups. Nationally known wood-carver Francis "Ted" Kempf was on the teaching staff and made marionettes for the performances.

Despite its benefits to the community, the WPA did not operate free from criticism. There were complaints about low wage scales, which ranged from 50 dollars a month for unskilled laborers to 95 dollars for supervisors. Charges of waste and politics were levied against the WPA. Some people ridiculed having traffic officers at intersections, even though many parents praised the safety patrols for their work near schools.

Its ardor for the New Deal cooled and by 1936 the *Post-Tribune* regarded most WPA projects as "boondoggles." After 75 workers walked off their jobs to protest the racism and favoritism of their foreman, the *Post-Tribune* claimed that they were striking because their boss made them work too hard and would not pay them for rainy days.

These snide attacks caused one reader to wonder whether Roosevelt's opponents had "ever experienced the heartbreak of losing family and home? Have they known sickness and hunger, and have they tried to exist on three dollars worth of groceries for two weeks? Have they considered that there are loafers in every mill, store or office; and that for every one loafer on the WPA, there are 25 hard-working people?"

By June 1938 New Deal agencies had pumped 35 million dollars into Lake County, about half of which went to Gary. The WPA had more than 5,000 area workers on its rolls, and a variety of other federal agencies were complementing its work.

The need for the WPA decreased with the onset of World War II. By May 1942 the county rolls had been reduced to 1,200 workers, and many of them were women. A year later, the state office closed, after having spent 315 million dollars in eight years.

"The WPA lifted my soul from the gloom of the depression," said one Garyite. "I don't know what we would have done without it," said another. Offering jobs rather than alms, the WPA allowed thousands of people to survive the hard times with a shred of their dignity intact.

JACOB L. REDDIX AND CONSUMER COOPERATIVES

One of the most practical community experiments of the 1930s was a consumer cooperative founded by Jacob Lorenzo Reddix. The youngest of nine sons born to illiterate former slaves in 1897, Reddix attended school for five years in a one-room church in his native village of Vancleave, Mississippi, before going to a trade school in Miller's Ferry, Alabama. Following graduation, he served as a corporal in an armed services band and taught for a while in Birmingham, Alabama, until he saved enough money to enroll at the Illinois Institute of Technology. In 1927 he graduated and got a teaching job in Gary. Three weeks after his arrival, the Emerson High School strike occurred. Within a few years Reddix was teaching mathematics and economics at Roosevelt High School, the all-black institution created in the wake of the Emerson strike.

Roosevelt's principal, Frederick C. McFarlane, a Columbia University graduate who was born in the Virgin Islands, emphasized individual instruction, including remedial programs, private tutoring, and special clubs and projects for advanced students. One of McFarlane's favorite slogans was, "I am what I am; by the grace of God I will make the best of it." He believed, as did Reddix, that all-black schools could foster pride, self-respect, and academic excellence better than if Negroes had "to sit in the back of white classes in a white school." Reddix admired the principal's zeal and "almost religious fervor" in building up a dedicated staff.

One of Reddix's most gratifying teaching experiences began when a shy student named Robert Lloyd entered his algebra class. Recognizing his unusual aptitude, he encouraged the youth to join the mathematics club and do advanced work on his own. Lloyd went on to earn a Ph.D. degree from Purdue University and became a nuclear engineer.

Under Reddix's guidance Roosevelt students established a savings bank. They elected officers, built teller windows, issued passbooks, set up Summer Vacation and Christmas Club plans, and deposited their receipts in the Gary State Bank.

Reddix's most important economic venture was the Gary Consumer Cooperative Trading Company. He had become interested in the consumer cooperative movement while in college and had looked into the activities of the National Negro Cooperative League. In January 1932, 20 families sought Reddix's advice on how to cope with the depression. Reddix persuaded them to form a buying club with an initial capital of 24 dollars. Each week a member collected orders and bought bulk quantities from a local black merchant. In December 1932 the group rented a storeroom to use for recording orders and storing supplies. This enabled them to buy more items wholesale. Gradually the facility was converted into a "bona fide" store.

The project's fate had remained in doubt during its first year. The company had to operate with an "ancient" delivery truck, "antiquated fixtures," and very limited stock. With the help of a women's guild, however, and the stimulus from Reddix's night course in cooperative economics, the number of members soon exceeded 400, each of whom owned at least one ten-dollar share of stock and had an equal vote at board meetings.

By 1936 Gary's Consumer Cooperative Trading Company was the largest black business of its kind in the United States. Members opened up a second store, operated a filling station and a credit union, and even formed a children's auxiliary that maintained an ice cream and candy store.

In 1937 another Gary cooperative was formed under the leadership of attorney Mario Tomsich; by 1940, however, it had collapsed due to overextension, undercapitalization, and disuse. Reddix's cooperative survived the depression, despite its scanty resources and the abject poverty in the Central District.

The principles embodied in the Gary Consumer Cooperative Trading Company exemplified Reddix's social philosophy. Black people needed "money power, political power, and educational power," he wrote, "in order to build a better life for themselves and their children." For Reddix, the "inspiring sight" of former mill hands and unschooled housewives "managing stores [and] controlling finance" promised a better future.

In 1940 Reddix left Gary to work with the Farm Security Administration. A few months later he was elected president of Jackson State College, a post which he held for 27 years. Maintaining his interest in the cooperative movement, Reddix founded a health and recreation resort in Mississippi and other similar ventures.

The Gary Consumer Cooperative Trading Company went into a slow decline after Reddix's departure and became a privately owned store in 1956. The company missed the expertise and crusading zeal of Reddix, who taught that it was more than a way to save money. Reddix died in 1973, shortly after completing his memoirs, which he called *A Voice Crying in the Wilderness.*

RUTH WALL NELSON

In 1928 Carl and Lydia Wall moved to Gary's Brunswick area in order to escape Indiana Harbor's noxious pollution. They bought a lot just north of the 5200 block of West 5th Avenue, across from an Italian neighborhood and in a sandy new settlement populated mainly by Swedes, Irish, and Poles. Selecting their house from a Sears, Roebuck, and Company catalogue, they paid 1,800 dollars for a model that contained an attic, a basement, a front and back porch, and six rooms.

Carl T. Wall was a hammersmith who made Ford hubcaps at Standard Forge. His wife was a devout Baptist who bore him eight children, two of whom died before reaching adulthood. Ruth Wall Nelson later recalled that her mother was a strict disciplinarian who forbade her daughters to dance, attend picture shows, play cards, or hit a baseball. Life would have been dreary had it not been for the nearby wooded areas, the beach at Pine Station, the dime stores downtown, and school activities.

West 5th Avenue School was a crude wooden portable, but as Ruth recalled later, it seemed "just the most exciting place in the world." The activities included auditorium, gymnasium, music, plays, movies, carnivals, the game "my day," and frequent special events on weekends and evenings. "The school was just my whole being," she concluded.

In ninth grade Ruth began attending Horace Mann High School. Handicapped by her family's perilous economic condition, for a while she had only one three-dollar dress to wear, which she washed every night. She encountered the snobbery of middle-class youths whose world revolved around football and basketball games, fraternity and sorority functions, and fashionable clothes and automobiles. Most teachers treated her with indifference; a few "mentioned that I didn't look good," she recalled. "I realized that I couldn't mingle with everybody."

Despite these drawbacks, Ruth enjoyed Horace Mann. She enrolled in a business program, played the piano for choral groups, and became a teaching assistant. Studying became her passion and consumed her energy; algebra and music were substitutes for nonexistent dates. Perhaps her strong-minded personality and overweight condition, the result of a depression diet of bread, potatoes, and rice, intimidated potential suitors. "A lot of people later told me they were afraid of me," she said 40 years later.

Graduating in June 1934, Ruth found no immediate employment because of the hard times. At a July Fourth picnic, her father broke his neck. The fact that he faced a long period of convalescence enabled her to obtain a FERA job as secretary to Albert Fertsch, the director both of Gary College and the school-city's adult education program. Her 55-dollar monthly salary "helped put food on the table" at home. Eighteen months later, when her father became a watchman, Ruth lost her work relief subsidy. The school system paid her ten dollars less, and she soon transferred positions to the Gary Credit Bureau. Missing the excitement of her old job, she returned a year later at the reduced salary.

Located at Horace Mann, Gary College had been formed in 1933 as part of Superintendent William A. Wirt's dream of providing higher education for needy urban youths. During the previous decade Indiana University had offered extension courses at Memorial Auditorium but had begun to channel its resources to its East Chicago center. Wirt gave the dedicated, German-born Fertsch a free hand in policy decisions. The director recruited professors to teach part-time and fought zealously to place his two-year students in prestigious universities. His three female assistants operated as clerks, typists, registrars, grade recorders, test administrators, and business managers. Among Ruth's multitudinous functions was the task of compiling the schedule. She used Indiana University course numbers even though there was no connection between the two institutions. Classes commenced at 4:05 in the afternoon and lasted until nine at night.

During the 1930s few Gary College students could afford tuition but were kept on anyway. For a time instructors were paid in scrip. Because the school board allowed free use of Horace Mann and paid the staff (due to their adult education functions), the only budget item was faculty salaries.

Only once did Ruth ever speak to Superintendent Wirt. Hoping for a raise, she obtained an interview. Wirt turned down her request, saying, "the class of people that you are dealing with and working with should compensate for the lowly salary."

On one occasion Gary College held a picnic at Marquette Park. The festivities were interrupted when a policeman ordered the lone black participant to leave. "Well, I just couldn't believe it," Ruth recalled. "It hurt me so much that I went up to him and said, 'Wait a minute. If you have to leave, I have to leave.' So we left together. The picnic went on without us."

In 1948 financial and accreditation problems led to Gary College's demise and rebirth as part of Indiana University. When Ruth was offered a lower salary, Fertsch got her reclassified as his administrative assistant to prevent the wage cut. The school occupied the City Methodist Church until 1959, when it moved to a building at the present site of 3400 Broadway. By then John C. Buhner had replaced Fertsch, and bureaucratic changes were complicating Ruth's position. She still performed a large variety of tasks in regard to purchasing, scheduling, veterans' affairs, and payroll. But because she was a woman and did not have a college degree, she was demoted to the position of manager of the university bookstore. Her male replacement earned twice her salary. Having married Elmer Nelson, Ruth briefly considered retiring but decided that running a bookstore would be challenging. Uncomfortable in the role of boss, she nonetheless built up close friendships with students and staff members and came to feel a kinship with the women's rights movement. In 1974 she declared: "I've got all the ideas of a liberated woman. Maybe I was born 30 years too soon."

PARTY STALWART: BARNEY CLAYTON

In 1934 the Democratic mayoralty candidate was 49-year-old Lee B. (Barney) Clayton, a former mill office manager and transfer company executive. Since 1930 the native of Owensboro, Kentucky, had been a deputy sheriff and president of the Calumet Advisory Board. With Ray J. Madden and Joseph E. Finerty he put together an effective political organization of "Young Democrats," which served as the springboard for his political rise.

On July 19, 1934, the Democrats were embarrassed by the murder of beer salesman Harry J. Hutchings in Clayton's home. Clayton later claimed that members of John Dillinger's old gang had killed Hutchings to stop him from telling the whereabouts of outlaw Homer Van Meter. Nonetheless, many observers believed that Hutchings was a bootlegger caught up in a local gang war which already had claimed a score of lives since the repeal of prohibition.

In August local Democrats suffered further discomfort over a planned presidential whistle stop. Twenty-five thousand people gathered at the station, but because Roosevelt's train was 80 minutes behind schedule, it went through Gary without even slowing down.

Despite this snub, the Democrats adopted the campaign slogan "Be Patriotic, Vote for Roosevelt and Clayton." Republican candidate John Holloway countered by calling for a "New Deal for Gary." Clayton narrowly won the 1934 election by 268 votes out of approximately 31,000 cast. Twice as many blacks (30 percent) voted Democratic than in 1932, and many of R. O. Johnson's supporters switched parties because of Holloway's conservatism.

During the campaign Clayton had promised to support civil service reform and economy in government, but after becoming mayor he fired parks superintendent William H. DeGan for refusing to add 12 Democrats to his staff. Alleging that the mayor was turning a nonpartisan agency into a political football, William P. Gleason resigned as chairman of the parks department. Clayton replied that the present staff was dominated by Republicans who had opposed his election. When the *Post-Tribune* protested, the mayor called it the "mouthpiece for a minority."

Clayton never acted upon his civil service promises, and he supported a state law enabling him to appoint school board members formerly selected by the City Council. The *Post-Tribune* warned that the "school grab" would "make political spoils out of Gary's far-famed school system."

Other sources of friction were the bookie joints at 645 Washington and 124 West 5th. The police allowed them to operate on the condition that they were orderly and unobtrusive. Patrolmen once killed three robbers trying to escape from 645 Washington, but Chief Lawrence T. Studness, a former sheet mill foreman and Democratic precinct committeeman, denied that there were any gambling establishments in Gary, prompting the *Post-Tribune* to label him "Our Leading Humorist." On another occasion, the police suppressed information regarding the burglary and bombing of a 13th Street casino and then denied knowledge of the incident, even though neighborhood power lines had been out for several hours.

In October 1935 gangsters murdered 23-year-old Councilman Daniel Perrotta, who had threatened to "blow the lid" on organized crime in Gary. Although cynics suspected that Perrotta had been more interested in personal profit than good government, his death dramatized the power of Gary's underworld. As in previous gangland slayings, the Perrotta case was never solved.

During Clayton's administration it was widely rumored that black policy czar Walter Kelly paid handsomely for the privilege of operating his numbers wheels and brothels in Gary's Central District. Juvenile court investigator Thelma E. Marshall charged that huge crowds gathered at Kelly's clubs on payoff nights and that young girls lured "the winners to their rooms."

After one of Kelly's managers shot a rival racketeer, the police listed his death as a suicide, eliciting this racist retort from a *Post-Tribune* reader: "Now tell me, Mr. Editor, have you ever known of a Negro committing suicide? . . . They'll sing when they're hungry and pray when they're sad and they'll cuss when things go against them, but they never grow so discouraged as to take their own lives."

In 1937 black Councilman Robert L. Anderson charged that Kelly's thugs had tried to murder him, whereupon a Clayton Democrat accused him of previous connections with a rival syndicate and then sponsored a motion to have Anderson gagged, which lost by a vote of 5 to 3. At the same meeting Chief Studness admitted: "It has been the policy of this administration to be as tolerant as possible and not to interfere with people in the Central District who enjoy gatherings at pool halls and taverns and having a sociable game of cards or partaking in amusements which are not malicious violations of the law."

Influential Northsiders railed against the immoral activities tolerated by the Clayton administration. William F. Hodges declared that "the forces of vice and crime in Gary never were so well organized in the history of the community as they are today." In a sermon entitled "Washing Up the World," the Reverend Frederick W. Backemeyer said that fruit vendors peddled bootleg liquor and that one "blind pig" catered to school children. In 1938 these law-and-order forces united behind the candidacy of Republican Ernst L. Schaible.

Clayton also faced opposition in the Democratic primary from labor leader Edward "Peg" Ennis and coroner J. Robert Doty. Having feuded with county officials over such matters as governmental contracts, liquor license permits, and patronage selections, Clayton now found them in Doty's camp. On April 13, 1938, Doty claimed that gamblers had offered him 20,000 dollars to quit the primary. Two weeks later, he accused Clayton of having politicized the WPA.

In his campaign Clayton took credit for the millions of dollars in federal money that had poured into Gary from New Deal agencies and for erasing the city's debt in spite of a tax reduction. He also frequently mentioned how efficient the garbage collections had become. In the primary Clayton received approximately 10,000 votes, compared to 7,000 for Ennis and 4,000 for Doty. Even so, the campaign tarnished his reputation, and there were accusations of wholesale vote fraud.

During the election campaign bookie joints closed down for 38 days. The *Post-Tribune* greeted their reopening with a pictoral display headed by the caption, "Street Guide for the Chief of Police."

In the general election, workers, poor people, and minority groups faced the dilemma of the more liberal candidate seeming to be corrupt. Some followed the lead of Edward Ennis and supported Clayton, but others were disgusted at stories of such Democratic tactics as the beating up of Republican workers with iron pipes, the confiscation of opposition literature, the demotion of Schaible supporters within the WPA, and references to the native-born physician as "Herr Schaible." As usual, the *Post-Tribune* actively aided the Republicans and urged residents to "Vote for Schaible if you want a real New Deal in Gary during the next four years."

Schaible won the election by 1,000 votes even though the Democrats swept all other contests except two council seats. Clayton had more than twice Schaible's vote in the Southside, although he lost the black fifth ward by 3,000 votes. As in previous elections, the Republicans did best in the Northside.

Mayor Schaible instituted a civil service law for police and firemen, but organized crime did not disappear from Gary. As one judge complained, only the "small fish" were brought into his courtroom.

Schaible's victory did end the career of Walter Kelly, however. Forced out of Gary in 1939, he was killed gangland-style in Chicago. In spite of the predatory nature of his profession, Kelly's charitable donations had won him admirers, and his successors in the Gary numbers racket were less honest in paying off winners.

The 1938 election did not signal a return to the old order. Rather than threatening Democratic ascendancy, it was merely a vote of no confidence for Clayton. Honest but unimaginative, Schaible was Gary's last Republican mayor. In 1942 Clayton lost the Democratic primary to his onetime ally Joseph E. Finerty. During the late 1940s he was twice elected sheriff. He died of a heart attack in 1959.

UNION STALWART: JOHN M. MAYERIK

In 1932 the prospects for unionization at the Gary mills seemed bleak. Given the depression pool of unemployed workers, the torpor of the national labor movement, and management's intransigence toward collective bargaining, few would have predicted a peaceful union settlement within five years.

Economic and political factors created a conducive environment for unionism. With Franklin D. Roosevelt in the White House and other Democrats in control of the state, county, and city machinery, government was less partial to big business than during the 1920s. In John L. Lewis, the founder of the Congress of Industrial Organizations (CIO), workers gained an aggressive, crafty leader who favored industrywide unions.

Corporations lost power and status during the depression, and U.S. Steel was particularly vulnerable because of its traditional concentration on producing heavy, unrolled steel products, which were no longer in great demand. By 1933, therefore, with its profits low and its prestige diminished, the elephantine corporation began to modify its repressive labor policies, which had become politically, economically, and socially untenable.

After Section 7 (a) of the National Industrial Recovery Act guaranteed workers the "right to organize and bargain collectively through representatives of their own choosing," U.S. Steel set up a company union called the ERP (Employee Representation Plan). Although worker delegates had little power, they gained valuable experience by participating in elections and discussing such issues as salaries, seniority, and "share-the-work" plans. Some representatives saw their interests as harmonious with management and were later rewarded with supervisory posts. Others were genuinely interested in collective bargaining and cast their lot with the AFL's Amalgamated Association of Iron, Steel and Tin Workers.

Unionization ultimately depended on rank-and-file militancy and sacrifices. John M. Mayerik, who later became union president at Gary Works for 15 years, concluded that changes were inevitable, given the intolerable working conditions. During the nonunion era, he said, if someone "didn't like you, you were fired. You didn't know if you had a job from day to day."

Another steelworker remembered a foreman who timed his men when they went to the bathroom. "If you stayed three or four minutes," the man said, "that guy would come runnin' in and tell you to get back to work or go home! Sometimes he'd wanta see proof that you hadn't just given him an excuse for takin' a little rest."

The 25-year-old Mayerik was one of 13 workers who met secretly in 1933 in a tavern basement to discuss ways of organizing for the Amalgamated. A native of Pennsylvania, whose Slovakian parents had moved to Gary in 1910, he worked in the electric shop as a coil winder at the age of 16. A few months later he was dismissed for arguing with the foreman. Hired in the wheel plant in 1927, he had moved up to the position of heater when the depression curtailed his work schedule to a day or so a week. Still he was more fortunate than his father who, unprotected by seniority, was laid off.

In 1934 the Amalgamated threatened to strike if management did not allow out-of-plant elections. Mill officials refused to negotiate and began arming their company policemen with machine guns. Realizing that the time was not ripe for a protracted struggle, the Amalgamated called off the strike.

Union stalwarts next concentrated upon building their strength within the ERP. Mayerik was elected to represent the wheel mill. In 1935 the ERP went on record as in favor of the Amalgamated. The following January, unionists formed the Rubicon Lodge, which was dedicated to organizing all laborers who worked north of the Grand Calumet River.

Thus, when John L. Lewis set up the Steel Workers Organizing Committee (SWOC), which superseded the Amalgamated, local workers were already making inroads toward unionization. The struggle was perilous, and many sympathizers backed away from joining SWOC for fear of reprisals. Company agents spied on union activities. In some departments a union button cost a man work time. Mayerik related later that the company offered to promote him if he stopped associating with an organization that "would only bring you trouble."

One incident that solidified the stalwarts was the suspension of Mike Ostroski and Edward Ennis after they attended a SWOC conference in Pittsburgh. Mayerik helped persuade the company to reinstate Ennis 18 days later, but Ostroski was fired, supposedly because he did not give notification that he was taking off from work.

To mollify discontent, U.S. Steel increased its wage scale ten percent in 1936, adopted a 48-hour week, and announced a one-week vacation plan. SWOC members on the ERP, who had been demanding a 40-hour week and a five-dollar day, took credit for winning these concessions while demanding still more. Thus, the move increased the prestige of SWOC rather than weakening it.

A further blow to the corporation was a decision by the National Labor Relations Board calling for the abolition of the ERP on the grounds that it was a company union. Mill officials formed the Steel Employees Independent Labor organization (SEIL), which SWOC members nicknamed the sugar-barrel union because of the casks set up at mill gates for use in soliciting members. Few people joined SEIL, and on March 2, 1937, U.S. Steel signed a collective bargaining contract with SWOC.

This historic development in labor-management relations developed after a chance encounter between John L. Lewis and steel executive Myron Taylor at the Mayflower Hotel in Washington, D.C. After engaging in amenities, they agreed to hold a series of secret meetings. Lewis eventually dropped his demand for a closed shop, and Taylor promised to restore fired union members to their jobs and grant a modest pay raise and the 40-hour week.

Both Lewis and Taylor took the most realistic course in agreeing to the settlement. SWOC was not yet strong enough to win a closed shop, but Lewis knew that the settlement would stimulate its membership drive. Realizing that sit-down strikes had disrupted the auto industry, Taylor did not want to jeopardize what promised to be the company's best year since 1929. In fact, the English were negotiating for large orders on the condition that the corporation guarantee "uninterrupted production." Finally, Congress had recently passed legislation mandating the 40-hour week for companies holding government contracts.

In 1937 Gary Works increased its share of the market during strikes against five of its competitors. Some historians have contended that U.S. Steel encouraged an antiunion counteroffensive by "Little Steel" as a means of maintaining the open shop. In any event, Gary unionists donated money and supplies to strikers and relieved them on picket lines. Mayerik attended the rally at Republic Steel Company at which Chicago policemen shot dozens of peaceful protestors in what became known as the Memorial Day Massacre.

In 1938 a business slump imperiled the Gary steelworkers union. U.S. Steel cut wages and began red-baiting SWOC leaders. A management spokesman told Mayerik, who had succeeded Joe Goin as president of Gary Works Local 1014, that there were too many Communists in the union. "If we have them, it's because you people hired them first," replied Mayerik, who went on to defend the CIO policy of unionizing all workers, whatever their race, religion, or politics.

The union survived the 1938 depression and gained strength during the defense-spending boom of 1940–41. Having won collective bargaining, the next objectives were higher wages, the closed shop, and dues checkoff. In February 1941 SWOC held a dues inspection "Round-up" at the mill gates, and demonstrators dissuaded nonunionists from going to work, sometimes by force. Production for the day was cut in half. The following month, SWOC threatened to strike if dues inspectors and pickets were barred from mill property. The union got its way upon promising that its men would be orderly. On April 14, 1941, a new contract guaranteed workers a ten-cent raise and included a no-strike pledge.

The checkoff increased the power of SWOC, which during the war changed its name to the United Steelworkers of America; but with the building up of a national union bureaucracy, the locals surrendered much decision-making power. In fact, during the late 1940s Joe Goin, who had been promoted to the Pittsburgh office, began red-baiting Mayerik when his former friend ran for district director against the national headquarter's candidate, Joseph E. Germano. As Myron Taylor had anticipated, recognition in the long run defused labor militance; and industrywide collective bargaining was more orderly than dealing with the rank-and-file at each plant.

CIVIL RIGHTS STALWART: JOSEPH A. PITTS

Joseph A. Pitts was a barber and tailor by trade, and a civil rights activist in his spare time. Born on August 8, 1900, in Forest City, Arkansas, he was the 24th child of a farmer who amassed a library of Negro history books from itinerant salesmen. Pitts had nine years of schooling before he started working full time. At the age of 16 he joined the NAACP as a result of reading its magazine, *The Crisis,* to which his father subscribed. After getting married and moving to a small hamlet that had no public school for black children, he emigrated north so that his offspring would have better educational opportunities. Arriving in Gary in 1923, Pitts obtained work hauling cement and doing janitorial work at the mill. After receiving his first paycheck and finding a suitable rooming house, he sent for his family.

Looking back upon his first years in Gary, Pitts later noted that "the reception was very poor." It was hard for his family to get used to the cold climate and the frequent moves, and three of his four children died of pneumonia. Pitts was passed over for promotion even though he passed a correspondence course in electricity and was as qualified as others with less seniority. As a result, he purchased a steam press on credit and ironed clothes after work. In 1926 he opened a barber shop, and four years later he quit his mill job.

In the mid-1920s in outrage over an incident of police brutality, Pitts joined the local chapter of the NAACP. As Pitts later described it: "A group of boys were shooting marbles in a sand hill and a policeman drove up. The youth broke and ran. There were no arguments or anything. The boy had not been here long and naturally was afraid of police cars and policemen; and when he ran, the policeman shot him in the back. I became a paid member [of the NAACP] that day."

In 1930 Pitts became president of the NAACP and fought to integrate a park near 15th and Connecticut which had been donated to the city by the Gary Land Company. When blacks tried to use the tennis court, baseball diamond, and wading pool, the subsequent confrontations were, in Pitts' words, "the nearest we had ever come to a riot in Gary." On one occasion three white youths and a policeman manhandled a black youth who went into the park. When a policeman told Pitts to cease his agitating, he told him to "Go to Hell." Mrs. Hallie Hayes, who took her children to the park, was frequently insulted. Pitts received numerous death threats. The parks department closed the wading pool temporarily rather than permit integration, but after several weeks it opened without fanfare and blacks started to use it.

In the wake of the controversy some mill officials sarcastically told prospective black workers to "eat grass in the park" or "go see Pitts." Employment manager H. O. Egeberg threatened to blacklist those involved in civil rights activities. The NAACP sent a written complaint to U.S. Steel chairman Benjamin F. Fairless, who reprimanded those responsible and apologized to Pitts.

The depression had forced most people in the Central District to buy on credit from merchants who often refused to hire black employees. Some people were so impoverished that they could not afford to buy anything but stale bread, dry milk, and meat skins that were cooked in a pot with homegrown greens to give them flavor. Taking advantage of the hard times, some grocers charged inflated interest rates, rigged their scales, weighed down their poultry with putty, and altered customers' credit books, especially when their children did the shopping.

Aware of the need for solidarity in combating this type of discrimination, Pitts launched boycotts against ghetto stores with offensive hiring practices. Shopper boycotts had been tried before without much success. In 1929 the Gary *American* had printed the names of businessmen who would not hire blacks. Under Pitts' direction, the NAACP persuaded ministers to have their members sign pledges not to shop at certain stores. In May 1931 a mass rally was held at Roosevelt High School to gain support for the cause, whose rallying cry was "Don't spend your money where you can't clerk." After four months of agitation, merchants hired 50 black clerks and cashiers.

Pitts temporarily curtailed his NAACP work after his wife Velva died in 1933. She had helped him run the clothes press until her health deteriorated and had been supportive of his civil rights work. With unemployment reaching staggering proportions in the Central District, few customers could regularly afford the price of pressed pants or a haircut. When he could, Pitts went back to the mill to supplement his income. Asked about his activities during the mid-1930s, Pitts said: "I was trying to live, to tell you the truth about it."

In 1938, when a measure of prosperity returned to Gary, Pitts again involved himself in community activities. On June 22, 1938, however, he was jailed in the aftermath of a racial incident in Glen Park which erupted following the Joe Louis-Max Schmeling boxing match.

Interest in this heavyweight bout had been building for weeks. Two years previously, the German pugilist had beaten the "Brown Bomber," who was now a seasoned champion. Louis' victory touched off wild celebrations in black ghettos all over America, including Gary's Central District. In Glen Park, where Negroes were unwelcome after dark, a mob gathered near Ridge and Broadway ready to throw tomatoes, eggs, and fruit at black celebrants rumored to be coming south.

Shortly before 9:30 P.M., the crowd spotted three black men in a green Chevrolet. At the wheel was Carl Carruthers. In the back seat was Percy Bell. Riding "shotgun" was Pitts. Stopped by a red light, the car quickly was surrounded by the jeering throng. Pitts brandished a pistol to clear a path, and it went off as he was pulling it back into the car.

The circumstances surrounding the firing of the gun were somewhat unclear. Some witnesses claimed that Pitts provoked the trouble. At first Pitts said he fired the gun in self-defense to scare off a man about to throw a huge rock through the car window. Later he said the gun went off accidentally as he was hit in the face by a tomato. At any rate, the bullet rebounded off a wall and struck 37-year-old

Florence Nehring. Her husband thought she had fainted until he saw blood oozing from her midsection. Ten days later she died.

The crowd's initial reaction to the shooting was a mixture of shock and rage. A patrolman disarmed Pitts, removed him from the car, and then abandoned him momentarily while he called for reinforcements. Pitts was saved from serious harm by off-duty policeman Millard T. Matovina, who tussled with several would-be assailants as cries rang out to "lynch the nigger." The green Chevrolet was overturned with Carruthers and Bell still inside.

After squad cars whisked the three black prisoners away, the crowd defied police orders to disperse for nearly three hours. One angry band went to a Glen Park apartment where a black custodian and his wife lived. Fortunately, neighbors had hidden them just before the mob arrived. Not until police reinforcements arrived from East Chicago, Hammond, and Chicago was order restored.

Shortly after Pitts was taken into custody, rumors that a lynch mob was preparing to descend on the city jail prompted his transfer to Crown Point. Suspicious that something might happen to him on the way, two black policemen followed the squad car carrying Pitts.

The *Post-Tribune* castigated municipal officials for not having taken precautionary steps to avert the incident. "Street brawls" involving "both colored and white hoodlums" had followed Joe Louis' last bout with Englishman Tommy Farr, the paper noted, and there had been talk that blacks planned to hold a victory parade if the "Brown Bomber" won the fight.

Mayor Barney Clayton, sensitive to this criticism, declared that nobody could have foreseen "that a man should suddenly open a car door and shoot into a crowd." His distorted version of the disturbance was accepted by many residents. In fact, the *Post-Tribune* characterized Pitts as an irresponsible "colored celebrant" who fired "point blank" into the crowd.

The passions aroused by Mrs. Nehring's death were a tremendous handicap for Pitts' defense counsel Milo J. Murray, a black graduate of Harvard Law School who had moved to Gary from Chicago during the late 1920s. Murray based his case on the premise that Pitts had acted in self-defense. Driving through Glen Park with a legally registered gun was no crime, he argued; other people provoked the trouble, not his client.

When the Pitts trial opened in October 1938, Murray vainly attempted to win a directed verdict on the grounds that the evidence against his client was entirely circumstantial and that the charge of murder was absurd in view of the fact that Pitts had not even known

Mrs. Nehring, much less intended to shoot her. In his questioning of eyewitnessess Murray established that the area around Ridge and Broadway had become littered with debris. One black man who had driven through the intersection a few minutes before the shooting testified that his car was so splattered with food that it took hours to remove the stains.

Pitts testified that he had intended to listen to the fight at his barber shop but that Carruthers and Bell had suggested they cruise around town to see how people were reacting to the event. "At the time," said Pitts, "I had my gun in my pocket. I got the gun to protect my business. I didn't intend taking it with me. I had no motive for taking it along." Pitts maintained that he had not meant to fire into the hostile mob but just to intimidate the people into backing away from the car.

Most members of the jury were unsympathetic toward Pitts' story. Nonetheless, after six hours of deliberation, two people held out for acquittal. The judge reluctantly declared a mistrial.

In December 1938 the case was retried. This time Pitts was convicted of second-degree murder and sentenced to life imprisonment. Appealing the decision of the all-white jury, Murray charged that blacks were systematically excluded from the county jury rolls, thereby infringing his client's Fourteenth Amendment rights. The Indiana Supreme Court rejected the motion for a new trial, claiming that no technical errors had been made.

During his incarceration at Michigan City prison, Pitts read voraciously, studied accounting and bookkeeping, joined the debating team, and worked in the tailor and barber shops. Meanwhile, his attorney persuaded the parole board to examine his case. Concluding that he should have been tried, at most, for involuntary manslaughter rather than murder, the board recommended that the remainder of his sentence be commuted. The governor concurred, and in 1943 Pitts was released after spending five years and two days behind bars.

Milo Murray noted in 1974 that Pitts was fortunate to get out of jail so soon, given the racism of the era. He remembered Pitts as a civic-minded man who was ready to "go to the front" on any civil rights issue.

Within two years after his release, Pitts remarried and opened a barber shop at 2518 Adams and a delicatessen next door. In the early 1950s he resumed the presidency of the Gary NAACP for five years. During that time the membership increased to more than 1,200, a youth council and women's auxiliary were established, and various desegregation campaigns were launched.

Failing eyesight and diabetes forced Pitts to retire from business in 1965, but he frequently participated in radio talk shows and supported Richard G. Hatcher's 1967 mayoralty campaign. He told friends: "If the opposition can keep you divided, they can beat you. With unity will come victory."

On September 13, 1974, Pitts died at the Simmons Nursing Home following a stroke. Shortly before, at an NAACP banquet he was honored as a "stalwart" freedom fighter who had overcome poverty and personal tribulations and had taught others to shake off the shackles of subservience, fear, and apathy. Pitts himself once explained his activism with this remark: "If I can't live in freedom, I might as well be dead."

THE OLD ORDER PASSETH

On February 12, 1935, Superintendent William P. Gleason, 70 years old and ailing from high blood pressure, retired from Gary Works. "I feel like an indulgent father," he said during a farewell banquet, "who would save his children from his own untoward experiences and failures."

Gleason promised to remain active in civic affairs, but the Democrats soon removed him from the parks department, which he had controlled with an iron hand for a generation. He also lost his position on the Crown Point Tuberculosis Hospital Board. Gleason, who claimed credit for founding the hospital, interpreted his ouster as evidence that base men had taken over leadership from the area's business aristocracy.

In March 1936, at the funeral of builder John McFadden, the Reverend Frederick W. Backemeyer wondered aloud what would happen to the community with so many of the original pioneers dying off. After the ceremony a reporter noticed the "bowed figure" of William P. Gleason walking away alone.

Three months later, Gleason died from a stroke. As he was buried in Joliet, Illinois, Gary mill workers observed a moment of silence and Mayor Barney Clayton closed down city hall for half a day. Among unionists and Democratic politicians, however, there were few tears over the passing of the autocratic steel baron.

After Gleason's death, a rotation system in management assignments began at Gary Works. Whereas Gleason had reigned for three decades, there were three different superintendents at Gary Works —Walter E. Hadley, Earl E. Moore, and Stephen M. Jenks—within a half-decade. While they were more realistic in their attitudes toward labor unions than Gleason had been, they were less interested in civic affairs.

On November 27, 1938, Horace S. Norton celebrated his 70th birthday and retired as general agent of the Gary Land Company. Having founded the Commercial Club and supported such local projects as City Methodist Church, Stewart House, and Gateway Park, Norton was Gary's preeminent civic leader—even though he had an "autocratic bent," to quote newsman Erwin Crewe Rosenau. Shortly after Norton's retirement, the Gary Land Company began divesting itself of residential holdings. As historian Richard Meister wrote: "The vices of paternalism were replaced . . . by the vices of an absentee landlord. No longer would there be great interest shown by the corporation concerning Gary parks or civic endeavors. . . . Gary was on its own."

Among the most prominent spokesmen for civic paternalism were the Snyder brothers, who in March 1935 celebrated their family's 25th anniversity as owners of the *Post-Tribune* and its predecessor, the *Evening Post*. During the depression the paper boosted such downtown events as "Buy Gary" days and the opening of Gordon's department store. Each January a dozen of the paper's advertisers gave away milk, flowers, bottle warmers, and feeding sets to the first white and black babies born in the New Year. To stimulate business, the *Post-Tribune* hired high wire artists Benny and Betty to perform their "dance of death" 100 feet above the newspaper building. Four performances attracted a total of approximately 175,000 people.

In 1936, in conjunction with two savings and loan companies, the paper urged residents to save their coins in "Thrift Banks." Horace S. Norton endorsed the idea, as did William A. Wirt, who had instituted savings plans for students in the public schools. Photographed holding a bank, Wirt repeated James J. Hill's dictum that the test of success was whether one could save money. Ironically, Wirt himself had failed in several business ventures, including banking.

Like Gleason, Wirt had lost prestige in the autumn of his life. The depression had wreaked havoc with the school budget, necessitating reductions in salaries, elective courses, and night classes. In 1934 Wirt charged that communist sympathizers had infiltrated the Roosevelt administration. He was called to appear before a Congressional committee and ridiculed as a reactionary. *Time* magazine wrote that his statements fell "flatter than a crepe suzette," and even his defenders lamented that he had been made to look foolish. In 1937 teachers threatened to strike if their salaries were not raised and their working conditions improved. To Wirt's chagrin the school board was forced to bargain with union negotiators to settle the dispute.

On March 12, 1938, Wirt died. Rabbi Garry J. August noted that the educator had worked "to keep the common schools clean of politics and to broaden their influence . . . for the education of young and old alike." Other eulogies poured in from nearly all segments of the community.

The Wirt system did not long outlive its founder. Critics claimed that his once-innovative programs were outdated. Purdue University educators carried out an 18-month "audit" of the Gary schools. Although director F. B. Knight labeled Wirt a man who welcomed change, the study was most critical of the very thing of which Wirt had been most proud: fiscal efficiency. The survey concluded that the work-study-play system was a failure in the primary grades, with many youngsters unable to read well or keep alert during the long school day.

On December 4, 1940, the school board voted unanimously to adopt the single-teacher concept in the grade schools. The following year there was a deemphasis in auditorium, perhaps the most well-known aspect of the Wirt system. Soon the curriculum in the Gary schools bore little resemblance to the work-study-play system.

LIFE AS A NEWSMAN: ERWIN CREWE ROSENAU

During the quarter-century that Erwin Crewe Rosenau was a reporter for the *Post-Tribune,* working conditions went through a gradual process of change. A high school dropout reared in Naperville, Illinois, who arrived in Gary in 1919, Rosenau got into journalism under unusual circumstances. After a brief stint as a cub reporter for the *Daily Tribune,* he worked for six years as an apprentice construction engineer and then as an insurance agent. From time to time he contributed to Tom Cannon's "Flue Dust" column under the pseudonym "The Grey Courier." Editor H. B. "Bud" Snyder came to admire Rosenau's style and in October 1927 hired him as a full-time reporter, supposedly for 40 dollars a week. His first paycheck, however, was a mere 30 dollars; and when he complained, he was told: "You'll get 40 dollars when you're worth it."

The *Post-Tribune's* managing editor, Rosenau discovered, was a petty tyrant who enjoyed holding staff meetings at speakeasies. Unable to hold his liquor, the man frequently became rowdy and knocked bottles off the bar with his cane. "He'd do all the buying like he'd been treating," said Rosenau, "but the next day he'd leave notes on our typewriters asking for our share of the expenses."

Along with the sports and city editors, Rosenau's boss put together a news bureau for the wire services. Reporters had to do extra work for this enterprise without remuneration and be on call at all times. "You had to get permission to take your wife into Chicago to see the planetarium, which was the only thing you could afford to take her to," Rosenau complained.

Rosenau recalled that "it was hard in those days to find enough local news to fill up the paper." Newsmen occasionally padded the "Voice of the People" column with fictitious letters and filed items gleaned from almanacs, encyclopedias, and record books. When an event like the Arlene Draves case broke, the paper stayed with it as long as possible.

During elections the staff usually stayed on the job all night, substituting coffee or alcohol for sleep. On many occasions, Rosenau recalled, when the time came "to put the paper to bed, there was only about one man left on the desk sober enough to do it. Everybody else was pie eyed."

During the depression applicants were willing to work for "coolie" wages in order to gain experience. The staff twice had their salaries reduced ten percent. Despite assurances that this was a temporary expediency, the reduction continued long after the economic situation improved and then was lifted on a selective basis. Except for a five-dollar raise when he got married in 1928, the only time Rosenau received a substantial wage increase was when he threatened to accept an offer from the Chicago *Herald-Examiner*.

Another source of irritation was expense money, which reporters first paid out of their own pockets. Compensation came weeks later, if at all. While assigned to cover the state legislature, Rosenau received almost no meal money and was not paid for tipping pages, a necessary expense in covering the bicameral legislature. "I was often forced to seek small loans from friendly senators and house members," he recalled. "I'd often even lack the wherewithal to buy stamps to mail my dispatches." One year his managing editor blue-penciled his reimbursement request for a garage parking bill, saying: "When I go to Indianapolis, I park at the curb."

On one occasion, the reporters rebelled when told not to use taxis. Unwilling to drive their own cars at a five-cent mileage rate, they rode trolleys to all assignments until they got their way.

"The Wagner Act about killed Ralph," Rosenau recalled in a reference to publisher J. Ralph Snyder's reaction to a 1935 law creating

the National Labor Relations Board (NLRB). Even though the press-
men and typographers were already unionized, Snyder declared that
the paper could not survive a newspaper guild. To forestall collective
bargaining, he created new executive positions and attempted to
manipulate staff members with threats and promises.

Efforts to form a guild in the 1930s failed. "It was rough," Rosenau
remarked of those struggles, "with the old Sword of Damocles hanging over you. . . . The Snyders threw all kinds of stumbling blocks in
our way."

One of the photographers instrumental in reviving the guild idea
was Elmer F. Budlove, who came to the paper in August 1936, for
15 dollars a week. "I had many suits burned out on me covering
fires," he remembered. Budlove received no compensation for that
occupational hazard, nor was he paid overtime after working 72
hours straight during an industrial accident.

Edward R. Brennan and Steve Ripley were the reporters most
responsible for getting the guild beyond the "idle talk" stage. After
recruiting members in Sharkey's saloon, they held a secret meeting
on December 3, 1941, and decided to merge with the Northwest
Indiana Newspaper Guild, which had been founded by Hammond
Times reporters. Brennan and Ripley did not approach Rosenau until
they had commitments from a majority of the staff for fear that he
would be cool toward their plans. Rosenau later became the guild's
controller and called it "the salvation of the newspaper craft."

Ralph Snyder knew nothing about the fledgling organization until
he received an election order from the NLRB and then became so
enraged that he almost fired the managing editor for having been
ignorant of the scheme. Despite much eleventh-hour politicking, the
staff voted overwhelmingly to affiliate with the Northwest Indiana
Newspaper Guild.

On the eve of contract negotiations, Brennan and Ripley obtained
a pledge from the typographers to honor pickets in the event of a
strike. AFL crafts unionists and CIO organizers from the steel and oil
workers unions lent moral support at the first bargaining session. The
Snyders agreed to nearly all their demands, and despite their earlier
doomsday predictions, the paper survived.

During the 1930s Rosenau coordinated the paper's Christmas Basket Fund. For weeks he solicited donations, acquired food and toys,
and put together an army of volunteers to investigate requests and
distribute as many as 1,100 baskets. Christmas relief had heretofore
been "a scattered, hit-or-miss business with perhaps a dozen different agencies trying to do the job, and none doing it very well," wrote

Rosenau. He recalled seeing one basket containing a loaf of bread, a pound of oleo, and a link of bologna, signed "courtesy of Mayor R. O. Johnson." Said Rosenau: "We packed four different size baskets, depending on the size of the family, with a good variety of food— enough to last a week in most cases—and proper toys for boys and girls."

One applicant, a struggling pianist, told Rosenau: "I spent more than $6,000 for my musical education, but now I consider myself in great luck if I can get one night's work a week in some second-rate tavern." In a newspaper article Rosenau wrote that this man had to get "all slicked up" in tuxedo and boiled shirt and pound out songs "for the entertainment of well-off night clubbers while . . . seething with a hundred horrors about the wife and kids back in the cold and cheerless flat."

Each Christmas Eve, as Rosenau was cleaning the Armory, Gary Land Company agent Horace S. Norton arrived in his limousine and handed him an envelope containing a hundred dollars as a gesture of appreciation. "I got more recognition from him than from the Snyders," Rosenau said half-jokingly. In 1947 Rosenau was a pall-bearer at Norton's funeral, which was sparsely attended considering his former position in the community. "You could have sprayed that chapel with a machine gun and wouldn't have hit 17 people," he recalled.

Rosenau covered school board meetings which sometimes lasted long past midnight, causing him to be up most of the night because of a rule forbidding reporters to sleep on their stories. Superintendent Wirt occasionally asked him to put down his pencil during "off the record" discussions. After one such meeting Wirt criticized Rosenau for publishing privileged information. The reporter replied that since he was never told when to resume taking notes, he had to use his own judgment. Thereafter, at the proper interval, Wirt unfailingly announced, "Mr. Rosenau, you can pick up your pencil now."

"Mr. Wirt was a very formal man and always called me Mr. Rosenau, rather than Rosey, as did everyone else," the reporter recalled. After one productive interview, the educator gave him a copy of George Santayana's *The Last Puritan* and showed him how to hold his pencil differently to avoid writer's cramp. Rosenau ignored the advice to his later regret. After Wirt's death, Rosenau wrote a long series of articles concerning the Purdue survey of the Gary schools, which he later claimed was his best piece of reporting, although it disappointed him that some people misinterpreted his articles as an attack upon Wirt, whom he admired.

One of Rosenau's toughest jobs was to cover mill events. The paper "killed stories about accidents regularly," he claimed. Having once groped up unlit, icy stairs as a coke plant timekeeper, Rosenau knew from firsthand experience about the safety hazards of Gary Works.

During the late 1930s an eyewitness told him about two men who climbed into a manhole and were overcome by fumes. A black worker rescued them but fell back into the pit himself and died unaided as others revived the two white men.

Before writing up his scoop, Rosenau contacted plant superintendent Walter Hadley, who first denied the incident and then dismissed it as not newsworthy. "Well, Rosey," the reporter remembered that he said, "this sort of thing happens in an industrial operation. I don't see any story in that."

To Rosenau's surprise, his superiors allowed the article to reach print uncensored. "Up to that time," he said, "the Snyders had always genuflected to the corporation. . . . They finally began to firm up . . . to the extent that they insisted on getting the news."

During a strike Rosenau's efforts at objectivity managed to alienate both labor and management. At a picket line he had his pencils snatched and his notes shredded and thrown in his face. A union leader took offense at a description of his Italian silk suit. Then mill officials "had me on the capret" for an imagined insult. Within ten days Rosenau was in the hospital with an ulcer.

In February 1952 Rosenau left his 7,000-dollar job to work for the Gary Chamber of Commerce. He tried to attract new industry to the city, but several agreements fell through at the last minute due, he believed, to opposition from U.S. Steel, which feared a competitive labor market. Because of its budget control, Rosenau maintained, "big industry had the chamber by the throat." Lamenting that the city was unable to diversify economically, Rosenau concluded: "That's the curse of Gary! . . . It's a one-industry town." During the decade prior to his retirement in 1973, Rosenau was business editor for the short-lived Lake County *Sentinel*, then a political speechwriter, and then an assistant director for the Northwest Indiana Crime Commission.

CHAPTER NINE

The Era of World War II

The war is old, the days are cold
A chill enfolds our heart—
So many fall at their country's call,
Are we, too, doing our part?
So many dreams must fade and die,
Young plans must go astray.
What are we doing to help the cause?
Help keep the American way?

—Lydia Fisher in "Flue Dust,"
January 10, 1944

WORLD WAR II WAS a boon for Gary's economy and provided a purpose behind which the city could unite. With so many important tasks ahead, people could shed their "Depression Blues" and ask, "What can I contribute to the winning of the war?" Seventeen days after the Japanese attack on Pearl Harbor, the following headlines appeared in the *Post-Tribune:* "Cheer Rules on Eve of Yule Observance . . . Holiday Finds City Busy Providing War's Sinews . . . Prices Up; Business Good." In time the ebullient mood became tinged with a measure of concern over the inadequacy of homefront sacrifices; but at the outset, as *Time* reported, "the war came as a great relief, like a reverse earthquake that in one terrible jerk shook everything disjointed, distorted, askew back into place."

THE GARY HOMEFRONT

The war dramatically increased the power and scope of the federal government. Draft board regulations, for example, caused anxiety and tears. For some a deferment meant a chance to start a successful business or pick up overtime money at the mill. An induction notice caused one Garyite such anguish, however, that he killed himself and his two sons and seriously wounded his wife.

The Office of Civilian Defense (OCD) was set up to guard against enemy attack, but its primary value lay in boosting morale, allaying fear, raising money, and collecting scarce war materials. On February 9, 1942, the OCD held a blackout drill between 1:30 and 2:00 A.M. It was judged successful except in the Central District, where cabaret life went on as usual and where the turning off of street lights caused a traffic jam.

Three months later, the OCD held a "United Gary Day" festival which raised four million dollars in War Bond pledges. Participating in the celebration were actress Dorothy Lamour and a squadron of fighter planes. One tavern owner sold "Rap-a-Jap" cocktails which consisted of a glass of water and a 25-cent defense stamp. Exotic dancers helped sell bonds by auctioning off their veils.

To stir up interest in its scrap iron drives, the OCD set quotas, devised competitive events, and awarded "V-Banners" to contest winners. One month, there was concern that Hammond would surpass Gary's effort, but the donation of nine memorial cannons increased the city's contribution by 20 tons.

In the fall of 1942 students competed so fiercely in a scrap iron drive that OCD wardens had to guard each school's scrap pile to prevent pilfering. One school rounded up an old cement mixer; another found a two-ton boiler under its playground. Aetna students won the grand prize when they discovered 200 tons of abandoned rails.

The Gary Finance Committee exhorted religious, racial, and ethnic groups to participate in War Bond drives as a means of demonstrating their patriotism. The Minutemen of America sold war stamps, as did senior citizens' groups and the American Legion. The Legion even hired conservative spokesman DeLoss Walker to deliver a series of lectures on the need for vigilance and sacrifice. He warned: "Our smug comfort and complacency is going to cost us this war if we don't abandon it—and I don't mean next summer."

When exhortation failed, coercion was sometimes used. In the midst of one bond drive, mill workers forced a Jehovah's Witness to quit his job so that their unit could claim 100 percent participation. "This is total war," one worker explained. "Exterminate or be exterminated."

During a newspaper series on immigrants who bought a conspicuous number of War Bonds, the *Post-Tribune* singled out George Kitahara, a Californian of Japanese ancestry who had been detained in an internment camp before obtaining a job in Gary. After an officer of the Gary chapter of the American Legion advocated the incarceration of all "Japs" for the war's duration, one "Voice of the People" respondent labeled his remarks "fascist" and another suggested that he go to the Pacific theater and fight to his "heart's content." Shortly afterwards, the members of the Gary Legion satisfied themselves that the eight Nisei currently employed by the Marbon Corporation in Tolleston and the Kraft Laboratories in Glen Park were trustworthy and did not oppose the release of a few more Japanese-Americans to work in Gary.

During wartime the government regulated rents, wages, work conditions, and food prices. Rationing became the means by which the Office of Price Administration (OPA) limited the consumption of scarce items after experiments with voluntary controls met with little success. "Gary drivers are still lone eagles," lamented columnist Roy G. Parry, after failing to convince residents to form car pools to conserve gas and rubber.

Sugar rationing began in the spring of 1942. On June 17 women flocked to City Hall to receive extra allotments for canning rhubarb, currants, and berries. As more and more food items went on the ration list, restaurants felt the pinch. According to one local joke, a man discovered his favorite eating place to be out of every menu item, so he pulled out three eggs and said, "Scramble these, will you?"

By the winter of 1942 signs of war were everywhere. "Uncle Sam Wants You" was the most ubiquitous poster, but there were "Careless Talk Costs Lives" ads issued by the Gary Committee on Security of War Information and countless decals signifying that a family member was in the service. The Gary Home Front Committee issued anti-black-market pledge sheets and distributed "Smash the 7th Column" leaflets (the 7th column referred to wastefulness; 6th columnists were rumormongers). The most frequently heard expression in many quarters was the accusatory refrain, "Don't You Know There's a War Going On?"

The war affected local politics. One of Gary's first draftees was the youngest member of the City Council, 28-year-old Edward B. Krieger. During the 1942 Democratic primary Ray J. Madden distributed literature emphasizing the failure of Congressman William T. Shulte to support many of President Roosevelt's foreign policies. Madden won the election and moved on to his first of 17 terms in the House of Representatives.

In Gary as elsewhere, according to Geoffrey Perrett, the typical homefront family "was donating blood, buying bonds, saving its tin cans and fats, collecting old newspapers, and hunting up scrap metal." More likely than not, both parents worked. Typical of the influx of women war workers was Mrs. Elizabeth Kish, an American Bridge Company employee during World War I who returned to the same plant and operated a drill press after 23 years as a homemaker. Humorist Roy G. Parry noted that there were "women, women, everywhere—on the streets, in our mills, in buses and street cars. Women dressed in every kind of garb."

Some men had trouble accepting the new situation and worried excessively about how it would affect efficiency and job security. Unions treated women as second-class citizens and agreed to separate and unequal wage scales on the basis of sex. In May 1943 Assistant School Superintendent Ralph L. Muller named Anna Visclosky and Cecelia Balucki to the two top custodial posts at Lew Wallace High School. "We still regard these positions as men's jobs," he announced, "and the women will serve only until men can be found to replace them."

The *Post-Tribune* "Women's Section" reflected the changing conditions. There were ads for work clothes and leg makeup (due to the stocking shortage), recipes for easy-to-prepare meals, hints on how to budget ration stamps, instructions on starting "Victory gardens," suggestions for making clothes out of shower curtains, auto upholstery, and flannel underwear, safety hints for women millworkers (especially regarding hair styles), and articles about club women participating in war-related charities.

Many newspaper advertisements included admonitions to buy bonds. Since automobile dealers had no new cars to sell, they stressed their service and repair facilities. Kroger's claimed that its Clock Bread, which cost 17 cents for two loaves, provided war workers with "energy vitamins" for "the needed extra vitality." An advertisement for Comay's Jewelers, claiming that "You Can't Ration Love," stated: "We will have war and weddings! We will have bombers and bullets . . . and babies, too! We're not going to stop the pursuit of happiness! We don't have to . . . We must not!" Appealing to families with loved ones overseas, Gordon's photo studio pictured a helmeted child saying, "Hi ya, Dad! Here's your soldier on the home front."

In the summer of 1943 the *Post-Tribune* sponsored a "Smokes for Yanks" drive in conjunction with the Gary Retail Grocers' Association and the Gary Drug Club. For each five-cent contribution, a serviceman was to receive a free pack. Expanding on the promotion a year later, the newspaper held a contest to select a "Miss Gary

Cigaret, the Paper Doll for Yanks Overseas." Because the largest amount of money was donated in her name, Irene "Cookie" Kuchta won the honor of having her pinup picture included in each carton of cigarets sent overseas. A mill draftsman who attended Gary College at night, Miss Kuchta told reporters that she had not gone away to school after graduating from Emerson because "I wanted to stay here and help win the war."

As World War II entered its third year, Garyites became increasingly impatient with homefront restraints, angry over inequalities of sacrifice, anxious for news from overseas, and worried about social dislocations caused by the conflict. Gone were the exhilaration and frenzy of the Pearl Harbor Christmas season. Because people tended to look after their own interests, there was no wartime suspension of partisan politics, corruption, vice, class conflict, intolerance, or greed.

An editorial entitled "Good Old Jim" captured the public indignation with slackers who avoided work, ignored scrap iron drives, and refused to buy bonds. This type of person, the *Post-Tribune* wrote, was "always ready with a joke, or a deck of cards or his latest comments on why we aren't winning the war. Good old Jim. We wish they'd shoot him at sunrise."

Equally despised by the public were the black market operators who made windfall profits from bootleg beer, beef, sugar, cigarets, electrical appliances, or rubber products. Tire thefts were common throughout the war, and several Garyites, including a grocer, a butcher, and a liquor distributor, were indicted for selling illegal goods and counterfeit ration stamps. Although few admitted it, probably a majority of Garyites engaged in black market dealings at one time or another.

Under these conditions organized crime thrived. The *Post-Tribune* noted in February 1944 that gamblers were "still doing business at the same old stands but in a very discreet manner." Prostitution, although labeled an "unhealthy and unpatriotic" profession by one local official, also flourished. A syndicate with good city hall connections allegedly assessed each lady-of-the-evening ten dollars a week.

On February 9, 1944, Republican County Prosecutor Charles W. Gannon arrested six men for transporting teen-age girls across state lines to Gary brothels. Gannon also staged periodic raids against bookie joints and numbers parlors but was voted out of office in the November election after drawing the wrath of church groups for raiding their bingo contests. Even while Gannon was in office, the syndicate had so many allies in city government that they neutralized his effectiveness.

The most shocking gangland action during the war was the killing of Lawrence E. Finerty, the mayor's brother, who had allegedly been involved in illegal dice games, county fair concessions, beer running, and slot machines. Along with Jack Doyle, he apparently had collected payoffs from numerous pool halls, cigar stores, and brothels. It was rumored that former associates of Al Capone killed him when he tried to get into racetrack betting.

At the outbreak of war both labor and management promised to put defense needs ahead of pecuniary interests. Steelworkers chafed under wartime wage controls, however, especially after U.S. Steel was convicted of price fixing. Dozens of short wildcat strikes took place at Gary Works, drawing the ire of the local press.

In 1943 the school board locked horns with the Building Service Employees Union over the issues of poor wages (50 cents an hour base pay for women, 75 cents for men), long hours (48 a week with no overtime for night work), lack of job security for departing servicemen, and the fact that janitors had to take orders from teachers. After a two-day strike in February, the school board granted most of the strikers' demands in return for an agreement against future work stoppages prior to arbitration.

A year later, 12 custodians forced Froebel to close for a day for lack of heat because a man had been hired who refused to join the union. Although the dispute was resolved that evening, it led to an attempt to break up the union. In March 1945 the school board rejected an eight percent wage increase request, broke off collective bargaining, claimed it had no power to sign a union contract, and offered janitors individual contracts calling for six percent raises. This action precipitated a bitter, week-long strike before the board signed an eight percent union contract.

War had disruptive effects on family life and produced, in the words of Lake County Circuit Court Judge T. Joseph Sullivan, a "spirit of recklessness" and a "psychology of daring." The crime rate for young people doubled between 1941 and 1943, as did school absenteeism. Increasing numbers of youngsters worked in bowling alleys, pool halls, taverns, diners, and other places where they were exposed to gambling, drinking, profanity, and lewd behavior. Thirteen-year-old waitresses were frequently propositioned. Juvenile court dockets registered an upsurge in sex crimes, shoplifting, gang fights, and vandalism. Cemeteries, parks, and churches were not immune to desecration. On one occasion, four youths armed with knives, clubs, rifles, and saws were caught trying to help five buddies escape from the city jail.

In response to the alarm created by the apparent juvenile crime wave, the Anselm Forum and the Gary Council of Churches held panel discussions on the impact of war upon young people. Residents debated the mental health of "latch key" children whose mothers worked. Probation officer Agnes Doyle noted with alarm that many women workers stopped off at taverns after their shifts and were in no condition to cook a meal or otherwise take care of their children afterwards. She believed that adult delinquency was the prime cause of juvenile delinquency.

At one panel discussion, Emerson coach Arthur J. Rolfe called for firm disciplinary measures to halt promiscuous trends among young people. Student leader Zonabelle Kingery challenged Rolfe's assumption that "the modern generation is going to the dogs" and argued that most young people simply wanted freedom and responsibility. Other young people complained of a lack of "hang-outs" where they could socialize without being "shoved around."

In June 1943 Mayor Joseph E. Finerty appointed a Committee on Juvenile Delinquency to study the problem. Its hearings had as much to do with moral issues as legal ones. Various witnesses analyzed the pernicious influences of post-prom parties, tattoo parlors, swoon music, B-movies, zoot suits, tight-fitting sweaters, ducktail haircuts, jitterbugging, and beer guzzling. On June 29, Mayor Finerty reported that "the situation is more serious than I thought. We have found things that have shocked me, youngsters 13 to 16 years old, unsupervised and apparently without morals."

In response to the committee's recommendations, the city set a ten o'clock curfew for unescorted children under the age of 15 and established a youth services board. Several organizations set up canteens modeled after USO centers with juke boxes, coke machines, and booths. Among the most popular were the Stewart House teen lounge and the YMCA Golden Nugget Club.

By 1944 there was a growing realization that, while the "live for today" war mood had caused children to grow up faster, the delinquent teen-ager was the exception rather than the norm. The wartime crime rate, while higher than during the depression, was equivalent to the equally prosperous 1920s. For every delinquent teen-ager, there were dozens of "All Out Americans" collecting scrap, phonograph records (for shellac), wastepaper (a half million pounds), and library books for servicemen; who were distributing "WAR WORKERS SLEEPING" signs, clean plate pledges, and anti-black market cards; and who were participating in child care, police training, fire prevention, and first aid courses.

The last year of the war was traumatic for Garyites. Hopeful of quick victory following the successful Normandy invasion in June 1944, residents saw the fighting intensify and drag on for another 14 months. During the 1944 Christmas season many people cashed in War Bonds despite the hue and cry that it was "Blood Money." On December 24 muggers stole combat medals from a Gold Star mother and Christmas gifts from two other women. A woman "Santa Claus" collapsed of a heart attack and died that day, and a man fractured his common-law wife's skull with a milk bottle. Families of deceased servicemen were bothered by a variety of hucksters selling plaques and burial plots. One man was arrested for mail fraud because he promised to produce lengthy newspaper clippings about the adventures of dead soldiers and then generally sent only the local obituary.

In the spring of 1945 two German prisoners escaped from a Canadian prison camp and made their way to Gary. Walking down Broadway hungry and without funds, they tried to pawn a watch at Busch Jewelers. A suspicious sales clerk named Freta Trainor refused to do business with them and notified policeman Peter Billick. He was on the phone alerting Stanley's, the next jewelers down the block, when they entered the store. Employee Helen Bonczek stalled then until Billick and officer Joseph Hopkins arrived and apprehended them. For the POWs, it had been their third escape and recapture. Police described them as knowledgeable about their legal rights and confident of a German victory.

War's end on August 14, 1945, found Garyites in a restrained but happy mood. There were no formal parades, but celebrants lit firecrackers, shot off guns, backfired their automobiles, honked their horns, and rattled scrub buckets. The mills closed for the first time in 26 years.

On the fourth anniversary of Pearl Harbor, the *Post-Tribune* listed Gary's casualty figures. Of the 16,103 men who served, 438 died, 686 suffered serious wounds, and 31 were missing. Later the death toll was revised upward to 460.

For those who came back, as well as for those who had never left, the period ahead would be a time of painful readjustment.

WAR HEROES: TOM HARMON AND JOHNNY BUSHEMI

During the first six months of World War II, American troops suffered many setbacks in the Pacific and did not begin fighting Germans until nearly a year after Pearl Harbor. In 1942, therefore, there were few tales of heroism to boost local morale. Individual soldiers seldom made the news except when they were drafted, went overseas, or became battle casualties. Nearly everyone supported the war, but because of the lingering residue of post-World War I disillusionment, there was little glamorization about it. In the words of one Garyite, it was "a dirty task that had to be done." Still, local residents wanted to think well of their fighting men, and the dominant image projected by the government and the news media was that they were brave, dedicated, well-trained professionals.

Gary's two most famous soldiers were Tom Harmon and John A. Bushemi. Harmon had achieved national fame as a result of his football prowess, and had it not been for his vanity and aloofness, he might have become Gary's most admired war hero. Instead that honor went to combat photographer Johnny Bushemi.

Harmon's public career resembled a Frank Merriwell story. The youngest of six children, he won his first prize—a pair of roller skates —in a bubble gum blowing contest at the Tivoli Theatre. Schoolteacher May M. Hake later recalled one afternoon when young Harmon came to her house selling copies of *The Saturday Evening Post*. "It was during the depression," she wrote, "and although the *Post* cost only a nickel or a dime then, I wasn't going to buy another one, so I said, 'I am sorry, Tom, I didn't know you were selling *Posts,* I'll buy one from you next week but not today. You see I bought one on my way home from school.' Tom looked at me suspiciously for a full minute and then demanded, 'Show it to me!' I knew right then that Tom would always know how to make money."

Athletics was the vehicle that propelled Harmon to fame and fortune. "I started playing football at Holy Angels parochial school when I was ten, on a playground surfaced with cinders," he later recalled. In 1933, when he was a 130-pound freshman at Horace Mann, the high school team lost every gridiron game. Three years later the "Horsemen" went undefeated, as Harmon scored 150 points and was selected as the best quarterback in the state. Harmon also was captain of the Horace Mann basketball team, pitched three no-hitters for the baseball team, and set a track record for the 200-yard low hurdles. Sixteen colleges offered him scholarships. On the advice of his coach, Doug Kerr, he chose the University of Michigan.

Harmon went on to become an All-American at Michigan in 1939 and 1940. Sportswriters referred to him occasionally as "Old 98" or "rhumba hips." After his senior year a Hollywood studio signed him to appear in an autobiographical film, and he courted an aspiring starlet named Elyse Knox. Just as Harmon was enjoying the fruits of his fame, the army drafted him. He obtained a deferment while the movie was being completed but failed to gain a permanent exemption on the grounds that he was the sole supporter of his parents. Reluctantly he joined the air force.

In April 1943 Harmon's name was in the headlines again when a tropical storm forced his plane to crash-land in Dutch Guiana. For six days the missing pilot made his way through thick jungle underbrush and crocodile-infested swamps, until weak from loss of food and water but unhurt except for minor cuts, he reached a friendly village. Afterwards, Harmon told reporters that he owed his life to football (for giving him a "pair of good legs"), to God ("I must have said a million Hail Mary's"), and to his loved ones ("I have got Mom, Pop, my gal—that's enough incentive for me").

Six months later, after having seen combat in Africa, Harmon was stationed in China when his P-38 was struck three times during a dogfight with Japanese Zeros. One shell landed between his legs, burning his pants from the knees down, setting his cockpit ablaze, and forcing him to eject. Opening his parachute at 5,000 feet, he floated dangerously amid encircling planes until he came to rest in a lake. Unscathed, he hid until the Japanese left.

For 32 days Harmon's fate was unknown to the outside world. "I can't believe that Tom has scored for the last time," declared his old coach, who showed reporters a recent letter in which Harmon bragged: "You can always outguess these Jap pilots because they fly like mechanical men." Shortly after his mishap, it turned out, Harmon was saved by Chinese villagers. According to a fellow pilot, he made a triumphant return to his base "riding in a sedan chair, carried by natives; and there followed an entourage which included four donkeys heavily laden with gifts of all kinds which had been showered on him by idolizing natives along the route...."

In America awaiting reassignment to public relations work, Harmon married Elyse Knox in Ann Arbor, where he had built his parents a house near the scene of his college exploits. The bride wore a gown made from his bullet-riddled parachute. She became pregnant a month later. Both events received ample publicity, as did a news release of Harmon catching a giant sting ray while making a training film off the Florida coast. The sea battle lasted longer than a football game and was the toughest physical challenge of his life, Harmon told reporters.

Despite these adventures, Harmon's reputation in Gary went into eclipse after he spurned an offer to participate in a local celebration and began making self-righteous statements about civilian apathy and greed. According to *Life*, he told a Detroit audience that had gathered to honor him "that he was ashamed of them and that what they needed most was a first-class bombing raid."

In 1967 Harmon consented to accept an award at a Gary Oldtimers' banquet. After reminiscing about summer jobs at the mill, jogging on lakeshore sand, and scrimmaging on Horace Mann's cement practice field, the honored guest, who had gone on to become a successful businessman and sportscaster in California, concluded: "I thank Gary for a lesson in toughness."

Johnny Bushemi was a combat photographer whose vibrant, daring personality caused local residents to consider him their "representative" soldier. Indeed, he was the inspiration for a *Post-Tribune* newsletter—called "Dear Johnny" and signed "Uncle Ed"—which summarized local events for soldiers overseas.

The seventh of nine children, Bushemi was 12 years old in 1930 when his Italian-born parents moved to Glen Park from Taylorville, Illinois. During the depression he boxed in Golden Gloves tournaments and earned spending money cutting hair in his basement. In his junior year at Lew Wallace High School he quit school and, like his father, went to work at the mill. Determined to become a professional photographer, he spent most of his savings on camera equipment.

In 1936 the *Post-Tribune* hired Bushemi as an apprentice photographer. His eagerness to learn and engaging personality soon earned him assignments with veteran reporters. During the next five years he became best known for his sports pictures but was equally at home racing to a disaster scene or capturing the tranquil beauty of the dunes.

In July 1941 Bushemi enlisted in the army and after basic training was assigned to Fort Bragg, North Carolina. One of his closest friends there was Marion Hargrove, whose best-selling book about army life made Bushemi a celebrity. In *See Here, Private Hargrove* (1942), Bushemi was described as having "an unfailing sense of humor." Hargrove added: "He has a good imagination and a sense of beauty, and he makes good pictures." Hargrove's readers learned how Bushemi outran most contestants in an obstacle race while photographing the action and how his feigned innocence and charm won over the author's girl. In a statement appreciated by Garyites, Hargrove wrote: "There is no need for me to visit Charlotte (North Carolina) again. . . . It's Bushemi's territory. If I ever get a furlough again, I'll probably have to go to Gary, Indiana."

Assigned to the staff of *Yank* magazine after his work was featured in *Field Artillery Journal*, Bushemi went to Hawaii in November 1942 to open its Pacific bureau. There he studied film making from Colonel Frank Capra, a former Hollywood director, but chafed at not being where the action was. "This is not a combat zone," he wired the *Yank* office in New York. "The only Japs you can smell here are the ones who ride beside you in Honolulu buses and streetcars."

In the spring of 1943 Bushemi island-hopped to such combat zones as New Georgia, Guadalcanal, Munda, and Vella LaVella, specializing in what his partner Merle Miller labeled "photography from a rifle's length vantage point." His colleagues thought him to be a little crazy but utterly fearless.

On January 10, 1944, Bushemi wrote to *Post-Tribune* reporter Edward Brennan about his experiences on Tarawa: "When we arrived there, we saw bodies floating around in the water—hundreds of them—all American marines. The courage of our marines was magnificent, and it made me proud that my brother, Sam, is a member of the corps."

On February 19, 1944, Bushemi was on the island of Eniwetok. His left arm was in a sling from having fractured his hand at Kwajalein. When the fighting became intense, most journalists retreated, but Bushemi remained at the front. Suddenly, as he was winding a movie camera, an enemy mortar shell exploded. Merle Miller heard him cry out: "Where's my camera?" Then to his horror he saw Bushemi's shattered legs and gaping neck wound. When medics arrived, Miller put his buddy's body on the stretcher.

Bushemi died less than three hours later. According to *Yank*, his last words were: "Be sure to get those pictures back to the office right away." *Time* magazine reported the death in its "Milestones" section in this manner: "Killed in action. Staff Sergeant John Aloysius Bushemi . . . probably the best known noncom in the Pacific area. . . ."

The news saddened the Gary community. He was a "dapper, darkly handsome youth," the *Post-Tribune* eulogized, "whose ready quip and irresistible grin were never to be denied." Gary coach Sam Catanzarite, who had been with him in Honolulu, said: "I figured he would get it sooner or later. He always went right in behind the front line troops to get his shots."

Reporter Erwin Crewe Rosenau drew the assignment of covering the memorial service for his former friend. His story began: "Under a gray and lowering sky which itself seemed to verge on weeping, hundreds of those who knew and loved Johnny Bushemi as an elfin boy, as a genial young man eager to make his mark in the world, and as a gallant soldier impatient to give his all to his craft and his country, filed into St. Mark's church this morning to bow their heads in memory of him."

Bushemi was not soon forgotten. Awards and buildings were named after him, and institutions exhibited his photos, some of which had appeared in the *New York Times* and *The Saturday Evening Post.* In 1947 his coffin was brought "home" from its shallow grave site on Japtan Island.

Johnny Bushemi became Gary's symbolic hero because in the public eye he reflected the aspirations and best traits of the community. Moreover, he exemplified the loyalty of its ethnic populace and performed his assignments with flair and professionalism but without the self-congratulatory fanfare of a Tom Harmon.

Had he survived the war, Bushemi might have come to believe, like Harmon, that he had outgrown Gary, but a mortar shell cheated him from making that decision. Unlike the image of most war heroes, who killed people, Bushemi was remembered as a man-child who combined cool professionalism with a basic, enduring innocence.

MAN OF STEEL: TONY ZALE

Prizefighter Tony Zale's background was similar to thousands of immigrants in Gary's Central District. Born in 1913 and christened Anthony Florian Zaleski, he grew up in a close-knit, Catholic family. Since his father died when he was two years old, the youngster's heroes, while he attended school at St. Hedwig and Froebel, were his older brothers, who were boxing in the amateur ranks.

At 15, Zale had his first bout at the Chicago Arena. The day of the fight, his mother fed him a fish dinner instead of his regular training meal because it was Friday. The debut was inauspicious. His experienced opponent pounded him so hard that Zale could not remember anything after midway through the second round. Afterwards, his brothers reassured him that he had fought well even though he lost.

In 1930, when Gary began holding Golden Gloves tournaments, Zale won the welter weight title, his first of four city championships. Moving up to the middleweight division, he fought over 200 amateur bouts before his twenty-first birthday.

Persuaded to turn professional in order, in his words, to buy his mother "a few luxuries," Zale signed with a manager who rushed his development too fast, overtrained him, and allowed him to fight while in pain from torn muscles. After splitting eight bouts, Zale retired in 1935 and worked full time at the mill in order to toughen his body. For two years, Zale requested such strenuous assignments as lifting beams, shoveling ore, and pouring slag. He said later: "I knew I'd never be any good as a fighter as long as my side bothered me. So I got the kind of work that would strengthen it."

Zale was back in the ring in 1937, but his lack of polish cost him several fights until he was signed for 200 dollars by managers Art Winch and Sam Pian, who had guided Barney Ross to three world titles. Impressed by Zale's stamina, courage, and body punching ability, they improved his style and, after several victories, secured him a nontitle bout with N.B.A. middleweight champ Al Hostak. By this time, Zale had attracted a considerable Midwestern following. Before the Hostak fight, held in January 1940, Mayor Ernst Schaible wired him: "Gary is proud of you. Get in and win."

Weakened by a recent viral disease, which had delayed the fight two weeks, Zale was floored in the first round and dazed by hard blows in the third and fifth. Nonetheless, he came back strongly and won a unanimous decision. When Hostak complained that he had broken his hand during the bout, manager Winch replied, "Maybe so, but Tony broke his heart."

Garyites regarded Zale as a conquering hero when he returned the next day. The Lions Club requested his presence at a luncheon, and the *Post-Tribune* eulogized him as "a great chap and a likeable one."

More accolades greeted Zale's second victory over Hostak on July 19, 1941, for the N.B.A. crown. Broadcast from Seattle, the 13th-round knockout sent hundreds of celebrants cascading down Broadway at two in the morning. Later at the Zale home reporters discovered a telegram of assurance that he was unhurt signed "The Champ, Tony."

The following week, columnist Roy G. Parry complained that Chicago newspapers were heralding Zale as one of their own, as had also been the case with Tom Harmon. Zale's achievements, Parry added, demonstrated the value of hard work, clean living, and a supportive family.

Zale's next opponent was George Abrams, still recognized by New York as the middleweight champion. A fungus infection caused Zale to postpone the match until November 1941. Slightly weak and nervous before the partisan New York crowd, Zale was floored for a nine-count in the first round but quickly gained the upper hand and became the undisputed champion.

World War II caused a suspension of title prizefights, and the only chance Zale had to capitalize financially on his fame was in an ill-advised match against heavyweight Billy Conn. Enlisting in the Navy, he worked as a fund raiser and physical education instructor while his skills atrophied. "I couldn't box with the kids," Zale later said of his war work. "I have to wade in and punch. I can't hold back. If I started pulling punches to protect the kids, I would never get over the habit. I would have lost my punch. So I simply didn't fight."

In 1946 Zale signed to defend his title against Rocky Graziano, a savage puncher-brawler who drew well at the box office in the East. During training Zale contracted pneumonia, forcing a postponement of the match. Then on the day of the fight he woke up with a sty but resisted efforts to move back the fight date again.

Held at Yankee Stadium on September 27, 1946, the Zale-Graziano bout was a classic confrontation between contrasting styles. In each of the first two rounds, Zale was on the canvas. He broke his right thumb, appeared wobbly, and looked over-the-hill. He took Graziano's best punches in the next three rounds, however, and turned the fight around in the sixth. After delivering several punishing body blows, Zale knocked out Graziano with a two-punch combination to the stomach and chin. Former heavyweight champion Gene Tunney called the comeback performance "the greatest exhibition of heart I have ever seen." Said Graziano: "All I heard was 8-9-10 and that count came up awfully fast."

Attending Zale's homecoming were 30,000 people, fully one-fourth of Gary's population, including well-wishers from Froebel and the Polish National Alliance of Silverbells. Mayor Schaible presented him with the key to the city. Four months later, at a Junior Chamber of Commerce banquet honoring Zale as Gary's "Outstanding Young Man of 1946," H. B. Snyder praised his work on behalf of the Red Cross and the Community Fund and concluded that "in a profession too often touched by sordidness, the Gary fighter has not been touched either physically or mentally."

Journalist Howard Roberts echoed these sentiments in a *Saturday Evening Post* article entitled "Hard-Luck Champion," which mentioned that Zale told boys' club audiences "to practice good sportsmanship and live cleanly." Zale neither smoked, drank, nor swore, Roberts asserted, and he believed that "this kind of missionary work is one of the duties of holding a title."

Zale was proud of, but a little uneasy about, his image as a "Man of Steel" with a "heart of gold." The publicity was a double-edged sword, as evidenced by the widespread coverage of his marital problems, an extremely sensitive subject to one of his religious faith.

In a return bout with Graziano, Zale lost his crown on a disputed, sixth-round technical knockout, without ever having been knocked down. Zale believed that the referee erred in stopping the fight, but the official told critics, "What do you want up there, murder?"

Zale won back his title with a third-round knockout over Graziano but retired in 1949 after a loss to Frenchman Marcel Cerdan. The challenger hurt Zale so badly that after the 11th round, Zale's managers would not let him continue. Zale called the defeat "one of those things ... you either have it or you don't."

Following his retirement from the ring, Zale worked as a CYO director and an adviser to the Boys' Club, the Mentally Retarded Olympics, cerebral palsy clinics, and veterans rehabilitation programs. He was named Gary's "Sportsman of the Decade" but was beset by a broken marriage, financial woes, and moods of depression. Many former admirers unfairly considered him to be little more than a punch-drunk pugilist. In November 1949 he claimed that he was too poor to meet his alimony payments; his only asset, he said, was a car given him the previous year by well-wishers.

After his remarriage in 1970, Zale, who worked in a boys' boxing program for the Chicago Park District, put in appearances at a variety of civic functions, including soccer and football games, beauty contests, and receptions for visiting dignitaries. On November 10, 1971, columnist Blaine Marz wrote that Zale "has had his share of the up-and-down routine ... since the championship days. But he's definitely up now."

MOSES TO HIS PEOPLE:
FATHER VENCESLAUS M. ARDAS

During World War II many ethnic families moved out of the Central District. Under the leadership of the Reverend Venceslaus M. Ardas, who was born in the village of Padolic in 1900, Gary's Croatian community remained a close-knit group. Ardas came to America in 1930 as a Franciscan missionary and traveled widely for seven years before taking over the pastorate of the declining parish of Holy Trinity Church at 22nd and Adams on the silver anniversary of its construction.

Combining a blend of Old World nationalism and New World

practicality, Ardas lured many Croatians back into the church. After celebrating his first mass, he told reporters: "While I am pleased to see Croatians retain a love for their native land, I also am glad that they are trying to be real Americans. In my work I have always attempted to have my countrymen appreciate the advantages offered them in the United States."

In 1941 Ardas purchased a large parcel of land at 44th and Delaware and carried out fund drives to relocate his church in Glen Park. Once while holding a Sunday picnic at 63rd and Broadway, Ardas was arrested because of the selling of intoxicating beverages. The confrontation with County Prosecutor Charles W. Gannon did not hurt his popularity, and his parishioners rallied to his defense. A parochial school was erected on the new land in 1943, a new church building was ready for Christmas Eve mass in 1944, a two-story rectory was built in 1947, and finally a new Gothic edifice was dedicated in 1956.

By then Father Ardas had retired to take over leadership of the St. Joseph Commissariat of Franciscan Fathers. At the time of his death in 1959, he was eulogized as a modern Moses who had led Gary's Croatians to a new home.

ANNA RIGOVSKY YURIN: SLOVAK-AMERICAN

Anna Rigovsky came to Gary in 1912 with her parents, John and Mary, and her two brothers. Although just three years old, she retained lifelong memories of the train ride from her birthplace in Clairton, Pennsylvania, and of the shack-like home at 10th and Jefferson where they first lived. Sent to kindergarten the following year, she spoke only Slovak and ran home when the teacher ignored her requests to use the washroom. After someone quelled her fears and spoke to the teacher, she returned only to be sent to the bathroom whenever she spoke. Because of the incident, she said later, "I learned and I learned fast, and pretty soon I was talking nothing but the American language."

For eight years Anna attended Holy Trinity School, built in 1913 with money that her father helped raise through door-to-door solicitations. Anna and her seven classmates studied English, Latin, and Slovak. One nun "thought she was a failure if she couldn't pound the stuff into you," Anna recalled. Referring to the nun's disciplinary tactics of ruler rapping, ear boxing, and hair pulling, she said: "I got it plenty because I was always on the bold side. I was never afraid of anybody or anything."

Anna grew up on the Southside, close to undeveloped marshes and frontier-like saloons. On Saturday nights, while the men drank away their problems, the wives stayed home. Some immigrant women were housekeepers for a dozen boarders. Others were mail-order brides. "Beauty didn't count in those days," Anna remembered. "How strong you were was what mattered."

At the time, Anna was only vaguely aware of Gary's "Wild West" atmosphere. The saloons were places to get free pretzels when you bought beer for your father. Anna remembered World War I as a time when the family often had to eat brown sugar. Likewise, the 1919 steel strike passed unnoticed except that she could not play on the Froebel schoolgrounds because the militia was encamped there. When Czechoslovakia achieved independence from Austria-Hungary, the congregation at Holy Trinity took up a special collection. Anna's father refused to donate anything, believing that the priest could either "send *his* money" or help poor people in his new homeland.

The Rigovsky household was religious and strict but not autocratic. Church was mandatory, however, and each year on Good Friday nobody could eat butter or milk. Anna's mother managed the finances and controlled the daily routine. She jokingly declared: "I believe everything your father says if it's to my advantage. Otherwise I don't believe it." Some of Anna's friends lived in terror of their fathers, but steelworker John Rigovsky was partial to his two daughters and never spanked them. "From mother it was a different story," Anna recalled. "One, two, three! I got it when I got out of line."

Once when Anna's sister played hooky from school, Mary told her husband to punish her with the razorstrap. Into the bedroom went the culprit and the reluctant patriarch, and through the door came screams. Fearing that John was overdoing it, Mary burst into the room to find him pounding the bed. "She took that razorstrap, and both of them got it," Anna recalled.

Anna's parents considered dating to be a prelude to marriage. They wanted to know who each suitor was, who his parents were, where he worked, how much he made, and whether he had honorable intentions. Anna would teasingly promise to get their pay stubs or would meet them on the way to parish dances, which featured old-country bands playing polkas, waltzes, and the czardas.

For two years Anna attended Froebel School before going to work at the Boston Clothing Store for a weekly salary of 13 dollars. Froebel's work-study-play curriculum was interesting but easy compared to Holy Trinity. She encountered no problems and said later: "Maybe I'm a little bit tougher than a lot of kids were. I've been that way and still am."

Leaving her job in the men's department at 10:00 P.M. Saturday nights, Anna and a friend, dressed in the "flapper" style of the 1920s, walked from Broadway through the "Red Light" district to Tyler Street. Nobody ever bothered them; their absence of heavy makeup distinguished them from the prostitutes.

In October 1926 Anna married Henry Yurin, whom she had met ten months earlier at midnight mass. John wanted her to wait until her 18th birthday but relented when she threatened to elope. By 1930 the couple had paid 2,000 dollars toward a house in Glen Park. But then the depression caused Henry his job at the mill, except for a day or two each month, and they lost the house with only 1,600 dollars remaining on the mortgage. They rented a roach-infested apartment downtown and later bought a snug four-family dwelling on 3rd and Harrison.

Life went on during the 1930s. Mrs. Yurin learned how to can vegetables and make peach butter from skins that she previously had thrown away. "What are you having for dinner?" a friend would ask. "Potatoes and beans? Why, we are having beans and potatoes." Relatives frequently visited, and while the women talked and minded the children, the husbands played cards for match sticks. Anna did not resent being excluded from the games because the men argued as if they were gambling for real money. They did not care how late the party lasted, Mrs. Yurin recalled, because nobody had to get up the next morning to work.

During the 1930s Henry Yurin helped organize millworkers, meeting secretly at first so as not to lose his job. Anna took an active part in Democratic campaigns, as did her mother, who was a precinct committeewoman. Once while in a Republican area, Anna was told that her candidate was a crook. In a reference to R. O. Johnson, she replied that at least Democrats did not nominate men who had served time in jail.

During World War II Anna worked in a machine shop after friends told her that it would be unpatriotic not to have a defense job. At first many men resented women co-workers because their exemptions from military service might be threatened as well as their egos. Women had to do the equivalent of a man's work, and some even became crane operators. When one draftee criticized her presence, Mrs. Yurin answered that she would quit the day he returned from the war.

On one occasion, Anna began questioning the necessity of wars when a German-American employee asked her to be quiet or government spies would hear the conversation. She replied that it was a free country and that she could speak her mind but changed the subject out of deference to his fears.

The horrors of war left their mark on Mrs. Yurin's family. When her youngest brother Steve left for France, her father advised him to shoot the "lords" rather than the common soldiers. Steve returned from the conflict partially disabled. A cousin in the Czech army disappeared shortly after he questioned the government's policies while home on leave. He was never heard from again. Anna's oldest son enlisted in the Navy in 1945; her second son was in the Korean War; her youngest son Henry served two tours of duty in Vietnam.

A member of many civic organizations—including the Slovak Auxiliary of the American Legion, the Isabellas, the Ladies Christian Benevolence Society, and the Archconfraternity of Holy Family— Mrs. Yurin has been most active in the Ladies Auxiliary of the Slovak Club. Founded in 1913, the Slovak Club was dedicated to fostering ethnic culture, language, and traditions. But the organization atrophied except as a place of male fellowship, until the Ladies Auxiliary started in 1948 with Mrs. Yurin as its first president. The auxiliary planned such family activities as dances and Christmas parties. Its most lucrative and popular function was the Friday night fish fry. Anna's mother helped prepare pierogi at the Slovak Club until she was in her mid-80s.

Mrs. Yurin credited her parents with teaching her to go after something when she wanted it. She said: "My father had a philosophy which I have tried to live by. It was that you never feel that you're any better than the other guy. You are not any uglier than the other guy, and you're not any dumber."

Proud of her ethnic heritage, Mrs. Yurin sent a son to Holy Trinity, hoping that he would learn the Slovak language. She lamented that Slovaks no longer participated in pageants at the International Institute. Nonetheless, she sympathized with a son who complained in 1961 that he could not understand the priest's eulogy at his grandfather's funeral, which was delivered in the Slovak language. In 1973 when she talked to her mother in the presence of her own grandchildren, they asked: "Why are you and Baba talking Spanish?" The experience reminded her how far removed those children were from their Slovak ancestry.

JEWISH REFUGEE: MARTIN ZELT

The story of Martin Zelt's evolution from a German law student to a professor at Indiana University Northwest was filled with the vicissitudes of fortune. He was born on January 3, 1906, in Berlin, the son of an urbane Jewish shoe factory owner. Reared to respect formal education, he received a philosophy of law degree at the University of Heidelberg in 1933 and was admitted conditionally to the bar. Ominously, these events coincided with Adolf Hitler's rise to power. The Nazi leader soon purged from his university post Zelt's former adviser, Professor Gerhard Anschuetz, a liberal who had helped author the Weimar Constitution. The Führer's gospel of anti-Semitism led to the ending of Zelt's law career.

For the next six years the Zelt family lived in a nightmare world of humiliation, impoverishment, and terror. The German government nationalized Joseph Zelt's shoe factory. He and Martin, working when and where they could, discovered that "the deeper one went down the social scale, the more difficult it was to overcome the great prejudice of the German people against Jews." As their savings evaporated and the abuses mounted, Martin's self-confidence waned. He "felt that this Jew was not so good" and had "the terrible feeling that something must be wrong with us." Marriage to Gerta Weinschenk in June 1937 alleviated the despair somewhat, as did his father's fierce pride. He was "the great encourager . . . that is what saved us," Martin recalled.

Before 1938 the Zelts avoided publicly opposing Hitler and wrongly believed that they could migrate to America if and when the situation deteriorated beyond repair. Concerning his family's political passivity, Martin later remarked that "we were unfortunately very ordinary people who, I regret to say, had never purchased weapons. . . . We were sitting there and waiting for it, so to speak." In 1924 the United States had limited immigration drastically, and the depression further tightened the quota regulations. The Zelts had neither the money nor the connections necessary to qualify.

Without warning or rational cause, the Reich Chancellor in June 1939 ordered Martin Zelt banished from Germany within three weeks on pain of arrest. Two strokes of luck saved him from probable death. The British, who had taken an interest in aiding German intellectuals, classified him as a professional eligible for asylum if he were not indigent. The necessary money came from a cousin in Danzig in gratitude for the Zelts having transferred his mentally ill sister out of a public institution where her life was in jeopardy. The cousin denied a request, however, for an additional hundred pounds for Martin's parents.

Martin faced his flight with misgivings. It meant separation from Gerta until she could obtain an entrance visa as a household employee (she arrived in England three days before World War II erupted), and it meant leaving his parents, an ordeal that gave him pangs of guilt. At first he refused to go, but Joseph Zelt insisted that it was the only way that he might raise enough money for them all to get out.

The Zelts' sojourn in England lasted ten months until they could be sent to America. Because the British forbade her husband to work, Gerta had to take menial jobs to support them. After they arrived in New York on June 1, 1940 (due to his father's prescience in reserving space on a Cunard Liner), the Hebrew Sheltering and Immigrant Aid Society located them in Terre Haute, Indiana. There Martin began working at "the most awful mixture of jobs" at such low wages as to frustrate his dream of financing his parents' escape. For awhile he taught Latin at Indiana State Teachers College after Gerta persuaded an acquaintance to get him the job. He later stated: "I knew so much about Latin because they had tormented me for years with translating law books." As a consequence of American entry into war against Germany, he lost that position because he was now classified as an enemy alien. There was bitter irony in the government treating a Jewish Latin teacher as a security risk. This incident and recurrent memories of his parents' exclusion clouded his otherwise bright impressions of the United States.

In 1942 the Zelts moved to Gary. Martin was employed at a series of jobs for which he had little aptitude. "I mostly ended up behind the eight ball," he recollected. At the Weiner Pants Company he lasted ten months and then, in his words, "they had to reject me like a machine rejects plug nickels." Making pants ever remained "a very mysterious process," and "the American effectiveness was very much hindered by me." Next Zelt lost a position at an iron store by dropping a stove. Then he became a not-so-handy handyman at a furniture shop in Indiana Harbor. Finally, the Washington National Insurance Company hired him as a salesman, a position he held for twenty years. Concerning his previous job failures, Zelt recalled: "I made mistakes, and they could not stand it."

The tragedy of his parents' deaths permanently scarred Zelt's memories of the war years. A thousand-dollar loan from Temple Israel in Gary enabled him to apply for a Cuban visa for them, but once Cuba entered the war on the allied side, the island could not be used as a transfer point by refugees. For four years, his father was a slave laborer (building streets) before dying in an extermination camp. His mother Franziska also perished. In 1949 the West German government offered Martin a post as a judge in Bonn. Unwilling to forget what the Germans had done to his parents, he refused it.

By this time, Zelt felt at home in America even though selling insurance in Gary did not make use of his academic background. "I became moderately successful and moderately happy," he said, adding that "to a great extent I had abandoned my dreams." In a poem entitled "I, Alone," he wrote:

> Yet who am I but all these countless masses
> Of thoughts and fears and dreams of other men,
> One hollow stalk in myriads of grasses.
> I am the sum of all that passed and passes;
> I am what others were before my ken.

At the University of Chicago Zelt studied German literature, which was his "lifelong passion"; his father had steered him into law. He wrote essays and delivered a scholarly paper on Nelly Sachs before the Deutsche Literarische Gesellschaft.

Zelt's association with the Deutsche Literarische Gesellschaft thrust him into contact with German-born intellectuals and led to his becoming a professor of German literature and language at Indiana University Northwest. In 1962 a fellow refugee named Frederick Ritter asked him if he wanted to be his part-time replacement at the university. He accepted and soon terminated his insurance job upon being offered a full-time appointment. Having been thwarted in a legal career by Hitler and then thrust during his years of peak productivity into an environment that had no use for his scholarly training, he was starting anew at an age when most people were in the twilight of their careers. He considered himself fortunate in comparison to other educated men displaced from the old country who never had a chance like his.

CHAPTER TEN

Postwar Strife

God of justice, save the people
From the clash of race and creed,
From the strife of class and faction
Make our Nation free indeed.
Keep her faith in simple manhood
Strong as when her life began,
Till it finds its full fruition
In the brotherhood of man.

—Official prayer of the Anselm
Forum

ONCE THE AXIS POWERS were defeated, most Garyites expected that their main concerns in the postwar world would be economic. The city did not return to the depressed conditions of the 1930s as some feared, but did undergo a racial crisis in the schools, a Red Scare, labor troubles in the mills, a wave of crime and juvenile delinquency, and a series of political crises. The war boom had brought an influx of newcomers from the South who had problems in adjusting to urban life. Out of the polarized environment emerged political boss George Chacharis, whose immigrant background and rough-hewn ways seemed representative of Gary, which one contemporary writer called a "raw young town."

During the 1950s the Democratic party was dominant locally, and the power of organized labor increased. There were approximately 25 active unions, including the teamsters, the American Federation of Teachers, the United Auto Workers, AFL building and trades unions, and, of course, the United Steelworkers of America. One writer described Gary as a union "bastion," with labor representatives automatically holding seats on governmental boards, playing a key role in Democratic party politics, and assuming leadership in the annual Community Chest drives. Political scientist Warner Bloomberg concluded that the CIO's subdistrict director was one of the city's six most powerful men, along with the superintendents at Gary Works and the Gary-Hobart Water Corporation, the mayor and city controller, and the owner-publisher of the *Post-Tribune*. No blacks were on the list; they would not come to the forefront until the 1960s.

THE FROEBEL SCHOOL STRIKE

On September 18, 1945, several hundred white students at Froebel School boycotted classes in an effort to have their black classmates transferred to other institutions. Alleging that Principal Richard A. Nuzum had been treating them like "guinea pigs" in "racial experiments," they demanded his ouster.

Tensions had been building at Froebel since the early years of World War II, when increasing numbers of black families had moved into the surrounding ethnic neighborhoods. In September 1943, 812 blacks and 1,607 whites enrolled for classes at Froebel, once known as Gary's immigrant school. Two years later, the figures were 1,070 blacks and 1,129 whites.

Traditionally, blacks at Froebel had been treated as outcasts and excluded from extracurricular activities except for sports. After Nuzum became principal when Charles S. Coons retired in 1942, the situation began to improve slightly, though some white parents feared that their children's "social integrity" was being threatened.

Nuzum altered his predecessor's policy of classifying large numbers of blacks as "incorrigibles" and then segregating them from normal school activities. He ordered a curtailment of corporal punishment, set up special programs for slow learners, made it easier for blacks to enroll in academic courses, integrated the student council and the boys's swimming pool, and enabled blacks to try out for the orchestra.

Use of the swimming pool had long been a source of friction. In the summer of 1943, when the school board had opened it to blacks in the afternoons, white parents pressured the board into rescinding the order so that blacks could only use it on Fridays, the day before it was cleaned.

Nuzum helped found a biracial Parent-Teachers' Association, and he asked the Bureau of Intercultural Education to recommend ways of promoting tolerance among young people. One local organization interested in this same goal was the Chamber of Commerce's Race-Relations Committee, which had been formed in the wake of the 1943 Detroit riot out of fear that a similar disturbance might erupt in Gary. Among its members were Mayor Joseph E. Finerty, Gary Works Superintendent S. M. Jenks, *Post-Tribune* editor H. B. Snyder, School Superintendent Charles D. Lutz, and several members of the school board. Ironically, the Chamber of Commerce was an all-white organization, but in 1944 the Race-Relations Committee added six black advisers and drew up a model code supporting equal opportunity and desegregation.

The pace of change was slow, and in 1945 the city's ministerial organizations and medical facilities were still segregated. Furthermore, the Froebel strike occurred just a month after World War II ended, at a time when a rash of strikes was taking place. There was a general boredom or disinterest in school. After Labor Day five percent of the school-age population failed to register for classes, as many teen-agers preferred to keep their summer jobs.

The Froebel strike, according to the *Post-Tribune,* resulted from a series of "minor irritations" having to do with the "changing status in the school." Eight students devised the idea in the aftermath of a football game that Froebel lost to Horace Mann, 19 to 0. Among other things, they were disgruntled over the performance of their team's black players and angered by a postgame fight which started when a white youth insulted some black coeds.

The following Monday, they demanded that Nuzum make Froebel an all-white institution. The principal replied that he had neither the power nor the desire to do so. The next morning, they picketed in front of the school entrances and persuaded approximately 500 of their classmates to follow them to Tyler Park. With the sun shining and students clustered on the grass, the rally had a holiday flavor. The crowd selected the eight ringleaders as its strike committee, rejected efforts to elect female leaders, and made plans to persuade other schools to hold sympathy strikes. Only at Tolleston did a few students join the boycott, and then only briefly.

On Tuesday evening, a hundred parents and teachers who were unsympathetic to the strike attended a school board meeting. The Reverend L. K. Jackson made an impassioned appeal to keep Froebel integrated. "We don't want any fascism in Gary," he concluded. Superintendent Lutz, a former Froebel teacher, condemned the strike but told board members privately that the overwhelming majority of Garyites believed in segregation.

Principal Nuzum thought the strike leaders were unrepresentative of Froebel's student body. An investigator for the NAACP called them " 'D' students, hooligans, zoot-suiters, and Klan sympathizers." Nonetheless, they came from a cross-section of ethnic backgrounds and soon had most white students observing the boycott.

The most important strike leader was 17-year-old Leonard Levenda, who had a flair for the dramatic and a history of poor grades and disciplinary problems. Exploiting his classmates' resentment against Northsiders, as well as their dislike for blacks, Levenda seized upon inequities in the school board's racial policies which had been in existence since the 1927 Emerson strike. Blacks in other districts were transferred either to Froebel or Roosevelt (an all-black school), leaving the other schools segregated.

Calling for equal treatment so that Froebel would not become a slum school, Levenda said: "If we must attend school with Negroes, so should all the other(s). . . . We'll stay out until every school in Gary . . . accepts Negro pupils."

More than the prejudice or immaturity of the participants, the fundamental cause of the strike was the degree to which segregation had been previously tolerated by the very businessmen, clergymen, city officials, and newspapermen who condemned it. Given that situation, both Levenda and the school board realized that an immediate order to integrate all Gary schools would precipitate a citywide school boycott.

If racial polarization caused the crisis, religious and class conflict exacerbated it. Rumors spread that Catholic clergy were using the strike as a means of launching a parochial school. A labor leader charged that mill personnel were fomenting trouble in order to weaken labor solidarity during contract negotiations. The Gary Teachers' Union was slow to rally behind Nuzum because of his previous hostility to some of its officers.

One of the first groups to condemn the strike was the all-black Interdenominational Ministerial Alliance, whose members signed an "appeal to reason" calling for decency and justice to prevail rather than a "manifestation of Hitlerism." Meeting with two of its officers, Mayor Finerty expressed the wish that all Garyites would respect the law. In that case, the Reverend Claude Allen replied, he should arrest the lawbreakers. "That is a difficult matter," Finerty replied.

School officials refused to meet with strikers until they started attending classes, but they neither expelled them nor ordered them arrested as truants. On September 25, in fact, the board agreed to hear their grievances when about half of them returned to Froebel for one day.

That evening Levenda amplified upon his charges of lax discipline and racial experimentation at Froebel, citing 13 instances where blacks insulted, threatened, or threw paper clips at whites. He complained also that whites had to share the same band instruments with Negroes and would soon probably be attending the same dances. Levenda rejected the suggestion that a biracial student committee could reduce tensions, declaring that the time for that had passed. He further claimed that it was unsafe for the strikers to return to Froebel.

No other group came forward at the board meeting in support of the strike except for a self-appointed Tolleston student who demanded a "long guarantee" that blacks not be sent to his school "and take away our democratic right to happiness." In contrast, numerous organizations went on record in opposition to the boycott, including the Anselm Forum, the Gary Civil Liberties Union, the Interdenominational Ministerial Alliance, the CIO, the Froebel PTA, and the Chamber of Commerce's Race-Relations Committee.

The school board rejected the strikers' demands, and the boycott continued into its second week. At this point sympathetic parents enlisted in the cause. On September 27 boycott supporters met at Spanish Hall to set up a Parents Committee of Thirteen, headed by John Jadrnak, to press for Nuzum's ouster.

Three days later, Jadrnak's forces reached an agreement with the school board by which three prominent outside educators would be selected to investigate the charges against Nuzum. Meanwhile, the principal would relinquish his duties to football coach Johnny Kyle, a man respected by all parties to the dispute.

Nuzum publicly welcomed the opportunity to vindicate his reputation but feared becoming a sacrificial lamb. Sharing this opinion, the Gary *American*, which had labeled the strike a "tragi-comic . . . hate show," wrote that "it is the way of the rabble to turn upon the just and the innocent when their plans for destruction come to naught."

Returning to class on October 1, 1945, the strikers were confident that Nuzum would never be back. According to a widely circulated story, Superintendent Lutz had told Jadrnak: "Nuzum's throat is cut."

The investigators spent three weeks studying conditions at Froebel and then exonerated Nuzum, categorizing him as an "effective administrator." The principal returned to his post; and after three days of fruitless discussions, the boycott resumed. Levenda blamed the second walkout on Nuzum's arrogance, a charge that the principal vehemently denied. "He told us he is boss, and the first thing he intends to do is open the girls' pool to Negroes," Levenda declared.

At this juncture the Anselm Forum arranged for singer Frank Sinatra to visit Gary. Founded in 1932 by Reuben E. Olsen, a Norwegian-American foreman at Gary Works, the nondenominational organization was dedicated to the promotion of interreligious, intercultural, and interracial fellowship. Historian Richard Meister wrote that "the Forum became a beacon showing through the bleak years of the depression and brought effective action through its weekly symposiums on problems affecting the various groups in the city."

During World War II the Anselm Forum had sponsored panel discussions on such issues as juvenile delinquency, the meaning of religion and brotherhood, and the place of women in modern society. Typical of its activities was an annual visit to the Indiana State Penitentiary, where members presented a program featuring a Jew reading Scripture from the New Testament, an Italian-born resident singing a Russian hymn, a. Welsh violinist playing a German folk ballad, songs by a black veterans' glee club, and inspirational speeches by Americans of Filipino and Japanese ancestry.

When the Froebel strike first began, Reuben Olsen and Anselm Youth Forum leader Harry Johnson inquired into the possibility of having Sinatra and heavyweight champion Joe Louis visit Gary to help defuse racial tensions. Sinatra had recently put on a "tolerance" benefit at a New York high school, while Louis had become famous as a good-will ambassador during World War II.

Other commitments prevented Louis from coming, but Sinatra cancelled a $10,000 engagement and arrived in Gary on November 1, 1945. High school students were given a holiday, and more than 5,800 young people crowded into Memorial Auditorium to hear him sing "Ole Man River" and "The House I Live In" and deliver an impassioned denunciation of bigotry. He labeled the strike "the most shameful incident in the history of American education," and suggested that the adults who fomented the trouble be run out of town.

Levenda met briefly with Sinatra and afterwards said that the singer was misinformed about the situation. Parents Committee spokesman Jadrnak called for a boycott of his records. Mayor Finerty personally apologized to two strike leaders whom Sinatra criticized by name.

Although Sinatra's visit frayed some oversensitive nerves and did not end the strike, it focused national attention on Gary. Three days later, cartoonist Bill Mauldin, poet Carl Sandburg, and novelist Edna

Ferber visited the city in support of a Victory Bond drive and echoed Sinatra's plea for an end to the strike.

The longer the deadlock continued, the more anxious the parents of the strikers became to find a face-saving way to resolve it. When State Superintendent of Public Instruction C. T. Malan promised to study conditions at Froebel on the condition that the students return to classes, Levenda and Jadrnak interpreted his remarks as a victory insofar as the strikers had succeeded in publicizing their grievances. On that note, after one final rally at Tyler Park, the Froebel strike ended on November 12, 1945.

Before long, however, rumors started that Levenda was organizing yet another walkout. It was difficult for him to relinquish the limelight, accept defeat, and get along with Nuzum. Few students shared his enthusiasm for another boycott, however, especially if it meant jeopardizing any basketball games. In fact, the Froebel student council voted unanimously against striking.

While Levenda put off his plans until after basketball season, his opponents took countermeasures to head him off. In February 1946 the school board, bolstered by resolutions from a half-dozen civic groups, turned down Levenda's request for an emergency meeting. The members also rejected a proposal by Councilman Paul Dudak (who had praised the strikers for conducting themselves "splendidly, without violence, and in a democratic manner. . . .") to fire Nuzum, whom he called the "symbol of dissatisfaction."

When the Parents Committee asked why all Gary's schools could not be integrated if Froebel had to be, board member Sophia Hill replied that "the adjustments can't be made as quickly as one, two, three. If you are sincere, as you say you are, you will help us work out the problem within [Froebel] first."

One person prepared to test that sincerity was Joseph C. Chapman, who had come from St. Louis the previous autumn to become executive secretary of the Gary Urban League. Quickly familiarizing himself with the crisis, he appeared on several panel discussions opposite Jadrnak.

Jadrnak came to respect Chapman and, anxious to demonstrate that he was not a racist, agreed to serve as a cochairman at a biracial public meeting on February 23, where all interested parties could express their views. The meeting was spirited but successful in bringing fears and false rumors into the open. At one point, a strike supporter challenged Nuzum to a fight and then waited outside for him. Jadrnak and Chapman kept the altercation purely verbal; and after more opinions were aired on the sidewalk, the last stragglers went home.

Chapman's master stroke was to persuade Levenda and his girl friend Mary Balles to meet with three black student leaders, thereby allowing the strike leader to regain the spotlight at a time when the school board would have nothing to do with him. After several meetings, the five students released a statement of principles advocating the desegregation of all Gary schools and equal access to "facilities, activities, clubs, and programs. . . ." The threat of a strike had passed. After the spring semester ended without further incident, one school official remarked that Froebel students were becoming "the most tolerant in the whole city."

It remained for the school board to remove the barriers of discrimination in other districts. In August 1946 William H. Stern drew up a resolution to that effect, but the board amended it so as to include initially only the primary grades and for implementation to be delayed a year until September 1947.

Segregationists attempted to make the antidiscrimination resolution an issue in the 1947 Democratic primary. Dropping out of the contest, Mayor Finerty announced: "The results of certain decisions of our school board have become controversial. Obviously, the problems . . . are more susceptible of solution by a mayor who is not a candidate for re-election."

In the primary Eugene Swartz, who had praised the antidiscrimination resolution, defeated Anthony E. Dobis, who had indicated opposition to it, by a mere 287 votes. He probably would have lost had the county election committee not thrown out the candidacy petition of a bowling alley proprietor named William H. Swartz on the grounds that he was attempting to "perpetrate a fraud . . . [and] confuse the voters."

Four months later, 116 black youngsters enrolled in five previously all-white schools, including 38 at Emerson. For ten days, 80 percent of the Emerson student body boycotted classes, and hundreds of demonstrators gathered each morning to jeer, curse, and threaten the few Negroes and whites who defied them. Even the threat of canceling Emerson's entire athletic program for the year did not deter the football team from unanimously supporting the strike.

Better organized and more prepared for trouble than in 1945, integrationists mobilized in support of the school board. The CIO informed its members that union bylaws prevented them from supporting racist actions, and the Gary Bar Association threatened to censure any attorney who aided the "mass truancy." Msgr. John A. Sullivan called the boycott un-Christian and undemocratic.

The school board refused to negotiate with the truants, and strike leaders were ordered to appear in juvenile court. The police even threatened to enforce a recently passed "racketeering in hatred" statute against adult strike spokesmen. These forceful actions overcame the boycott. Back in school, the strikers gained amnesty on the condition that they made up their back work but were not allowed to participate in extracurricular activities, including football, until after the first grading period.

In November, because Republican Clarence H. Smith failed to endorse the school board's policy, many segregationists supported him for mayor. The issue was not clear-cut, however, because Dobis supported Swartz; and the *Post-Tribune,* a supporter of the school board, endorsed Smith. Swartz won by 1,500 votes, and Emerson never again was an all-white school.

Although moderation prevailed in the school crisis, the result was but a small step forward for integration, however, because Gary's ghettoized housing patterns drastically limited its practical consequences.

THE ANXIOUS DECADE

On January 21, 1946, a steel strike began which was the result of problems inherent in converting from a wartime to a peacetime economy. The United Steelworkers of America (USWA) sought wage increases totaling 25 cents per hour to compensate for inflation and the loss of take-home pay resulting from a declining work week (down from an average of 45 hours in 1945 to 37 hours in 1946). The steel industry demanded guarantees that the government would amend its price guidelines to cover the contemplated increase in production costs. After federal mediation broke down, President Harry S Truman recommended a pay increase of 18.5 cents coupled with a review by the Office of Price Administration of the industry's requested price hike. The USWA accepted Truman's terms, but the steel industry rejected them, precipitating a walkout. A month later, when the government accepted a five dollar per ton price increase, the steel companies agreed to the 18.5 cents wage increase.

Historian William T. Hogan wrote that the 1946 strike signified the growing impact of government policy in the collective bargaining process and set a precedent for settling disputes through higher wage and price levels. By 1946, Hogan concluded, "the union had become an accepted institution, since strikebreaking and other potentially violent tactics that had been used in other disputes with the union were absent."

On January 27, 1946, Sergeant Mike Sofranoff, who had been held prisoner by the Japanese for 40 months following his capture on Corregidor, received his discharge from the Marines. Two months later, "fed up with the general confusion" of strikes, inflation, housing and food shortages, and the lack of advancement opportunities at the mill, Sofranoff reenlisted.

Other Gary veterans shared Sofranoff's frustration and disillusionment, despite efforts by the federal government to provide them with home-loan and educational benefits. Some did not get home until a year after V-E day; in the summer of 1946 the *Post-Tribune's* "Janey" was still writing newsletters to "G.I. Joe." Readjustment was especially hard on those whose wives no longer loved them or whose children no longer knew them. The newspapers recorded numerous automobile accidents involving inebriated veterans who had been driving at high speeds.

Gary's crime and divorce rates mounted in 1946. On May 22 the *Post-Tribune* reported that vandals had uprooted or defaced street signs, smashed toilet bowls at Buffington Park, pushed urns off the Marquette Park rotunda, thrown benches into the nearby lagoon, and desecrated the War Memorial at 6th and Pennsylvania.

In 1947 the American Social Hygiene Association labeled Gary a "wide open town" with at least seven brothels in operation ten hours a day and soliciting occurring in taverns after nightfall. The Knights of Columbus decried the pornography sold at newsstands and launched a campaign against erotic literature.

On January 1, 1948, Mayor Joseph Finerty was succeeded by Eugene H. Swartz, a respectable, consensus-minded politician who in his younger days had been a pilot, a saxophonist in the Eddie Hawkins dance band, a "Flue Dust" poet, and an actor with the Civic Repertory Theatre (his favorite role was John Dillinger). Noting the similarities between Finerty and Swartz, the *Post-Tribune* wrote: "Both were twice elected to the office of Lake County auditor; both favor double-breasted suits; both love to play the chef over an outdoor barbeque; and both live on Rush street in Miller, within hailing distance of each other."

Finerty campaigned for Swartz, who upon taking office retained Millard T. Matovina as police chief. Known as "Clean Gene," Swartz made some effort to contain gambling and prostitution, whereas

Finerty left his $8,000-a-year job to administer a personal estate worth more than three million dollars—according to the St. Louis *Post-Dispatch*—including two yachts, two mansions, an airplane, and real estate in Florida.

In 1948 U.S. Steel faced its most serious labor shortage in four decades. During the summer the company airlifted over 500 Puerto Ricans to Gary, housing most of them in Palace cars on a stretch of mill property nicknamed Pullman City. The following winter several thousand displaced persons from Eastern Europe sought work at the mills, easing the labor problem.

In October 1948 Gary police arrested two members of the Progressive Party who were critical of Harry S Truman's foreign policies. The men were held six hours on an antinoise ordinance violation for informing workers at the mill gate about an upcoming rally. No such arrests befell those who trumpeted the arrival of President Truman's campaign train a short time later. Truman delivered a blistering speech at Memorial Auditorium, denouncing the Republicans as a bunch of "special privilege boys" who "took you to the cleaners in 1929 and want to do it again."

During the 1948 Christmas season Gary shops, for the first time in seven years, were well stocked with freezers, pop-up toasters, imported perfume, nylon stockings, and battery-operated toys. With the city preparing to install meters the following year, it was the last Christmas that shoppers enjoyed free parking downtown. The cost of living was at a record high—the price of haircuts, for example, had risen to $1.25—but the availability of millwork and consumer items made the holiday season the most bountiful in 28 years.

Looking back on the year 1948, Garyites took pride in the accomplishments of Patti Grubbs, who was crowned Miss Indiana, and Robert LaFayette Burns, a seven-year-old "quiz kid" radio celebrity. But 1948 also witnessed the beginning of a "Red Scare" hysteria that infected both national and local politics. Immigration officials began deportation proceedings against several alleged local Communists who had been denied citizenship because of their politics. Two years later, the city required municipal workers and public housing project tenants to sign loyalty oaths. Dr. Frank W. Neuwelt, a part-time staff member at the health department's venereal disease clinic, was fired for refusing to comply with the edict. The *Post-Tribune* ran articles on "How to Protect Self if the A-Bomb Falls" and on the difference between Communism and Americanism. As late as 1958, the House Un-American Activities Committee held hearings at City Hall in an effort to discredit radicals within the labor movement.

The Red Scare not only threatened people's civil liberties, it obscured more relevant threats to Gary's political, economic, and social well-being, such as the deterioration of the downtown business district, segregation, pollution, corruption, juvenile delinquency, and overcrowding in the public schools—which necessitated half-day shifts in some districts.

In the autumn of 1955 repeated incidents of "rowdyism" forced high schools to cancel night football games. The following year, according to the press, gangs embarked on a reign of terror, stealing cars, breaking into stores, crashing parties, and mugging old people and young children. The number of unwed mothers increased, as did the instances of ungovernable behavior among pupils between the ages of six and nine.

As a result, juvenile court officers began meting out harsher penalties against offenders. One intoxicated youth who tried to climb the Gilroy Stadium fence to avoid paying admission received 90 days at the penal farm. Teen-agers apprehended after a "rumble" were forced to shave their heads. Juvenile referees commonly ordered parolees to attend church and be off the streets after dark. One 13-year-old girl was forbidden to wear makeup, jeans, or Bermuda shorts. In an age of conformity, as was the 1950s, public authorities generally interpreted rebellious behavior as indicative of individual shortcomings rather than civic failure.

MORE STEEL STRIKES

Four steel strikes took place between 1949 and 1959. The first centered on pension and insurance benefits and lasted 42 days. Steel officials had balked at financing programs without contributions from individual workers. In the end, the settlement provided for a noncontributory pension program and a contributory package covering sickness, accident, hospitalization, and life insurance benefits.

The 1949 strike disrupted Gary much more seriously than the 1946 walkout. After four weeks people were doing less shopping, seeking extensions on their debts, flocking to the township relief office, and heading south to stay with relatives. Some picketers took their families to the free kitchen for strikers at the Philip Murray Hall. Reporter James O'Gara wrote that the strike "did not succeed in making Gary a ghost town. . . . [but] did show to a frightening degree how real that threat is to Gary and any town like it."

Two years later, the USWA sought substantial raises in pay and fringe benefits, plus a union shop contract. When steel spokesmen demanded prior approval by the government of a price boost, USWA President Philip Murray declared that steel profits were sufficient to cover labor's demands.

Just before the old contract expired on December 31, 1951, President Truman persuaded Murray to postpone a strike until the Wage Stabilization Board had time to suggest an equitable compromise. That agency ultimately recommended that management accept the union shop and grant a 26 cents per hour raise.

Murray praised the proposals, but the steel companies rejected them. A strike was averted only by Truman's seizure of the mills on the grounds that uninterrupted production was vital to the Korean War effort, the atomic energy program, and the health of the economy. When the Supreme Court ruled on April 2 that Truman's action was unconstitutional, a 55-day walkout ensued.

During the strike Truman pushed unsuccessfully for legislation permitting him to take over the mills. The Senate urged the President to use the Taft-Hartley Act to force a postponement of the dispute, but Truman refused on the grounds that its provisions were unfair to labor.

On July 24, 1952, Truman called Murray and steel spokesman Benjamin Fairless to the White House and demanded a settlement in the interest of national security. A two-year contract was signed later that day calling for a 21.5 cents increase in wages, more fringe benefits, and a modified union shop, whereby new members had the option of quitting between their 15th and 30th days on the job. The steel industry won permission to raise its tonnage prices $5.20.

David J. McDonald became USWA president following the death of Philip Murray in November 1952. A beefy, white-haired man with the tastes and demeanor of an aristocrat, he had long been an aide to Murray but was an unknown quantity to many steelworkers. Some viewed him as a "management type." He had once called CIO President Walter Reuther a "hot-headed, socialist s.o.b." Following ratification of a new contract in 1953, he toured the mills with Fairless and spoke about a "new era of amity" between labor and management.

In bargaining held during the summer of 1955, McDonald refused to state his terms publicly. This caused some anger among Gary workers when the contract expired without a settlement. Said one worker, "I've always been a good union man, but this time I think they're pulling a boner if they strike." Another worker declared, "Who in hell wants to face a month or two without work for three or four lousy cents?"

A compromise settlement was reached in 1955 without the need for a strike. A year later, however, a 34-day strike ensued over the issues of overtime pay for weekends and wage increases. Because the strike took place during the summer, unionists occupied their time with fishing trips, house repairs, and family vacations. In August the parties agreed to an unprecedented three-year contract providing for a gradual 45.6 cents increase in hourly wages.

McDonald's "new era of amity" was shattered by the 1959 steel strike, which revived memories of 1919 and the 1930s. It was an unwelcome, unexpected reminder of how dependent Gary was on events unfolding far from its borders.

Under pressure from President Dwight D. Eisenhower to hold the line on inflation, the steel industry opposed wage increases in 1959 unless accompanied by new work rules designed to increase efficiency and preserve "management's right to manage." When contract talks began, the steel industry proposed to reduce alleged instances of featherbedding, to forbid wildcat strikes, and to establish labor-management plant committees empowered with the authority (subject to binding arbitration) to alter work schedules and review seniority regulations in the interest of increasing productivity.

McDonald declared that these provisions would wipe out labor's gains of the past generation. Advocating a shorter work week and three-month-paid vacations every five years, he argued that steel profits were so "fabulous" that without raising prices the companies could raise wages, thereby giving the slumping economy a "shot in the arm."

The old contract expired on June 30, 1959, with steel negotiators still refusing to amend their position. Aware that his adversaries had been stockpiling supplies, McDonald complained that the companies wanted a strike in order to blame labor for anticipated price hikes and to unload their surplus inventory. Eisenhower pursuaded Mc-Donald to postpone a strike for two weeks, but when conditions remained unchanged, he called a walkout.

The mood in Gary as the strike commenced in mid-July was one of calm resignation. On the picket lines there was little passion or anger, and strikers played horseshoes and baseball or relaxed in tent stations equipped with cool refreshments and televisions. Art Link-letter's "House Party" and Jack Bailey's "Queen for a Day" attracted the largest audiences except during baseball games (the Chicago White Sox went on to win a pennant in 1959 for the first time in 40 years).

By August Gary Works employees had received their last pay-checks for work done before the strike and were becoming disturbed at the lethargic pace of the negotiations. Most strikers supported the walkout, however, especially after U.S. Steel reported record earnings for the six-month period ending June 30. The more the debate raged regarding work rules, the more anxious laborers became about their job security. The average worker was in his mid-40s and still had vivid memories of the depression. Since World War II, steel production had increased 25 percent while the work force had declined almost 50 percent. With rumors afloat of new automated processes of steelmaking, there was a recognition of the need for solidarity. Although McDonald himself declared that he did not oppose automation, to most workers the "work rules" provisions seemed fraught with peril. "I would much rather take in my belt another notch and starve some more in a fight to the end," one worker declared, "than to sell my job away for 'seven pieces of silver.'"

The arrogance of management negotiator R. Conrad Cooper solidified the union cause. Once when McDonald suggested that they discuss pensions, Cooper replied: "Let's talk about potatoes." Later he told the union president: "Unless you change your attitude, Dave, we are going to destroy you." Afterwards Cooper compounded his gaffe by saying that he did not mean McDonald personally but rather the union.

By October the 11-week strike had begun to cause severe hardship in Gary. Save for the opening up of 27 parks department jobs, the city had no special relief program. To qualify for township assistance, one could not own a home and had to be seeking employment. Local 1014 had a half-million dollar strike fund, but the maximum amount available to a registrant who could demonstrate extreme need was 30 dollars. One steelworker took his entire family to Michigan to pick vegetables rather than stay in Gary.

In an article appearing on October 4 regarding the human effects of the strike, the *Post-Tribune* interviewed Mrs. Andrew Terek. Her three children had skipped their dentist's appointments and were tiring of soup and spaghetti, she said. A son was forced to miss his Little League banquet, and she feared that it would be a gloomy Christmas. "If we didn't have a grocery charge account," she added, "I don't know how we'd get along."

Despite the increased budget-consciousness, downtown merchants reported no drastic reduction in sales. Businessmen extended liberal credit terms, including deferred payment plans to begin a month after the strike ended. Nonetheless, merchants echoed the lament that if things did not change, the Christmas season would not be merry.

On October 9 President Eisenhower invoked the Taft-Hartley Act, which set procedures in motion to halt the strike for 80 days. The USWA appealed the action on the grounds that the strike was not yet endangering the nation, but a month later the Supreme Court approved the government injunction, 8 to 1.

Locally, both labor and management had mixed feelings about the reopening of the mills after 116 days. They were expensive to operate for a short time, and supervisors feared that disgruntled workers, entering the gates on November 7 wearing mourners' arm bands, would engage in slowdowns. Most workers were unhappy at the method by which they were forced back on the job and were disappointed that the dispute remained unsettled. Nevertheless, they were relieved to be earning money again. As one said, "It's no fun seeing your family eating only half of what it should be eating."

Six weeks later, McDonald spoke before 5,000 workers at Memorial Auditorium. He said that as he walked along Broadway earlier in the day, he prayed for a settlement by Christmas but not of the type that would turn the USWA into a company union. Then he asked how many men wanted to accept management's terms. Three people stood, amidst jeers and catcalls.

Throughout December McDonald hinted that the union might engage in piecemeal strikes once the 80-day injunction ended. By Christmas the momentum had turned against management. The Eisenhower administration did not want the strike to resume, and Vice President Richard M. Nixon warned steel officials that further intransigence might lead to legislation requiring compulsory arbitration. Under this pressure, the companies agreed to a 30-month contract providing for gradual hourly increases totaling 32.8 percent in wages and benefits. Management failed to win binding agreements on amending work rules or preventing wildcat strikes. Company victories lay in the length of the contract (the union would have preferred a two-year contract) and in the dropping of the cost-of-living "escalator" clause.

Automobile executive George Romney charged that the settlement was a "national catastrophe,' while columnist Walter Lippmann called it a "political fix." Nonetheless, there was general relief in Gary when it ended. It cost each side a billion dollars. The average steelworker lost about 2,000 dollars in take-home pay. In Gary, things were back to normal as the new decade began, but there was a general consensus that such a protracted dispute should not be allowed to happen again.

MARY CHEEVER AND
THE WOMEN'S CITIZENS COMMITTEE

On the night of March 3, 1949, Mary Cheever, a popular, 45-year-old language teacher at Lew Wallace High School, was returning from a PTA meeting to her apartment on West 8th Avenue. After she parked her car in a nearby alley, a man grabbed her shoulder purse. When she resisted, he shot her in the back and dragged her to a lighted stairway. A neighbor heard three screams, saw the assailant flee, and then noticed Mary Cheever's body lying in a pool of blood. She was dead on arrival at Mercy Hospital.

The murder shocked the community. "Her loss to the school system is irreparable," mourned Principal Verna M. Hoke. The Gary Teachers' Union offered $500 for information leading to the killer's apprehension, and other pledges quickly raised the reward to nearly 5,000 dollars. "Gary has earned an evil reputation," the *Post-Tribune* editorialized, "and the reputation will remain until the people of the community do something about it."

On March 7, 1949, nearly 2,000 women assembled at Seaman Hall to form the Women's Citizens Committee (WCC). Blaming Mary Cheever's death on lax standards of law enforcement, they marched on a council meeting at City Hall and demanded that Gary rid itself of its criminal element. The women jeered a councilman who told them not to get hysterical, hooted an official who denied that there had been a breakdown in law enforcement, and gave Mayor Eugene H. Swartz two weeks to clean up the town. "It's up to you to do something and do it quickly," declared Mrs. Ida Saks. Added Mrs. Mary Wiseman: "Can we not make Gary the best rather than the worst mill town in the world?"

Although the mayor said it would make more sense to eradicate the crime-breeding slums and disarm the "gun and knife toters" than to padlock a "few vice or gambling dens," the WCC demanded that the latter action be taken. It was common knowledge that Gary's bookies, card dealers, policy operators, and brothel managers were linked with an East Chicago syndicate headed by Warren J. "Sonny" Sheetz and William "Peck" Gardner. The syndicate boss in Gary was Jack Doyle, whose contacts allegedly reached deep into City Hall and the police department. Operating from the Green Front Casino, which was located within "a stone's throw" of City Hall, Doyle provided services ranging from prostitution to gambling. More than a dozen bookies got racetrack bulletins from his headquarters.

The situation did not change much following the March 7 council meeting. To quote *Time* magazine, "The cops put the ax to one horse parlor, [and] picked up seven Negro prostitutes. A policeman from nearby East Chicago caught a man molesting a woman on the streets of Gary and shot him dead. Otherwise Gary was the same old Gary, even if the truth hurt."

On March 14 the WCC set up a 21-member executive committee and a board of delegates representing 300 women's groups. Plans were made for vigilante squads to monitor the police and for another march on City Hall a week later.

In response to WCC pressure, Police Chief Millard Matovina set up an eight-man vice squad headed by the respected crimefighter Peter Billick. The vice squad's freedom of action was inhibited, however, by orders requiring Billick to be present during each raid and to prepare every court case himself. The WCC brought out these and other grievances at the March 21 council meeting.

Dissatisfied with the excuses of local politicians, a delegation of women called on Governor Henry F. Schricker four days later. Scheduled for a 15-minute visit, the women talked with the governor for four hours. Mrs. Russell Griffith told him that things were so bad "that no woman dared appear on the streets of Gary alone after dark. If she did, it wasn't a case of whether or not her purse would be snatched, it was merely a case of when."

The WCC also sponsored a crime commission modeled after a private Chicago organization. The Reverend Bernard Spong, who was instrumental in persuading the women to fund the investigative agency, said: "This is going to be a dirty fight. What we need is citizens with the courage to go right down into the rat holes and fight it out."

These pressures curtailed Doyle's operations. In fact, he began searching for possible sites outside the city limits to relocate his headquarters, such as an abandoned roller rink at 63rd and Broadway or the old Bailly homestead in Porter County. Dice games were more surreptitious, slot machines less regularly used, and policy writers less conspicuous. Most brothels closed down, bringing the prostitutes out into the taverns. It was even rumored that the syndicate was offering a 10,000 dollar reward for the capture of Mary Cheever's killer. One syndicate man guessed, however, that the heat would soon be off, just as "it always has in the past." He added, "Why, we're running a poor man's Monte Carlo!"

In July 1949 the WCC launched "Operation Shoe Leather" in reaction to complaints of continuing syndicate activities. "We know we're holding a bobcat by the tail," Mrs. Ida Saks declared, "but we're not letting go. And we're not afraid." For two days several hundred volunteers braved steaming temperatures and picketed 18 of the most notorious brothels, saloons, and gambling houses. "People jeered at us, called us names, or simply stood by and stared," Mrs. Frank H. Collins said. "One tavern owner was so angry he rolled back his awning so we wouldn't get any of its shade." Several volunteers received threatening phone calls. One man told Mrs. Griffith, "This isn't funny business. You girls lay off the heat or there may be a funeral."

In January 1950 Chief Matovina disbanded the special vice squad and transferred Captain Billick to the Records Bureau. At a rally held on the first anniversary of Mary Cheever's death, WCC officers criticized the city administration, read telegrams of support from Eleanor Roosevelt and J. Edgar Hoover, and heard Republican candidate for prosecutor David P. Stanton endorse their methods and goals.

"Operation Shoe Leather" was the high point of the women's crusade. Afterwards, the WCC deemphasized mass demonstrations in favor of political action. In 1950 its highest priority was ousting incumbent county prosecutor Benjamin Schwartz. In an effort to obtain evidence of malfeasance against him, the crime commission bugged the office of his Gary deputy Blaz A. Lucas and recorded conversations he had with Doyle and other racketeers. After Lucas discovered the taping device, the Gary Bar Association censured the crime commission lawyers who had "invaded his privacy." Nonetheless, the WCC printed and distributed 200,000 copies of "The Microphone Speaks," a booklet containing the incriminating transcripts.

As election day neared, the WCC organized a network of poll watchers and campaigned openly for Stanton, a 46-year-old *magna cum laude* graduate of Notre Dame law school, who had previously served under Mayor Ernst Schaible and Prosecutor Charles W. Gannon. Ten thousand voters split their tickets, and Stanton was swept into office despite a Democratic landslide in other county contests. "I asked for a mountain to climb; now I must figure out how to climb it," the victorious candidate declared. Newsman Ed Mills wrote: "Most everyone knows 'The Microphone Speaks,' but it took Tuesday's vote to indicate how loudly it had spoken." Mrs. Griffith joked that she might finally be able to heed her detractors' advice to stick to her knitting, but added that "the way we knit now is like Madame Defarge."

Hiring Democrat Metro M. Holovachka as special prosecutor and Captain Peter Billick as special investigator, Stanton closed down the main syndicate headquarters in East Chicago and Gary. Virtually all wrongdoers escaped prosecution, however, due to problems Stanton had with Lake Criminal Court Judge William J. Murray, who dismissed some indictments and suppressed a grand jury report as "full of political hokum." Murray twice banned Stanton from his courtroom for unethical actions and remarks impugning his honor. It took considerable time for Stanton to get these rulings overturned. Meanwhile, the prosecutor castigated the judge as the "political beneficiary of the syndicate," while Murray branded Stanton as "King David, the gutless liar," who could not win a case "except in the newspapers."

In 1951 the WCC concentrated its energies on the city elections. WCC officer Hylda Burton finished third in the Democratic mayoralty primary, but the WCC ousted Gary City Judge John M. Ruberto by publicizing statistics gathered by its court watchers that purported to show that Ruberto gave out an unconscionable number of suspended sentences to habitual criminals. Prior to the November election, the WCC attempted to win pledges of cooperation from mayoralty candidates Peter Mandich (Dem.) and Clarence H. Smith (Rep.). Smith promised to seek their counsel, but Mandich spurned them, saying, "I am vigorous and can work all the time, night and day if necessary."

The victorious Mandich surprised reformers by appointing the respected crimefighter James W. Traeger as police chief. For five months, according to the press, "the lid was on." Then Traeger was fired, and the WCC went into open rebellion against the administration. Mandich accused the women of engaging in partisan politics and said: "If they think they can come in to pressure me, they are just crazy."

In the 1952 election Judge Murray won another term while Prosecutor Stanton was defeated by his onetime aide Metro Holovachka, who had become anathema to the WCC. Stanton self-righteously blamed his defeat on "illiteracy, ignorance, the fear of complicated election machines, and the tremendous power of lawless elements. . . ."

It was slight solace for reformers when syndicate lieutenant Jack Doyle went to prison for tax evasion on the strength of evidence gathered by Senator Estes Kefauver's Rackets Committee. In 1953 a half-dozen storefront bombings signified that Doyle's would-be successors were fighting for territory. By 1954 at least 15 pinball arcades had sprung up within a two-block radius of City Hall.

On January 19, 1954, the WCC forced the City Council to hold hearings after a nine-year-old child was molested near Froebel

School. The following evening several women had their purses snatched. A councilman subsequently asked Chief Detective Thomas V. Curley whether Gary was experiencing a crime wave. "What is a crime wave?" Curley responded, adding glibly, "Gary has always had a good, robust crime rate."

Born in the wake of tragedy, the WCC succeeded for awhile in curtailing vice and gambling but failed to elect enough allies to sustain its goals. Despite the sacrifices, in the 1950s Gary gained national notoriety as a wide-open city. In fact, the publicity generated by the WCC contributed to that image.

Social and political conditions thwarted the WCC. Many residents enjoyed syndicate-supplied services. Others dismissed the crusaders as affluent, Republican amateurs with less to offer than traditional Democratic politicians. One opponent labeled them "WASP biddies" whose real dislike was immigrant participation in politics. Unfair though this categorization was, it was believed by many Southsiders who distrusted the rhetoric of law-and-order and who viewed as hypocritical the denial of innocent pleasures to poor people that rich people were enjoying in the privacy of their own social clubs.

Mary Cheever's killer was never apprehended. Several mentally unbalanced men confessed to the crime, but in each case the admission turned out to be a fabrication.

STORMY CAREER OF METRO HOLOVACHKA

On January 1, 1952, Mayor Peter Mandich appointed 43-year-old Metro M. Holovachka to the post of city controller. Holovachka's Ruthenian-born father mined coal in Pennsylvania for ten years before moving to Gary in 1906 and becoming a pipe fitter at the mill. Anxious for his family to get ahead in America, Basil Holovachka believed in thrift and hard work, values transmitted to his son Metro, who was a newsboy at the age of six. By the time he graduated from Froebel School in 1927, Metro had earned money as a manual laborer, a truck driver, and an agent for *Liberty* magazine.

Holovachka spent two years at Purdue University as an engineering student before working for the township assessor and then for a Republican congressman. While attending George Washington law school, he worked for the Capitol architect.

Returning to Gary in 1935 when the New Deal was in full swing, Holovachka became a Democrat. "Lake County politics was no game for amateurs," he said later, but it offered "a way of meeting a lot of people, of enhancing my law business, and of getting an entry to things a lawyer might need."

A deputy to three Democratic prosecutors, Holovachka ran for the office himself in 1948 against Benjamin Schwartz after the incumbent refused to close the syndicate-run "Big House" casino in East Chicago. "I was opposed to big-time gambling," Holovachka said later, "because you have thieves, thugs, and murderers involved. People would come out of the mills, cash their checks there, and before they knew it, spend most of their money."

Regarded as a neophyte by party regulars, who nicknamed him "Hold-a-bicycle" and "Hola-bob-cha" for the way his ever-present bow tie bobbed when he gesticulated, Holovachka caused a storm by addressing a large throng in front of the the Big House. To attract attention and emphasize his points he banged on a bass drum. Schwartz won the election by 1,300 votes, a margin that Holovachka believed was provided by the syndicate. Two years later, he almost unseated Schwartz.

During the 1950 primary, a man pulled up beside Holovachka's car and brandished a sawed-off shotgun. "I took off," Holovachka recalled. The incident was not unusual in local politics; in fact, eight years later, someone shot out his front window.

In the general election Holovachka supported Republican David Stanton, who rode to victory in the wake of the Mary Cheever slaying. Holovachka became his special prosecutor. "We had an understanding that I might run against him later," he recalled, "but Stanton hired me anyway because of my expertise regarding organized crime."

In mid-December 1950 the Big House shut down, and Gary's "Green Front" soon followed suit. In 1951 Holovachka obtained indictments against corrupt officials in East Chicago and Whiting, before resigning at year's end to become Gary's controller.

In June 1952, while Mayor Mandich was in Florida, Holovachka assumed the duties of acting mayor and fired Police Chief James Traeger, whom he had originally recommended for the job. His explanation was that Traeger's chief detective, Herald S. Swaim, had been indiscreet and heavy-handed in harassing immigrants. The "final straw" came when two detectives "nearly caused a tragedy" by crawling into the second story of a Lithuanian hall at 2:00 A.M. "I wasn't that damn interested in breaking up 'nickel and dime' card games or after hours drinking in social clubs," Holovachka recalled, "especially when somebody could have been killed. I gave Traeger 24 hours to transfer Swaim, and when he refused I told him he was no longer chief."

Almost immediately, a large delegation from the Women's Citizens Committee stormed City Hall to castigate Holovachka. The *Post-Tribune* claimed that he had "opened the lid" on vice and gambling in order to win machine support for his upcoming candidacy for prosecutor. Despite being branded a traitor to good government, he defeated Stanton. On his first full day in office he dismissed indictments which he had prepared as Stanton's special prosecutor. By this time the WCC and the *Post-Tribune* were his bitter enemies, but Holovachka appeared secure in his power.

In July 1954 the crime commission declared that Gary had once again become a "wide open" city. Holovachka offered a hundred dollars to "anyone who can find a real, open house of prostitution" in Gary and promised to prosecute all legitimate cases that the sheriff or any good-government group brought to his attention. "It's not the prosecutor's duty to police the streets," he said.

When Holovachka ran for reelection, the *Post-Tribune* charged him with malfeasance during his tenure as controller for having monopolized the purchase of Barrett neighborhood improvement bonds. According to the newspaper, Holovachka had allowed contractors to submit inflated estimates in return for a guarantee that they would sell him the Barrett bonds at a 20 percent discount. Contractors had shied away from projects in slum neighborhoods until Holovachka assured them a market for their bonds if they wished to sell them. In 1952 there were more Barrett bond projects underway than in the previous seven years combined. "What I did was good policy, good politics, and strictly legal," Holovachka claimed, adding that the 20 percent discount covered the risk factor, since the city was not liable for improvement bonds.

Nonetheless, the *Post-Tribune* questioned Holovachka's ethics and implied that the money he used to buy all the bonds (and a new house besides) was obtained illegally. Many residents came to believe that his office shielded a plethora of tenderloin activities and that bagmen collected money from hundreds of disreputable establishments. "I had opportunities to take pay-offs," Holovachka said later, "but none would have made me rich. The thing is, nobody enjoys paying a bribe, and sooner or later they'll squawk about having paid it."

In October 1954 a coalition of independent Democrats endorsed David Stanton for prosecutor. Holovachka called them "sore losers" —several had been defeated in primary races—and formed a "Republicans for Holovachka" club.

Holovachka won reelection in 1954 and again in 1956. He prided himself on his high conviction rate and on being in the courtroom more than any of his predecessors. A believer in capital punishment, he obtained Indiana's first death sentence verdict against a woman (later commuted to life) and successfully prosecuted rapist-murderer George P. Brown, labeling him a "demon" who deserved "the hot seat." He also gained publicity for censoring the movie "Baby Doll" and various "girlie" magazines. Renowned as a showman who could invoke a tone of righteous anger and cross-examine defendants with ruthless efficiency, Holovachka's appearances before the bench attracted large crowds.

Holovachka declined to seek reelection in 1958 but stayed on as chief deputy to Floyd C. Vance. A few months later, the Senate Rackets Committee, under the chairmanship of John McClellan, began investigating charges that he had allowed a pinball machine syndicate to amass a 12-million-dollar monopoly in Lake County. At the committee hearings, which Gary radio station WWCA broadcast live, Holovachka claimed that he had not received "one thin dime" from any syndicate. Branding the proceeding a "public lynching," he complained that chief counsel Robert F. Kennedy asked gangsters insinuating questions—such as: "Have you had dealings with Holovachka?"—knowing in advance that they would refuse to answer any questions. In its final report the McClellan committee castigated Holovachka for aiding and abetting the pinball monopoly, and Robert F. Kennedy suggested in his book *The Enemy Within* that local authorities take appropriate action against him.

Claiming that committee investigators "were interested in smearing me personally," Holovachka believed that he was victimized for not having supported John F. Kennedy for Vice President at the 1956 Democratic convention when the Massachusetts Senator barely failed to win the nomination. "I had a few delegates in my vest pocket, so to speak," Holovachka recalled, "so Bobby met privately with me. When I held out for Estes Kefauver, he said, 'I'm going to even up the score with you, and I'll do it in spades!' "

According to Holovachka, a few hours after the Senate Rackets Committee first contacted him, campaign manager Hy Raskin asked him to support John F. Kennedy's upcoming presidential bid. "I told him I wouldn't support the son of a bitch, and within days there were three dozen agents combing the county looking for someone who gave me a bribe. They couldn't find any, so they pressured a brothel madame into committing perjury."

Within a week after the release of the Senate Rackets Committee report, 1,200 people met at Seaman Hall to form the Northwest Indiana Crime Commission. Its chief investigator was former FBI agent Francis E. Lynch; and one of Lynch's assistants was Herald

Swaim, whose dismissal as chief detective originally pitted Gary's good-government groups against Holovachka.

Following Robert F. Kennedy's appointment as Attorney-General in 1961, Lynch enlisted the aid of the Justice Department, which had already been examining Holovachka's income tax returns. Kennedy put a crack investigative team on the case. The agents tapped Holovachka's phone and threatened to prosecute people who had dealings with him if they did not cooperate. They subpoenaed his son while he was attending college classes and his father-in-law, the Reverend Alexander Papp, while he was in church with his congregation.

In the winter of 1961 a grand jury indicted Holovachka for evading taxes in excess of $39,000 (later lowered to $32,000) between 1955 and 1957. The trial lasted over three weeks. Claiming to have lost most of his financial records, Holovachka argued that the apparent discrepancy sprang from nontaxable gifts and loans from three people who had since died—his father, his mother-in-law, and Judge William J. Murray. The prosecution case relied on convincing the jury that the large amounts of money recorded in Holovachka's bank statements came from other sources. In the absence of hard evidence of specific graft payments, the key prosecution witness was Paul Boyle, a government tax expert whose statistic-laden testimony linked Holovachka and his wife with cash transactions totaling $352,776 within a five-year period.

The most dramatic part of the trial was when Holovachka took the stand. Maintaining his innocence, he gave an account of his rise in politics, stressing his dedication to law and order. At times serene and at other times flushed with anger, he had to endure a grueling cross-examination. Near the end of one long session he apparently suffered a heart seizure but soon recovered his combative spirit. He bristled when the prosecution aired suspicions about his father amassing a $27,000 estate between 1945 and 1951, while Holovachka listed him as a dependent. And he was outraged when Prosecutor Vincent P. Russo hinted that he had hidden money in the estates of friends and relatives.

After listening to closing arguments and the judge's charge, the jurors deliberated for a little over four hours. Residents from the Lafayette and South Bend area, they had been impaneled over the objections of the defense team, which argued for a panel composed of Lake County residents whose ethnic and social background more closely resembled Holovachka's.

On February 21, 1962, Holovachka was found guilty on three

counts of tax evasion. Reporter David Samuels noted that the defendant "blanched as he heard the verdict and left the courtroom with his arm around his son, Demetri." Blaming unscrupulous agents who "have destroyed me fully and completely," Holovachka later said, "I could have had a fairer trial from Hitler or Stalin."

Sentenced to three years in prison and a $10,000 fine, Holovachka remained free on appeal throughout 1962. Meanwhile, crime commission chief Francis Lynch moved to have him disbarred. Holovachka claimed he was too "ill and nervous" to attend the hearing, but in his absence he was pilloried for a decade of alleged misdeeds, including the firing of Police Chief Traeger, the Barrett bonds transactions, the quashed indictments against Whiting and East Chicago politicians, the alleged pinball connections, the cash transactions with the contractor who built his house in Miller, and even his "offensive" conduct before the McClellan committee. Charging him with "utter depravity and moral turpitude of the rankest sort," Judge Newell A. Lamb ruled that his name be "forever stricken from the roll" of licensed attorneys in Indiana.

On June 24, 1963, Holovachka entered a federal penitentiary at Milan, Michigan. Subsequently transferred to Missouri, Tennessee, and Florida—for his own safety, the government claimed; to inconvenience his wife, Holovachka charged—he served 25 months, the maximum amount considering time off for good behavior.

Holovachka worked for a Chicago brokerage firm following his release in August 1965, but his reputation remained tarnished. Few people sympathized with his claim to have been a scapegoat of the Boston Irish political maxim to which Bobby Kennedy subscribed: "Don't get mad, get even." Like Mayor Chacharis, he had once wielded great power, but unlike the former city boss, who admitted taking payoffs to reward faithful party workers, he did not have a "Robin Hood" image to fall back upon.

"Metro was his own worst enemy," said a former colleague, who believed that he had been unfairly maligned. "He had a terrible temper, and it got him in trouble with the wrong people."

THE RISE OF GEORGE CHACHARIS

Like most effective politicians, George Chacharis loved people and power. He rose from the ethnic wards of the Central District to become one of Gary's most popular mayors. There was even talk in 1961 of his becoming ambassador to Greece. But instead of returning triumphantly to his native land, he was sent to prison for conspiring to commit income tax evasion. "The story of George Chacharis," *The Saturday Evening Post* wrote, "has all the elements of a Greek tragedy: ambition, success, and a tragic flaw that brought the hero to his ruin. . . ." Said one resident: "He was a saint and a sinner at the same time."

Chacharis was born in Thebes on February 11, 1908. His father Demetrius was a cattle buyer who spoke seven languages and traveled widely in the course of his business, including three trips to America. At the outbreak of World War I, the family moved from an estate in Edessa to Athens, where his wife Paraskevi became ill with tuberculosis and died soon afterwards in a sanitarium. Fearful of being drafted into the Greek army and becoming separated from his three sons, of whom George was the youngest, Demetrius fled to Italy. In August 1918 the family boarded an Italian steamer bound for America. During the voyage the danger of German submarine attack produced some anxious moments. After landing in New York, the family took a train to Gary, where friends lived. Obtaining a job at the mill, the elder Chacharis labored 12 hours a day and then assumed the duties of a parent at night. Never remarrying, he died in 1951 at the age of 83.

The biggest problem that ten-year-old George Chacharis faced in Gary was the language barrier. Previous moves had forced him to learn Turkish and Italian, however, and he adjusted quickly to the ethnic environs of the Central District. He became an altar boy at SS. Constantine and Helen Greek Orthodox Church and a student at Froebel, where he was a manager for the football and basketball teams and was involved in several school plays. In his spare time he held various jobs, such as working in a Greek coffeehouse, delivering Greek-language newspapers, and becoming a sports reporter for the *Post-Tribune.*

Following his graduation in 1926, Chacharis attended the University of Athens for a year. His father was contemplating a return to Greece if all went well. Within a year, however, the younger Chacharis left Athens to avoid conscription into the Greek army. Returning to Gary, he took a job at the mill as a roll greaser. He was subsequently made a typist and then a steel charger, but with the onset of the depression he was laid off for a year. In 1933 he was rehired as a typist in the engineering department and within a decade had received promotions to expeditor, valuation clerk, estimator, and then chief project engineer.

In October 1932 Chacharis organized Club SAR, which was dedicated to promoting social, athletic, and recreational activities in the depression-ridden Central District. Starting with 22 members in an empty storefront, Chacharis lured people to meetings with free hot dogs and doughnuts in order to interest them in such activities as holding a charity benefit, collecting old shoes or clothing for needy children, gathering firewood on Gary Land Company property, putting together a basketball squad, or supporting a youth baseball team.

In time Club SAR became noted for dispensing Christmas baskets to depression victims, for sponsoring swimmers, prizefighters, and track stars, for holding fund-raising dances, and for producing successful politicians. "At first we weren't much better than hoodlums," a charter member recalled, "and we might have ended up worse if Pete (Mandich) and George didn't get us all careers in politics."

"The reason Club SAR was so successful," Chacharis said later, "was that it represented so many nationalities, with its members being leaders in their respective ethnic organizations and churches." Many residents believed that Chacharis' leadership was the essential ingredient which allowed it to flourish. There were other clubs involved in politics, such as the Silver Bells and the Sportsmen's Club, but none was so successful as Club SAR.

"Unemployment was what got me into politics," Chacharis said later, adding that his admiration for Franklin D. Roosevelt made him a Democrat. In 1934 he became a campaign manager for coal dealer Isaac Bloom, who had donated a ton of coal to Club SAR. Chacharis coined the slogan, "Gary Will Boom with Bloom" and hired a network of campaign workers. Many went over to Barney Clayton's camp, however, when Bloom reneged on paying them. Although Bloom finished third in the Democratic mayoralty primary, the Democratic landslide in the general election signaled a new era in local politics.

At first politics was primarily an outlet for Chacharis' abundant energies and his love of competition. But during the New Deal he began to regard public office as a path to respect and social mobility for people of foreign extraction whose interests had been neglected by the large property interests which held such a tight grip on Gary.

As World War II approached, Chacharis defended President Roosevelt against such isolationist critics as Congressman Hamilton Fish, who addressed a local "America First" meeting in September 1941. In a letter to the *Post-Tribune* he described Fish as a Nazi sympathizer with a "stinking, labor-baiting record" and his followers as "appeasers, fifth-columnists, dupes, molly-coddling parents, publicity seekers, and blind pacifists."

In the 1946 township election Chacharis put together a victorious ethnic slate consisting of such Club SAR members as Peter Mandich for trustee, Steve Gersack for assessor, and Nick Schiralli for constable. Chacharis subsequently resigned from Gary Works ("there was no future there for someone without a college degree," he said later) and purchased the General Coal and Oil Company. Within a year he was earning more money than he had ever made at U.S. Steel and had secured contracts with such clients as Methodist and Mercy hospitals, the county poor farm, and the township relief office.

In 1951 Chacharis helped manage Peter Mandich's mayoral candidacy against Republican Clarence Smith, whose campaign, Chacharis felt, was being directed by the *Post-Tribune.* The paper accused Mandich of having connections with the syndicate, of having given preferential treatment to Chacharis' General Coal and Oil Company, and of prevaricating on the issues of law and order and taxes. During the 1949 steel strike the trustee's relief policies had ingratiated him with organized labor.

On September 23, 1951, the state police raided Club SAR headquarters on 515 West 11th and confiscated 28 fifths of whiskey, 24 bottles of wine and 5 cases of beer. Chacharis was infuriated at the front-page coverage given to the incident in contrast to the ignoring of a previous raid against the Gary Country Club.

A few days later, the newspaper reprinted portions of a speech by Republican Paul Cyr charging that Chacharis "pulls the strings that guide the thinking and direct the affairs of the Democratic candidate for mayor." To answer the charge, the officers of Club SAR took a full-page advertisement in the *Post-Tribune.* Written by Chacharis as an open letter to "Country Club Clarence Smith," it predicted that "justice will triumph over the shortcomings of politics on November 6, 1951, when your name will sink into promiscuous obscurity as just another Smith, private citizen. We blush with shame for you and your ilk."

Near the end of the campaign, the Republicans charged that Mandich opposed integration of Marquette Park. At a forum held by the League of Women Voters, Mandich had endorsed equal access to all city facilities but added that he would ensure public safety by preventing riots. In response to the same question, Clarence Smith said cryptically: "Would you ask the mayor if it's right for you to take a bath on Saturday night?" When Republicans began telling black voters that their candidate was more liberal on the race issue, Metro Holovachka placed an anonymous telephone call to Smith. Claiming to be a "concerned Miller property owner," he questioned the candidate on his integrationist remarks. Unaware that his answer was being recorded and would later be played in black neighborhoods, Smith said that his statements were just politics and that he was on the caller's side.

Mandich won the election and a year later appointed Chacharis controller and president of the Board of Public Works and Safety. An affable, self-effacing former football star at Froebel, Mandich left much of the governmental routine to his political mentor. "Mandich was not a figurehead and sometimes had heated arguments with George," a former colleague recalled, "but they generally saw eye to eye."

While Mandich was mayor, the city negotiated many Barrett bond improvement projects. Gilroy Stadium was built at Gleason Park at a cost that critics believed was far in excess of its real worth, and land was donated to Indiana University for the purpose of creating a Northwest extension. An enthusiastic promoter of the Gary campus, Chacharis had originally favored donating the airport site on the West Side. When Indiana University Trustee Ray C. Thomas held out for the Gleason Park site—which Chacharis viewed as too swampy —and threatened to locate the extension in South Bend, the city deeded over the property, despite the protests of some Glen Park residents.

During the mid-1950s, wrote political scientist Thomas F. Thompson, the controller's anteroom bustled with activity, with scores of people coming to "spend a minute" with Chacharis in a single day, including aides, contractors, councilmen, irate citizens, journalists, merchants, salesmen, hangers-on, patronage seekers, and people needing a permit for a church bazaar or a zoning variance. Chacharis generally had time for everyone. He was reputed to be an "easy mark" for hard-luck stories but "iron-tough" when it came to negotiating with businessmen.

The *Post-Tribune* was highly critical of the city administration for tolerating vice, gambling, and corruption. Articles on bookie joints, B-girls, and brothels appeared regularly. Chacharis regarded the hostile press coverage as the result of a "Rule or Ruin" mentality on the part of publisher H. B. Snyder. On one occasion, the controller had turned down an oil company's request to run a pipeline through park property, even though he had recommended an alternative site adjacent to the Wabash tracks, which the company rejected. The *Post-Tribune* headlines indicated that Chacharis told the company "to get out of town."

Once while Mandich was out of town, Chacharis installed parking meters in front of the paper's delivery entrance, necessitating that each roll of paper be carried inside the building on a stretcher. The *Post-Tribune* cited its First Amendment rights and obtained an injunction against the acting mayor. To avoid a court summons, Chacharis went downstate to hear Metro Holovachka try a murder case. When Mandich returned to Gary, Chacharis advised him to expect a call from the paper and recommended that he "show them you're a good sport and remove the meters."

On another occasion, Chacharis told an elderly missionary of Father Divine that while he was a devout churchgoer, he knew two souls in need of saving. As a practical joke, he wrote the names of publisher H. B. Snyder and editor Arnold A. Coons on the back of calling cards and directed the woman to the *Post-Tribune* building just when Coons and Snyder were working hard to get out the afternoon edition.

In 1955 Mandich became the first Gary mayor to win two successive terms, defeating pharmacist Emery A. Badanish by almost 9,000 votes. It was a "fun campaign," remembered one resident, complete with picnics, rallies, banquets, solicitations, and the usual pranks. The Democrats put "That's My Dad" decals on baby carriages, because Mandich's wife had recently had a baby. On the morning after the election, Chacharis took two large bottles of iodine to Snyder's office and told the startled publisher that it might be easier for him to swallow the contents than Mandich's victory.

In 1958 Chacharis opposed the reelection bid of his close friend, Steve Gersack, for township assessor because the latter opposed raising U.S. Steel's tax assessment. From working 20 years at the mill, Chacharis was convinced that the company's property holdings were undervalued, thereby depriving the city of millions of dollars. In 1957 U.S. Steel had thrown the city into financial insolvency and disrupted governmental processes for several weeks by terminating its custom of paying taxes in January and instead paid them on their last due date. Chacharis filed a brief with the state tax board that resulted in a ten million dollar assessment increase. This was less than ten percent of what he wanted, however.

During the Democratic primary, therefore, Chacharis supported fellow Club SAR member Tom Fadell, who campaigned for a "fairer" evaluation of mill property. U.S. Steel instructed its supervisors to work for Gersack. More than 80 percent of the voters on the far East Side, a traditional Republican stronghold, crossed over to the Democratic Party and voted for Gersack. Even so, Fadell won by

2,000 votes. "It was the 'Last Hurrah' for the mill as a dominant force in Gary politics," Chacharis later said.

In the 1958 primary Pete Mandich won nomination for county sheriff and announced his intention to resign as mayor, paving the way for Chacharis to become Gary's first foreign-born chief executive. Some viewed the move as a tactic to get Chacharis into the mayor's office without going the election route. They felt Chacharis would stand a better chance of being elected mayor in 1959 if he ran as the incumbent.

"This city has been my world," Chacharis told 600 well-wishers at his inauguration on July 16, 1958. "Here I have spent all but a few years of my life." Promising to be a "people's" mayor whose decisions would be made without regard to race, color, or creed, he concluded: "I must not fail, for only by succeeding will I have fulfilled my obligation to a beloved community."

CHACHARIS: THE PEOPLE'S CHOICE

Chacharis' ascension to the office of mayor seemed a natural consequence of a quarter-century of political preparation, even though he had never held elective office. A prerequisite to fulfilling his ambitions, however, required winning a mandate from the people in the 1959 election.

Chacharis was a very visible mayor. Whether milking a cow at the county fair, serving lunches to needy children for the March of Dimes, honoring "Music Man" actor Forrest Tucker, dedicating a portrait of General Casimir Pulaski at a school named in his honor, appearing at an AAU basketball game, raising funds for the Olympics, forming a Committee of 100 to revitalize the business district, extending greetings to a convention of police chiefs, socializing on the picket lines during the 1959 steel strike, wading into Lake Michigan with Illinois Senator Paul H. Douglas bearing a "Save the Dunes" placard, or cutting a ceremonial ribbon at a street opening, he was seldom out of the public eye.

Unlike his predecessor, Chacharis attended to the most minute administrative matters, even to the appointing of lifeguards, parking attendants, and school-crossing patrolmen. He claimed to know 10,-000 Garyites by name and 30,000 others by sight. He gave gifts to countless charitable causes and friends in need, from folding chairs for SS. Constantine and Helen Church to tuition money for deserving students. After working late with his staff, he often treated them to dinner. City employees donated two percent of their wages to a flower fund which was used for weddings and funerals.

A bachelor, Chacharis lived modestly with his brother and sister-in-law. When at home he answered telephone calls personally from residents who might have had their car stolen, lost a wallet, suffered a cat bite, had a storm sewer back up, or needed a favor. "I had many tragic cases," he later said, "and I always tried to take care of them." On Halloween hundreds of children capped off their evening by receiving "king size" candy bars from "Cha Cha."

Black people, constituting 40 percent of Gary's population, were a part of the Chacharis organization. The mayor attended many civic functions in Midtown, dispensed patronage to deserving Negroes, approved David Mitchell's election as president of the City Council, and appointed Gary's first black cabinet member, City Attorney Harry O. Schell. Endorsing the overall goals of the civil rights movement, he welcomed Dr. Martin Luther King, Jr., during his several visits to the city and predicted that within a decade Gary would have a black mayor.

In the summer of 1958 Chacharis traded in the mayor's limousine for a garbage truck in order to dramatize his commitment to improving general services. He reorganized the garbage collection system and equipped the 36-truck fleet with snow plows. When maintenance workers struck for higher wages, he refused to negotiate until they returned to their jobs, and then made a generous settlement.

A lifelong sports enthusiast who had helped found the Gary Tennis Club, Chacharis put together an ambitious recreation program which included opening school facilities in the evenings and refurbishing city playgrounds. Additional tennis courts were built at Gleason Park and plans drawn up for a new fieldhouse and an ice skating rink. The city also installed a boat launching ramp on Lake Street as the first stage in expanding the harbor and beach facilities at Marquette Park.

Chacharis believed that taxation inequity and traffic congestion were Gary's biggest problems. In his first 14 months in office, he secured two rate reductions for homeowners while pressing for higher corporate assessments. Solving traffic problems required building downtown parking garages, securing state and federal cooperation on highways, and constructing more access roads to and from the mills, such as the Harrison-Buchanan and Indiana-Tennessee throughways. Supplementing these plans were a traffic safety program; the resurfacing, widening, and illuminating of streets; and the improvement of mill entrances at Virginia Street and Broadway.

When Chacharis ran for a full term in 1959, the Gary Democratic Central Committee published a 40-page booklet entitled "A Mayor for All the People," which listed his accomplishments and future plans to redeem Gary's promise as the "City of the Century." Against Republican Elmer K. Bailey he garnered 72 percent of the vote, the greatest landslide in the city's history, and Democrats swept every councilmanic race. "The dimensions of the Democratic victory are truly amazing," the *Post-Tribune* editorialized. At a huge victory rally Chacharis ridiculed Bailey's "decency and efficiency" platform, saying that "no single party has a corner on decency. We love our city, and we will govern it well. And if they raise this issue of decency again, we'll beat them four to one instead of three to one."

Flushed with confidence, Chacharis moved to implement a campaign pledge to have the city take over the Gary-Hobart Water Company. In 1932 Gary's water works was purchased by the Northern Indiana Public Service Company (NIPSCO). Nineteen years later it was sold to a company controlled by Charles S. Mott, a major stockholder in General Motors Corporation. When Mott refused a 20-million-dollar offer for the water works, Chacharis petitioned the City Council to approve a referendum authorizing its condemnation and purchase. At his inauguration on January 1, 1960, the mayor alleged that corporate directors used "rigged bookkeeping . . . defended by rigged Madison Avenue propaganda" to charge "bloated" rates which were twice as high as the city-owned facilities in Hammond and East Chicago. Why should windfall profits go off to Flint, Michigan, Chacharis asked, when under a nonprofit municipal agency the people could have water at fair rates? "It is food snatched from your tables," he declared, "and it is milk denied to your children, in order to feed the insatiable appetite of an absentee plutocrat."

Mott had no intention of parting with his profitable investment without a fight, even after Chacharis offered to name a park for him. "I own six or eight or ten, I guess, water companies," Mott once said, "and they're the easiest things to run. . . . If they want water and don't pay, all you have to do is apply to the courts and demand payment. You'd collect."

After a private poll revealed that two out of three Garyites initially favored municipal ownership, the company spent large sums of money to defeat the referendum. A public relations firm warned that the health of Gary's youth was in jeopardy. Meter readers asked voters to save their jobs. One full-page advertisement warned: "Don't let the politicians get their dirty hands on your water!"

The *Post-Tribune* opposed the purchase on the grounds that it would politicize the water company, endanger service to the suburbs, and be too costly to allow rate reduction. In one cartoon the paper represented the mayor carrying a huge bottle labeled "$50,-000,000.00 in Bonds and Interest." A nearby voter, pictured carrying away a little bottle marked "Water Bill," said, "You mean I have to buy that one, too?"

Post-Tribune reporter Jim Driscoll put together a 20-part series on the issue which was highly critical of Chacharis. Categorizing the mayor as "a man of tremendous vitality and intelligence who is not using his natural gifts as well as he might," Driscoll compared him to "a brilliant man, with the potential to find a cure for cancer, who turns away from his potentialities and becomes the world's best player of contract bridge." Driscoll's series was carried on the front page from its inception in mid-January of 1960 until its conclusion on February 1, two weeks before the referendum.

Chacharis lashed out at the "iron curtain of news disseminating agencies" and chided the water company for not hiring many blacks or Gary residents. Nonetheless, the suspicion remained that city ownership was dangerous. One councilman said later: "Chacharis believed in good, solid patronage politics, and he sought influence wherever he felt he could help the organization."

Right before the referendum, Chacharis played host to John F. Kennedy during the presidential candidate's two-day visit to Gary. He arranged meetings with labor leaders and clergymen at the Hotel Gary and a tour of Gary Works—even though, in his opinion, he "was public enemy number one to U.S. Steel." When the company tried to transport the delegation in a vehicle adorned with the slogan "Vote NO on the Referendum," Chacharis exclaimed, "I'm not getting on that bus!" He and Kennedy made the trip by automobile. Kennedy apparently enjoyed the mayor's combative spirit for he introduced his major address at Hellenic Hall with a quip about the bottled water Chacharis had obtained for the banquet tables.

The referendum lost, 26,539 to 10,723, and proved to be a serious political miscalculation on Chacharis' part, raising as it did the fury of the *Post-Tribune*, the Chamber of Commerce, good-government organizations, U.S. Steel, and the utility company itself. Chacharis agreed to abide by the people's decision but noted that "future generations will appreciate my efforts." Later in the year, however, his power seemed secure. He helped Kennedy win the presidential nomination at the Democratic National Convention, raised tens of thousands of dollars for the campaign, and helped deliver a 60,000-

vote Democratic plurality in Gary in the general election even though Kennedy failed to carry Indiana. When Republican Governor Harold W. Handley questioned the legitimacy of the Lake County vote count, Chacharis said he would welcome an investigation into charges of fraud and categorized the governor's remarks as ignorant, arrogant, intemperate, and prejudiced.

THE FALL OF MAYOR CHACHARIS

In April 1961 President Kennedy invited Chacharis to attend a White House reception for Greek Prime Minister Constantine Kara- manlis. The mayor brought back an autographed picture of the Presi- dent, which adorned his office alongside citations from the Optimist Club and the United Steelworkers of America. Three months later, however, Justice Department agent Jay Goldberg began investigat- ing evidence of kickbacks paid to contractors during the Mandich administration. At first sent to Gary by Attorney-General Robert F. Kennedy in order to build a case against Metro Holovachka, Chacha- ris' predecessor as city controller, Goldberg became angry at the lack of cooperation from municipal officials. An Internal Revenue Service agent provided him with check stubs from corporations doing busi- ness with the city which implicated Chacharis and other members of the Mandich administration. Goldberg then expanded the scope of his probe.

Described in Victor Navasky's book *Kennedy Justice* as a publicity- conscious zealot, Goldberg threatened to "throw the book" at any- one who withheld evidence about kickbacks. He warned one city employee that a ten-ton truck marked "Federal Government" was coming down the road and that, in effect, the man could either remain silently in its path or talk and therefore get safely onto the sidewalk.

Goldberg came under pressure to contain the probe short of City Hall, or at the least, to show Chacharis the evidence against him and allow him to explain his actions away from the public eye. According to Navasky, the Kennedys believed it likely that Chacharis had not used graft money to enrich himself personally and that, therefore, "by his *own* code he had not really been doing anything wrong."

During the grand jury investigation, Goldberg returned to Wash- ington, and rumors surfaced that President Kennedy was going to halt the probe in order to win Congressman Ray J. Madden's support on a crucial piece of legislation. Chacharis' attorney asked that the matter be adjudicated as a civil case, since it involved campaign funds. Goldberg's local supporters then mailed coconuts to the White House with the message, "Friendly natives of Gary need help." This was a deliberate copy of President Kennedy's use of them when he sought help following the sinking of his P-T boat during World War II.

Since the investigation had received so much attention, partly as a result of wire-service articles emanating from the *Post-Tribune*, the point had been reached, according to Navasky, where the embarrassment to the Kennedy administration "of bringing it before a grand jury was countervailed by the greater embarrassment of not bringing it."

The grand jury began hearing evidence again during the winter of 1961–62. Meanwhile, the mayor lashed out at the "Anglo-Saxon clique" of absentee corporate landlords who regarded Gary as their personal fiefdom. Chacharis singled out publisher H. B. Snyder for special denunciation, labeling him "The Duke of Dune Acres," whose neighborhood was so exclusive that guards kept uninvited visitors away. Snyder blew the case open, some people believed, out of pique that Chacharis was being considered for an embassy post. According to an offshoot of this interpretation, U.S. Steel and Gary-Hobart Water Company added their influence to cut down an adversary who was getting "too big for his breeches."

On February 21, 1962, the grand jury indicted Chacharis and five others for conspiring to avoid the payment of taxes on money collected illegally from firms doing business with the city. The trial was set for November 1962.

The pretrial publicity did not diminish Chacharis' vote-getting power in the county elections. The Republicans put together a reform slate featuring David Stanton for prosecutor and James Traeger for sheriff. "Dave Can Do the Job with a Traeger Finger," the *Post-Tribune* declared, but both Stanton and Traeger went down to defeat.

By the time the trial began in Hammond Federal Court in November 1962, Prosecutor Jay Goldberg had compiled a list of 75 witnesses, including businessmen willing to testify (with immunity) that they had paid kickbacks totaling more than $226,000 for a multitude of licenses, variances, permits, contracts, and consultant fees. The most damaging evidence concerned the payment of $110,350 by a construction company in 1956 for the rights to excavate sand while working on the Indiana toll road.

In the middle of the trial Chacharis resigned as mayor and pleaded guilty of conspiring to avoid tax payments. Charges were then dropped against all other defendants except city engineer Harold Zweig and accountant Willmar Chulock.

Returning to court on January 18, 1963, Chacharis was sentenced to three years in prison and fined $10,000. Federal Judge Robert A. Grant declared that there was no evidence of an "avaricious greed for money on his part, but there was an avaricious greed for power." Chacharis maintained that his record as mayor was "unblemished" and vowed to "devote the rest of my days to rectify those mistakes," which he made while controller.

Four days later, Chacharis traveled to South Bend where he was put under federal custody and transferred to a penitentiary in Milan, Michigan. The previous evening, Chacharis had advised Gary City Judge A. Martin Katz to "get out of politics and go back to private law practice." Elected mayor in November with machine support, Katz later said that no mayor in his memory had as much vision for the city as did Chacharis. "Chacharis was extremely energetic and capable," Councilman Glen W. Vantrease later recalled, "but there's no doubt he did a great many things because there was money involved."

There was strong sympathy for Chacharis in Gary even after his admission of guilt. One steelworker said that if he "was to run tomorrow, he'd win. He's the best mayor we ever had." Another resident stated: "He's a friend to all the people—not the elite but the people who don't have much. Whatever he took, he hasn't got it now. He never had it. He took the rap for the others."

The Gary *American* declared that Chacharis was "the most outspoken friend of the Negro people" and accomplished "an insurmountable amount of good." The black newspaper concluded that "the Negro people kept faith with George by supporting his political program, and he kept faith with us by giving us recognition and jobs of importance."

Nationally, Gary's reputation suffered. *Time* wrote that "Corruption is a kind of custom in Gary, Ind.—to the point that about the only mistake a politician can make is failing to report his bribes on his federal income tax return." "The recent publicity given to Gary's political deviltries is awful," one traveler wrote Anselm Forum President Reuben Olsen. "The image of the city is about as ugly as the inside of a vacuum cleaner."

While in jail Chacharis served as a clerk-typist. He was paroled on December 18, 1964. When he returned to Gary, friends sponsored a "Gorge For George" benefit to help him settle some of his debts. Remaining a force in local politics, he later held a staff position in the office of Calumet Township Assessor Tom Fadell until 1977.

Prostitution, gambling, political patronage, and special relationships among contractors and officeholders had existed in Gary from its inception and continued during the administrations of Republicans such as R. O. Johnson and Democrats such as Barney Clayton. In fact, funding from these sources was a way politicians could build organizations that were not totally dependent upon U.S. Steel and the news media. When he entered public office, Chacharis accepted these arrangements, believing he could contain them so as not to politicize such departments as the school board nor impair proper law enforcement against drug pushers or other dangerous felons.

Chacharis' critics argued that his methods infected city government with the taint of corruptibility which bred disrespect for the law and cynicism toward all government projects, whether they involved the building of a new stadium or control over public utilities. "He taught immigrants that they could get ahead," said one resident, "but he also taught them they could do anything they wanted, no matter how illegal or unethical it was."

In the end, Chacharis paid for his mistakes, and most of his goals for Gary did not come to pass. One accomplishment that Chacharis cherished, however, was playing a part in saving the Dunes National Park area from corporate exploitation. "One of my cardinal beliefs throughout my years as a steel employee, businessman, and public servant," he said, "was that human rights should take precedence over property rights."

Senator Paul H. Douglas wrote that the uncompromising way in which Chacharis fought against "the marauding steel companies" who wanted "to ring the lake front from Gary to Michigan City with steel, cement, and chemical factories and electrical plants" reminded him of John Hay's poem about the steamship captain Jim Bludso:

> He weren't no saint,—but at jedgment
> I'd run my chance with Jim,
> 'Longside of some pious gentlemen
> That wouldn't shook hands with him.

CHAPTER ELEVEN

The Rise of Black Power

Let us dare to make a new beginning. Let us shatter the walls of the ghetto for all time. Let us build a new city and a new man to inhabit it.

—Richard G. Hatcher, Inaugural
Address, January 1, 1968

DURING THE 1960s there was a growing impatience and militance among Gary's black people and a more keenly felt sense of power and purpose. There were antecedents to Gary's civil rights movement, however. Preparing the way were lawyers such as Louis Caldwell, educators such as H. Theo Tatum, community leaders such as Jacob L. Reddix, black power activists such as Joseph A. Pitts, settlement house workers such as Frank S. Delaney, social workers such as Thelma E. Marshall, politicians such as Robert Anderson, and ministers such as L. K. Jackson. The Urban League had documented evidence of racial injustice in numerous reports; the Interdenominational Ministerial Alliance had drawn attention to the injustices; the NAACP had demonstrated against segregated public facilities; and the Gary *American* had brought these social issues to the attention of the black community.

Nonetheless, Gary's black residents were second-class citizens until the 1960s—economically, politically, and socially. They were poorly housed, denied access to job advancement, and inadequately educated. Perhaps only in sports did blacks have equal opportunity to excel, and the accomplishments of basketball player Dick Barnett, football player Fred "The Hammer" Williamson, Olympic boxing champion Charles Adkins, and track star Lee Calhoun are testimonials to their excellence.

270

During the 1950s *de facto* segregation existed in almost all public schools. Froebel became nearly all black, and the phenomenon of changing neighborhoods caused black enrollment at Tolleston and Emerson to rise and white enrollment to decline. On the tenth anniversary of the Froebel strike, the Public Administration Service released a yearlong school survey that resulted in the dismissal of Superintendent Charles Lutz. The report concluded that the schools were deteriorating and that administrators had "perpetuated the disadvantages of the Wirt system while having lost whatever advantages it may have had."

In 1960 black parents protested the mistreatment of their children at Emerson and the absence of black teachers there. Charging that pupils could not join clubs or participate in student government and that Nazi crosses had been drawn on school property, they brought forth grievances reminiscent of the World War II era at Froebel.

During the next three years the NAACP tried in vain to force the school board to modify its neighborhood school concept in favor of obtaining more racial balance. On April 17, 1964, the Civil Rights Coordinating Committee sponsored a "Freedom Day" boycott in protest against *de facto* segregation. Although Superintendent Lee R. Gilbert encouraged students to attend class and the *Post-Tribune* labeled the boycott "ill-advised and ill-timed," almost 75 percent of Gary's 25,000 black pupils participated. Many attended black culture workshops, set up at 24 sites. In the fall of 1964, in response to this pressure, some blacks were transported to Horace Mann to attend seventh grade classes.

THE OLD PROPHET DR. L. K. JACKSON

On March 31, 1943, the members of St. Paul Baptist Church at 1938 Adams Street held a welcome service for their new pastor, 48-year-old Lester Kendel Jackson, who was succeeding the Reverend William F. Lovelace. Keynoting his sermon with the verse, "I am come that they might have life and have it more abundantly," Jackson vowed to wage war on the "inhuman, barbaric, and ungodly" forces of bigotry that existed in Gary.

Reared in Clay County, Georgia, Jackson had held pastorates in Lynchburg, Virginia, and Passaic and Long Branch, New Jersey. A self-proclaimed "Hell-Raiser from the East," he had fought to integrate public beaches in New Jersey and had worked with the Reverend Adam Clayton Powell, Jr., to get jobs for blacks by boycotting the New York regional transit authority. Before long, he established a reputation as one of Gary's most outspoken civil rights leaders.

Jackson's first accomplishment, carried out in conjunction with the Interdenominational Ministerial Alliance, was to force the Gary Transit Company to hire black conductors and motormen. When the company superintendent claimed that union policies tied his hands, Jackson declared: "We're going to work and drag folks off these cars until you get some sense." By evening the company had hired Clifford Smith, whose uniform and union membership card were paid for by the ministerial alliance.

The following autumn, a parishioner told Jackson that his children had been turned away from Roosevelt School for lack of space. At first incredulous, Jackson vowed to "raise hell until Gary jumps off her foundations" after Principal H. Theo Tatum confirmed that hundreds of children were siphoned off to mobile units and other substandard quarters. The minister harangued school officials until work commenced on a new wing for the all-black school.

The circumstances surrounding the expansion of Roosevelt demonstrated, however, that more was needed than agitation alone. Working quietly through channels cultivated over the course of a generation, Tatum got Congressman Ray J. Madden to use his influence to obtain the necessary federal funds.

"When I came to Gary," Jackson said later, "a Negro could not empty a waste basket at the YMCA, much less use its facilities." This disturbed him profoundly, especially since he had started his lifework as a YMCA secretary. When the YMCA commenced a citywide appeal for donations, Jackson denounced its racist policies in an advertisement in the *Post-Tribune.* Within days the board of directors informed him that blacks would be welcome at the YMCA.

One of Jackson's favorite anecdotes concerned a talk he had in 1944 with *Post-Tribune* editor H. B. Snyder. "A decent Negro could move the mountains of right and righteousness, and you would never hear a word about it," he allegedly said, "but some no-good, trashy scamp could steal a box of sardines, and it would be on your front page." Snyder claimed the problem lay in the lack of qualified black reporters. Before the week passed, Jackson found him one.

In the pulpit Jackson frequently spoke out against the corruption, ignorance, and apathy that seemed to extend from City Hall to the ghetto and from syndicate-bought ministers to the ranks of his own congregation. "If we stopped back-biting, shooting, cutting, and stabbing one another and unite in serenity, understanding, and brotherhood," he preached, "we can get anything we want out of this community and the nation." Jackson's broadsides against bookie joints, numbers runners, and prostitutes resulted in his being offered generous terms on a new church site if he ceased condemning under-world activities. After rejecting the bribe, he had to fight off a factional struggle to oust him as pastor.

The dual approach of appealing to an adversary's conscience and threatening economic reprisals enabled Jackson to integrate several downtown stores which heretofore had not even allowed blacks, in his words, "to clean out the cuspidors." After the Gary National Bank rejected a parishioner's loan application, Jackson told President W. W. Gasser that it was his moral obligation to act more brotherly if he expected to remain in the good graces of God and his many black depositors. "Gasser took my talk to heart and liberalized his policies after that," Jackson asserted.

The pace of change was slow, however, and some restaurants even had signs that read, "We Cater To White Trade Only." Grocers commonly prevented black youths from drinking soda pop in their stores, and blacks were not allowed in most cocktail lounges. One of the few integrated establishments was the Hotel Gary.

During the 1946 Christmas season Jackson noticed the disparity between the number of black shoppers and white workers at Gold-blatt's department store, especially the absence of black teen-agers working part-time. A few hours later, he told manager George Lapping: "I was in your store this morning, and it was all I could do to keep from going to your office and cursing you out."

According to Jackson, Lapping replied: "I know that you are right. I know the existent conditions are an insult to the intelligence of your people. I want you to come down here after Christmas, and we will work something out for the common good of all your people."

Not only did Lapping hire some black clerks, he invited Jackson to speak to the Retail Merchants Association, of which he was president. In Jackson's opinion, because of Lapping's cooperation, "many Jim Crow practices took the wings of the morning and fled the sacred borders of our city."

In January 1948 Paul Robeson was invited to speak at Roosevelt High School as part of a program to help aliens threatened with deportation because of their political activities. During World War II a visit by Robeson to Memorial Auditorium had drawn 4,000 people, raised $1,200 for the Gary War and Community Chest, and received the praise of editor-publisher H. B. Snyder. The Cold War, however, had produced such a climate of suspicion that Robeson's admiration for the Soviet Union caused the American Legion, the Chamber of Commerce, and the *Post-Tribune* to pressure the school board to rescind permission for him to speak at Roosevelt. Black

Councilman Terry C. Gray labeled the withdrawn invitation "an insult to the intelligence and patriotism of Negro citizens. We are perfectly capable of deciding for ourselves the merits of anything Robeson or the others may have to say, compared to capitalism as we know it. We are not children. . . ."

Jackson then invited Robeson to speak at St. Paul Baptist Church. On January 12, 1948, approximately 300 people attended the three-hour program, in which Robeson sang several protest songs and spirituals and made a plea for racial tolerance (earlier in the day he addressed members of the United Public Workers Union, which withstood pressure to cancel its luncheon). Jackson's action provided his enemies with an excuse to label him a Communist agitator. For him it was a simple question of free speech. Three years later, under similar circumstances, he arranged for W. E. B. DuBois to appear at a peace rally at a Midtown skating rink.

In 1949 Jackson endorsed the "Beachhead for Democracy," an integrated rally at Marquette Park to commemorate the fifth anniversary of the World War II landing at Salerno Beach. On August 22 he asked Mayor Eugene Swartz to guarantee the safety of the participants. Swartz agreed that blacks had a right to use all city facilities but refused to promise police protection. During the week before the rally the *Post-Tribune* urged that the demonstration be called off on the grounds that it was Communist-inspired and would lead to a riot. This prompted the Gary *American* to accuse its rival of "the most vicious piece of red-baiting which we've seen in many a day."

On August 28 a hundred demonstrators assembled at City Hall and set out for Miller. Along the route people hurled rocks and vegetables at the caravan; a mob armed with bats, iron pipes, and clubs awaited at Marquette Park. The demonstrators got into the parking lot with some difficulty and unfurled an American flag on the beach. Three people ran into the water before police arrived and closed the beach "to prevent trouble."

Disappointed at the police action but relieved that nobody was hurt, Jackson believed that "God had disappointed the racists." For the next several days, however, vandals burned crosses and damaged property belonging to the "Beachhead" organizers.

Beach incidents occurred during each of the next four years, culminating in the mistreatment of six black women who went to Marquette Park to have a picnic. Chief John F. Foley blamed the trouble on "professional left-wingers," but Jackson charged that park police commonly beat blacks until their heads "nearly turned to jelly." In

1954 the City Council affirmed the right of all residents to use park and beach facilities, but blacks did so at their own risk.

In July of 1956, when Jackson returned to Marquette Park, a youth kept darting in front of his car to provoke a confrontation. Jackson finally made his way past sullen onlookers to the beach; but when he returned to his car, it had been broken into and his hat, resting on the front seat, had been slashed. So were his tires, and his side lights and aerial had been broken. While waiting for a tow truck, jeering youths "tried their darndest to goad me into physical combat."

Seven years later, when 21-year-old Murray Richards took three female companions to Lake Street Beach, a mob broke his jaw, lacerated his face, and beat him so badly with clubs and bottles that he had to be hospitalized. All the while, a nearby policeman, ignoring the women's screams, looked the other way and took off his badge. After Richards broke away from his attackers, he thumbed his nose at the policeman, who allegedly put his hand on his gun and said: "Don't get smart with me, boy!"

The all-white Police Civil Service Commission investigated charges against the "blind" policeman but found no conclusive evidence of negligence. Jackson was furious. At a council budget hearing on August 28, 1961, he suggested canceling the police appropriation until laws were properly enforced.

Interrupting Jackson, Councilman Paul Dudak said: "I'm not going to sit here and listen to what I've listened to 20 times in the past 18 months." Jackson replied: "What is the need of talking about something new until we've done something about the old?"

By 1963 a host of civil rights activists were championing goals which "The Old Prophet," as Jackson liked to call himself, had been advocating for 20 years. One such group was Hilbert L. Bradley's Fair Share Organization, which asked Jackson to distribute leaflets against Henry C. Lytton Clothing Company. Jackson later remembered saying: "Save your propaganda. I think we can get some blacks hired without throwing a brick or saying a nasty word about anyone." Bypassing the local manager, he arranged a meeting with the Chicago-based directors, who bowed to the Fair Share Organization's demands. Calling Jackson a "pioneer and solo fighter," Bradley later said of the Lytton disputes: "We had the muscle, and Jackson was in a position on the ministerial alliance to wield some influence and to threaten to cancel accounts."

On May 2, 1963, St. Paul Baptist Church burned to the ground. Jackson charged that it was in retaliation for his crusade against political corruption and underworld activity. During the next four years he raised money and supervised construction of a new church at 2300 Grant Street. Soon after it was finished, he suffered a stroke and heart attack. On the silver anniversary of his arrival in Gary, Jackson retired as pastor. The congregation honored him with a 15-day jubilee whose theme was: "I have fought the good fight. I have kept the faith. I have finished my course."

Throughout his career, Jackson had supplemented his local crusades by sending long messages of advice and criticism, published at his own expense as ads in the paper, to such national leaders as Everett M. Dirksen, Dwight D. Eisenhower, Barry Goldwater, Roy Wilkins, John F. Kennedy, and Richard M. Nixon. He was a delegate to conventions of the Baptist District Association and the National Council of Churches and worked for state and federal legislation to rid southern Indiana of such obnoxious road signs as: "Nigger, don't let the sun go down on you here."

A lifelong Republican who signed his letters "The Servant of the Lord's Servant," Jackson supported Democrat Richard Gordon Hatcher in Gary's 1967 mayoralty election. On October 4 he wrote an open letter to Democratic County Chairman John Krupa, who had thrown his support to Republican Joseph B. Radigan, accusing him of undemocratic, irresponsible, poisonous, and incendiary utterances which sullied all Negroes and threatened to set off a racial "powder keg."

Four years later, he remained loyal to Hatcher despite his regret that the mayor had not consulted him more often. "Hatcher has not ushered in the millennium," Jackson said, "but he divorced city government from the rotten political vultures, and he is not an Uncle Tom. Gary has suffered too long at the hands of Uncle Toms and Aunt Sallys."

In 1973 several religious and civil rights organizations sponsored a testimonial banquet for Jackson. Dr. Martin Luther King, Sr., who had once called him "the Daddy of the militant civil rights movement," was the guest speaker. Mayor Hatcher congratulated "The Old Prophet" for "a recognition well deserved" and added: "You will always be remembered in Gary for your never ending battles against discrimination and racial injustice in this city. Your face silhouetted against the night as your church burned years ago will never be forgotten as never will your determination to let the then blackballed Paul Robeson speak in St. Paul Baptist Church. You have come a long way Reverend L. K. Jackson for your belief in what's right and you have come with your head unbowed."

Retired but still in contact with friends, Jackson in 1975 said that progress never comes without struggle. One of his favorite anecdotes concerned the person who told him, "God has given you a wonderful garden." He replied, "You should have seen what this field was like before God and I got together on it."

DEMANDING A FAIR SHARE

During the Froebel strike of 1945, Mayor Joseph E. Finerty set up an advisory committee on race relations. His successor, Eugene Swartz, followed his precedent. In 1950 sixteen organizations, including the NAACP, the Anselm Forum, the Urban League, and the CIO, supported the creation of a permanent Fair Employment Practice Commission (FEPC) in order to ensure that "no person shall be denied the right to work because of race, color, religion, national origin or ancestry." Rabbi Adolph J. Feinberg predicted that such a commission would reduce unemployment and welfare costs because a fourth of Gary's job openings were presently closed to a third of its residents.

On November 20, 1950, the City Council voted, 6 to 2, to set up a five-member FEPC. During its 15-year existence it was rendered ineffective by inadequate funds, uneven leadership, and lack of enforcement power. The FEPC made few inroads against the discriminatory practices of craft unions, large corporations, and the police and fire departments. Charitable, sectarian, and fraternal organizations and private businesses with less than eight employees were excluded from the ordinance's provisions; and employers retained the authority to be the sole judge of applicants' qualifications. If they rejected mediation, the FEPC's only weapons were to threaten to hold public hearings or levy fines not exceeding 300 dollars. This latter course was never taken.

Not until 1953 did the City Council appropriate enough funds for a full-time administrator. Then, just as director Waitstill H. Sharp was setting up effective publicity and conciliation procedures, he was removed at the insistence of conservative council members, allegedly because of his association with the American Civil Liberties Union. Commissioners Adolph J. Feinberg and Thelma E. Marshall vigorously protested Sharp's ouster and the subsequent four-year tenure of Rudolph R. Bobella, whose do-nothing policy also alienated the NAACP, the Gary Ministerial Fellowship, the Frontiers Club, and several Midtown citizens groups. In 1954, for example, the FEPC helped obtain jobs for only four people (out of 35 applicants) and made little effort to publicize its services. By 1958 even Bobella's original sponsor, Eli Mandich, admitted he was wasting the taxpayers' money.

In 1958 former Urban League official Edward E. Smith replaced Bobella. "We now have an opportunity to get somewhere," said Commissioner Andrew A. Means. Smith publicized the FEPC in newspaper columns, at school workshops, and on a Saturday radio show. Unable to make independent probes into the hiring, promotion, and firing policies of employers, he believed that a conciliatory approach was essential to cultivating a good relationship with Gary's business community.

Smith's gradualist profile came under attack from Hilbert L. Bradley's Fair Share Organization, which demonstrated against "unfair" employment practices. On August 2, 1961, pickets appeared at the Anderson Company, which had only three Negroes on its 1,250-member staff. One placard asked: "Mr. Anderson, Why does Gary's FEPC tolerate your unfair hiring policies?"

Meeting personally with John W. Anderson, Smith tried to persuade the old patriarch to stop selecting applicants on the basis of recommendations from present employees. Anderson was cordial but noncommital. Unhappy with the slow pace of change, the Fair Share Organization and the NAACP Young Adults Council picketed City Hall, demanding that Smith hold public hearings. Smith ultimately took this course and secured an agreement from the company to accept an open application system of hiring. The Fair Share Organization demanded further prosecution, but Smith declared that Anderson should have the opportunity to demonstrate his good faith. The NAACP subsequently filed another suit charging that the company did not live up to its promises. Before the dispute was resolved, the FEPC had been superseded by a more effective agency, the Human Relations Commission (HRC).

The HRC came into existence largely as a result of pressure from the Combined Citizens Committee on Open Occupancy (CCCOOO), a coalition of more than 20 civil rights groups, including the NAACP, the Fair Share Organization, the Frontiers Club, Muigwithania, the Indiana Civil Liberties Union, and the Urban League. The CCCOOO was primarily interested in housing, but it also pressured Mercy and Methodist hospitals into integrating their staffs and facilities and held freedom rallies to integrate the schools. Inspired by the goals and tactics of Dr. Martin Luther King, Jr., the CCCOOO was dedicated to eradicating racism in Gary.

The first effort to enact an open housing bill was made in July 1962. The City Council, voting along strict racial lines, rejected the proposed ordinance, 6 to 3, with Councilman Paul Dudak leading the opposition on the ground that it would abridge property owners' "freedom of choice." CCCOOO spokesman George Neagu called the vote shameful and concluded that Gary did "not yet appreciate the significance of its democratic heritage."

The following April Dudak's abstention killed a similar measure. Nonetheless, some Glen Park residents were so angered by civil rights activists that they formed a National Association for the Advancement of White People. The topic of open occupancy dominated bar rooms, radio talk shows, cocktail parties, and lunchroom debates at the mill. Worried about the growing polarization, Bishop Andrew G. Grutka released a pastoral letter on August 9, 1963, which denounced segregation as "immoral" and approved the tactic of peaceful demonstrations to combat discrimination.

Meanwhile, after some of its members participated in the "March on Washington," at which Martin Luther King gave his "I have a dream" speech at Lincoln Memorial, the CCCOOO organized a demonstration to protest Gary's ghettoized housing conditions. On September 14 thousands of people assembled at 25th and Broadway behind a coffin emblazoned with the words "Segregated Housing." Carrying banners and singing "We Shall Overcome," they marched to City Hall, where comedian-activist Dick Gregory satirized their critics. "Man, you depreciated my soul for 300 years," he said. "I couldn't give a damn about your bricks."

In the absence of open housing legislation, black people were blocked by realtors, insurance companies, banks, and white homeowners from purchasing homes in white neighborhoods. In September 1963, for example, a black teacher bought a house in the Ryan subdivision. When she and her 85-year-old mother moved in, according to the Gary *Crusader,* ten men threatened to fire-bomb the house. Next evening, 50 shouting demonstrators assembled in front of her property. The police observed the scene but did not disperse the crowd. A day later, the woman decided to move out of concern for her mother's health.

On January 1, 1964, Mayor A. Martin Katz took office, succeeding John Visclosky, an opponent of open occupancy legislation. Implementing a campaign pledge, Katz established a 26-member Advisory Committee on Human Relations headed by Bishop Grutka. After lengthy deliberations, Grutka's committee drew up an omnibus civil

rights bill with provisions for a permanent Human Relations Commission empowered to combat discrimination in education, employment, public accommodations, and housing.

In 1964 the City Council was evenly divided on the omnibus bill.
Louis Karras and the three black council members—Cleo Wesson,
Mrs. Jessie Mitchell, and Richard G. Hatcher—supported it; Paul
Dudak, Theodore B. Nabhan, Eugene P. Carrabine, and Paul F. Guist
opposed it; and Councilman E. Hugh McLaughlin was torn between
his personal tendency to favor the bill and the hostile feelings of his
Glen Park constituents.

At the beginning of the year McLaughlin had cast the deciding
vote to elect Hatcher council president. Three months later, he
helped defeat a bill to give the FEPC subpoena power. After the
vote, Hatcher warned that, as much as he would regret it, "Gary
Negroes will go into the streets and take the law into their own hands
if they do not receive redress from their elected officials."

On September 23, 1964, the omnibus civil rights bill passed first
reading by a 5 to 4 margin despite Councilman Nabhan's charge that
Grutka's committee did not represent the "average working citizen
who lives here and has his life savings invested in his property."
Councilman McLaughlin, who cast the deciding vote, needed a police escort to leave the meeting.

During the next six weeks, support for the bill dwindled due to
opposition from the Gary Board of Realtors and the Chamber of
Commerce. Mayor Katz tried to arrange a compromise whereby the
proposed Human Relations Commission would not have the power
to subpoena records nor conduct independent investigations and
complainants would be faced with a 60-day statute of limitations and
be penalized for unfounded charges. The amendments angered the
black council members and did not satisfy opponents of the bill.

On November 13, 1964, the City Council met for six hours to
decide the issue. "Let us dare to make a new beginning. Let us build
a new city and a new man to inhabit it," Councilman Hatcher declared. Before the vote, 32 spokesmen endorsed the bill and four
opposed it. Bishop Grutka warned that a haze was "hovering over
Gary, which if it descends and envelopes the city will blur and smear
this communal picture." After spirited debate the council voted
along racial lines to weaken the omnibus bill by adopting the mayor's
suggestions. Then, with McLaughlin again casting the critical vote,
the council rejected it anyway. Katz later described his reaction to
the proceedings as one of despair, frustration, and disappointment.
The Gary *American* referred to the event as "Black Friday."

In the wake of the defeat was born the "Gary Freedom Movement," an effort organized by the Reverend Julius James to take economic reprisals, such as a Christmas shopping boycott, against businesses that had opposed the bill. Six days after the vote several prominent black leaders, including Coroner-elect Alexander S. Williams, Reverend John E. Hunter, and Police Commissioner Randall C. Morgan, resigned from the Chamber of Commerce.

Pickets appeared in front of Gary National Bank protesting the negative vote cast by Councilman Paul Guist, who was manager of the Tolleston branch bank. Blacks were urged to withdraw their money from Gary National. Guist subsequently resigned his elective office, leaving the choice of a successor up to the deadlocked council. Mayor Katz recommended John Armenta, a supporter of open occupancy, and used a variety of patronage inducements to arrange his appointment.

On May 18, 1965, the showdown arrived. "Tonight may go down in Gary's history as a turning point," declared the *Post-Tribune,* which supported the measure despite doubts about giving subpoena power to the proposed Human Relations Commission. "Some will make the immediate claim," the editorial added, "that it will mark the beginning of the end for the 20th century's most rapidly growing city. Others will claim that the date will mark another progressive step toward building a truly metropolitan city capable of leadership and of handling 20th century problems."

Councilman Hatcher led the successful fight against adding amendments which would have decreased the commission's investigatory power. Armenta's support tipped the balance in favor of passage despite the last-ditch efforts of Councilman Paul Dudak, who had said in a public letter urging "the white people of Gary [not to] take this sitting down," that under the proposed ordinance one might go to jail for talking his neighbor "out of selling his home to a Negro" or "for trying to *move out of Gary.*" He added that "if I were to write a letter of this nature after its passage, I would be put in jail. IS THIS DEMOCRACY?"

The final tally was 5 to 3, with McLaughlin, Nabhan, and Carrabine voting against the measure. Dudak was not present to register his dissent. During debate he had launched into a speech about "forced integration," prompting Council President Louis Karras to rule that his remarks were not germane. Refusing to yield, Dudak said: "I challenge you to throw me out." Karras responded by having him ejected.

After the vote, the following statement was released by Mayor

Katz, who had come under attack both from white opponents and black proponents of the omnibus civil rights bill: "There is no need to fear progress in the field of human relations. Changes in the old established order are sometimes painful, often uncomfortable, but frequently necessary. This is a necessary change to accommodate the broad progress of the concept of equality for all people." In the wake of the dispute, Councilman Theodore Nabhan made a short-lived attempt to require FBI checks of HRC nominees and to block appropriations for the commission. The Board of Realtors unsuccessfully challenged its constitutionality.

The HRC superseded the FEPC, and under the leadership of Director Charles H. King it did battle with apartment owners, the news media, the steel mills, and the school board, as well as working with teen-age gangs and operating a rumor-control center to prevent riots. Problems remained, however. Public hearings proved an impractical method of responding to ordinance violators, and grievance proceedings could be stalled in the courts for years. Massive white flight from the city frustrated efforts at integration. In 1972, for example, the HRC sponsored an ordinance which banned "For Sale" signs in the hope of stabilizing neighborhoods. By that time busing to Horace Mann High School had ceased because the changing racial composition of the neighborhood had turned it into a predominantly black school. Overall, the HRC proved useful to individuals with legitimate grievances but failed to achieve racial harmony in Gary.

THE RISE OF RICHARD G. HATCHER

"Let's Get Ourselves Together"—on that double-edged appeal to black unity and civic harmony Richard Gordon Hatcher changed the course of local politics in ways hardly imaginable in 1959 when he arrived in Gary as a 26-year-old law school graduate. Aided by the political demise of George Chacharis, the recent black migration into Gary, and the support of a small but significant number of white liberals, he became within eight years Gary's first black mayor.

"The logic of black power is irrefutable . . . only its direction is in question," Hatcher stated on several occasions. In 1967 he put together a "black united front" by espousing the militant but optimistic message that it was possible to work within an unfair political system without succumbing to its evils. The path to equality, he believed, was through black unity and "ballot power."

Born on July 10, 1933, Hatcher was the youngest of 14 children, 7 of whom died before reaching maturity. He grew up in a small waterfront ghetto area in Michigan City, Indiana. His father Carlton, a wheel molder at the Pullman Palace Car Company, was a shrewd, Georgia-born Baptist deacon who could neither read nor write. His mother Katherine worked at a foul-smelling "hair" factory, plucking pigs' tails for cushion stuffing.

During the depression, the family sometimes lived on a welfare diet of powdered milk, powdered eggs, margarine, dried prunes, and potatoes, supplemented by handouts of small fish provided by trawler captains. "I didn't even know we were on relief," Hatcher said later. "I thought that was the way life was."

A childhood accident left Hatcher blind in one eye, and there were times when he stayed home from school for lack of shoes. For spending money he collected junk, scavenged for coins at an amusement park, did yard work at beach homes, or ran errands for a black attorney who employed his older sister Gladys as a secretary. Hatcher could not join the YMCA or play American Legion baseball, and counselors at Michigan City Elston discouraged him from taking academic courses even though he wanted to be a doctor or lawyer. A shy, introverted student who stuttered badly, Hatcher excelled on the football field and set a school track record in the 220-yard dash.

In 1950 a restaurant manager who employed Hatcher as a dish washer refused to serve a black couple unless they ate with the hired help. Outraged, Hatcher stalked out the door. Later his father told him that "to get where you want to go, you'll sometimes have to take things you don't like." The next day he went back to work but with a new sense of alienation and heightened feelings of racial consciousness. Two years later, he participated in a sit-in which desegregated the establishment.

An athletic scholarship plus help from his two older sisters and two black churches enabled Hatcher to attend Indiana University in the fall of 1951. Unprepared for college courses, he struggled to avoid the fate of most black freshmen—flunking out. He dropped off the football team but worked part-time in a dining hall. In the spring he ran track in order to keep his scholarship and participated in an NAACP demonstration against a segregated restaurant located near the campus.

After graduation Hatcher attended Valparaiso Law School while working full-time as a psychiatric aide at Beatty Memorial Hospital. In 1958 he and several friends went to Brownie's Griddle in Michigan City and tried unsuccessfully to get some coffee. The next day they went back and were served. Reporter Ernie Hernandez wrote:

"There were no placards, no marches, no arguments, and no publicity. Just success."

When Hatcher ran for justice of the peace in 1958, his home-town newspaper asked him for a capsule biography. Hatcher wrote: "I have grown up in a Christian home, where honesty is accentuated." Out of ten candidates, he finished fourth. Admitted to the bar in 1959, Hatcher became a deputy county prosecutor after winning an important extradition case involving a black youth from Mississippi charged with aggravated assault for allegedly insulting a white woman.

The vehicle through which Hatcher entered Gary politics was Muigwithania, an organization which began as an informal discussion group consisting of Hatcher and a dozen friends, including attorney Jackie Shropshire, bus driver John Gibson, probation officer Houston Coleman, and businessmen Dozier T. Allen and John Lawsche. Inspired by John F. Kennedy's call for citizen involvement and by the emerging nations of Africa (in Swahili, *Muigwithania* means "We are together"), its members held social functions to raise money for deserving community projects. In this way they gained support in their struggle to obtain more responsive and independent black leadership. Their first venture into politics was an attempt to unseat ten precinct committeemen which ended in utter failure. Nonetheless, Muigwithania established a reputation as a progressive force for change within the ghetto.

Elected president of Muigwithania in 1962, Hatcher resigned as deputy prosecutor and moved his law practice from East Chicago to Gary. He worked at the juvenile court, argued a school integration case for the NAACP, represented ghetto residents before the Police Civil Service Commission, and was a leader in the open housing movement.

In 1962 friends urged Hatcher to run for state representative, but he demurred out of respect for the black incumbent James S. Hunter. The following year, he entered the Democratic primary for councilman-at-large. During the campaign his car was rammed at an intersection. After it was towed to a garage, someone poured liquor on the upholstery, and threw whiskey bottles inside. Pictures were taken for the press. The trick backfired, however, because it was common knowledge in the ghetto that Hatcher was a lifelong teetotaler. Winning election by polling 99 percent of the black vote, he was chosen by his colleagues to be council president, an unprecedented honor for a freshman councilman.

Politics was in flux between 1964 and 1967, with a vacuum having

been left by Chacharis' indictment. Anxious to retain the black vote
and avoid a race riot, Mayor A. Martin Katz advocated open housing,
established the Human Relations Commission, appointed Negroes to
his staff, and helped Alexander S. Williams become county coroner.
Some whites resented Katz for being too friendly to blacks; others
credited him with "keeping the lid" on the city. On March 25, 1966,
Katz vetoed a loyalty oath bill requiring garbage workers to pledge
that they were not members of the Communist party. Three weeks
later, it passed into law anyway by a 6 to 3 vote, with Gary's three
black councilmen dissenting.

The following month Muigwithanian Dozier T. Allen finished a
close second to incumbent Tom Fadell in the Democratic primary
for township assessor. Allen carried Gary, indicating a diminution in
power of the regular Democratic machine.

Mayor Katz tried to keep politics away from the school and parks
boards, but to the chagrin of the Northwest Indiana Crime Commission and other good-government groups he winked at vice and gambling. When an Indiana University graduate student, John Sopsic,
wrote a thesis on syndicate activities, Katz quipped: "It sounds to me
like the boy has just discovered prostitution exists in the world." On
May 14, 1966, several hundred teen-agers marched to Gateway Park
with placards reading "Gary is the SteAl City" and "Not All the Dirt
in Gary Is in the Mill." Uninvited, Katz joined the anti-crime demonstration after police banned a sign saying: "When the Mice Are Away,
the Katz Will Play."

In the fall of 1966 a group of organization Democrats promoted
Lake County Treasurer Leslie O. Pruitt for mayor. Katz refused to
bow out of the race, confident that his civil rights record would carry
him to victory in a fashion similar to the 1963 primary when he
polled only ten percent of the white votes but received huge majori-
ties in the Central District.

Pruitt eventually dropped out of the contest, but Hatcher's candidacy upset Katz's plans. Combining the issues of civil rights and clean
government, Hatcher charged that Katz gave blacks only token benefits rather than jobs, integrated schools, or decent living conditions.
"Are the slums any prettier? Are our schools any less crowded?" he
asked.

Three events had caused many blacks to lose faith in white political
leadership. The 1964 Democratic presidential primary, in which segregationist George C. Wallace carried every white precinct in Gary,
sometimes by 4 to 1 margins, was a reminder of white intransigence
to change. Second, there was "Black Friday"—November 13, 1964

—when white councilmen weakened an omnibus civil rights bill at Katz's urging and then voted it down anyway. When Hatcher announced his mayoral candidacy at Baber Youth Center, he chose to do it on a "Friday the 13th" in remembrance of that day. Finally, there was the issue of public housing in Glen Park. In November 1966 Hatcher squared off at a planning commission hearing against his onetime ally, Councilman E. Hugh McLaughlin. At issue was a rezoning proposal to allow low-cost public housing at two Glen Park sites. Arguing that the projects would upset existing neighborhoods, McLaughlin claimed to know at least 78 homeowners who were ready to put up "For Sale" signs. Unimpressed, Hatcher vowed that blacks would "penetrate the iron curtain" of the Little Calumet River. "We've been confined to living with rats, roaches, and bed bugs long enough," he said. "We need decent housing." The commission passed the proposal, but the City Council voted along racial lines to block the projects. None was built until after the 1967 election.

GARY'S 1967 ELECTION

On January 5, 1967, Mayor A. Martin Katz formally announced his candidacy for reelection. "We, in this city, have peacefully met problems that other communities have not been able to cope with," he said.

Eight days later, Richard G. Hatcher launched his "New Freedom" campaign for the Democratic nomination, pledging to rid Gary of the "shackles of graft, corruption, inefficiency, poverty, racism, and stagnation." He pleaded that the contest not degenerate into a "black-white" conflict and said that honest government and equal rights were the real issues. Chiding U.S. Steel for polluting the air and not paying its fair share of taxes, Hatcher said that the corporation "has taken much from the people of this city, and given little in return."

In addition to Hatcher and Katz, a third major candidate, Bernard W. Konrady, joined the race. Konrady was a political maverick who believed that his late brother Emery had been cheated out of beating Katz in 1963 by illegal machine activities. Claiming to have been offered a bribe to drop out of the race, he said: "You may be able to beat a Konrady, but you can never buy a Konrady." Hatcher also claimed he was offered a bribe by a rackets czar if he would quit the race. Support for Konrady was strongest among segregationists, but Hatcher benefited from his candidacy since he split the white vote and kept up a barrage of criticism against Katz, whom he labeled a pawn of George Chacharis.

Katz portrayed himself as a moderate and his opponents as extremists. Singling out Hatcher's campaign manager Jesse E. Bell as a militant, Katz said: "Gary has no room for people who wish to be catapulted into public office on the rocket ship of violence, using the fuel of race hatred." For his speech writer Katz hired Chuck Stone, a former aide to Harlem Congressman Adam Clayton Powell, Jr. The mayor enjoyed the support of most precinct committeemen and such black politicians as Alexander Williams, Hoyt Brown, and Curtis R. Strong. The help of Martin Luther King, Jr., was solicited, but the civil rights leader expressed hope that Hatcher would win. Heavyweight champion Muhammad Ali, singer Harry Belafonte, and Georgia legislator Julian Bond all campaigned for Hatcher, whose aides referred contemptuously to Katz's Negro supporters as "Uncle Toms, Aunt Sallys, and paid political prostitutes" who would "sell their souls . . . for a hot dog and a bottle of beer."

Hatcher's hopes rested upon 2,000 volunteers, about 80 percent of whom were black. Many of the rest had responded to an appeal by Miller residents Arthur Daronatsy, Fred Stern, and Burton D. Wechsler, who had written on February 10 that it "would be a major set-back for this city were he to be completely shunned by the whites and gain election with only the support of black people. The problems faced by any mayor of Gary are overwhelming—a mayor who had no connections or support from half his constituents would indeed be in an untenable position." Hatcher sought help from black community leaders—in some cases pastors, civil rights activists, and teachers but often steelworkers, taxi cab drivers, youth leaders, nursery school workers, secretaries, and others without previous political experience. Press secretary Chuck Deggans organized a zealous band of canvassers called the "Shock Troops."

To overcome the apathy and cynicism common to Gary elections, Hatcher defined the issue in messianic terms as a battle between good and evil. "Each and everyone of us will sing in unison in one huge chorus in one polling booth after another," he told blacks. "No longer will we be stampeded to the polls like a bunch of cattle by a cynical, corrupt political machine. Plantation politics is dead. The day the machine can come to us with satchels full of stolen and extorted money and buy our votes is, thanks to God, over and gone."

Katz was favored to win, but Hatcher received more than a 3,000 vote plurality (20,272 to 17,190 with Konrady receiving 13,133 votes). Even though Katz won more than 30 percent of the black vote, Konrady's large vote in white neighborhoods lost Katz the contest. Hatcher received 4.5 percent of the white vote. The results set off a jubilant block party along Broadway, halting traffic for four hours. Konrady was happy that Katz had lost and at the end of his concession speech shouted, "Emery, we did it!" Mayor Katz called Hatcher an honorable man and wished him well, as did Konrady.

The Republican candidate, furniture dealer Joseph Radigan, admittedly had little taste for politics. Since Gary was nearly a one-party city, the Republican nomination would have been meaningless had Hatcher not been a black antimachine candidate. Two weeks after the primary, Democratic County Chairman John Krupa, who had risen in local politics to the position of Lake County Clerk through his leadership in the American Legion, referred to Hatcher as "Gary's Next Mayor." Behind the scenes, however, he told Hatcher that it was traditional for the county organization to select Gary's controller and police chief as the price for its support. When Hatcher refused to agree to these terms, he was allegedly told, "The trouble with you people is you're not willing to wait your turn. You're too impatient."

Having pledged to eradicate corruption, Hatcher launched a "Dollars for Decency" drive to finance his campaign independent from Krupa's control. Using almost all his reserve funds, he placed a full-page advertisement in the *New York Times*. It included a picture of a white policeman beating a Negro and a plea for concerned Americans to help end bigotry, ignorance, and violence in Gary. "Hatcher is making a career out of being a Negro," Krupa sniped, but the advertisement attracted nationwide attention and support.

Krupa then accused Hatcher of having called American pilots who flew bombing missions over North Vietnam war criminals. Hatcher denied it and said that "Krupa had no monopoly on patriotism." After Krupa called on Hatcher to denounce the violence-prone philosophy of Stokely Carmichael and H. Rap Brown and the antiwar positions of Martin Luther King, Jr., folksinger Joan Baez, and actor Marlon Brando, Hatcher replied that Krupa was injecting irrelevant issues into the campaign and, in any event, "wouldn't support me if I stood on my head." Refusing to repudiate any black leader and thereby threaten his black united front, Hatcher nonetheless denied that he was a radical, an extremist, or a separatist and defined himself as a "progressive minded person who believes in the rights of all people."

By September most white Democratic precinct committeemen were helping Radigan, and Krupa's remarks became more intemperate. "I feel I'm standing shoulder to shoulder with the boys in Vietnam," he told one audience. "They're fighting Communism, and I'm fighting it here." Krupa's red-baiting, however, hurt Hatcher less, wrote Edward Greer, than a "false accusation, that he was secretly engaged to a white campaign worker—and it was so damaging in the black community that special pains had to be taken to overcome it."

Partially because of Krupa's tactics, Hatcher attracted support from national Democrats. At a fund-raising reception in Washington, D.C., attended by Senators Birch Bayh and Robert F. Kennedy, Vice President Hubert H. Humphrey called Hatcher a "man of merit" who deserved to be mayor. Hatcher said that he believed in "building up, not burning down" and pledged to work for an urban environment where "persons of different backgrounds can play, work, and live together in peace and harmony."

Locally, Hatcher received endorsements from Congressman Ray J. Madden, CIO Director Joseph A. Germano, and Mayor A. Martin Katz. E. Hugh McLaughlin, who had lost his council seat in the primary to a segregationist, stumped Glen Park on Hatcher's behalf despite receiving considerable abuse. On several occasions, Hatcher's sixth district headquarters was pelted with rocks and splattered with paint. Hatcher's opponents attempted to exploit the racial fears of white residents, even though, as Richard M. Dorson pointed out, "the machine turned against Hatcher, not because he was a Negro but because he would not do their bidding."

After his trip to Washington, Hatcher stated that racketeers, slum lords, corporate tycoons, and dishonest politicians had "blighted the city" through "years of neglect and pillage. To rebuild it, to transform it into a thing of beauty, is not an easy task. It cannot be wrought overnight, nor without enormous federal aid." A prerequisite to receiving aid, he added, was honest and progressive leadership.

Radigan claimed that Gary's problems could best "be solved by the people of Gary, because our only difficulties came from outsiders." The implication was that Hatcher was an untrustworthy newcomer. Republican billboards described Radigan as a "100 percent American." The Republicans also criticized Hatcher's use of motorcycle gang members as bodyguards. It was a precautionary measure, Hatcher replied, because he had gotten death threats but received no extra police protection from Chief Conway "Moon" Mullins, a Radigan supporter, who denied that Hatcher had asked for any.

As secretary of the board of election commissioners and the board of canvassers, Krupa sent extra registrars to white precincts but refused to cooperate with "Operation Saturation," a Midtown voter registration drive. He purged 5,286 blacks from the rolls and accepted more than a thousand other names later found to be fraudulent.

Apprised of illegal registration procedures in Glen Park by Marian Tokarsky, a Polish-American committeewoman who had been told that the tactics were necessary to stop Communism, Hatcher filed suit in federal court charging Krupa with violating the 1965 Voting Rights Act. FBI investigators were sent in to examine the roll books. Under pressure Krupa added the 5,286 Midtown residents to the list of eligible voters; and on election eve a panel of judges ordered 1,096 "ghost" names stricken.

Hatcher still feared that Krupa would try to "steal" the election, and the mood was so tense that Governor Roger D. Branigin put 5,000 National Guardsmen on alert. There were open predictions of a riot if Hatcher lost. Some black teen-agers enjoyed asking whites for matches and watching their reactions.

On election morning when Hatcher went to vote, hundreds of supporters swarmed around him shouting, "We'll dance in the streets tonight!" During the day he checked out reports concerning defective voting machines and the harassment of poll watchers. When told that no stops were being pulled to beat him, the normally mild-mannered candidate snapped: "If I lose this election, I'm going to let my hair grow long."

It was a close race, but Hatcher won by 1,865 votes out of 77,759 cast, receiving approximately 96 percent of the black vote and 12 percent of the white vote (there were 2,000 more whites registered to vote even though blacks constituted 55 percent of the population). "The glaring way the Democratic party in Gary tried to defeat Hatcher probably tipped the scales and gave Hatcher some white votes he wouldn't have received otherwise," one observer wrote. Hatcher himself believed that Krupa's tactics played into his hands but attributed the result, in large part, to the dedication of his workers and the determination of ghetto residents to make Gary a decent city.

Shortly after midnight, Mayor Katz congratulated Hatcher and noted with some exaggeration that it had been the most peaceful election in Gary's history. A half-hour later, John Krupa confirmed the vote result from Crown Point; and after a few moments of reflection, Hatcher greeted a crowd in council chambers. After thanking his workers and cautioning against too riotous a celebration, he evoked a vision of a "New Gary" beyond the horizon. "We shall lead the way for the whole country to follow," he promised. "We shall prove that urban America need not wallow in decay, that our cities can be revived and their people rejuvenated. Yes, we shall prove that diversity can be a source of enrichment, that at least the people of

one city in the nation have decided, finally, to get themselves together."

"Mayor Hatcher's election has taught black youngsters one important thing," a resident said: "The only thing standing between my
being mayor or fire chief or city engineer or city attorney is education. If I get an education I can get a job. The proof of the pudding
is in the tasting. I don't believe my son can be president until I see
a black president. . . . But I can encourage him to be Richard Hatcher
because Hatcher is Black—and we tried to get the blackest one we
could find so white folks couldn't claim him."

THE CHALLENGES OF OFFICE

In his inaugural address at the Gary Armory on January 1, 1968,
Mayor Hatcher talked about the need for harnessing the community's resources in order to build a new, livable city with an honest,
responsive government. Near the end of his speech, he recalled the
words of black poet Arna Bontemps:

> We are not come to make a strife
> With words upon this hill;
> It is not wise to waste the life
> Against a stubborn will
> Yet we would die as some have done,
> Beating a way for the rising sun.

Then he said: "Gary is a rising sun. Together we shall beat a way;
together, we shall turn darkness into light, despair into hope and
promise into progress. For God's sake, for Gary's sake—let's get ourselves together."

Gary's bitterly contested election of 1967 had aroused great fears
and expectations among different segments of the population, but
Mayor Hatcher lacked the power to institute immediate social or
economic changes. Symptomatic of his problems were the chaotic
conditions at City Hall, with some employees not coming to work and
others wondering if they still had jobs. Well-wishers and job seekers
swarmed about, and incoming phone calls went unanswered until a
switchboard operator was found. There were almost no office supplies, and police cars and garbage equipment were in such disrepair
as to suggest sabotage or looting.

To the chagrin of some supporters, Hatcher retained a number of
holdovers from the Katz administration in positions where their

knowledge of operations was needed to prevent a deterioration of city services. Having criticized the patronage politics of his predecessor, Hatcher moved cautiously in personnel matters and the letting of contracts and tried to make good his pledge to have a multiracial administration that stressed talent. "The joke around the mayor's office," said one disgruntled supporter, "is that he climbed to the top and pulled the ladder up behind him."

Less than a week after Hatcher took office, a delegation of Midtown residents complained that he had not provided enough jobs or done anything to clean up the slums. The mayor asked for their patience and their trust. Having promised an "open" administration, Hatcher held weekly press conferences, published occasional columns in the *Post-Tribune*, attended club luncheons, walked the streets, and started a mayor's access program to establish contact with neighborhood organizations.

In a "state of the city" address delivered on February 1 at Hotel Gary, Hatcher said: We can never be what we must become until we face up unflinchingly to what we are: not in self-pity, not in despair, but in the pragmatic spirit of those who examine the real world in order to change it."

Although blacks comprised more than 55 percent of the population, he told the assembled civic leaders, they were confined to one-fourth of the city's housing units, which were generally substandard and overcrowded, and were twice as likely as whites to be without jobs. After outlining similar inequities in the areas of health, education, and recreation, Hatcher asked his constituents to respond affirmatively to challenges ahead. He appealed to those who had recently moved away because of the crime and corruption to come back "and help us to bring the culture and arts and the parks, the beauty and the grandeur upon which we can all thrive."

Hatcher directed his new police chief, James F. Hilton, to take personal charge over an enlarged antivice squad. After going on a raid against the Venus Cafe, Hatcher said: "We want the citizens of Gary to know where the mayor's office stands on this sort of thing." Those affected by the crackdown complained that it threatened the livelihood of many black people and just transferred the lucrative industry to other areas, such as East Chicago. Hatcher replied that strict enforcement was necessary for honest government and a healthy moral environment.

Hatcher's most significant accomplishment in 1968 was attracting millions of dollars from foundations and the federal government. Among the private agencies contributing technical assistance or "seed money" for social programs were the Ford Foundation, the Field Foundation, the Potomac Institute, the Congress of Racial Equality, the Cummins Engine Foundation, the National Alliance of Businessmen, the Carnegie Foundation, and the Metropolitan Applied Research Center.

Federal agencies pledged more than 35 million dollars for programs ranging from a Neighborhood Youth Corps (NYC) to a beautification program. Gary became known as an "urban laboratory" for President Lyndon B. Johnson's "Great Society" experiments, and its Model Cities programs became the most extensive in the country for cities of comparable size.

Almost all cabinet-level departments in Washington contributed something in Gary. For example, the Commerce Department furnished a youth coordinator, and the Justice Department sent a special assistant for public safety. The Department of Health, Education, and Welfare funded early learning centers and bilingual clinics. The Department of Labor financed a drug rehabilitation center (Marona House) and a Concentrated Employment Program (CEP) to train ghetto youths as dental hygienists, secretaries, plumbers, and the like. The Department of Housing and Urban Development (HUD) approved two urban renewal projects, Midtown West and Small Farms. HUD money also stimulated the private housing market and financed public housing projects for the elderly and the poor. In 1970 a 60-member Model Cities Resident Committee assumed responsibility for planning and coordinating neighborhood projects.

The Office of Economic Opportunity (OEO) supported Metro Corps, Gary's primary antipoverty agency. The OEO originally funded money through the county government, but after Hatcher argued that two-thirds of the eligible recipients lived in the city, the money went directly from Washington to Gary. Metro Corps administered "Operation Head Start" for preschool children as well as senior citizen centers and emergency food and medical services. Its most controversial venture was Soul, Inc., a project that paid gang members to operate a skating rink, a theatre, and a cultural center. "We can ignore the gangs and leave them to their own destructive impulses," Hatcher said, "Or we can work with them and try to reform them. I prefer the latter."

With the annual city budget a mere 12 million dollars and the tax base stagnant, Hatcher had to seek this outside help, but the flow of money and consultants into Gary was a mixed blessing. According to Edward Greer, it created a dependence on distant bureaucrats, separated Hatcher from his grass-roots followers, raised expectations artificially, and provided "endless opportunities for nepotism and even thievery." As one official said: "Whatever program we thought up, they sent us the money for it; and if we couldn't think up a program, why, they sent us the money anyway."

During the spring of 1968 Hatcher's inclination to scrutinize personally all administrative decisions created serious staff problems and delays. With over 20 department heads directly responsible to him, it was impossible to find time for all of them. After much deliberation, a new chain of command was devised that created three "superadministrators," to whom departments reported: one for matters of public safety and law enforcement, a second for housing and community development, and a third for fiscal and personnel matters.

Hatcher's first year in office was marked by labor disputes involving police, firemen, garbage collectors, and social workers and several near riots. After the assassination of Martin Luther King, Jr., about 200 students stormed out of school. Soliciting help from the Roosevelt championship basketball team, Hatcher persuaded them to return to classes. Three days later, he closed schools for a day of prayer and mourning. A year after King's death, Hatcher paid tribute to the slain leader, saying: "He represented a kind of order—to use a dirty word—in the civil rights movement, a kind of reasonableness and willingness to forgive people that maybe a Rap Brown or an Eldridge Cleaver would not have."

Several weeks later, a downtown fire precipitated incidents of rock throwing and minor looting which resulted in 127 arrests. Hatcher visited the scene, alerted the National Guard, imposed an after-dark curfew, and met with some of the gang leaders rumored to be involved in the trouble.

In May 1968 the Concerned Citizens for Quality Education (CCQE) organized a week-long school boycott involving 20,000 students in protest against the alleged segregationist policies of Acting Superintendent Clarence E. Swingley. An antiboycott group, the Citizens to Save Our Schools (CSOS), then vowed to march on City Hall. Warned that black gangs were ready to attack the CSOS demonstrators, Hatcher convinced CCQE organizer Steve Morris, a clerk in the school lunch program, to call off the boycott, thereby avoiding the confrontation. Hatcher later appointed Morris to a CEP staff position and defended the school boycott as an example of "our community speaking to us, loudly and clearly, about the need to . . . reorder our priorities on the educational scene."

In the fall of 1968 six youths mugged and robbed a Serbian priest. A delegation from St. Sava Orthodox Church demanded a City Council investigation. Lake County Prosecutor Henry S. Kowalczyk, already angry about a police crackdown on pinball and slot machines, called Mayor Hatcher and Chief Hilton "cry babies" who "won't stand up to their responsibilities." After probing Gary's police department and juvenile gangs, the City Council passed an "unlawful assembly" ordinance that forbade loitering in public places. Hatcher vetoed it on the grounds that it would impede civil rights demonstrations, but the council overrode him, 8 to 1.

Despite such programs as "Operation Crime Alert" and "Operation Safe Gary," the city crime rate rose precipitously in 1968 (11 percent, not counting auto thefts, of which there was an epidemic). One black leader linked the problem with the antivice crusade, saying: "Cut off a man from running policy slips, working in an after-hours joint and a cathouse and he's got to make it some other way."

Despite the alarm over street crime and some grumbling in white neighborhoods about the deterioration of garbage service, Hatcher generally received praise after his first year in office. "If any administration in the country gave the Washington money tree a good shaking in 1968, it was the one right here in Gary," wrote *Post-Tribune* reporter Joe Hopkins. Councilman Paul Dudak conceded that Hatcher "has done as well as should be expected" and deserved praise for maintaining "good race relations" and "giving a dollar's worth for a dollar spent on public services. . . . "

In March 1969 Washington correspondent Bernard D. Nossiter described Hatcher as an earnest, well-meaning, quietly moralistic man with "a kitful of Band-Aids where massive surgery is needed." Hatcher talked of exciting new changes, Nossiter wrote, but "this ugly agglomeration of railroad tracks, steel mills, dirty streets, and mean, low lying buildings mocks his words."

Hatcher told Nossiter: "When I was running for office, I had a simplistic solution for everything. In 13 months I've learned there are some problems that have no solution."

Noting how little control Hatcher had over U.S. Steel, county politicians, or semiautonomous agencies, and how he had to deal with the sullen hostility of whites and the cynical street-corner "nihilism" of blacks, Nossiter concluded: "Mayor Hatcher fits almost any detached observer's description of a good man. Honest, intelligent, energetic, he has a deep and wise perception of his city's needs. But Gary appears beyond the competence of one man, even armed with the battery of federal aid he has mobilized."

TRIUMPHS AND TRAVAILS OF MAYOR HATCHER

During his first 18 months in office, Mayor Hatcher had frequent disputes with the City Council. Most councilmen complained that he treated them like junior partners or rivals and seldom consulted them in matters of patronage or policy. Councilman Dozier T. Allen, Hatcher's former Muigwithania ally, claimed that the mayor had "incurred a time-table problem in getting things done" and was not coming down hard enough on lawless elements that were giving Gary "such a foul reputation as to halt all progress."

A public confrontation occurred in the spring of 1969 when Councilman John Armenta proposed that the council, rather than the mayor, appoint nine of the 15 members of the Human Relations Commission. When the measure came up for final passage on May 17, hundreds of protestors filed into council chambers, including spokesmen for the NAACP, the League of Women Voters, and various youth gangs. During the public debate a teacher drew loud applause when he told a councilman that "your effort to attack my mayor is going to hasten your slide into Hell." The president of the Sin City Disciples warned that if the mayor needed help, all he had to do was "pull our string and we bark and bark loud." The most threatening speech was delivered by a dashiki-clad youth who identified himself as Elemi Olorumfummi. To the accompaniment of black power salutes from the audience, he said: "What do you want us to have? Nothing? You crawin' with us. And we're tired. Tired of playing. The game is over. We make this clear, this is not a threat. This is a promise."

During recess several councilmen complained that they felt intimidated. Paul Dudak demanded police protection. Eugene M. Kirkland said that he was "in no mental condition" to think clearly, much less vote. Hatcher rejected a suggestion to caucus privately and told Dudak: "That's the first time you've seen black people come down here and speak their mind—the truth, and you get shook."

The council voted down Armenta's bill, 6 to 2. The mayor's "gunboat diplomacy" worked, the *Post-Tribune* wrote. Hatcher refused to dissociate himself from his exuberant supporters and said: "We now have some very enlightened councilmen. They are not going to go down there anymore and just vote black people down the river without even thinking about it twice. They will never be the same again."

Ten days later, Governor Edgar D. Whitcomb was scheduled to speak at a Republican function at the Gary Armory. Before he arrived, more than a hundred members of the Aid for Dependent Children Mothers' Club entered the banquet room and demanded an audience with him to protest his recent veto of a welfare measure. More orthodox methods to see him had failed. Hatcher persuaded them to leave but not before some of the children helped themselves to food.

Hatcher's critics seized upon the "eat-in" as exemplifying a breakdown in law and order. It was Gary's "Day of Infamy," charged Councilman William McAllister. It showed that Gary was undergoing a "reign of terror," said Attorney General Theodore L. Sendak. "Somehow, children eating pie do not call up an image of terror," replied Hatcher. Nonetheless, Bernard Konrady released a public statement accusing Hatcher of driving white people out of town. George Chacharis joined the attack after one of his relatives was mugged, claiming that the streets were no longer safe. One visitor to the city later wrote that "gloom, ugliness, and apprehension set the tone of Gary."

In Glen Park petitions circulated calling for disannexation in order to block low-cost housing projects and the busing of black students to Lew Wallace High School. Proponents of secession took heart from a recent ruling that had affirmed a special state law allowing the incorporation of Merrillville, located south of the city. Hatcher opposed disannexation, saying, "Gary has become a fish bowl, and the eyes of the nation are upon us."

At neighborhood meetings sponsored by the Glen Park Information Committee, Police Chief James Hilton and Hatcher's special assistant Glen W. Vantrease (a former councilman and controller under Mayor Katz) spelled out the advantages of remaining part of Gary. Vantrease later estimated that he spoke before a hundred different groups in a month and that his most telling arguments were that Glen Park had an insufficient property valuation to support city services and that the area would still remain under the jurisdiction of Gary's school and parks boards. The disannexation movement eventually fizzled out after failing to win support in the state legislature.

In September 1969 Hatcher attended an Institute for Black Elected Officials in Washington, D.C. Addressing several hundred officeholders, he spoke about the need for cultivating "a healthy vital black nationalism . . . that encourages, develops, subsidizes, and pays attention to its own culture, that takes pride in its past, that rids itself of self-hate and self-doubt, [and] that does not mirror and ape white society, especially the worst of it. . . . When we gain strength and unity, we shall from time to time, as situations arise, and when we can be no less than equal partners . . . ally ourselves on specific issues with nonblack groups who share our purposes and commitment."

Hatcher went on to say that black elected officials must not only work for reforms but should view "the struggle around reforms as a means for radicalizing people's consciousness. . . ." Perhaps inspired by the Glen Park disannexation fight, he concluded: "We don't abandon to George Wallace the white working class; they are fearful, confused, battered by inflation, barely making their mortgage payments. We point out to them the real enemy. We explain to them patiently, tirelessly, day in and day out, that the Establishment fears nothing so much as working-class whites and working-class blacks getting themselves together. Because when that day comes, brother, the system is going to change."

Hatcher's national press coverage was generally much better than the treatment he received locally. On several occasions in 1969 the *Post-Tribune* faulted Hatcher for starting press conferences behind schedule, for going out of town too much, and for being a poor administrator. Hatcher said the paper was "constantly abrasive" and "reckless in wielding power because it is free from competition." He charged that, like the segregationists and the machine politicians, the news media was trying to undermine confidence in his administration.

In 1970, Hatcher complained that the paper's coverage of his "Goals for Gary" commission was less than of a flag patch dispute between Police Chief Charles E. Boone (who had succeeded Hilton) and the Fraternal Order of Police. Siding with Boone, Hatcher said that the insignias could be interpreted as an "anti-Negro symbol."

Perhaps in response to Hatcher's criticism, the *Post-Tribune* published a favorable four-part series by George Crile that emphasized Hatcher's success in obtaining federal money. "His performance has perhaps been poorest in the area of public relations," Crile wrote, adding: "And this is peculiar because the achievements of the Hatcher administration are numerous."

Hatcher suffered a number of political setbacks in 1970. He campaigned for an independent slate of candidates for county office in the Democratic primary. Not only did they fare poorly, but Hatcher lost to Dozier T. Allen in a bid to become city chairman of the Democratic party.

Many black ministers were disenchanted with the mayor for ignoring their advice and refusing to be deferential to them. Too often in the past, Hatcher believed, clergymen had hindered progress. The frayed relations threatened the fragile "black united front," which he had put together in 1967. As one Midtown resident put it: "The [black] community will never be the same again. Those who hate him really hate him, and those who love him really love him. And I guess all strong leaders have people with an ambivalence toward them."

That winter, journalist Joseph McLaughlin sampled public attitudes toward the mayor. "Sure, I'll vote for Hatcher again. We haven't had any riots here," a Polish-American steelworker said. A bartender disagreed, saying the streets were so unsafe after dark it was ruining business.

In an article published in *Trans-Action* magazine (January 1971) entitled "The Liberation of Gary, Indiana," former aide Edward Greer credited Hatcher with having freed the city from a corrupt machine but warned that he was losing his "local mass base," because "the promise of vast change after [he] took office came to be seen as illusory."

To compound Hatcher's problems, there was a slow erosion of federal support for urban programs under President Richard M. Nixon. On the second anniversary of Robert F. Kennedy's death, Hatcher declared that "the war on poverty has become a mere skirmish, and we're beating a hasty retreat. The reality of today is that there are two Americas—one white, comfortable, and free, the other black, captive, and without opportunity." Hatcher feared that revenue sharing, Nixon's main urban program, would not be accompanied by nondiscrimination clauses and that the money would come in such small amounts as to dictate that it be spent on salaries and police equipment rather than on the poor. That Daniel P. Moynihan, one of Nixon's few "liberal" advisers, advocated a policy of "benign neglect" toward black people increased Hatcher's concern.

On February 1, 1971, Hatcher delivered a "Partners for Progress" report on the "state of the city" which summarized his administration's housing, job training, and model cities programs and promised new initiatives in restoring the central business district, helping senior citizens, meeting the needs of the growing Latin population, and reducing crime, pollution, and poverty. He noted that thousands of abandoned cars had been removed from the streets during the past year, that the crime rate was down, that the number of housing inspections was up, that a downtown Holiday Inn was about to open, and that the City Council had recently passed a coke oven ordinance as a result of pressure by such citizens groups as the Calumet Community Congress (CCC) and Community Action to Reverse Pollution (CARP).

Hatcher reiterated these themes in his campaign for renomination against Negro Coroner Alexander S. Williams and maintained that he was best qualified to "reverse the blight and deterioration in the community." "The real issue," the mayor said, "is an honest government of three years or a return to the corrupt politics of people who raped Gary and stole everything not nailed down." Williams charged that Hatcher was a divisive extremist who "fiddled while Gary burns." When the mayor said he was a front man for George Chacharis, Williams replied that Hatcher was a front man for Valparaiso University law professor Burton Wechsler.

As in 1967 Hatcher enlisted the aid of national celebrities such as Harry Belafonte, Sammy Davis, Jr., Bill Cosby, Dick Gregory, and Jesse Jackson. Singer Nancy Wilson campaigned so zealously that rumors spread of her impending marriage to the "city's most eligible bachelor." These luminaries emphasized that Hatcher was an important national figure who had received honorary degrees (from Valparaiso and Fisk universities), had spoken at prestigious conferences, and had been featured in *Life* and *Ebony* magazines.

A laudatory biography by Alex Poinsett, entitled *Black Power Gary Style,* appeared in print in time for the campaign. It described the mayor as "so spartan he neither smoked, drank, nor used profanity, so dedicated he worked 14 to 18 hours a day, so religious he prayed in church on New Year's Eve while others partied, so committed his Gary soul brothers saw him as 'a beautiful, black, together cat.' "

Near the end of the primary campaign a rumor spread that Williams tried to withdraw from the race but that George Chacharis slapped him and said, "Nobody quits on me." Whether the story was true or not, the slogan "unbought, unbossed, and unslapped" solidified Hatcher's strength among blacks.

Although most analysts predicted a close contest, Hatcher beat Williams handily, 34,371 to 20,834, with Mexican-American Councilman John Armenta receiving 2,880 votes. Four months later, Gary's precinct committeemen unanimously chose the mayor to be city Democratic chairman. Even County Chairman John Krupa gave his blessing.

In November Hatcher won reelection by 20,000 votes over Republican Theodore D. Nering, who had conducted a "silent campaign" in the wan hope that he might lull Hatcher's supporters into staying away from the polls.

During the summer of 1971 Gary Works built up a large stockpile of finished products in anticipation of a long strike. Then after signing a union contract, the company cut back production. The layoffs left an estimated 43 percent of the city's work force temporarily unemployed. Gary received more than a million dollars under the Emergency Employment Act, but the slump betrayed Hatcher's prediction that Gary was "on the edge of an economic boom."

In 1972 Hatcher proposed the construction of a farmers' market and a civic center. Hope was expressed that Charles O. Finley, a former Gary resident, would move his ailing Memphis basketball franchise to the city. In an effort to demonstrate Gary's potential as a convention center, Hatcher arranged for the first National Black Political Conference to be held at West Side High School.

On March 22, Hatcher welcomed 3,500 delegates to the three-day conference. In a spirited speech entitled "For We Must Pave the Way," he called for a black united front against racism and social injustice. "Yes, we support all avenues to liberation. . . . We know full well that political action is not the whole answer. But political action is an essential part of our ultimate liberation," he concluded.

As Hatcher was hosting the conference at West Side, the Indiana High School Athletic Association (IHSAA) was deliberating over incidents that had taken place during the state basketball tournament in Bloomington. In the final game Connersville upset the West Side Cougars, as the referees called 31 personal fouls against the Gary team, plus two technicals against West Side Coach Ivory Brown, compared to nine personal fouls against Connersville. Hatcher called the officiating "lousy" but typical of the traditional bias by downstate referees against teams from the Calumet Region. At the end of the game several fights broke out in the stands, and black youths allegedly assaulted white spectators with belts and chains. One schoolbus had a window shattered by a rock allegedly thrown by someone on a Gary Transit Authority bus.

After receiving approximately 90 complaints, the IHSAA suspended West Side for a year on grounds of unsportsmanlike conduct. Hatcher called the action excessive insofar as West Side students were being punished and denied chances for athletic scholarships as a result of events beyond their control. He added that to blame West Side for the misdeeds of unnamed black people was unfair. An area judge enjoined the IHSAA from enforcing the decree, and West Side went forward with its football program in the fall of 1972. After the third game of the basketball season, however, an appeal board upheld the IHSAA, halting West Side's athletic program until March 17, 1973, despite the protests of Hatcher and other community leaders.

If the West Side incident hurt Gary's pride, the Nixon administration's freeze of federal funds in January 1973 torpedoed its housing and antipoverty programs. Already there had been cutbacks involving the Concentrated Employment Program and Metro Corps; the freeze threatened to deny Gary up to 20 million dollars. Hatcher warned the Senate Intergovernment Relations Committee that "the nation as a whole cannot long endure without cities such as Gary remaining vital. . . ." In April 1973 city employees held a one-hour strike to protest the freeze.

Nixon's action was intended to prod Congress into replacing the categorical grants of most federal programs with a system of revenue sharing that made use of block grants not tied to specific programs. Hatcher feared that the new policy would discriminate against cities such as Gary whose special problems had caused them to get a lion's share of the categorical grants. Revenue sharing money was later used to set up a city ambulance corps, to take over a municipal bus line, and to build a new firehouse in Miller. Even so, since less money came to the city than previously, Hatcher had to scrap some antipoverty programs.

The Nixon freeze also set back local HUD programs for more than a year. At the Midtown West project, for example, buildings had been razed and sewers laid, but there was no money for the proposed housing units. "Over the past half decade," Hatcher stated in May 1974, "federal policy has moved from Operation Breakthrough to Operation Breakdown." In August Congress passed a compromise housing bill which released some HUD funds. Hatcher called the legislation a "fresh start" but still far short of what was needed.

The movement of middle-class families to the suburbs during the early 1970s not only reduced Gary's tax base but resulted in a majority of its residents either being less than 21 years old or over 65. "These are the dependent rather than the independent," Hatcher said.

During Hatcher's second term a long article by Godfrey Hodgson and George Crile appeared in the Washington *Post*. Entitled "Gary: Epitaph for a Model City," it predicted a bleak future for the exurban laboratory. When asked whether Gary could be revived, Mayor Hatcher said: "It's a very fair question and a very important question. My answer would be, at this point, yes, we can make it, but not without some very significant changes in how we relate to Washington, and how we relate to U.S. Steel. . . ."

Objecting to the gloomy tone of the Hodgson and Crile article, urban planners James O. Gibson and Geno Baroni presented "Another View" of Gary in a subsequent issue of the Washington *Post.* They wrote that "Gary, like other central cities in America, faces an immediate crisis in unemployment and crime and in its schools and changing neighborhoods. It needs outside assistance during this period, and the current federal administration moves are not encouraging. But unlike too many other cities, Gary has developed depths of local competence previously lacking, and new capacities for long-range planning that enable it to better pursue its own economic development. Gary is probably further along than most jurisdictions in its ability to utilize revenue sharing funds constructively."

In addition to the funding crisis, Hatcher suffered further setbacks in 1974. His "super slate" of county candidates failed to win nomination in the Democratic primary; a nepotism scandal tainted the summer Neighborhood Youth Corps program; and the state legislature blocked his touted civic center project. Several powerful local black politicians—including Calumet Township Trustee Dozier T. Allen, Gary City Judge Frederick T. Work, Councilman Thomas J. Crump, and State Representative Jewell G. Harris—formed an anti-Hatcher coalition in preparation for the 1975 election.

In spite of threatened economic reprisals from the National Black Political Conference, Sears closed its downtown store in 1974, following the example of the Palace Theatre, Gordon's department store, Comay's jewelers, Radigan's furniture store, and W.T. Grant (the Holiday Inn closed in 1975). Gary-born realtor Daniel W. Barrick said: "It seems like everyone wants to leave. I feel like an outcast in my own home town. I don't want to live here. I don't like working here. And, most of all, I feel like they don't want me here."

Gary's homicide rate spiraled during Hatcher's second term, due in large part to drug-related crimes and well-publicized gang warfare among narcotics suppliers. *Time* magazine reported on December 30, 1974, that "thugs have invaded church services and meetings to rob and, in one case, even rape parishioners. Clergymen of several denominations recently organized a committee to fight this barbarism. The New Mount Olive Baptist Church took more direct action this month, after bandits shot up the church during a heist. Some New Mount Olive parishioners armed themselves and now stand guard while dressed in their Sunday best."

Graduate student Bradley J. Beckham wrote in 1975 that some

policemen participated in the heroin traffic and that Illinois Bell's service personnel refused to go into Midtown except between 10:00 A.M. and 2:00 P.M. "Gary's future is as grey as the sky that blankets it . . . the eleventh hour has come and gone," Beckham concluded. "Frankly I don't have time for the prophets of doom," Hatcher said defensively. "Too many things are being planned for Downtown to take seriously the comments of people who don't even live here of a dead Downtown."

Hatcher's chief rival in the 1975 Democratic primary was Dozier T. Allen, who stressed that he was a lifelong resident of Gary with more compassion for the city than his politically ambitious opponent from Michigan City. Hatcher labeled the contest "a referendum on freedom," accused his opponent of being a pawn of George Chacharis, and claimed credit for 4,000 new public housing units (with another 6,000 by 1976), and for bringing technical skills to 38,000 young people. "If there is such a thing as 'the solution' to the urban crisis, it'll be found in Gary," he said.

Hatcher defeated Allen by nearly 8,000 votes. In the summer he coordinated a successful Founder's Day Festival, lured the Miss Black America pageant to Gary, and appointed a citizens' task force to study ways of revitalizing the city. In November he defeated former Police Chief James Hilton by more than 17,000 votes.

The following month, his task force recommended, among other things, creating a downtown mall, hiring an outside professional as police chief, and attracting visitors by offering tours of the mills and the dune areas. "Some will say that it is too late to begin a drive to 'save Gary,'" the *Post-Tribune* wrote. "They are wrong. It is late, true. But the energy shown by those on the study groups proves that there is plenty of life in 'the old girl.'"

As Hatcher began his third term in 1976, it was still uncertain whether Gary would again be "on the move." In part, its fate rested upon how committed the American people became toward the goals of economic justice, civil rights, and saving cities. Hatcher once said he hoped to be mayor on the day when Americans decided that cities were worth saving. In eight years he had instituted a plethora of antipoverty programs but could not bring the sweeping social and economic changes necessary for full racial equality. He had calmed troubled racial waters but could not halt white flight to the suburbs. He had brought millions of dollars into Gary but could not reverse the deterioration of its downtown business district. His tribulations reflected the general plight of American cities. As he said in his third inaugural address on January 1, 1976: "A minister alone cannot build a church. A general alone cannot fight a battle. A mayor alone cannot create a community."

Hatcher kept alive the dream of progress, however, that had sustained Gary in the past. "Yes We Can," would be the motto for this third administration, he said, and the bywords would be "independence" and "interdependence." Despite its obvious problems, as Gary celebrated its 70th anniversary during America's bicentennial year, the city was probably less polluted, better governed, less a pawn of U.S. Steel, and more responsive to the needs of black people than at any point in its history.

"We have, all of us, come a long way since 1968," Hatcher said while on the campaign trail in 1975. "We have come a long way since the time when Gary was a national synonym for corruption and municipal malfeasance. We have come a long way since the time when new housing for senior citizens was a blue print promise: when decent public housing for all citizens was deemed an unattainable dream. I say forward together, backward never. Together we can continue building a new Gary, a marvel of a metropolis, right here on the shores of Lake Michigan."

BIBLIOGRAPHY

A. Books

1. Alinsky, Saul D., *John L. Lewis* (1970).
2. Allen, Frederick Lewis, *Only Yesterday: An Informal History of the 1920's* (1931).
3. Altrocchi, Julia Cooley, *Wolves Against the Moon* (1940).
4. Appleton, John B., *The Iron and Steel Industry in the Calumet District: A Study in Economic Geography* (1925).
5. August, Garry J., *God's Gentleman* (1932).
6. Ball, Timothy H., *Northwestern Indiana From 1800 to 1900* (1900).
7. Ban, John, *Governments of Lake County, Indiana* (1966).
8. Banfield, Edward C., and James Q. Wilson, *City Politics* (1963).
9. Barnhart, John D., and Donald F. Carmony, *Indiana, From Frontier to Industrial Commonwealth*, 2 vols. (1954).
10. ——, and Dorothy L. Riker, *Indiana to 1816: The Colonial Period* (1971).
11. Bernstein, Irving, *Turbulent Years: A History of the American Worker, 1933–1941* (1971).
12. Bourne, Randolph S., *The Gary Schools* (1916).
13. Bowers, John O., *Dream Cities of the Calumet* (1929).
14. ——, *The Old Bailly Homestead* (1922).
15. Brennan, George A., *The Wonders of the Dunes* (1923).
16. Brody, David, *Labor in Crisis: The Steel Strike of 1919* (1965).
17. ——, *Steelworkers in America: The Nonunion Era* (1960).
18. Brooks, Robert R., *As Steel Goes* (1940).
19. Callahan, R. E., *Education and the Cult of Efficiency* (1962).
20. Cannon, Thomas H., Hannibal H. Loring, and Charles J. Robb (eds.), *History of the Lake and Calumet Region of Indiana Embracing the Counties of Lake, Porter and LaPorte*, 2 vols. (1927).
21. Case, Roscoe D., *The Platoon School in America* (1931).
22. Chudacoff, Howard P., *The Evolution of American Urban Society* (1975).
23. Cooper, Courtney R., *Ten Thousand Public Enemies* (1935).
24. Cotter, Arundel, *The Authentic History of the United States Steel Corporation* (1916).
25. Cromie, Robert, and Joseph Pinkston, *Dillinger: A Short and Violent Life* (1962).
26. DeBedts, Ralph F., *Recent American History: 1933 Through World War II* (1973).
27. Douglas, Paul H., *In the Fullness of Time* (1972).
28. Fitch, John A., *The Steel Workers* (1910).
29. Flexner, Abraham, and F. P. Bachman, *The Gary Schools—A General Account* (1918).

30. Flinn, John J., *The Standard Guide to Chicago for the Year 1891* (1891).
31. Foster, William Z., *The Great Steel Strike and Its Lessons* (1920).
32. Girdler, Tom M., *Boot Straps* (1943).
33. Glaab, Charles N., and A. Theodore Brown, *A History of Urban America* (1976).
34. Goldfield, David R., and James B. Lane (eds.), *The Enduring Ghetto* (1973).
35. Goodspeed, Weston A., and Charles Blanchard (eds.), *Counties of Porter and Lake, Indiana* (1882).
36. Gulick, Charles A., Jr., *Labor Policy of the United States Steel Corporation* (1924).
37. Handlin, Oscar, *The Uprooted* (1951).
38. Hargrove, Marion, *See Here, Private Hargrove* (1942).
39. Heller, Peter, *In This Corner . . . !* (1973).
40. Hoffman, Abraham, *Unwanted Mexican Americans in the Great Depression: Repatriation Pressures, 1929–1939* (1974).
41. Hofstadter, Richard, *The American Political Tradition* (1948).
42. Hogan, William T., *Economic History of the Iron and Steel Industry in the United States* (1971).
43. Howat, William F. (ed.), *A Standard History of Lake County, Indiana and the Calumet Region*, 2 vols. (1915).
44. Howe, Frances R., *The Story of a French Homestead in the Old Northwest* (1907).
45. Hughes, Elizabeth, and Lydia Roberts, *Children of Preschool Age in Gary, Indiana* (1925).
46. Jackson, Kenneth T., *The Ku Klux Klan in the City* (1967).
47. Janowitz, Morris (ed.), *Community Political Systems* (1961).
48. Janson, Florence E., *The Background of Swedish Immigration, 1840–1930* (1931).
49. Kaplan, Richard S., *History of the Gary Bar Association, 1907–1964* (1964).
50. Kennedy, Robert F., *The Enemy Within* (1960).
51. Kennedy, William, *Civil Rights Made Me a Criminal* (1972).
52. Komaiko, Jean, and Norma Schaeffer, *Doing the Dunes* (1973).
53. Leech, Harper, and John C. Carroll, *Armour and His Times* (1938).
54. Levinson, Edward, *Labor on the March* (1938).
55. Lingeman, Richard R., *Don't You Know There's A War On?* (1971).
56. McConnell, Grant, *The Steel Seizure of 1952* (1960).
57. Millender, Dolly, *Yesterday in Gary: History of the Negro in Gary, 1906–1967* (1967).
58. Mohl, Raymond A., and James F. Richardson (eds.), *The Urban Experience: Themes in American History* (1973).
59. Moore, Powell A., *The Calumet Region: Indiana's Last Frontier* (1959).

60. Murray, Robert K., *Red Scare: A Study in National Hysteria, 1919–1920* (1955).
61. Nash, Jay R., *Dillinger: Dead or Alive?* (1970).
62. Navasky, Victor, *Kennedy Justice* (1971).
63. Nelson, William E., *Black Politics in Gary: Problems and Prospects* (1972).
64. Olds, Marshall, *Analysis of the Interchurch World Movement Report on the Steel Strike* (1922).
65. Parton, Mary F. (ed.), *Autobiography of Mother Jones* (1925).
66. Perrett, Geoffrey, *Days of Sadness, Years of Triumph* (1973).
67. Phillips, Clifton J., *Indiana in Transition: The Emergence of an Industrial Commonwealth, 1880–1920* (1968).
68. Poinsett, Alex, *Black Power Gary Style: The Making of Richard Gordon Hatcher* (1970).
69. Quimby, George I., *Indian Life in the Upper Great Lakes: 11,000 B.C. to A.D. 1800* (1960).
70. Randel, William P., *The Ku Klux Klan* (1965).
71. Raybeck, Joseph G., *A History of American Labor* (1959).
72. Reddix, Jacob L., *The Cooperative Movement: Pathway to Economic Independence* (1954).
73. ——, *The Negro Seeks Economic Security Through Cooperation* (1937).
74. ——, *A Voice Crying in the Wilderness* (1974).
75. Reps, John W., *The Making of Urban America: A History of City Planning in the United States* (1965).
76. Richardson, James F., *Urban Police in the United States: A Brief History* (1974).
77. Ritzenthaler, Robert E., and Pat Ritzenthaler, *The Woodland Indians of the Western Great Lakes* (1970).
78. Sandburg, Carl, *Smoke and Steel* (1920).
79. Schlesinger, Arthur M., Jr., *The Politics of Upheaval* (1966).
80. Sheehan, Bess, *History of Campbell Friendship House: Gary, Indiana 1912–1940* (1943).
81. Sklar, Robert (ed.), *The Plastic Age: 1917–1930* (1970).
82. Tarbell, Ida M., *The Life of Elbert H. Gary: The Story of Steel* (1925).
83. Taylor, Graham R., *Satellite Cities: A Study of Industrial Suburbs* (1915).
84. Taylor, Myron C., *Ten Years of Steel* (1938).
85. Taylor, Paul S., *Mexican Labor in the United States: Chicago and the Calumet Region* (1932).
86. Taylor, Philip, *The Distant Magnet: European Emigration to the U.S.A.* (1971).
87. Terrell, John U., *American Indian Almanac* (1971).
88. Tipton, James H., *Community in Crisis* (1953).
89. Toland, John, *The Dillinger Days* (1963).

90. Urofsky, M. I., *Big Steel and the Wilson Administration: A Study in Business–Government Relations* (1969).
91. Vanderbilt, Cornelius, Jr., *Farewell to Fifth Ave.* (1935).
92. Westley, William A., *Violence and the Police: A Sociological Study of Law, Custom and Morality* (1970).
93. Wilson, James Q., *Varieties of Police Behavior* (1968).
94. Woods, Sam B., *The First Hundred Years of Lake County, Indiana* (1938).
95. Writers' Program of the Works Projects Administration, *The Calumet Region Historical Guide* (1939).
96. Yellen, Samuel, *American Labor Struggles* (1936).

B. Unpublished dissertations on Gary

97. Balanoff, Elizabeth, "A History of the Black Community of Gary, Indiana: 1906–1940," University of Chicago (1974).
98. Beckham, Bradley J., "City for a Century," University of Notre Dame (1975).
99. Bloomberg, Warner, "The Power Structure of an Industrial Community," University of Chicago (1961).
100. Carlson, Martin C., "A Study of the Eastern Orthodox Churches in Gary, Indiana," University of Chicago (1942).
101. Cheadle, Queen, "Gary—A Planned City," University of Chicago (1938).
102. Cutright, Phillips, "Party Organization and Voting Behavior," University of Chicago (1960).
103. Fisher, William D. "Steel City's Culture: An Interpretation of the History of Gary, Indiana," Yale University (1941).
104. Jones, James T., "Political Socialization in a Midwestern Industrial Community," University of Illinois (1965).
105. Lutz, Charles D., "Pupil Achievement in Platoon and Non-Platoon Schools," University of Chicago (1932).
106. Maloney, James A., "To Strike at Steel: Gary, Indiana and the Great Steel Strike of 1919," Harvard University (1972).
107. Meister, Richard J., "A History of Gary, Indiana: 1930–1940," University of Notre Dame (1967).
108. Potts, John F., "A History of the Growth of the Negro Population of Gary, Indiana," Cornell University (1937).
109. Quillen, Isaac J., "Industrial City: A Study of Gary, Indiana, to 1929," Yale University (1942).
110. Thompson, Thomas F., "Public Administration in the Civic City of Gary, Indiana," Indiana University (1960).
111. Turner, A. Michael, "Gary, Indiana: The Establishment and Early Development of an Industrial Community, 1906–1930," University of Keele (1971).

C. Interviews

112. Alice, Edna (April 1975).
113. Allen, Dozier T. (Mar. 1969). Conducted by David G. Nelson.
114. Anchors, Nellie E. (Feb. 1974).
115. Anderson, Robert L. (June 1975).
116. August, Garry J. (Aug. 1974).
117. Bell, Peter (Feb. and July 1975).
118. Benjamin, Adam (Nov. 1975).
119. Blackwell, Symantha B. (Mar. 1975).
120. Bradley, Hilbert L. (Nov. 1975).
121. Brennan, Edward R. (April 1975).
122. Budlove, Elmer F. (April 1975).
123. Caesar, Victoria (Nov. 1974).
124. Callis, W. Maurice (May 1974).
125. Carr, Fred (July 1974).
126. Castellanos, Hope (Aug. 1974).
127. Cessna, Mary Ellen (May 1975).
128. Chacharis, George (Nov. and Dec. 1975).
129. Clary, Marcella (Mar. 1975).
130. Cohan, George (Nov. 1974).
131. Cohen, Ronald D. (Mar. 1976).
132. Coleman, Henry (Mar. 1969). Conducted by David Nelson.
133. Cope, Garrett (Sept. 1975).
134. Costo, Charles C. (June 1973).
135. Cotten, Stanley (Sept. 1974).
136. Crawford, Hazel (April 1975).
137. Curtis, Harriet (Mar. 1974).
138. Davis, Arthur W. (June 1974).
139. Doering, E. C. (Jan. 1973, July 1974, and Feb. 1975).
140. Eichhorn, Julia (Nov. 1975).
141. Evans, Al (Mar. 1976).
142. Feister, Louis C. (Dec. 1973, and Feb. 1976).
143. Feldman, Herman (Nov. 1975).
144. Fonville, Mrs. A. C. (June 1974).
145. Gasser, Robert (Nov. 1975).
146. Gianpoulos, William (Oct. 1975).
147. Giorgi, Mrs. Paul (Feb. 1974).
148. Grady, Lydia (Dec. 1975).
149. Hatcher, Richard G. (Jan. 1976).
150. Holovachka, Metro M. (Sept. and Oct. 1975).
151. Holovachka, Mrs. Metro M. (Oct. 1975).
152. Holtz, Leona (Sept. 1975).
153. Housekeeper, Donald (Jan. 1974).
154. Howson, Louis R. (July 1974).
155. Ingersoll, Carl (Mar. 1974).
156. Jackson, L. K. (Sept., Oct., and Nov. 1975).
157. Jensen, Emily (Feb. 1974).
158. Jones, Harry (Dec. 1975).
159. Joshua, Corrine (Sept. 1975).
160. Kalusak, Joseph (April 1974).
161. Katz, A. Martin (Oct. 1975).
162. Keener, John S. (April 1974).
163. Knight, Dolores (Dec. 1973).
164. Krstovich, George (July and Aug. 1973, and Feb. 1976).
165. Kyle, John W. (Dec. 1973).
166. Lewman, Helen Bonczek (Aug. 1975).
167. Linstrom, Ruth (Sept. and Oct. 1974).
168. Martin, W. Lee (Sept. 1975).
169. Marz, Blaine (July 1974).
170. Mayerik, John M. (June 1975).
171. Mayerik, Mrs. John M. (June 1975).
172. McDaniel, Geneva (July 1974).
173. McDaniel, Hazel (Dec. 1973).

174. McNough, Polly (Nov. 1974).
175. Merwald, Herbert (May 1974).
176. Miller, Carl I. (Mar. 1976).
177. Monterrubio, Paulino (May 1973).
178. Morris, Steve (Mar. 1969). Conducted by David Nelson.
179. Murray, Milo C. (April 1974).
180. Neil, William B. (Mar. 1975).
181. Nelson, Ruth Wall (April 1973).
182. Norrick, Joe (Nov. 1974, and May 1975).
183. Novak, Ed (April 1974).
184. O'Rourke, Terence (Oct. and Nov. 1975).
185. Peterson, William (May 1974).
186. Petroski, Louis J. (Nov. 1974).
187. Pierson, Esther (July 1974).
188. Pilzer, John E. (July 1974).
189. Pitts, Joseph A. (Mar. 1973). Conducted by Judy Smith.
190. Polizotto, Don (Jan. 1976).
191. Powell, Nettie (July 1974).
192. Prete, Armand (June and Oct. 1974).
193. Reddix, Daisy S. (Dec. 1974).
194. Reddix, James D. (Sept. 1974).
195. Reed, Dortha (Sept. 1973).
196. Reese, Jesse B. (Nov. 1974).
197. Reissig, Henry O. (June 1974).
198. Reshkin, Mark (Jan. 1976).
199. Rosenau, Erwin Crewe (July 1975).

200. Saks, Mrs. Benjamin (Oct. 1975). Conducted by Ronald Cohen.
201. Scanlon, Charles (June 1975).
202. Seaten, Carole (Mar. 1974).
203. Sikes, D. E. (Aug. 1973, and Feb. 1976)
204. Silverman, Ivan (Nov. 1975).
205. Stern, Frederick C. (Dec. 1975).
206. Stern, William H. (July 1975).
207. Stiles, Harold E. (May 1974).
208. Strietelmeier, John (Sept. 1971, in Valparaiso, Indiana).
209. Tarailo, Nikola (June 1974).
210. Tatum, H. Theodore (Nov. 1975).
211. Traver, Nina (Sept. 1974).
212. Urice, Ted (June 1974).
213. Vantrease, Glen W. (Dec. 1975).
214. Voyles, Mary (Sept. 1974).
215. Washington, Lorraine Duncan (Mar. 1974).
216. Wiltrout, E. C. (Oct. 1974).
217. Wise, Edith (Oct. 1974).
218. Wood, Alvin F. (June, July, and Aug. 1974, and Jan. 1975).
219. Young, Mayola Spann (June 1974).
220. Yurin, Anna P. (Sept. 1973).
221. Zelt, Gerta (Jan. 1974).
222. Zelt, Martin (Dec. 1973, and Jan. 1974).

D. Magazine and Journal Articles

223. "Back to Work," *Time*, 74 (Nov. 16, 1959).
224. "Backlash, Backstab," *Newsweek*, 70 (Sept. 29, 1967).
225. Betten, Neil, and James B. Lane, "Nativism and the Klan in Town and City: Valparaiso and Gary, Indiana," *Studies in History and Society*, 4 (Spring 1973).
226. ——, and Raymond A. Mohl, "The Evolution of Racism in an Industrial City, 1906–1940: A Case Study of Gary, Indiana," *Journal of Negro History*, 59 (Jan. 1974).
227. ——, "From Discrimination to Repatriation: Mexican Life in Gary, Indiana, during the Great Depression," *Pacific Historical Review*, 42 (Aug. 1973).

228. "Black Power," *Newsweek,* 69 (May 15, 1967).
229. "Black Power in Office," *Time,* 93 (Feb. 28, 1969).
230. Bliss, Don C., "Platoon Schools in Practice," *Elementary School Journal,* 20 (Mar. 1920).
231. Bloomberg, Warner, "Five Hot Days in Gary, Indiana," *Reporter,* 13 (Aug. 11, 1955).
232. ——, "Gary's Industrial Workers as Full Citizens," *Commentary,* 18 (Sept. 1954).
233. ——, "State of the American Proletariat," *Commentary,* 19 (Mar. 1955).
234. Bonner, M. G., "School Riots and the Gary System," *Outlook,* 117 (Oct. 31, 1917).
235. Branch, Taylor, "The Ben Bradlee Tapes," *Harper's,* 251 (Oct. 1975).
236. Bro, Margueritte H., "Up By the Bootstraps: Negro Co-operators," *Christian Century,* 53 (Apr. 1, 1936).
237. Brook, Anthony, "Gary, Indiana: Steel Town Extraordinary," *Journal of American Studies,* 9 (Apr. 1975).
238. Buffington, Eugene J., "Making Cities for Workmen," *Harper's Weekly,* 53 (May 8, 1909).
239. "The Case of the Crooked Mayor," *Saturday Evening Post,* 236 (Jan. 19, 1963).
240. Cohen, Benjamin, "Lake County Before the Railroad Era," *Indiana Magazine of History,* 32 (June 1936).
241. Cohen, Ronald D., "Urban Schooling in Twentieth-Century America: A Frame of Reference," *Urban Education,* 8 (Jan. 1974).
242. Connell, E. T., "Women Run the Rascals Out of Gary," *American Magazine,* 149 (May 1950).
243. "Consumers' Co-operation among Negroes," *Monthly Labor Bulletin,* 72 (Feb. 1936).
244. Cools, G. Victor, "Gary's High School Strike," *School and Society,* 26 (Nov. 26, 1927).
245. Coons, Charles S., "Teaching of Science to Children in the Gary Schools," *School and Society,* 1 (April 17, 1915).
246. Crile, George, "A Tax Assessor Has Many Friends," *Harper's,* 245 (Nov. 1972).
247. Cullison, S. W., Jr., "Central Purchasing," *American City,* 54 (June 1939).
248. Dillon, John B., "The National Decline of the Miami Indians," *Indiana Historical Society Publications* (1897).
249. Dorson, Richard M., "Is There a Folk in the City?" *Journal of American Folklore,* 83 (Apr. 1970).
250. Edmonds, Anthony O., "The Second Louis-Schmeling Fight—Sport, Symbol, and Culture," *Journal of Popular Culture,* 7 (Summer 1973).
251. Edmondson, Edna Hatfield, "Juvenile Delinquency and Adult Crime: Certain Associations of Juvenile Delinquency and Adult Crime in Gary, Indiana, with Special Reference to the Immigrant Population," *Indiana University Studies,* 8 (June 1921).

252. Flower, Elliott, "Gary, the Magic City," *Putnam's,* 5 (Jan.–Mar. 1909).
253. Fowler, Bertram B., "Miracle in Gary," *Forum and Century,* 96 (Sept. 1936).
254. Frady, Marshall, "Gary, Indiana," *Harper's,* 239 (Aug. 1969).
255. Frakes, Margaret, "They Put Meaning into Brotherhood," *Christian Century,* 66 (Feb. 16, 1949).
256. "The Fraud that Failed," *Time,* 90 (Nov. 17, 1967).
257. Frost, Stanley, "The Klan Shows Its Hand in Indiana," *Outlook,* 137 (June 4, 1924).
258. Fuller, Henry B., "An Industrial Utopia: Building Gary, Indiana, to Order," *Harper's Weekly,* 51 (Oct. 12, 1907).
259. Galenson, Walter, "The Unionization of the American Steel Industry," *International Review of Social History,* 1 (Part 1, 1956).
260. Garver, F. B., "Pittsburgh Plus," *American Economic Review,* 14 (March 1924).
261. "Gary Clean-up," *Newsweek,* 33 (Mar. 21, 1949).
262. "Gary: Largest and Most Modern Steel Works in Existence," *Scientific American,* 101 (Dec. 11, 1909).
263. "Gary School Strike," *Literary Digest,* 95 (Oct. 22, 1927).
264. "Gary's All-Out Americans," *Public Welfare in Indiana,* 54 (Feb. 1944).
265. "Gary's Bootlegging Administration," *Literary Digest,* 127 (April 21, 1923).
266. "Gary's Liquor Scandal," *Outlook,* 133 (April 18, 1923).
267. Greer, Edward, "Black Power in the Big Cities," *Nation,* 219 (Nov. 23, 1974).
268. ———, "The Liberation of Gary, Indiana," *Trans-Action,* 8 (Jan. 1971).
269. Grow, Raymond, "De King Is Daid! Gary and Chicago Have Lost Their Negro Robin Hood of the Numbers Game," *American Mercury,* 48 (Oct. 1939).
270. "Guilty in Gary," *Time,* 80 (Dec. 21, 1962).
271. Hadden, Jeffrey K., Louis H. Masotti and Victor Thiessen, "The Making of the Negro Mayors 1967," *Trans-Action,* 5 (Jan. 1968).
272. Haig, Robert M., "The Unearned Increment in Gary," *Political Science Quarterly,* 32 (March 1917).
273. Harrison, Morton, "Gentleman from Indiana," *Atlantic,* 141 (May 1928).
274. Hatcher, Richard G., "Black Role in Urban Politics," *Current History,* 57 (Nov. 1969).
275. ———, "For We Must Pave the Way," *Vital Speeches,* 38 (1972).
276. ———, "My First Year in Office," *Ebony,* 24 (Jan. 1969).
277. "Hatcher's Landslide," *Newsweek,* 77 (May 17, 1971).
278. Henry, Nelson B., "War Course Required of Seniors, Horace Mann School," *School Review,* 51 (Sept. 1943).
279. Hernandez Alvarez, José, "A Demographic Profile of the Mexican

Immigration to the United States, 1910–1950," *Journal of Inter-American Studies*, 8 (July 1966).

280. Hickey, Margaret, "What Women Did in Gary," *Ladies Home Journal*, 68 (Oct. 1951).

281. Higdon, Hal, "Gary's Next Mayor: White, Pink, or Black?" *Reporter*, 37 (Nov. 2, 1967).

282. Holmes, Henry W., "The Gary System Examined," *American Review of Reviews*, 59 (June 1919).

283. Hough, Emerson, "Round Our Town," *Saturday Evening Post*, 192 (Feb. 14, 1920).

284. "An Interpretive Report on the 1959 Steel Strike," *Iron Age*, 184 (Oct. 1, 1959).

285. Jacobs, Stanley S., "Brotherhood Solves Gary's Problems," *Coronet*, 27 (Nov. 1949).

286. Kaplan, John, "Segregation, Litigation and the Schools: Part III: The Gary Litigation," *Northwestern Law Review*, 59 (May–June 1964).

287. Klauser, A. P., "Steel Town Frustration," *Christian Century*, 76 (Aug. 12, 1959).

288. Klein, Paul L., "Gary School Strike," *Nation*, 165 (Oct. 4, 1947).

289. Klein, Joseph, "How Good a Show Town is Gary, Indiana," *Variety*, 254 (Mar. 26, 1969).

290. Lardner, John, "This Here Now Harmon," *Newsweek*, 16 (Oct. 21, 1940).

291. "A Lawyer Takes On a Corrupt Steel Town's Machine," *Life*, 63 (Oct. 13, 1967).

292. Lynd, Staughton, "Guerrilla History in Gary," *Liberation*, 14 (Oct. 1969).

293. Meyer, Alfred H., "Circulation and Settlement Patterns of the Calumet-South Chicago Region of Northwest Indiana and Northeast Illinois," *Proceedings of the International Geographical Union* (1932).

294. "Model Cities Program Summary," *Residents' Voice*, 2 (Mar. 1970).

295. Mohl, Raymond A., and Neil Betten, "Ethnic Adjustment in the Industrial City: The International Institute of Gary, 1919–1940," *International Migration Review*, 6 (Winter 1972).

296. ——, "The Failure of Industrial City Planning: Gary, Indiana, 1906–1910," *Journal of the American Institute of Planners*, 38 (July 1972).

297. ——, "Gary, Indiana: The Urban Laboratory as a Teaching Tool," *History Teacher*, 4 (Jan. 1971).

298. ——, "Paternalism and Pluralism: Immigrants and Social Welfare in Gary, Indiana, 1906–1940," *American Studies*, 15, (Spring 1974).

299. "Mr. Gary and His Times," *Nation*, 125 (Sept. 7, 1927).

300. "Mr. Gary Moralizes," *Nation*, 109 (Oct. 11, 1919).

301. Mumford, John K., "This Land of Opportunity: Gary, the City That Arose from a Sandy Waste," *Harper's Weekly*, 52 (July 4, 1908).

302. "Negro Students in a Gary High School," *School and Society*, 26 (Oct. 8, 1927).

303. "No Gain: Student Strike in Gary," *Time,* 50 (Sept. 15, 1947).
304. Nock, Albert J., "Adventure in Education," *American Magazine,* 77 (April 1914).
305. O'Donnell, William C., "The Gary System in the Crucible of a Political Campaign," *Educational Foundation,* 29 (Jan. 1918).
306. O'Gara, James, "Big Steel, Little Town," *Commonweal,* 51 (Nov. 25, 1949).
307. Petit, Benjamin M., "The Trail of Death," *Indiana Historical Society Publications* (1944).
308. Pickens, Valerie, "Urban Life," *Steel Shavings,* 1 (1975).
309. "Plea from Gary," *Time,* 90 (Sept. 15, 1967).
310. Pollak, Louis H., "The Steel Injunction," *New Republic,* 141 (Nov. 23, 1959).
311. Ratcliff, John D., "It's Murder," *Saturday Evening Post,* 220 (Jan. 24, 1948).
312. "Return of the Glow," *Time,* 74 (Nov. 30, 1959).
313. Roberts, Howard, "Hard-Luck Champion," *Saturday Evening Post,* 220 (July 5, 1947).
314. Rossi, Peter H., and Phillips Cutright, "Party Organization in Primary Elections," *American Journal of Sociology,* 64 (Nov. 1958).
315. Sarber, Oliver B., "A Forward Look," *Gary Baptist Bulletin* (Jan. 1924).
316. Schott, Carl P., and Arthur Perrow, "Boxing," *Colliers' Encyclopedia,* Vol. 4 (1974).
317. Shockley, Ernest V., "County Seats and County Seat Wars in Indiana," *Indiana Magazine of History,* 10 (March 1914).
318. Smith, Dwight L. (ed.), "A Continuation of the Journal of an Emigrating Party of Potawatomi Indians, 1838," *Indiana Magazine of History,* 44 (Dec. 1948).
319. "Stand on Principle," *Time,* 74 (Oct. 12, 1959).
320. Starkey, Otis P., "Cities Built on Sand," *Survey,* 68 (Oct. 1, 1932).
321. "Steel Shock Waves," *Newsweek,* 55 (Jan. 18, 1960).
322. Sternberger, Estelle M., "Are Our Foreign-Born Emigrating?" *Survey,* 43 (Feb. 7, 1920).
323. ——, "Gary and the Foreigner's Opportunity," *Survey,* 42 (June 18, 1919).
324. Sutliffe, Ruth, "Gary, An Industrial City with a Fine Recreation System and Exceptional Park Buildings," *American City,* 40 (Mar. 1929).
325. Taylor, Alva W., "What the Klan Did in Indiana," *New Republic,* 52 (Nov. 16, 1927).
326. "Terrible Tommy," *Time,* 34 (Nov. 6, 1939).
327. "Tom Harmon," *Newsweek,* 23 (Feb. 7, 1944).
328. "Tougher Than Football," *Saturday Evening Post,* 214 (Oct. 25, 1941).
329. Vance, Jim, "Let's Give Credit Where It Is Due: Some Thoughts on the National Black Political Convention," *Negro History Bulletin,* 35 (May 1972).

330. "Vandergrift, A Workman's Paradise," *Iron Age*, 68 (Nov. 21, 1901).
331. "Vote Power," *Time*, 89 (May 12, 1967).
332. Wakstein, Allen M., "The Origins of the Open-Shop Movement, 1919–1920," *Journal of American History*, 51 (Dec. 1964).
333. "What Happened to One 'Model' High School," *U.S. News and World Report*, 68 (April 27, 1970).
334. "Who Killed Mary Cheever?" *Time*, 53 (Mar. 21, 1949).
335. Widick, B. J., "Big Steel's Blunder," *Nation*, 189 (Nov. 28, 1959).
336. Wilhelm, Donald, "Judge Gary, of the Steel Trust," *Outlook*, 107 (Aug. 22, 1914).
337. Wirt, William A., "Utilization of the School Plant," *National Conference of Charities and Correction Proceedings* (1912).
338. Wolff, Max, "Segregation in the Schools of Gary, Indiana," *Journal of Educational Sociology*, 36 (Feb. 1963).

E. Newspapers

339. Calumet *Voice* (1969).
340. Chesterton *Tribune* (1894, 1922, 1925).
341. Chicago *American* (1930–1931, 1962).
342. Chicago *Daily News* (1945).
343. Chicago *Tribune* (1922, 1925–1927, 1930–1931, 1962).
344. *Fiery Cross* (1923). On Microfilm at the IUN Library (Gary).
345. Gary *American* (1926–1936, 1945–1947, 1962).
346. Gary *Daily Tribune* (1910–1921).
347. Gary *Evening Post* (1909–1921).
348. Gary *Post-Tribune* (1921–1976).
349. Gary *Sun* (1927).
350. Glen Park *News* (1929–1931).
351. *Info* (1972).
352. Lake County *Star* (1925, 1930–1931).
353. New York *Times* (1945, 1947, 1949, 1959, 1962, 1967).
354. *Northern Indianian* (1907–1908).
355. Valparaiso *Daily Vidette* (1923–1924).

F. Newspaper Articles of Special Importance

356. Crile, George, "Distrust of Press Shrouds Non-Politician Mayor Hatcher," *Post-Tribune* (Aug. 30, 1970).
357. ——, "Hatcher Administration: City Departments Were Revised But . . . ," *Post-Tribune* (Aug. 29, 1970).
358. ——, "Hatcher Changes Character of Government in Gary," *Post-Tribune* (Aug. 26, 1970).
359. ——, "Housing, Jobs Get Top Priority in Hatcher Administration," *Post-Tribune* (Aug. 27, 1970).

360. Custer, Janice, "It's Golden Jubilee Time for U.S. Movie Theaters," *Post-Tribune* (July 2, 1955).
361. Driscoll, Jim, "Interview with August Sabinske," *Post-Tribune* (Nov. 12, 1958).
362. Drury, John, "Big Cattle Market Once Planned on Site of Gary," *Post-Tribune* (Nov. 6, 1954).
363. Falk, Alex E., "Bethel Lutheran Church Founded in 1874," *Post-Tribune* (May 20, 1956).
364. Gasser, W. W., "The Best Way Out of This Depression," *Post-Tribune* (Jan. 6, 1933).
365. Gengler, Jerry, "Majestic Is Opened; Vaudeville Pleased," *Post-Tribune* (Mar. 15, 1959).
366. Gibbons, Roy J., "How a New Church Has Set About Installing Christ in a City's Heart," Kokomo *Tribune* (Oct. 23, 1926).
367. Gibson, James O., and Geno Baroni, "Gary: Another View," Washington *Post* (Mar. 19, 1973).
368. Hatcher, Richard G., "Martin Luther King," Chicago *Tribune* (Mar. 3, 1969).
369. Hodgson, Godfrey, and George Crile, "Gary: Epitaph for a Model City," Washington *Post* (Mar. 4, 1973).
370. Lester, James W., "Orchids and Tumbleweeds: Dune Folk of Indiana," *Post-Tribune* (Jan. 12, 1929).
371. Marz, Blaine, "On the Go," *Post-Tribune* (Nov. 10, 1971, and July 23, 1972).
372. McLaughlin, Joseph, "Gary's Mayor Hatcher: New Breed of Politician," Chicago *Tribune* (Dec. 20, 1970).
373. Nossiter, Bernard D., "A Black Mayor's Struggle," Chicago *Sun-Times* (Mar. 9, 1969).
374. Parry, Roy G., "Gary Merry - Go - Round," *Post-Tribune* (July 18 and 25, 1929).
375. ———, "Remember 'Way Back When," *Post-Tribune* (Feb. 8, 1940, and Nov. 6, 1941).
376. Perry, Alfred G., "Associate of Tom Cannon on Early Gary Newspapers Recalls Exploits," *Post-Tribune* (Sept. 4, 1936).
377. Rosenau, Erwin Crewe, "Drusilla Carr Again Faces Loss of Land," *Post-Tribune* (Jan. 10, 1930).
378. ———, "Gleason's Death Ends Myriad Steel City Activities," *Post-Tribune* (June 15, 1936).
379. Samuels, Dave, "Prison Term Starts Next Wednesday," *Post-Tribune* (Jan. 18, 1963).
380. Smith, Diane, "Diana and Alice: A Young Girl's Pilgrimage from Progress," *Post-Tribune* (April 23, 1970).
381. ———, "In or Out of History? Bailly Homestead," *Post-Tribune* (Feb. 12, 1970).
382. Stanley, John, "Mayor Chacharis at Apex of Long Political Career, *Post-Tribune* (Nov. 8, 1959).

383. Van Dusen, Harold, "The 20 Years War Along the Little Calumet," *Post-Tribune* (Nov. 13, 1955).
384. Weisman, Joel D., "Every Major Problem Seems More Acute in Gary," Washington *Post* (Dec. 2, 1974).
385. Wilson, Douglas, "The Gary of the Future," *Post-Tribune* (July 29, 1932).

G. Materials Found in the Indiana Room of the Gary Public Library

386. Anselm Forum Collection. Containing scrapbooks, letters, clippings, and pictures.
387. Bailey, Louis J., "The Founding and Growth of Gary," 1911.
388. Banner, Warren M., *A Study of the Social and Economic Conditions in Three Minority Groups in Gary, Indiana* (1955).
389. ———, and J. Harvey Kerns, *A Study of the Social and Economic Conditions of the Negro Population of Gary, Indiana* (1944).
390. "Bethel Lutheran Church ... First 100 Years," 1974.
391. Bushemi (John) File. Containing pictures, booklets, and clippings.
392. Business History Society (ed.), *Addresses and Statements by Elbert H. Gary* (1927).
393. Cannon, Thomas H., "Old Frontiers and New," 1929.
394. Carlson, Donald O., "The Story of the Bethel Evangelical Lutheran Church and Miller in Gary, Indiana," 1954.
395. Chamber of Commerce, "Gary Forges Prosperity," 1925.
396. Concentrated Employment Program, *Annual Reports* (1969 and 1971).
397. Delaney, Frank S., *Seventeenth Annual Report of John Stewart Memorial Settlement House* (1937).
398. ———, *Tenth Annual Report of John Stewart Memorial Settlement House* (1930).
399. Feld, Rose, "Growing Up with Gary," *Success* (Oct. 1923).
400. Fertsch, Albert, "Adult Education from the Viewpoint of a City," *National Education Association Addresses and Proceedings*, 66 (1928).
401. *Final Report of the Gary Redevelopment Commission: Community Renewal Program* (1968).
402. Gary *City Directory* (1908–1909, 1920).
403. Gary Fair Employment Practice Commission, *Annual Reports* (1952, 1955–1958).
404. Gary Principals' Association (comp.), "The Taxpayer and the Gary Public Schools," 1934.
405. Gary Works *Circle* (Aug.–Sept. 1919).
406. "Gary, 1917–1918."
407. Gibson, David, "Wirt School System," *Common Sense* (June 1912).
408. Greater Gary Committee of 100, *Progress Report* (1960).

409. "Greater Gary Theatrical News," Weekly Programs for V.U. Young's Theatres (1926–1927).
410. Gross, Harriet, "An Analysis of Segregation in the Gary Public Schools," 1967.
411. Hall, Harry, "My Story," 1953.
412. Halstead and Phillips, "History of the Negro Race in Gary," n.d.
413. Howe, James C., "The History of Gary," n.d.
414. Illinois Steel Company, *Short History, General Statistics and Views of Gary Works* (1928).
415. Interchurch World Movement, Commission of Inquiry, *Report on the Steel Strike of 1919* (1920).
416. Janowski, Barbara R., "The Bailly Homestead," *DAR Magazine* (Jan. 1961).
417. Jones, Henry D., "Twenty Years of Neighborliness," 1929.
418. Joseph, Sister Mary, *Pioneer Fur Traders of Northwestern Indiana* (1932).
419. Lester, James W. (ed.), "Gibson Inn Material," 1923.
420. Martin (Joseph) Interview on Tape (1956).
421. "The Microphone Speaks," Gary Crime Commission Pamphlet (1950).
422. Northwest Indiana Crime Commission, *Annual Report* (1963).
423. Northwest Indiana Regional Planning Commission, "The Industrial Heritage of Northwestern Indiana," 1974.
424. Old Settler and Historical Association of Lake County (ed.), *History of Lake County,* vol. 11 (1934).
425. "An Outline of Information about Gary, Indiana," School City of Gary pamphlet (1963).
426. Parry, Roy G., "When They Came to Gary," n.d.
427. Purdue Survey Committee, *Final Report for the Gary Board of Education to the President and Board of Trustees of Purdue University* (1943).
428. Shumway, Arthur, "Gary, Shrine of the Steel God; The City that Has Everything, and at the Same Time Has Nothing," *American Parade,* 3 (Jan.–Mar. 1929), in booklet with letters to the *Post-Tribune* and Rabbi Garry J. August's reply.
429. Smith, Edward G., "Great Gary," 1908 booklet in a collection entitled *Gary, Indiana, America's Magic City.*
430. "Steel-O-Rama" Jubilee booklet commemorating Gary's Silver Aniversary (1956).
431. "Tolleston Gun Club," Tolleston Centennial Booklet (1951).
432. U.S. Congress. Senate. Select Committee on Improper Activities in the Labor Management Field. Hearings Before the Committee June 2, 3, 4, 8, 9, 10, and 11, 1959.
433. Vrooman, Bess, "Gary in the World War," 2 vols. (1923).
434. Walley, William V., "Selected Sources for a Social History of Gary, Indiana, prior to 1940, A Bibliographical Essay," 1969.

435. Wilson, Douglas, "Joseph D. Martin; First Police Chief of Gary," *Biographical Sketches of Gary and Lake Residents,* vol. 7 (n.d.).
436. Winter, Jacqueline C., "A History of Miller Station," 1967.
437. Wirt, William A., "The Great Lockout in America's Citizenship Plants," 1937.
438. World War I Scrapbooks (14 vols.).
439. World War II File.
440. Zale (Tony) Interview on Tape (1956).

G. Articles Found in "Papers By Various Hands" (compiled by the Gary Historical Society). The Two-Volume Manuscript is in the Indiana Room.

441. Demmon, Alice Mundell, "The Rhodes Family of Glen Park."
442. Earle, William, "The Earle Family in Lake County."
443. Gleason, William P., "The Gary Works of the Indiana Steel Company."
444. Graham, Ruby M., "Historical Report of the Gary Region."
445. Green, Silas E., "Jerusalem, or East Tolleston: A Town Founded on the Site of Gary."
446. Hamilton, W. J., "Notes on the 'Tolleston Tragedy.'"
447. Lester, James W., "Mrs. Drusilla Carr Tells of Early Days at Miller Beach."
448. ———, "Mrs. Ella Knotts Relates Her Experiences as a Pioneer."
449. Melton, Arthur P., "Early Recollections of Gary."
450. Nimitz, John F., "The Experiences of a Poacher."
451. Pinneo, George M., "Story Told by Fred Carr."

H. Materials Found in the Library of *The Post-Tribune.*

452. 1931 Commemorative Issue.
453. 1956 Commemorative Issue.
454. National Black Political Convention Steering Committee, "The National Black Political Agenda," 1972 booklet.
455. *Post-Tribune* Biographical File (clippings, typescripts, booklets, reporters' notes, pictures, etc.).
456. *Post-Tribune* Historical File (clippings, typescripts, booklets, reporters' notes, pictures, etc.).
457. *Post-Tribune* Subject File (clippings, typescripts, booklets, reporters' notes, pictures, etc.).

I. Materials Found in the Calumet Regional Archives (IUN-Gary).

458. Albert L. Anchors Collection. Contains diaries, photos, autobiographical typescript, and financial records.
459. City Methodist Church Collection. Contains letters, scrapbooks, pic-

tures, "Church History Notes," pamphlets by William G. Seaman entitled "Our Church" and "The City Church," and Beatrice Lewis'
"Methodism in Gary."

460. Gary Neighborhood House Collection. Contains minute books, pictures, pamphlets, and letters.
461. Richard G. Hatcher Collection. Contains letters, typescripts, pamphlets, and pictures.
462. L. K. Jackson Collection. Contains brochures, letters, booklets, typescripts, and memorabilia.
463. David G. Nelson Collection. Contains dissertation notes, including
HRC minutes, transcripts of interviews, copies of ordinances, pamphlets, and typescripts.
464. Erwin Crewe Rosenau Collection. Contains clippings, account book,
and memorabilia.
465. School City of Gary Collection. Contains File on the Froebel School
Strike.
466. Turk Riot File. Contains copies of depositions and transcripts of *State
of Indiana vs. Mike Jurich,* Case No. 777 in the Superior Court of Lake
County (March term 1908).
467. Women's Citizens Committee File. Contains magazines, clippings,
and notes.

**The following documents are in the Calumet Regional Archives
miscellaneous file.**

468. Edward Brennan to Elmer Budlove, undated letter outlining the history of the *Post-Tribune* newspaper guild.
469. "Chronology of Steel Strikes, 1892–1959," undated typescript.
470. Paul Dudak to "Friends," May 10, 1965.
471. "History of St. Joseph the Worker Parish," 50th Anniversary Booklet
(1962).
472. Indiana University Northwest *Bulletin* (1975–1976).
473. "In Honor of President Jacob L. Reddix," booklet published upon his
retirement as President of Jackson State College (1967).
474. "Jacob L. Reddix: Scholar, Educator, Administrator and Human-
itarian," booklet of the Jackson State College Ninety-fifth Founders'
Day Convention (1972).
475. Key, Barbara, and Pat O'Reilly, "Early Gary as known by Publisher A.
B. Whitlock," 1956 typescript.
476. "A Mayor for All the People," 1959 Campaign Booklet.
477. Nelson, David G., "Black Reform and Federal Resources," undated
typescript.
478. Nelson, William E., "Political Mobilization in Gary, Cleveland and
East Saint Louis: A Preliminary Assessment," undated typescript.
479. Reck, Samuel H., "Alice Gray: Diana of the Dunes," 1936 typescript.
480. Roser, Mark C., "This Is Our Story," Anselm Forum Brochure.

481. Schuster, Joseph J., "A History of Banking in Gary," 1974 typescript.
482. Waitkus, Joy, and Ed Cohn, "William Westergren," 1936 typescript.
483. "When the Tidal Wave Took the Dance Floor, 1927," undated typescript.

J. Manuscript Collections (located in Gary unless noted otherwise).

484. Alvord, Burdick, and Howson Collection (Chicago). Contains pamphlets, pictures, and the booklet "Public Works Designed or Executed," by John W. Alvord.
485. Garry J. August Collection. Contains pictures, autobiographical notes, and memorabilia.
486. Bethel Lutheran Church Collection. Contains scrapbooks, pamphlets, pictures, and typescripts.
487. John A. Bushemi Collection in possession of Mary Ellen Cessna. Contains scrapbooks, pictures, clippings, and memorabilia.
488. Central Baptist Church Collection. Contains minute books, scrapbooks, photos, the pamphlet "65 Years in Gary: 1901–1974," and Mrs. Frank Traver's "Historical Sketch of First Baptist Church."
489. City Hall Archives. Contains brochures, ordinances, and Minutes of the Gary Common Council and the Miller Town Board.
490. Gary-Hobart Water Company Collection. Contains scrapbooks, pictures, pamphlets, and John W. Alvord and Charles B. Burdick's 1917 "Inventory of the Water Works Properties of the Gary Heat, Light, and Water Co."
491. Gary Human Relations Commission Collection. Contains scrapbooks, ordinances, FEPC minutes, brochures, case notes, and typescripts.
492. Gary National Bank Collection. Contains bulletins, untitled speeches by W. W. Grasser, pictures, and an unsigned "History of the Gary National Bank."
493. Dr. Antonio Giorgi Collection in possession of Mrs. Paul Giorgi. Contains scrapbooks and memorabilia.
494. Indiana Supreme Court Records (Indianapolis), Nov. Term 1939, No. 27226 (Joseph Pitts Case).
495. Indiana Women's Prison (Indianapolis), File No. 1389 (Anna Cunningham).
496. Ruth Lindstrom Collection. Contains Minute Books and ledgers of the Swedish Evangelical Church.
497. John M. Mayerik Collection. Contains letters, pamphlets, and memorabilia.
498. Jonas Rhodes Collection in possession of Louis Feister. Contains tax receipts, citizenship papers, pictures, and memorabilia.
499. Stewart House Collection. Contains pamphlets, memorabilia, Frank S. Delaney's "History of Trinity Church," and Arthur W. Davis' "History of Stewart House."

500. Superior Court of Lake County Records (Crown Point).
501. Ted Urice Collection. Contains pictures, memorabilia, and manuscripts.
502. Martin Zelt Collection. Contains poems, articles, pictures, and memorabilia.

K. Letters to Author.

503. Owen W. Crumpacker (March 12, 1975).
504. John Cuson (April 3, 1975).
505. Druscilla Defalque (Aug. 11, 1974).
506. May M. Hake (Aug. 25, 1975).
507. Eugene Knotts (Feb. 20 and March 12, 1974).
508. Reuben E. Olson (Sept. 26, 1975).
509. Allen B. Rice (Oct. 2, 1974).
510. Erwin Crewe Rosenau (May 15, 1975).
511. Joseph J. Schuster (Aug. 3 and 12, 1974).
512. Melvin Sikes (Oct. 13, 1973).
513. Jeanette Strong (March 26, 1975).
514. Samuel W. Witwer (Dec. 4, 1974).

L. Unpublished Articles by IUN students.

515. Andrejevich, Milan, "Herman, Joe, and Nick," 1974.
516. Baker, Bruce J., "The Machinery of American Politics: A Study of Tammany Hall's Tweed Ring and George Chacharis' Gary Democratic Organization, 1972.
517. Bencze, Alex R., "Praying for Things to Get Better," 1974.
518. Costo, Charles C., "A History of a Steelworker," 1972.
519. Hughes, Bill, "Living in Glen Park," 1974.
520. Janott, David, "The Gary Steel Strike of 1919," 1972.
521. Murphy, Dennis M., "Gary and the Red Scare," 1972.
522. Renslow, Alfred L., "The Immigrants' Climb to Legitimacy: The Rise of George Chacharis, Gary's Immigrant Mayor," 1976.
523. Smith, Judy, "Joseph A. Pitts," 1973.
524. Tarailo, Nick "The Life of Nikola Tarailo," 1974.
525. Webb, Yvonne, "The Slovak Club," 1972.
526. White, Burnetta, "The Neighborhood House," 1972.
527. Wray, Betty, "Mrs. P.," 1974.
528. Yards, Frank, "A Bitter Experience," 1974.

SOURCES AND NOTES:
The Numbers Correspond to the Listings in the Bibliography.

Chapter 1: ANTECEDENTS

Introduction: 15, 52, 59, 98, 198, 348.
Potawatomi: 9, 10, 43, 59, 69, 77, 87, 197, 248, 307, 318, 348, 444.
Marie Bailly: 3, 6, 14, 44, 381, 416, 418.
Dream Cities and a Millionaires' Playground: 6, 13, 20, 30, 53, 59, 94, 240, 293, 317, 340, 362, 383, 419, 423, 424, 431, 442, 445, 446, 450, 453, 456.
Svanti A. Nordstrom: 48, 86, 167, 363, 390, 394, 436, 452, 453, 482, 486, 496.
Diana of the Dunes: 15, 59, 192, 212, 346, 347, 348, 370, 380, 456, 479, 501.
Drusilla Carr: 15, 59, 125, 144, 169, 187, 192, 361, 377, 447, 451, 453, 455, 483, 505.

Chapter 2: TWENTIETH-CENTURY CITY

Introduction: 59, 67, 83, 109, 395, 453.
Company Town: 33, 58, 59, 67, 75, 83, 98, 101, 109, 111, 237, 238, 258, 262, 272, 296, 320, 330, 401, 449.
Providing Water: 33, 59, 109, 111, 154, 188, 252, 354, 413, 452, 484, 490.
Town Divided: 34, 45, 59, 83, 101, 237, 251, 296, 297, 298, 323, 375, 411, 429, 453.
Elbert H. Gary: 16, 59, 82, 90, 95, 109, 218, 299, 300, 336, 392, 402, 456.
William P. Gleason: 59, 107, 199, 201, 238, 345, 346, 348, 378, 430, 443, 456.
Thomas E. Knotts: 59, 106, 209, 296, 301, 346, 347, 393, 413, 430, 434, 448, 507.
Joseph D. Martin: 59, 354, 375, 420, 435, 452, 453, 466, 500.
Moe and Young: 59, 95, 103, 346, 360, 365, 374, 402, 453, 455, 456.
Working 84 Hours a Week: 4, 17, 24, 28, 36, 37, 59, 134, 209, 262, 322, 323, 347, 414, 429, 518, 524.
Neighborhood House: 80, 109, 160, 295, 298, 323, 346, 417, 452, 453, 460, 526.

Chapter 3: PIONEER LIFE

Introduction: 67, 94, 248, 297, 411, 453, 480.
Albert L. Anchors: 114, 157, 301, 346, 387, 399, 411, 426, 449, 453, 455, 458.
William A. Wirt: 12, 19, 21, 29, 105, 131, 165, 230, 234, 241, 245, 282, 304, 305, 337, 346, 347, 374, 407, 437, 506.
Johnny Kyle: 88, 165, 190, 347, 348, 455.
Black Immigration: 57, 59, 97, 108, 137, 202, 215, 226, 346, 347, 387, 412, 456.

Mexican Immigrants: 40, 85, 107, 126, 177, 227, 279, 295, 348.
Jovo Krstovich: 100, 109, 164, 182, 249, 348, 453.
Antonio Giorgi: 95, 123, 147, 189, 207, 226, 346, 347, 455, 493, 523.
Tom Cannon: 41, 139, 199, 216, 347, 348, 376, 393, 438, 455.

Chapter 4:   World War I and its Aftermath

Introduction: 59, 78, 109, 225.
Most American City: 59, 97, 107, 346, 347, 406, 433, 438.
1919 Steel Strike: 16, 17, 31, 60, 64, 65, 96, 106, 109, 218, 283, 300, 323, 332, 346, 347, 405, 415, 520, 521.
Ku Klux Klan: 46, 70, 97, 107, 109, 208, 225, 226, 257, 265, 273, 325, 344, 346, 347, 348, 355, 489.
Paul P. Glaser: 49, 106, 122, 130, 139, 174, 182, 196, 201, 340, 343, 346, 347, 348.

Chapter 5:   Boom Years

Introduction: 59, 98, 260, 272, 348, 402.
Augustan Age: 59, 95, 107, 109, 139, 324, 347, 348, 401, 430, 453, 489.
Bob Lewis: 95, 124, 175, 185, 211, 315, 341, 348, 488.
William Grant Seaman: 57, 95, 107, 109, 139, 153, 163, 173, 348, 366, 457, 459, 509, 514.
Sales Gimmicks: 2, 81, 117, 207, 348.
At The Cinema: 289, 346, 347, 348, 409, 453, 457.
D. E. Sikes: 195, 203, 512.
Images of Gary: 5, 103, 109, 116, 141, 199, 320, 348, 428, 455, 485.
R. O. Johnson: 104, 109, 265, 345, 348, 350, 456.

Chapter 6:   Law and Justice in the Steel City

Introduction: 109
William A. Forbis: 58, 76, 92, 93, 109, 117, 155, 218, 345, 347, 348, 453, 455.
Anna Cunningham: 214, 340, 343, 348, 352, 495.
Emerson School Strike: 97, 107, 109, 131, 162, 189, 244, 263, 286, 302, 343, 345, 348, 349, 475.
Prohibition: 104, 155, 183, 192, 199, 216, 265, 266, 346, 347, 348.
Arlene Draves Case: 112, 125, 139, 218, 341, 348, 352, 457, 503, 504.

Chapter 7:   The Onset of the Depression

Introduction: 26, 207, 348, 519.
Hard Times: 79, 91, 107, 174, 220, 348, 385, 515, 517, 519, 528.
Depression Entertainment: 107, 164, 181, 199, 289, 348, 457.

W. W. Gasser: 107, 129, 136, 139, 145, 180, 217, 348, 364, 481, 492, 511.
R. O. Johnson's Third Term: 107, 109, 128, 220, 345, 348, 350.
Frank S. Delaney: 57, 97, 138, 139, 172, 191, 210, 219, 345, 348, 397, 398, 425, 457, 499.
John Dillinger: 23, 25, 61, 89, 117, 130, 174, 348, 457.

Chapter 8: GARY IN TRANSITION

Introduction: 11, 22, 107, 348.
WPA: 26, 107, 121, 203, 348, 455, 456.
Jacob L. Reddix: 72, 73, 74, 97, 107, 135, 193, 194, 236, 243, 253, 348, 473, 474.
Ruth Wall Nelson: 180, 181, 348, 400, 472.
Barney Clayton: 22, 99, 107, 115, 128, 146, 247, 269, 348, 455, 456.
John M. Mayerik: 1, 11, 18, 32, 54, 84, 170, 171, 182, 186, 232, 259, 292, 348, 497.
Joseph A. Pitts: 57, 97, 108, 119, 122, 179, 189, 199, 226, 250, 345, 348, 494, 500, 513, 523.
Old Order Passeth: 99, 107, 116, 139, 199, 324, 348, 378, 404, 427, 464.
Erwin Crewe Rosenau: 121, 122, 199, 348, 453, 464, 468, 510.

Chapter 9: THE ERA OF WORLD WAR II

Introduction: 55, 348.
Gary Homefront: 55, 66, 127, 278, 348, 439.
Frayed Wartime Nerves: 55, 66, 166, 216, 264, 348, 386, 439.
Harmon and Bushemi: 38, 66, 121, 127, 199, 290, 326, 327, 328, 348, 391, 453, 455, 487, 506.
Tony Zale: 39, 117, 152, 313, 316, 371, 440, 455.
Father V. M. Ardas: 100, 348, 455, 471.
Anna Rigovsky Yurin: 220, 348, 455, 525.
Martin Zelt: 221, 222, 455, 502.

Chapter 10: POSTWAR STRIFE

Introduction: 8, 99, 104, 110, 311, 348, 386.
Froebel School Strike: 88, 107, 133, 156, 159, 165, 168, 206, 255, 285, 288, 303, 342, 345, 348, 353, 386, 389, 410, 457, 465, 480, 508, 527.
Anxious Decade: 42, 102, 156, 205, 311, 348, 456.
More Steel Strikes: 8, 42, 56, 71, 104, 223, 231, 232, 233, 284, 287, 306, 310, 312, 319, 321, 335, 348, 457, 469.
Mary Cheever and the WCC: 92, 150, 200, 242, 261, 280, 334, 348, 421, 457, 467.
Metro M. Holovachka: 50, 51, 62, 128, 146, 150, 151, 161, 184, 235, 348, 422, 432, 457.

Rise of George Chacharis: 110, 118, 128, 158, 161, 184, 348, 379, 382, 457, 476, 522.

People's Choice: 7, 47, 62, 102, 110, 118, 128, 143, 161, 184, 213, 314, 348, 382, 408, 457, 476, 516, 522.

Fall of Chacharis: 27, 128, 150, 161, 184, 213, 239, 246, 270, 341, 343, 345, 348, 379, 386, 457, 522.

Chapter 11:   THE RISE OF BLACK POWER

Introduction: 115, 156, 286, 333, 338, 348, 410.

Dr. L. K. Jackson: 120, 145, 148, 156, 176, 205, 210, 345, 348, 388, 462, 491.

A Fair Share: 110, 118, 120, 140, 141, 149, 161, 176, 249, 345, 348, 388, 403, 457, 463, 470, 491.

Rise of Richard G. Hatcher: 68, 149, 161, 271, 281, 291, 348, 457.

1967 Election: 63, 68, 149, 161, 224, 228, 249, 256, 268, 271, 281, 291, 308, 309, 331, 348, 353, 457, 461, 478.

Challenges of Office: 63, 68, 113, 132, 149, 178, 184, 229, 249, 268, 276, 294, 348, 356, 357, 358, 359, 368, 373, 396, 455, 457, 461, 463, 477, 478.

Triumphs and Travails: 63, 68, 113, 149, 178, 204, 249, 254, 268, 274, 294, 339, 348, 356, 357, 358, 359, 372, 384, 396, 455, 457, 461, 463, 477.

Hatcher's Second Term: 149, 204, 267, 275, 277, 329, 348, 351, 367, 369, 384, 454, 457, 461.

INDEX

Mott, Charles S., 264
Moynihan, Daniel P., 299
Muigwithania, club, 278, 284–85, 296
Muller, Ralph L., 211
Mullins, Conway, 289
Murray, Milo J., 199–200
Murray, Philip, 243
Murray, William J., 250, 255
Myers, Fred, 181

Nabham, Theodore B., 280–82
National Association for the Advancement of
　Colored People (NAACP), 70, 270; Emerson
　strike, 146; Froebel strike, 234; Pitt's stew-
　ardship, 196–201; 1960s activities, 271, 277,
　278, 283, 284, 296
National Council of Defense, 88
National Industrial Recovery Act, 170, 183, 193
National Labor Relations Board (NLRB), 195,
　204–5
National Tube Company, 105
National Youth Administration, 176
Naughton, Mike, 33
Navasky, Victor, 266–67
Neagu, George, 279
Nehring, Florence, 199–200
Neighborhood House, 56–58, 74
Neighborhood Youth Corps (NYC), 293, 303
Neil, Martha, 168
Nelson, Christina M., 17
Nelson, Elmer, 189
Nelson, Jack, 181
Nelson, Ruth Wall, 187–89
Nering, Theodore D., 300
Netherton, Ross, 65
Neuwelt, Frank W., 241
New Deal, 56, 124, 170, 173–74, 182–85, 192,
　251, 258
New Mount Olive Baptist Church, 303
Nicklason, Nicklas, 17
Niestadt, Frederick A., 184
Nigrelli, Jack, 77
Nixon, Richard M., 246, 276, 299, 302
Nordstrom, Svanti A., 16–20
Northern Indiana Public Service Company
　(NIPSCO), 264
Northern Indianian, 49, 82
Northside, area, 44, 71, 79, 87, 95, 125, 127,
　130, 142, 191, 192, 234
Northwest Indiana Crime Commission, 207,
　254, 285
Northwest Indiana Newspaper Guild, 205
Norton, E. Miles, 100–2
Norton, Horace S., 34, 41, 43–44, 47, 50, 74, 85,
　88, 92, 106, 113, 121, 144, 202, 206
Nossiter, Bernard D., 295
Nuzum, Richard A., 67–68, 232–37

Office of Civilian Defense (OCD), 209
Office of Economic Opportunity (OEO), 293
Office of Price Administration (OPA), 210, 239
O'Gara, James, 242
Ogden Dunes, Indiana, 21

O'Hara, Barrett, 155–57
Old Sauk Trail, 4
Oldham, Ronald, 157
Olds, William H., 100
Olessio, Albino, 99–100
Olorumfummi, Elemi, 296
Olsen, Reuben E., 236, 268
O'Malley, William P., 178–79
Operation Head Start, 293
Optimist Club, 112, 266
Orpheum Theatre, 47, 52, 114
Ostroski, Mike, 194
Ottawa Indians, 4, 6–11
Owen, Chester A., 153, 155

Palace Theatre, 106, 121, 164, 303
Palm, Signe, 18
Papp, Alexander, 255
Parents Committee of Thirteen, 235–37
Parents-Teachers' Association, 232, 235, 247
Parks, 26, 33, 42, 69, 71, 107, 184, 189, 197,
　201–2, 213, 240, 245, 263, 274–75
Parry, Roy G., 48, 210, 211, 221
Patch, area, 34, 36, 48, 69, 108
Pattee, Frank B., 25
Patterson, James A., 114
Peradovic Choir, Croatian, 166
Perrett, Geoffrey, 210–11
Perrotta, Daniel, 191
Petit, Benjamin M., 7
Petite Forte, stockade, 6
Petrovich, Olga, 165
Petrowski, John, 99–100
Pian, Sam, 221
Pickford, Mary, 120
Pierce, Thomas S., 126
Pierpont, Harry, 177–78, 181
Pine Station, area, 187
Piquett, Louis, 179–80
Pitts, Joseph A., 146, 196–201, 270
Pitts, Velva, 198
"Pittsburgh Plus," 105
Poinsett, Alex, 300
Poles, 55–56, 73, 76, 123, 174, 187, 220–23, 258,
　290, 299
Police, 48–50, 69, 74–75, 90, 96, 99–100, 110,
　121–22, 127, 130–35, 143, 147, 153, 163–64,
　172, 173, 178, 190–92, 197, 199, 214–15, 240,
　248, 250, 252, 274–75, 277, 285, 291, 294–95,
　304
Police Civil Service Commission, 275, 284
Polish National Alliance, 222
Popovich, Joe, 99–100
Porter County, Indiana, 9, 11, 112, 154, 158,
　248
Potawatomi Indians, 3–8, 10, 24
Powell, Adam Clayton, 271, 281
Preston, John, 68
Prete, Armand, 21, 25, 26
Progressive party (Bull Moose), 47
Progressive party (1940s), 241
Prohibition, 44, 83, 94–95, 108–10, 113, 126,
　130–35, 147–54, 158, 177, 190